Microsoft® Office 97

Updated Edition

At a Glance

Microsoft® Press

Microsoft Office 97 Updated Edition At a Glance

Published by **Microsoft Press**
A Division of Microsoft Corporation
One Microsoft Way
Redmond, Washington 98052-6399

Library of Congress Cataloging-in-Publication Data
Microsoft Office 97 At a Glance / Perspection, Inc. -- Updated ed.
p. cm.
Includes index.
ISBN 1-57231-891-0
1. Integrated software 2. Microsoft Office. I. Perspection, Inc.
QA76. 76. I57M4553 1998
005.369--dc21
98-9289
CIP

Printed and bound in the United States of America.

5 6 7 8 9 QEQE 32109

Distributed to the book trade in Canada by Macmillan of Canada, a division of Canada Publishing Corporation.

A CIP catalogue record for this book is available from the British Library.

Microsoft Press books are available through booksellers and distributors worldwide. For further information about international editions, contact your local Microsoft Corporation office. Or contact Microsoft Press International directly at fax (425) 936-7329. Visit our web site at mspress.microsoft.com.

For Perspection, Inc.
Managing Editor: **Steven M. Johnson**
Writers: **Robin Geller, Ann Shaffer**
Production Editor: **David W. Beskeen**
Series Editor: **Jane Pedicini**
Developmental Editors: **Robin Geller, Ann Shaffer**
Technical Editor: **Ann-Marie Buconjic**

For Microsoft Press
Acquisitions Editor: **Kim Fryer**
Project Editor: **Maureen Williams Zimmerman**

Contents

"How can I get started quickly in Office?"

see page 6

Get help with the Office Assistant
see page 14

Use a hyperlink
see page 48

"How can I view my documents effectively in Word?"

see page 63

"How can I save time with templates?"

see page 90

Special publishing effects
see page 114

"I want to create a formula!"

see page 126

9 Designing a Worksheet with Excel 97 137

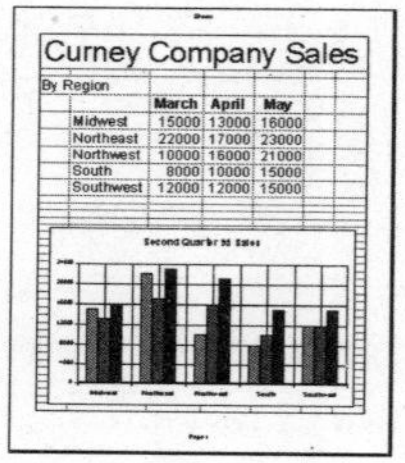

Create a chart
see page 140

10 Creating a Presentation with PowerPoint 97 157

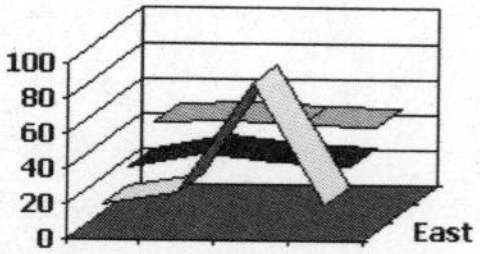

Insert a chart in a slide
see page 182

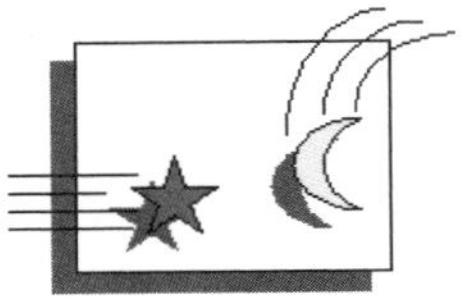

Add slide animation to a presentation
see page 190

"How can I create a query quickly and easily?"

see page 210

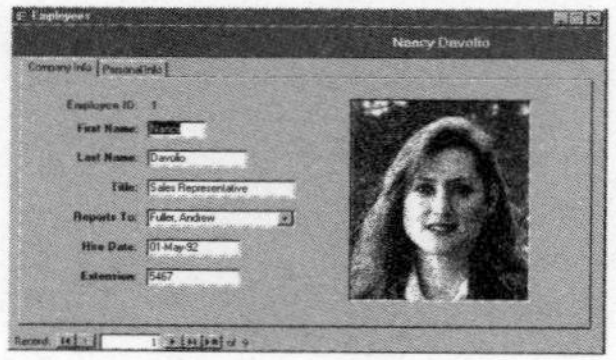

Create a form the easy way
see page 228

Move around Outlook 97
see page 233

Move around Outlook 98
see page 270

"How do I subscribe to a newsgroup?"

see page 306

"I want to create a presentation using my Word document!"

see page 320

Acknowledgments

The task of creating any book requires the talents of many hard-working people pulling together to meet impossible deadlines and untold stresses. We'd like to thank the outstanding team responsible for making this book possible: the co-writers and co-editors, Robin Geller and Ann Shaffer, the series editor, Jane Pedicini, the technical editor, Ann Marie Buconjic, the production team, Steven Payne, Patrica Young, and Gary Bedard, and the indexer, Michael Brackney. We'd also like to thank Liz Reding, Joan and Patrick Carey, and Marie Swanson for their contributions to this book.

At Microsoft Press, we'd like to thank Kim Fryer for the opportunity to undertake this project and Maureen Zimmerman for editorial expertise with the At a Glance series.

Perspection

Perspection

Perspection, Inc. is a technology training company committed to providing information to help people communicate, make decisions, and solve problems. Perspection writes and produces software training books, and develops interactive multimedia applications for Windows-based and Macintosh personal computers.

Microsoft Office 97 Updated Edition At a Glance incorporates Perspection's training expertise to ensure that you'll receive the maximum return on your time. With this staightforward, easy-to-read reference tool you'll get the information you need when you need it. You'll focus on the skills that increase productivity while working at your own pace and convenience.

We invite you to visit the Perspection World Wide Web site. You can visit us at:

http://www.perspection.com

You'll find a description for all of our books, additional content for our books, information about Perspection, and much more.

1

About *At a Glance*

IN THIS SECTION

Microsoft Office 97 Updated Edition At a Glance is for anyone who wants to get the most from their computer and their software with the least amount of time and effort. You'll find this book to be a straightforward, easy-to-read reference tool. With the premise that your computer should work for you, not you for it, this book's purpose is to help you get your work done quickly and efficiently so that you can get away from the computer and live your life.

No Computerese!

Let's face it—when there's a task you don't know how to do but you need to get it done in a hurry, or when you're stuck in the middle of a task and can't figure out what to do next, there's nothing more frustrating than having to read page after page of technical background material. You want the information you need—nothing more, nothing less—and you want it now! And it should be easy to find and understand.

That's what this book is all about. It's written in plain English—no technical jargon and no computerese. There's no single task in the book that takes more than two pages. Just look up the task in the index or the table of contents, turn to the page, and there's the information, laid out step by step and accompanied by a graphic that adds visual clarity. You don't get bogged down by the whys and wherefores; just follow the steps, look at the illustrations, and get your work done with a minimum of hassle.

Occasionally you might want to turn to another page if the procedure you're working on has a "See Also" in the left column. That's because there's a lot of overlap among tasks, and we didn't want to keep repeating ourselves. We've also scattered some useful tips here and there, and thrown in a "Try This" once in a while, but by and large we've tried to remain true to the heart and soul of the book, which is that information you need should be available to you at a glance.

Useful Tasks...

Whether you use Office 97 for work, play, or some of each, we've tried to pack this book with procedures for everything we could think of that you might want to do, from the simplest tasks to some of the more esoteric ones.

...And the Easiest Way To Do Them

Another thing we've tried to do in *Office 97 Updated Edition At a Glance* is to find and document the easiest way to accomplish a task. Office often provides many ways to accomplish a single end result, which can be daunting or delightful, depending on the way you like to work. If you tend to stick with one favorite and familiar approach, we think the methods described in this book are the way to go. If you like trying out alternative techniques, go ahead! The intuitiveness of Office invites exploration, and you're likely to discover ways of doing things that you think are easier or that you like better. If you do, that's great! It's exactly what the creators of Office 97 had in mind when they provided so many alternatives.

A Quick Overview

This book isn't meant to be read in any particular order. It's designed so that you can jump in, get the information you need, and then close the book and keep it near your computer until the next time you need it. But that doesn't mean we scattered the information about with wild abandon. If you were to read the book from front to back, you'd find a logical progression from the simple tasks to the more complex ones. Here's a quick overview.

First, we assume that Office 97 is already installed on your machine. If it's not, the Setup Wizard makes installation so simple that you won't need our help anyway. So, unlike most computer books, this one doesn't start out with installation instructions and a list of system requirements. You've already got that under control.

Sections 2 and 3 of the book cover the basics: starting Microsoft Office 97 programs: working with menus, toolbars, and dialog boxes; getting help; displaying the Office Shortcut Bar; saving documents; and exiting programs.

Section 4 describes tasks for exploring the Internet with Office 97 programs: inserting and using hyperlinks; navigating hyperlinks, searching the Web, getting documents from the Web; and creating HTML documents.

Sections 5 through 7 describe tasks for creating documents with Microsoft Word: changing document views; formatting text for emphasis; creating and modifying tables; checking your spelling and grammar; and printing documents.

Sections 8 and 9 describe tasks for creating spreadsheets with Microsoft Excel: entering labels and numbers, creating formulas, creating charts, creating lists, and creating PivotTables.

Sections 10 and 11 describe tasks for creating presentations with Microsoft PowerPoint: creating a new presentation; developing an outline; inserting slides, clip art, pictures, sounds, and movies; applying color schemes; and creating slide shows.

Sections 12 and 13 describe tasks for creating databases with Microsoft Access: planning and creating databases; finding, sorting, and modifying data; and creating and modifying forms and reports.

Sections 14 and 15 describe tasks for managing information with Microsoft Outlook 97: creating and sending e-mail messages; scheduling and changing events and appointments; planning and managing meetings; and managing tasks and information.

Sections 16 and 17 describe tasks for managing information with Microsoft Outlook 98: installing Outlook 98; creating and sending e-mail messages; scheduling and changing events and appointments; planning and managing meetings; managing tasks and information; and subscribing and reading newsgroup messages.

Section 18 describes tasks for integrating information from Office 97 programs: embedding and linking files between programs; creating Word documents with Excel data; creating PowerPoint presentations with Word text; and analyzing Access data in Excel workbooks.

A Final Word (or Two)

We had three goals in writing this book, and here they are:

- Whatever you want to do, we want the book to help you get it done.
- We want the book to help you discover how to do things you *didn't* know you wanted to do.
- And, finally, if we've achieved the first two goals, we'll be well on the way to the third, which is for our book to help you enjoy doing your work with Office 97. We think that would be the best gift we could give you as a "thank you" for buying our book.

We hope you'll have as much fun using *Office 97 Updated Edition At a Glance* as we've had writing it. The best way to learn is by doing, and that's what we hope you'll get from this book.

Jump right in!

2

Getting Started with Office 97

IN THIS SECTION

Microsoft Office 97 is simple to use so you can focus on the important challenges—your work. What's more, all the Office 97 programs—Binder, Word, Excel, Access, PowerPoint, and Outlook—function alike in many ways.

Working Efficiently with Office 97

Every Office 97 program contains several identical commands and buttons, which allow you to perform basic actions the same way, no matter which program you happen to be working in. For example, when you click the Open button on the Standard toolbar in Word, Excel, PowerPoint, or Access, the same Open dialog box appears. Similarly, the Close button for any program or document in Office 97 is identical.

In Office 97, you can perform many common tasks in several different ways. The method you choose depends on your personal preference. For example, suppose you need to start a program and open a document. You could start the program first and then open the file from within the program window. Or you could open the file and its associated program at the same time. The choice is yours.

Starting an Office 97 Program

All Office 97 programs start in the same two ways: either from the Windows 95 Start menu or from the Office Shortcut Bar. The Office Shortcut Bar is probably more convenient because it saves a few mouse clicks. By providing different ways to start a program, Office 97 enables you to customize the way you work and to switch from program to program with a click of a button.

TIP

Load the Office Shortcut Bar. *The Office Shortcut Bar loads automatically only during a complete installation. If you do a typical installation and want to use the Office Shortcut Bar, you must install it separately.*

Start an Office 97 Program from the Start Menu

1. Click the Start button on the Windows 95 taskbar.
2. Point to Programs.
3. Click the Office 97 program you want to open.

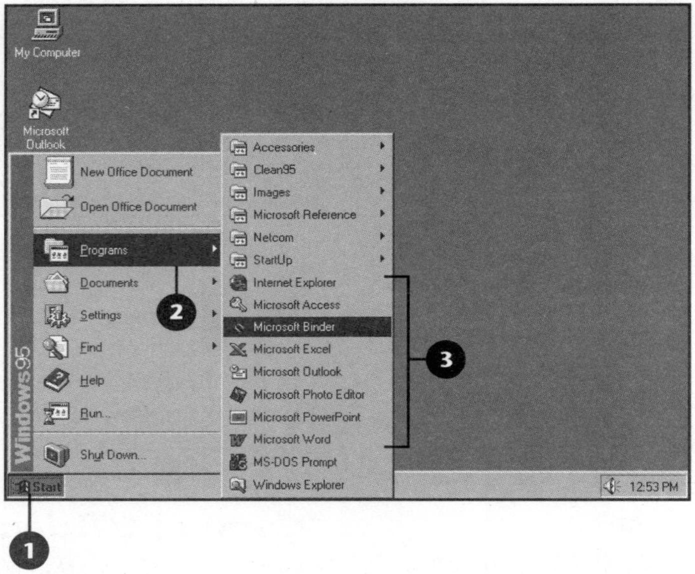

Start an Office 97 Program from the Office Shortcut Bar

1. Click the Office 97 program button on the Office Shortcut Bar for the program you want to start.

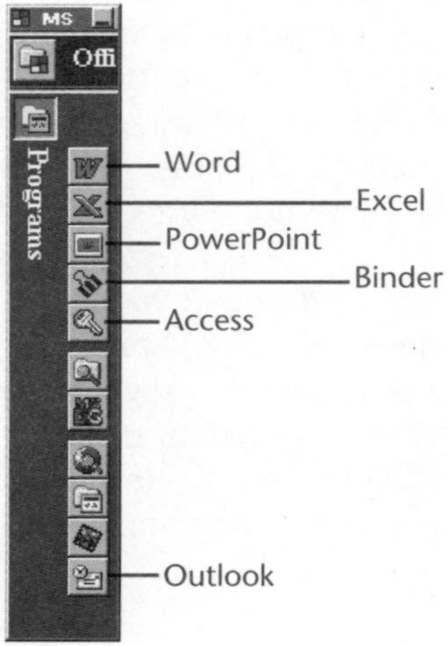

Start button

TIP

Start any Office program and a new document from the desktop. *Right-click the desktop, point to New, and then click the type of Office 97 document you want to create. The program starts and a new document opens.*

SEE ALSO

See "Displaying the Office Shortcut Bar" on page 18 for information about adding different toolbars to the Office Shortcut Bar.

Start an Office 97 Program and Open a New Office Document

1. Click the Start button on the taskbar.
2. Click New Office Document.
3. Click the tab for the type of document you want to create.
4. Double-click a document icon to start the program and open a new document.

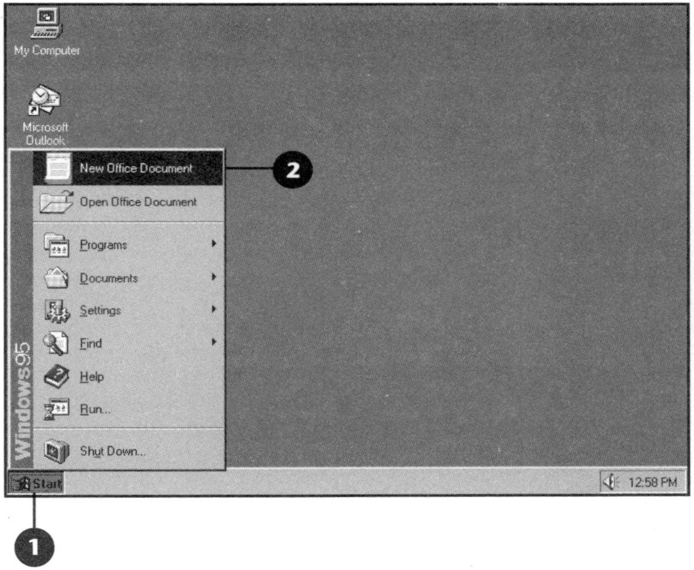

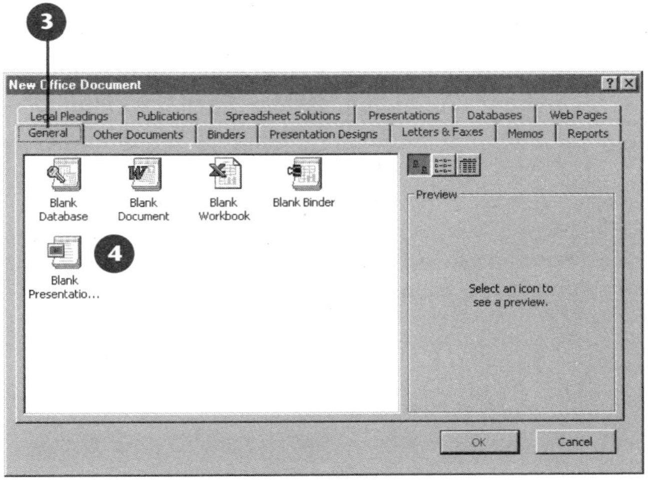

2

Opening an Existing File

Before you can begin working, you need to open a document to work on. There are two common ways to open an existing file: open the file and the program in which it was created at one time, or open the file from within its Office 97 program. If you have difficulty remembering where or under what name you stored a particular file, you can locate the file using the Find options in the Open dialog box.

Open button

TIP

Use the File menu to open a recent file. *You can open any of the four most recent files on which you worked in any Office program by clicking the appropriate filename at the bottom of the File menu.*

Open an Existing File from the Start Menu

1. Click the Start button on the taskbar, and then click Open Office Document.
2. Click the Look In drop-down arrow.
3. Click the drive where the file is located.
4. Double-click the folder in which the file is stored.
5. Double-click a filename to start the program and open that file.

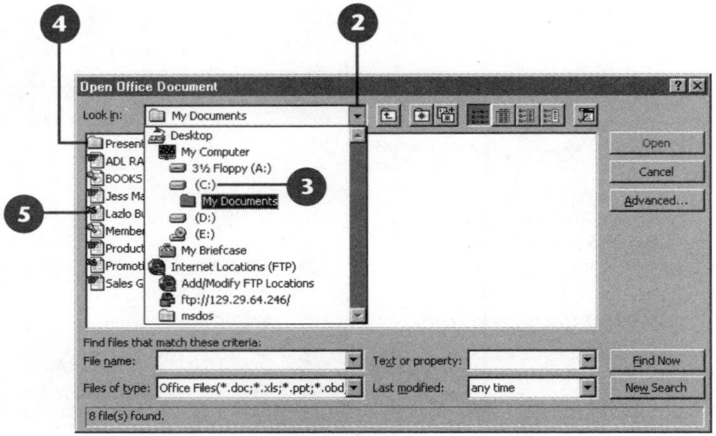

Open an Existing File from an Office 97 Program Window

1. Click the Open button on the Standard toolbar.
2. Click the Look In drop-down arrow, and then click the drive where the file is located.
3. Double-click the folder in which the file is stored.
4. Click the Files Of Type drop-down arrow, and select the type of file you want to open.
5. Double-click the file you want to open.

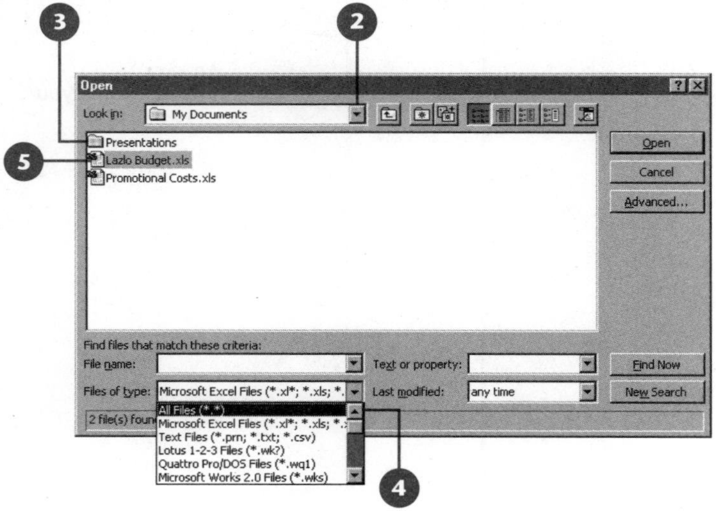

TIP

Use wildcards to search for filenames. *When you recall only part of the filename of the file you want to open, type a question mark (?) for any single character or an asterisk (*) for two or more characters of which you are unsure.*

SEE ALSO

See "Choosing Menu and Dialog Box Options" on page 20 for information about using dialog boxes.

TRY THIS

Locate a specific group of files. *Find all the files you worked with yesterday. Find all the Word files you worked with five days ago.*

Find a File Quickly Using the Open Dialog Box

1. Click the Open button on the Standard toolbar.
2. Click the Commands And Settings button, and then click Search Subfolders.
3. Click the Look In drop-down arrow.
4. Click the drive you want to search.
5. Enter as much information as you recall about the file you want to find in the text boxes at the bottom of the Open dialog box.
6. Click Find Now.
7. Double-click the file you want to open.

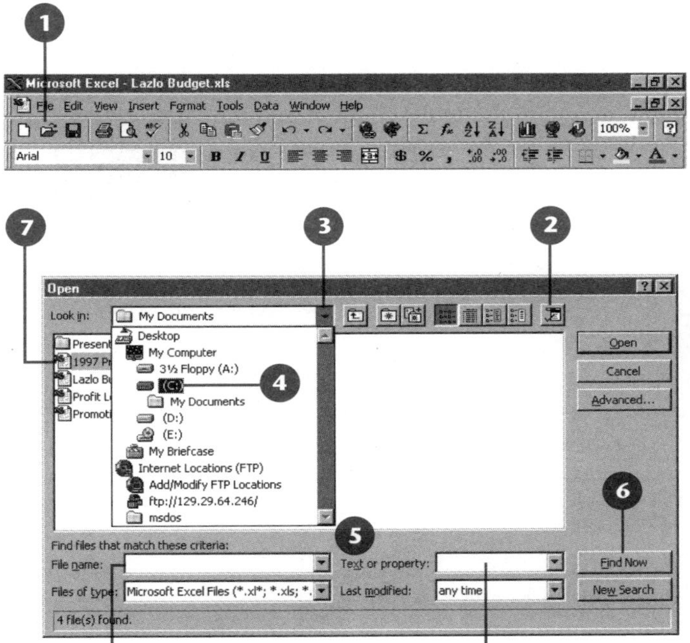

Type a complete or partial name to find all files with that letter combination or name.

Type a certain word or phrase to find all files that contain that word or phrase.

Saving a File

Saving your files frequently ensures you don't lose work in case of an unexpected power loss. The first time you save, you must specify a filename and folder in the Save As dialog box. The next time you save, Office saves the file with the same name in the same folder. If you want to change a file's name or save it in a new folder, you must use the Save As dialog box again, which actually creates a copy of the original file. If you haven't saved your work before you close a file, a dialog box opens asking if you want to save your changes.

TIP

What's the difference between the Save and Save As commands. *The Save command saves a copy of your current document to a previously specified name and location. The Save As command creates a copy of your current document with a new name, location, or type.*

Save a File for the First Time

1. Click the Save button on the Standard toolbar.
2. Click the Save In drop-down arrow, and then click the drive where you want to save the file.
3. Double-click the folder in which you want to save the file.
4. Type a name for the file or use the suggested name.
5. Click Save.

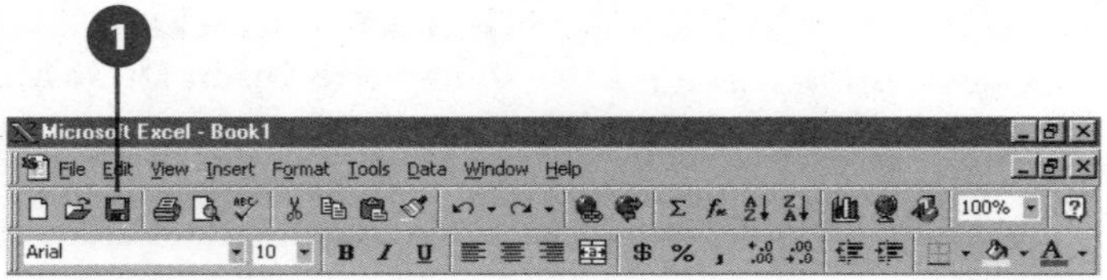

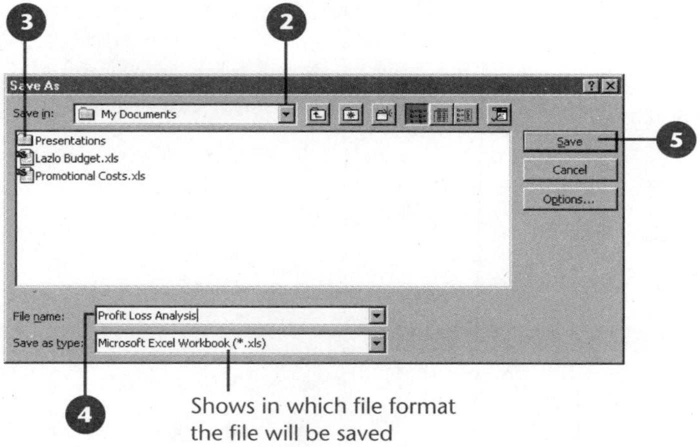

Save a File with Another Name

1. Click the File menu, and then click Save As.
2. Type a new filename in the File Name box.
3. Click Save.

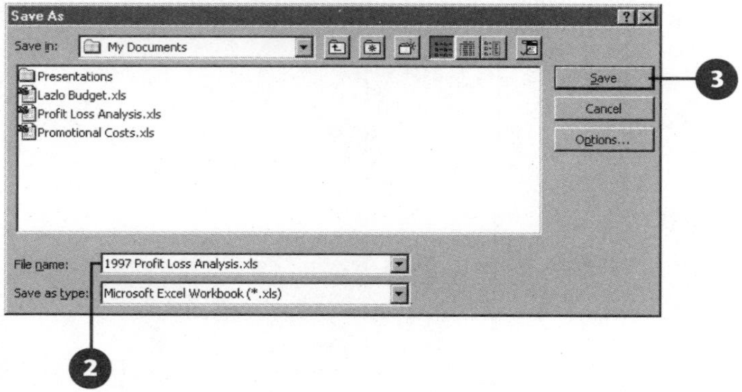

TIP

You don't have to worry about file extensions. *When you name a file, you do not have to type the file extension. The Office program automatically adds the correct file extension to the name you give your file.*

TIP

Use file types to save a file. *A file type specifies the document format (for example, a template), program and the version in which a file was created (for example, Word 7.0). You might want to change the document format or program and version if you're sharing files with someone who has an earlier version of a program.*

SEE ALSO

See "Importing and Exporting Files" on page 312 for more information about saving a document as another file type.

Save a File in a Different Folder

1. Click the File menu, and then click Save As.
2. Click the Save In drop-down arrow.
3. Click the drive to which you want to save the file.
4. Double-click the folder in which you want to save the file.
5. Click Save.

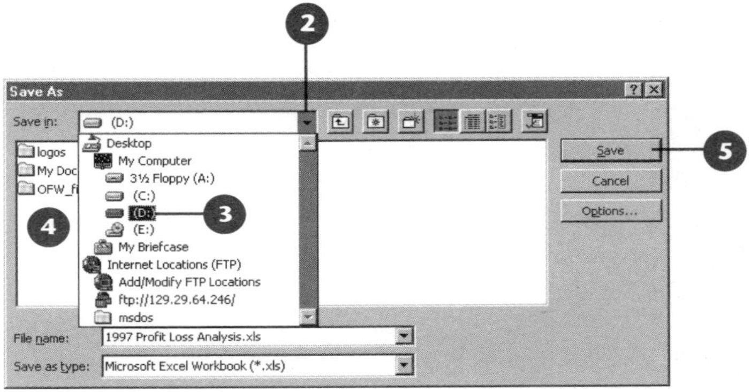

Save a File as a Different Type

1. Click the File menu, and then click Save As.
2. Click the Save As Type drop-down arrow.
3. Click the file type you want.
4. Click Save.

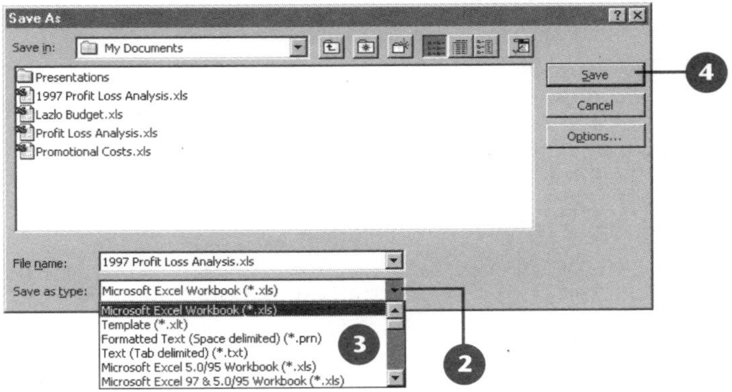

Getting Help in an Office 97 Program

At some point, everyone has a question or two about the program they are using. Office 97's online Help system provides the answers you need. *ScreenTips* are a mouse-click away whenever you want information about anything you see on the screen or in a dialog box. You can get a ScreenTip by holding down the Shift key and pressing F1, or clicking the Help button on dialog box title bars. You can also search an extensive catalog of Help topics to locate specific information.

Help button

TIP

Use the mouse pointer to view toolbar ScreenTips. *You can hold the mouse pointer over any toolbar button to see its name.*

Get a ScreenTip

1. Press Shift+F1 or click the Help button on a dialog box's title bar to display the Help pointer.
2. Click the Help pointer on any item or menu command to display a definition box.
3. Click anywhere to close the definition box.

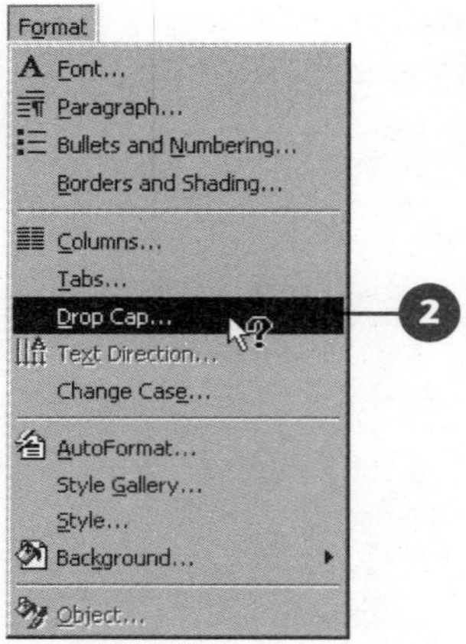

Format
Font...
Paragraph...
Bullets and Numbering...
Borders and Shading...
Columns...
Tabs...
Drop Cap...
Text Direction...
Change Case...
AutoFormat...
Style Gallery...
Style...
Background...
Object...
2

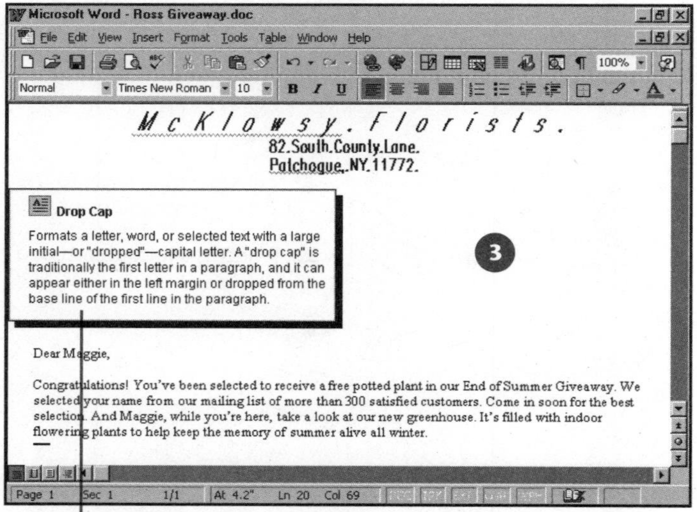

Microsoft Word - Ross Giveaway.doc
File Edit View Insert Format Tools Table Window Help
Normal
Times New Roman
10
100%
McKlowsy.Florists.
82.South.County.Lane.
Patchogue,.NY.11772.
Drop Cap
Formats a letter, word, or selected text with a large initial—or "dropped"—capital letter. A "drop cap" is traditionally the first letter in a paragraph, and it can appear either in the left margin or dropped from the base line of the first line in the paragraph.
3
Dear Maggie,
Congratulations! You've been selected to receive a free potted plant in our End of Summer Giveaway. We selected your name from our mailing list of more than 300 satisfied customers. Come in soon for the best selection. And Maggie, while you're here, take a look at our new greenhouse. It's filled with indoor flowering plants to help keep the memory of summer alive all winter.
Page 1
Sec 1
1/1
At 4.2"
Ln 20
Col 69

A description of the selected item appears.

SEE ALSO

See "Getting Help from the Office Assistant" on page 14 for information about finding out how to accomplish a certain task.

TRY THIS

Get information about the Web. *In every Office 97 program, you can get information about the World Wide Web. Click the Help menu, point to Microsoft On The Web, and then click the topic you want to read.*

Locate Information about a Particular Topic

1. Click the Help menu, and then click Contents And Index.
2. Click the Index tab.
   - Use the Contents tab to search for information from the Help table of contents
   - Use the Find tab to perform a detailed search of the Help topics.
3. Type a word about which you want more information. As you type each letter of the word or topic, the topics list scrolls.
4. Double-click a topic that relates most closely to the information you want.
5. If necessary, double-click a topic in the Topics Found dialog box.
6. After reading the Help window, click the Close button.

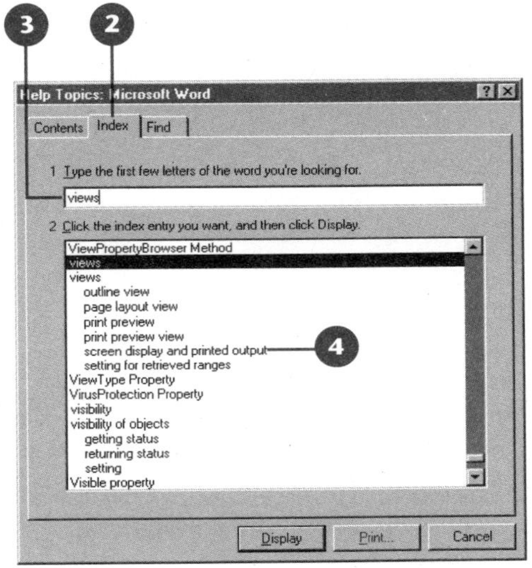

3
2
Help Topics: Microsoft Word
Contents
Index
Find
1 Type the first few letters of the word you're looking for.
views
2 Click the index entry you want, and then click Display.
ViewPropertyBrowser Method
views
views
outline view
page layout view
print preview
print preview view
screen display and printed output
setting for retrieved ranges
ViewType Property
VirusProtection Property
visibility
visibility of objects
getting status
returning status
setting
Visible property
4
Display
Print...
Cancel

Click to look up another topic.

Click to display more options.

Click words with a dotted underline to see a definition.

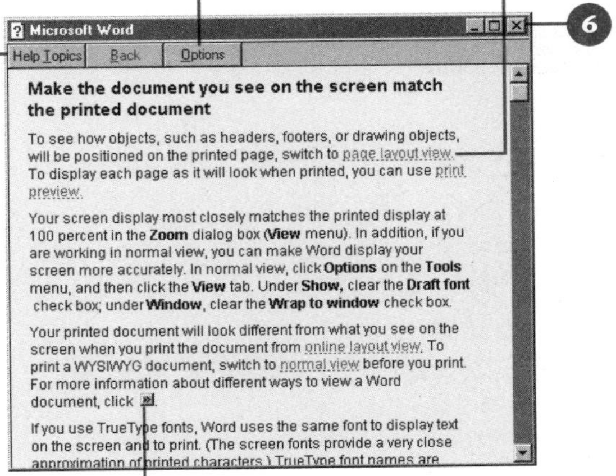

Microsoft Word
Help Topics
Back
Options
6
Make the document you see on the screen match the printed document
To see how objects, such as headers, footers, or drawing objects, will be positioned on the printed page, switch to page layout view. To display each page as it will look when printed, you can use print preview.
Your screen display most closely matches the printed display at 100 percent in the Zoom dialog box (View menu). In addition, if you are working in normal view, you can make Word display your screen more accurately. In normal view, click Options on the Tools menu, and then click the View tab. Under Show, clear the Draft font check box; under Window, clear the Wrap to window check box.
Your printed document will look different from what you see on the screen when you print the document from online layout view. To print a WYSIWYG document, switch to normal view before you print. For more information about different ways to view a Word document, click
If you use TrueType fonts, Word uses the same font to display text on the screen and to print. (The screen fonts provide a very close

Click to display another Help window.

Getting Help from the Office Assistant

Often the easiest way to learn how to accomplish a certain task is to ask someone who knows. Now, with Office 97, that knowledgeable friend is always available in the form of the Office Assistant. You just tell the Assistant what you want to do in everyday language, and the Assistant walks you through the process step by step. And if Clippit's personality doesn't appeal to you, you can choose from a variety of other Assistants.

Office Assistant button

Ask the Office Assistant for Help

1. Click the Office Assistant button on the Standard toolbar.
2. Type the task you need help with in the box.
3. Click Search.
4. Click the topic you want help with.
5. After you're done, click the Close button on the Help window.
6. Click the Close button on the Office Assistant.

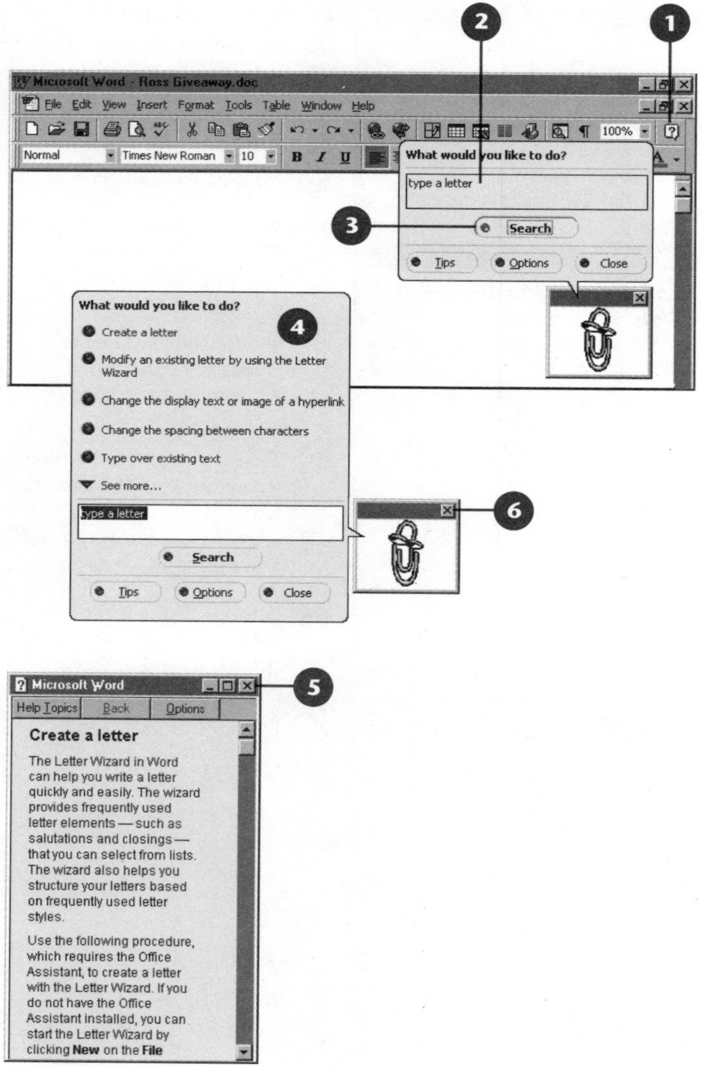

TIP

Use the Office Assistant to get help at any time. *When you begin to create a common type of document (such as a letter), the Office Assistant will appear and offer you help. You can have the Office Assistant walk you through the process or choose to complete the task alone.*

Clippit:
An Office Assistant

TIP

Use the Office Assistant to get useful tips. *When a light bulb appears on the Office Assistant button in the Standard toolbar or in the open Office Assistant window, the Assistant has a suggestion for a simpler or more efficient way to accomplish a task. Just click the Office Assistant button or window to see the suggestion.*

Choose an Assistant

1. Click the Office Assistant button on the Standard toolbar.
2. Click Options.
3. Click the Gallery tab.
4. Click the Next and Back buttons to preview different Assistants.
5. Leave the Assistant you want to use visible.
6. Click OK. If you are prompted, insert the Office 97 CD-ROM in your drive, and click OK.

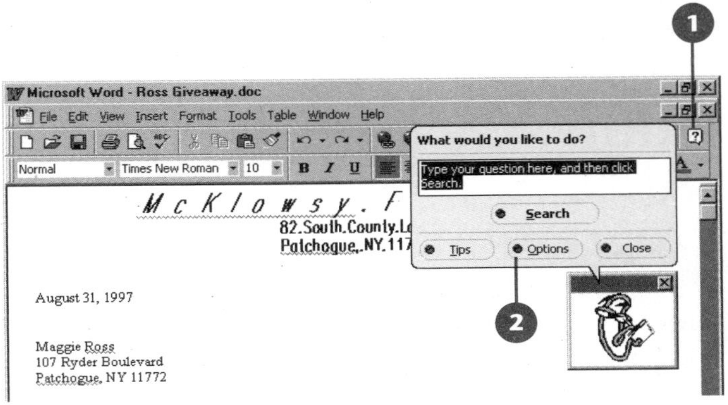

Use this tab to customize the Office Assistant with more advanced features.

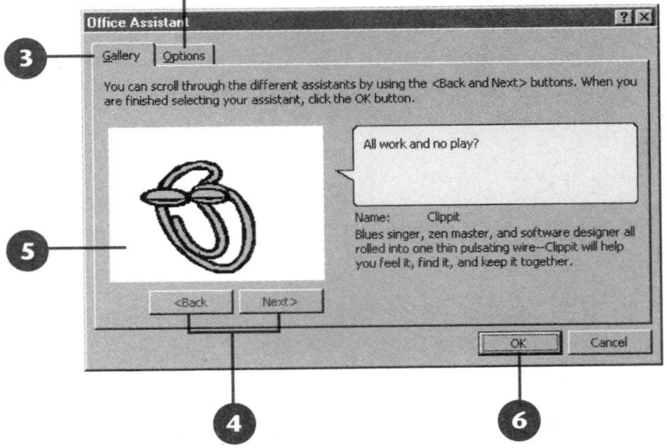

Closing a File and Exiting an Office 97 Program

When you finally decide to stop working for the day, the last things you need to do are close any documents that are open and close any programs that are running. You can close each document and its program separately. Or you can close everything at once by exiting the program. Either way, if you try to close a document without saving your final changes, a dialog box appears, asking if you would like to do so.

SEE ALSO

See "Saving a File" on page 10 for information on saving changes to your documents.

Close button

Close a File

1. Click the Close button on the document window menu bar, or click the File menu and then click Close.
2. If necessary, click Yes to save your changes.

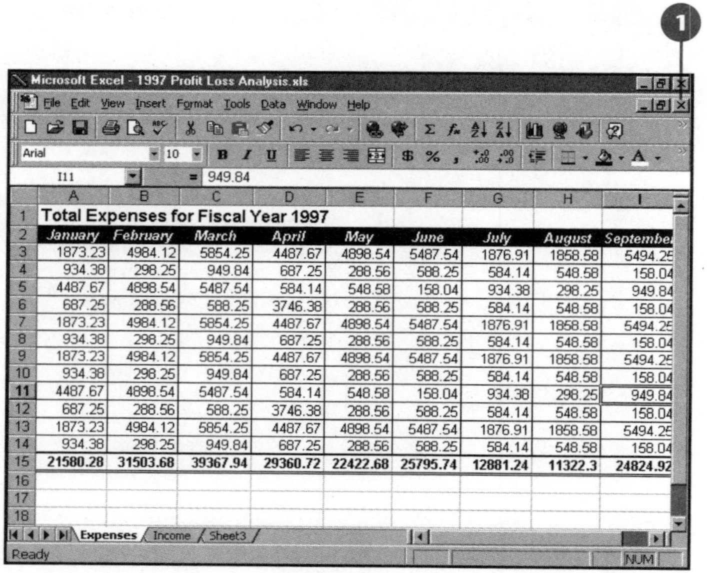

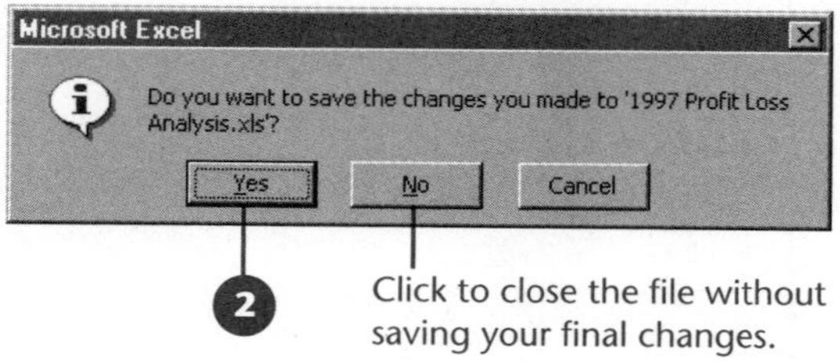

Click to close the file without saving your final changes.

TRY THIS

Exit a program and close any open files. *Try exiting a program and closing all open files at one time. Just click the Close button on the title bar without closing any files first. All saved files close immediately and the program exits. If you haven't saved your final changes, click Yes to save the changes, close the file, and exit the program.*

Exit an Office 97 Program

1. Click the Close button on the program window title bar, or click the File menu and then click Exit.
2. If necessary, click Yes to save any changes you made to your open documents before the program exits.

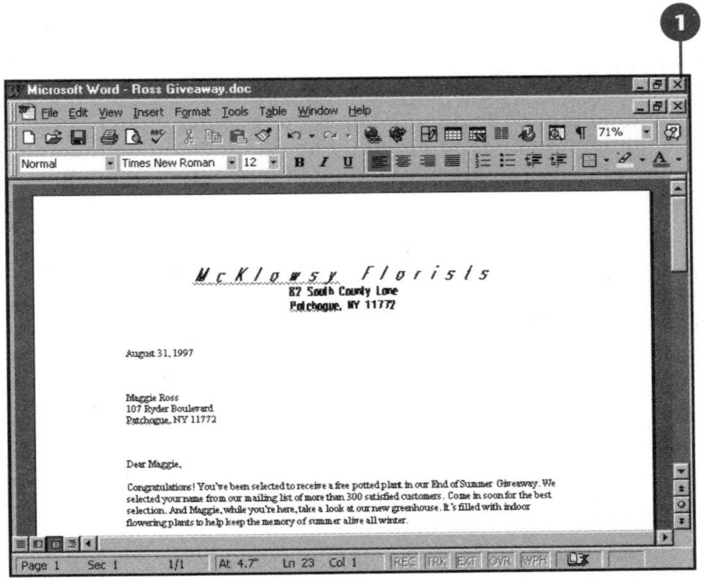
1
Microsoft Word - Ross Giveaway.doc
File Edit View Insert Format Tools Table Window Help
Normal
Times New Roman
12
71%
McKlowsy Florists
82 South County Lane
Patchogue, NY 11772
August 31, 1997
Maggie Ross
107 Ryder Boulevard
Patchogue, NY 11772
Dear Maggie,
Congratulations! You've been selected to receive a free potted plant in our End of Summer Giveaway. We selected your name from our mailing list of more than 300 satisfied customers. Come in soon for the best selection. And Maggie, while you're here, take a look at our new greenhouse. It's filled with indoor flowering plants to help keep the memory of summer alive all winter.
Page 1 Sec 1 1/1 At 4.7" Ln 23 Col 1 REC TRK EXT OVR WPH

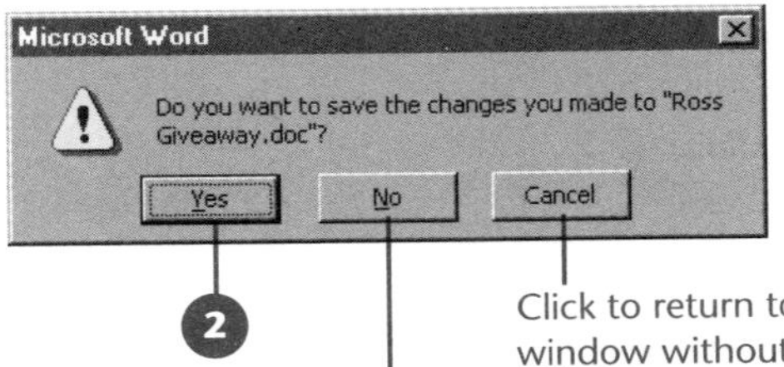
Microsoft Word
Do you want to save the changes you made to "Ross Giveaway.doc"?
Yes
No
Cancel
2

Click to return to the program window without saving the latest changes to your document.

Click to close the program without saving your latest changes to the document.

Displaying the Office Shortcut Bar

The Office Shortcut Bar provides access to all the programs on your system with one or two clicks of a button. You can display one or more toolbars on the Office Shortcut Bar. The Office Shortcut Bar itself can be *floating*, not attached to any part of your screen, or *docked*, attached to the left, right, or top edge of your screen. When the Office Shortcut Bar is docked, you can turn on *Auto Hide* so the Office Shortcut Bar appears only when you point to it.

TIP

Use the mouse pointer to display the shortcut menu. *If the Microsoft Office Shortcut Bar title bar is not displayed, you can right-click the Office icon to display its shortcut menu.*

Displaying Different Toolbars on the Office Shortcut Bar

1. Right-click anywhere on the Office Shortcut Bar.
2. Click the name of the toolbar you want to display.

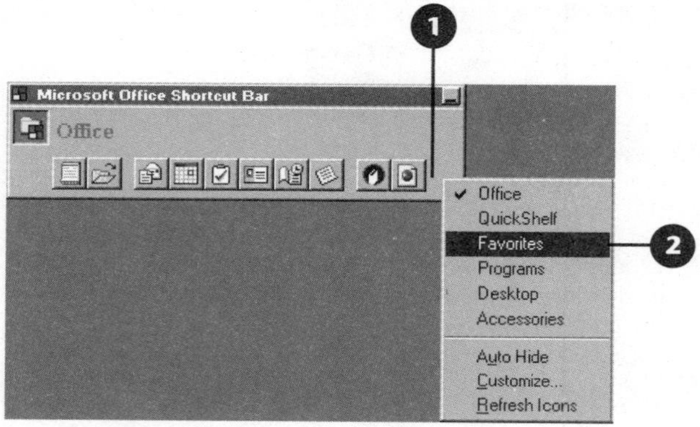

Hide the Office Shortcut Bar

1. Click the Office icon on the title bar.
2. Click Auto Hide.

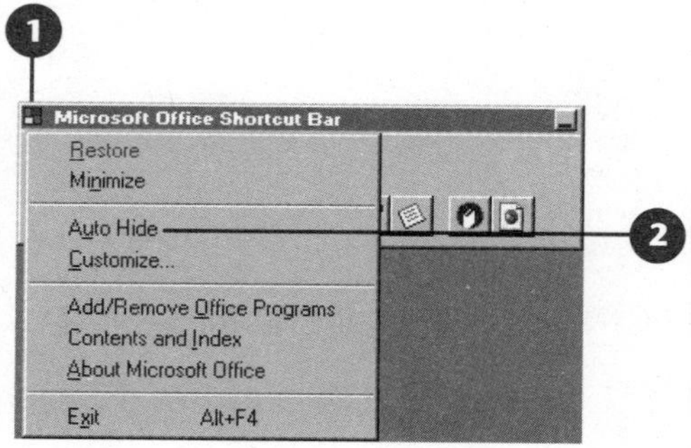

Close the Office Shortcut Bar

1. Click the Office icon on the title bar.
2. Click Exit.

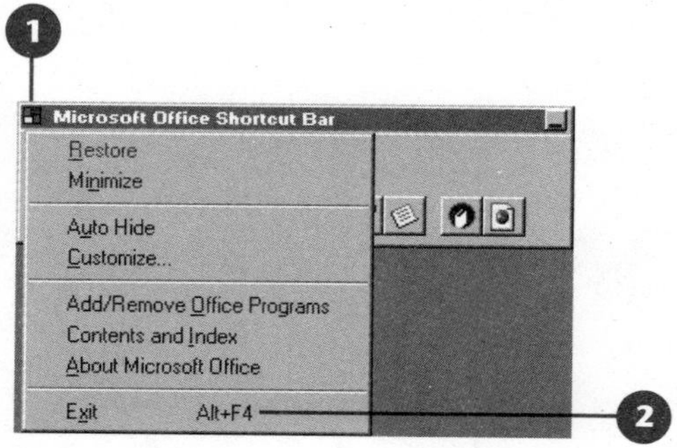

3

Using Shared Office 97 Tools

IN THIS SECTION

The great advantage of the many programs that make up Microsoft Office 97 is that they're designed to work together to allow you to focus on *what* you need to do, rather than *how*.

Similar Look and Function

When you start an Office program, a program window opens, which contains a menu bar (access to the program's commands) and several toolbars (with buttons for the most commonly used commands). Each program window also contains sizing buttons (which allow you to resize the program window instantly) and a document window, where you create spreadsheets, letters, presentations, or reports, depending on the program.

Once you learn to use menus, toolbars, dialog boxes, and sizing buttons in one Office Program, you can apply the same techniques to all other Office programs. If you perform a task one way in Word 97, you probably already know how to perform the task in Excel 97, PowerPoint 97, or Access 97. Go ahead and give it a try!

Choosing Menu and Dialog Box Options

A *menu* is a list of related commands. For example, an Edit menu contains commands for editing a document, such as Delete and Cut. A *shortcut menu* opens right where you're working and contains commands related to a specific object. Clicking a menu command that is followed by an ellipsis opens a *dialog box*, where you choose various options and settings and provide necessary information for completing the command. As you switch between programs, you'll find that all Office menus and dialog boxes look similar and work in the same way.

> **TIP**
>
> **What are shortcut menus?**
> *A shortcut menu is a group of related commands that appears when you right-click an item. The commands change depending on the item you right-click.*

Choose Menu Commands

1. Click a menu name on the menu bar at the top of the program window, or right-click an object (such as a toolbar, spreadsheet cell, picture, or selected text).
2. If the menu command you want is followed by an arrow, point to it to open a submenu of related commands.
3. Click a menu command to select that command or open a dialog box.

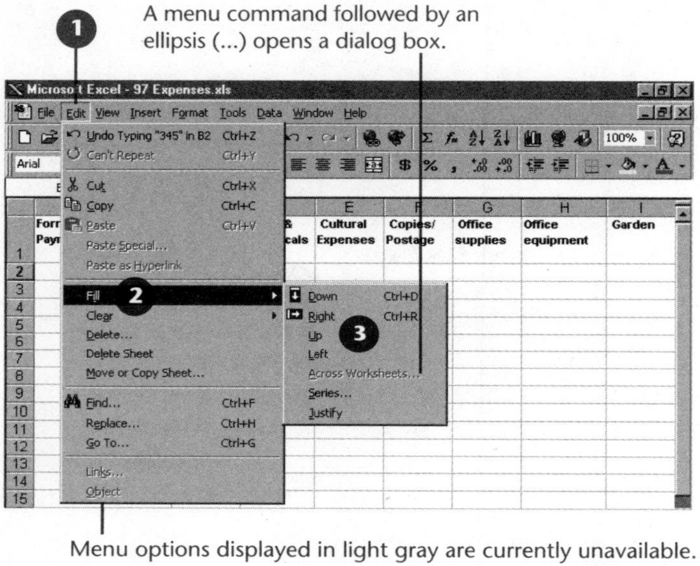

Choose Dialog Box Options

An Office 97 dialog box can be extremely simple with only a few options or very complex with several sets of options on different tabs. Regardless of the number of choices, all dialog boxes look similar and use the same types of buttons, boxes, and lists, including:

- Tabs: Each tab groups a related set of options. Click a tab to display its options.
- Option buttons: Click an option button to select it. You can usually select only one.

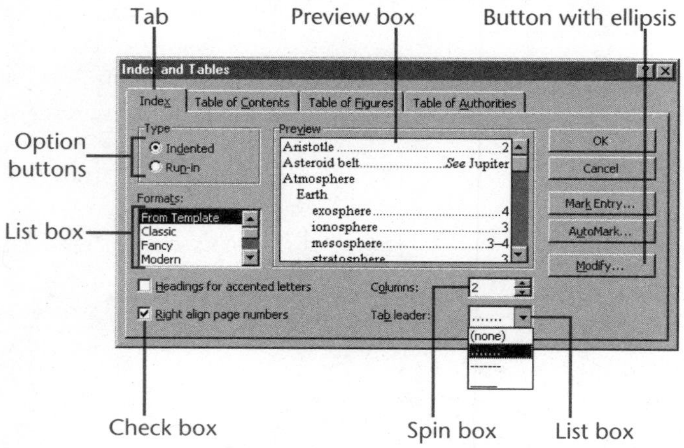

> **TIP**
>
> **Use toolbar button as alternatives to menu commands.** *If you see a toolbar button icon to the left of a menu command, you can access the command faster by clicking that button on the toolbar. In addition, keyboard shortcuts (such as Ctrl+V) appear to the right of their menu commands. To use a keyboard shortcut, press and hold the first key indicated (such as Ctrl), press the second key (such as V), and then release the keys.*

> **TIP**
>
> **Use the Tab key to navigate a dialog box.** *Rather than clicking to move around a dialog box, you can press the Tab key to move from one box or button to the next.*

- Spin box. Use this box to specify a value by clicking the up or down arrow to increase or decrease the number, or by typing the number you want in the box.
- Check box. Click the check box to turn the option on or off. A check means the option is selected; a cleared box means it's not.
- List box. The list box contains a preset list of options. Click the drop-down arrow to display the list, and then click the option you want. You might need to scroll to see all the available options.
- Text box. Click in the box and then type the specified information (such as a filename).
- Preview box. Many dialog boxes contain an image that changes to reflect the options you select.
- Button. Click a button to perform a specific action or command. The most common button is the OK button, which confirms your selections and closes the dialog box. When you click a button whose name is followed by an ellipsis (...), another dialog box opens.

Several dialog boxes require you to select a file or folder. Click the drop-down arrow and then select from a list of drives and folders on your computer.

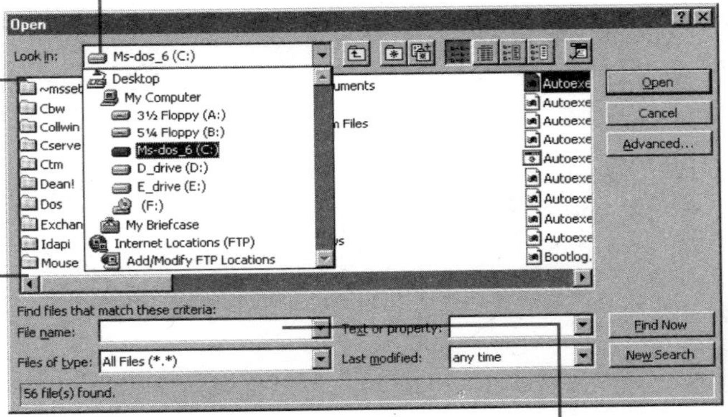

Lists the folders and documents available in the selected drive or folder. Double-click the one you want to open.

Text box

Working with Toolbars

Office *toolbars* give you quick access to frequently used menu commands with the click of a button. Most programs open with a Standard toolbar (with commands like Save and Print) and a Formatting toolbar (with commands for selecting fonts and sizes). You can also display toolbars designed for specific tasks, such as drawing pictures, importing data, or creating charts, as necessary.

SEE ALSO

See "Displaying the Office Shortcut Bar" on page 18 for information on working with the Microsoft Office Shortcut Bar.

Display and Hide a Toolbar

1. Right-click any visible toolbar.
2. Click the name of the toolbar you want to display or hide.

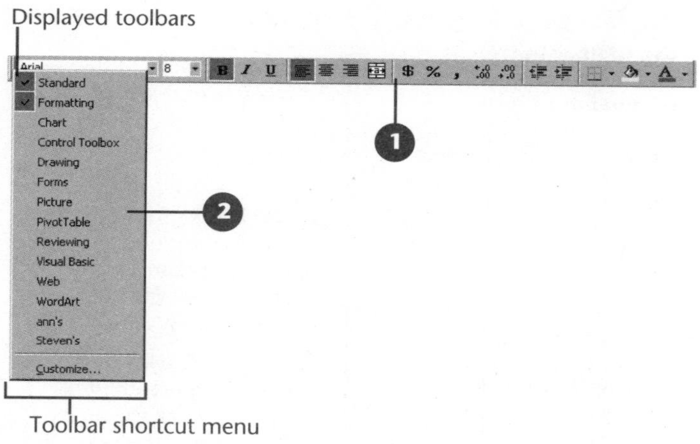

Move and Reshape a Toolbar

- To make a toolbar that is *docked* (that is, attached to one edge of the program window) float over the program window, double-click the gray bar on the left edge of the toolbar.
- To move a *floating* (unattached) toolbar, click its title bar and drag it to a new location.
- To change the shape of a floating toolbar, drag any border until the toolbar is the shape you want.
- To return a floating toolbar to its previous docked location, double-click its title bar.

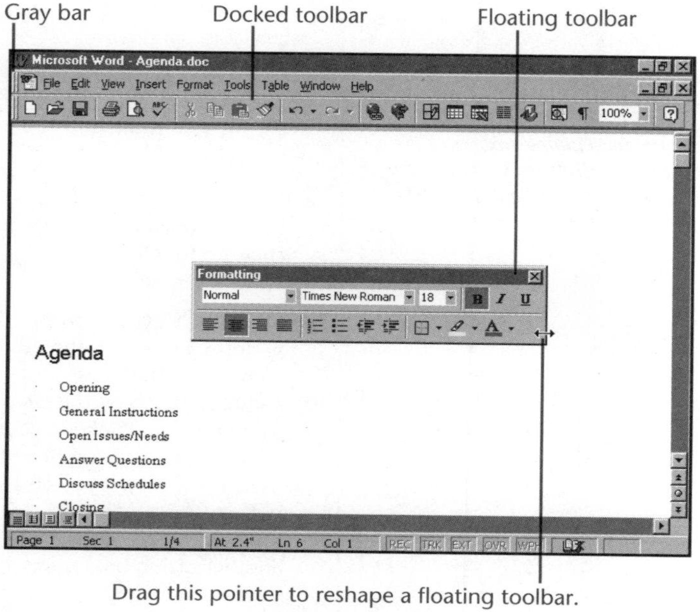

TIP

Displaying the name of the toolbar button. *To find out the name of a toolbar button, position the pointer over the button on the toolbar. The name of the button, or ScreenTip, appears below the button.*

TRY THIS

Hide ScreenTips. *To hide ScreenTips, click the View menu, point to Toolbars, click Customize, click the Options tab, clear the Show ScreenTips On Toolbars check box, and then click OK.*

TRY THIS

Customize your Excel Chart toolbar. *Display the Chart toolbar in Excel. Customize it by adding the Spelling toolbar button from the Tools category and several of the toolbar buttons from the Format category.*

Customize a Toolbar

1. Right-click any toolbar you want to change, and then click Customize.
2. If the toolbar you want to customize is not displayed, click the Toolbars tab, and then click the appropriate check box to select it.
3. Click the Commands tab.
4. To add a button to a toolbar, click the type of button you want to add in the Categories box, and then drag a button from the Commands box to the toolbar where you want it to appear.
5. To move a button, drag it to a new location on any visible toolbar.
6. To remove a button from a toolbar, drag it off the toolbar.
7. When you're done, click Close.

Use this tab to display or hide large icons, ScreenTips, or shortcut keys, and to select how menus open.

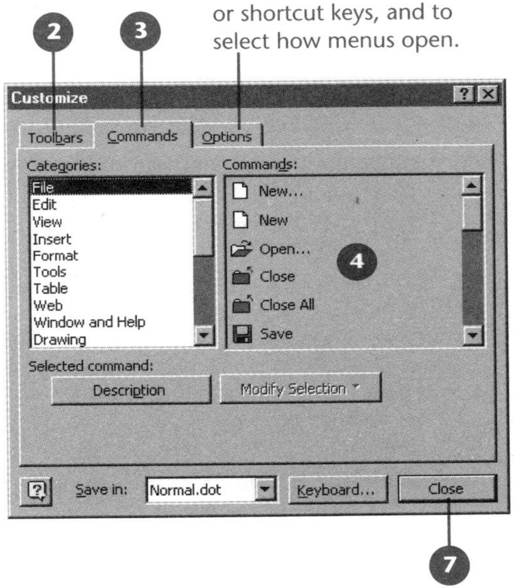

3

Working with Windows

Every Office program opens inside a *program window*. The program window, in turn, contains the *document window*, where you create and edit your various documents. In most situations, you'll probably have only one window filling the entire screen at once. But when moving or copying information between programs, it's sometimes easier to see several windows at once.

TIP

Use the mouse pointer to resize and move a window. *Drag a window's borders and title bar to resize and move it as necessary.*

SEE ALSO

See "Working with Multiple Documents" on page 66 for information on viewing multiple document windows within a program window.

Resize and Move a Window

Both the program and document windows contain the same sizing buttons:

- ◆ Maximize button

  Click to make a window fill the entire screen.

- ◆ Restore button

  Click to reduce a maximized window to about half its full size.

- ◆ Minimize button

  Click to shrink a window to an icon. To restore a program window to its previous size, click the appropriate taskbar button. To restore a document window, click its Maximize button.

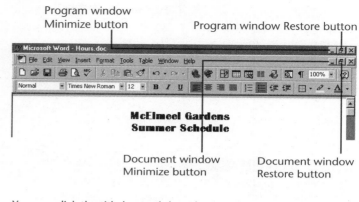

Program window Minimize button
Program window Restore button
Microsoft Word - Hours.doc
McElmeel Gardens
Summer Schedule
Document window Minimize button
Document window Restore button

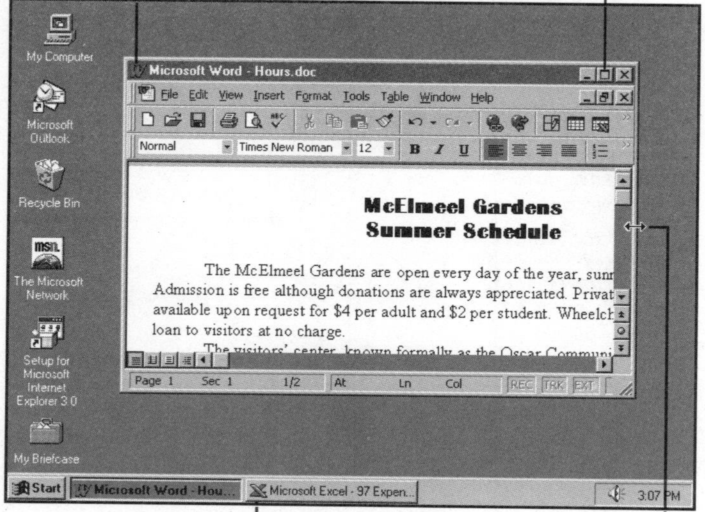
You can click the title bar and drag the entire program window to a new location on the desktop.
Program window Maximize button
Microsoft Word - Hours.doc
McElmeel Gardens
Summer Schedule
Click to restore the Excel program window to its previous size.
Use this pointer to drag the top, side, or corner borders to increase or decrease the size of the window.

TIP

Use shortcuts keys to work with windows. *You can open and close windows, and switch between windows using keyboard combinations. To close the active document window, press Ctrl+W. To switch to the next document window, press Ctrl+F6, and to switch to the previous document window, press Ctrl+Shift+F6.*

TIP

Use shortcut keys to resize windows. *To minimize the document window, press Ctrl+F9, and to maximize the document window, press Ctrl+F10. To restore the active document window, press Ctrl+F5.*

SEE ALSO

See "Closing a File and Exiting an Office 97 Program" on page 16 for information on closing a program or document window.

SEE ALSO

See "Moving Around in a Document" on page 65 for information on scrolling, paging and browsing through a document.

Open and Close Multiple Program Windows

1. Right-click the taskbar anywhere except on a program button.
2. Click Tile Horizontally or Tile Vertically.
3. Right-click the taskbar and then click Undo Tile to return to a single window.

Excel and Word program windows tiled

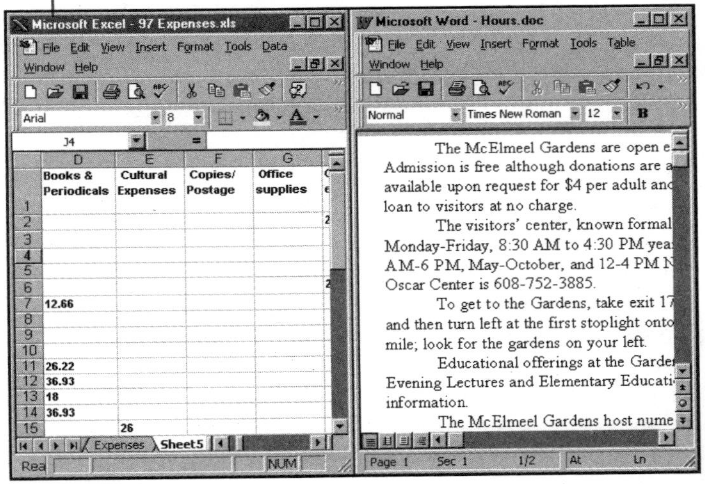

Choosing Templates and Wizards

Office 97 makes it easy to create many common documents based on a template or using a wizard. A *template* opens a document (such as a letter) with predefined formatting and placeholder text specifying what information you should enter (such as your address). A *wizard* walks you through the steps to create a finished document by asking you for information first. When you click Finish, the wizard creates a completely formatted document with the text you entered.

TRY THIS

Create your own letterhead. *Try using the Memo Wizard to create a professional-style interoffice memo or personal letterhead.*

Choose a Template

1. Click the New Office Document button on the Office Shortcut Bar.
2. Click the tab for the type of document you want to create, such as a letter.
3. Click the template you want to use.
4. Check the Preview box window to make sure the template will create the right style of document.
5. Click OK.
6. Type text for placeholders such as "[Click here and type your letter text]" as indicated.

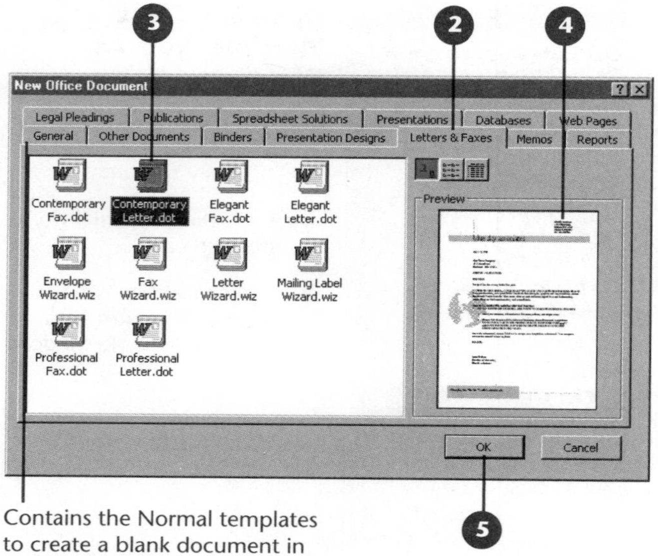

Contains the Normal templates to create a blank document in any Office Program

TIP

Use a wizard to create complete documents. *While you might think using a wizard to create a memo or fax takes more time than it's worth, wizards ensure that you include all the necessary information in your document.*

TIP

How does Word create a document using a Wizard? *If you create a Word document using a wizard, Word bases the document on the Normal document template. However, the styles used in the document reflect the formatting that you select when responding to the wizard.*

SEE ALSO

See "Applying a Style" on page 93 for information about styles used in templates.

Choose and Navigate a Wizard

1. Click the New Office Document button on the Office Shortcut Bar.
2. Click the tab for the type of document you want to create.
3. Double-click a wizard icon you want to use.
4. Read and select options (if necessary) in the first wizard dialog box.
5. Click Next to move to the next wizard dialog box.

   Each wizard dialog box asks for different types of information.
6. Continue to select options, and then click Next.
7. When you reach the last wizard dialog box, click Finish.

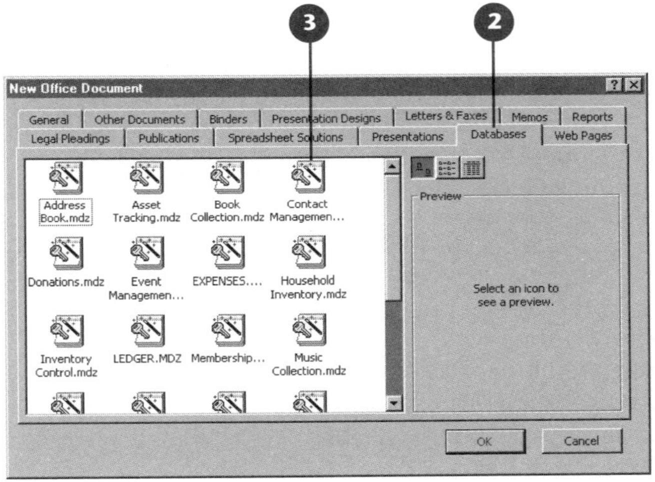

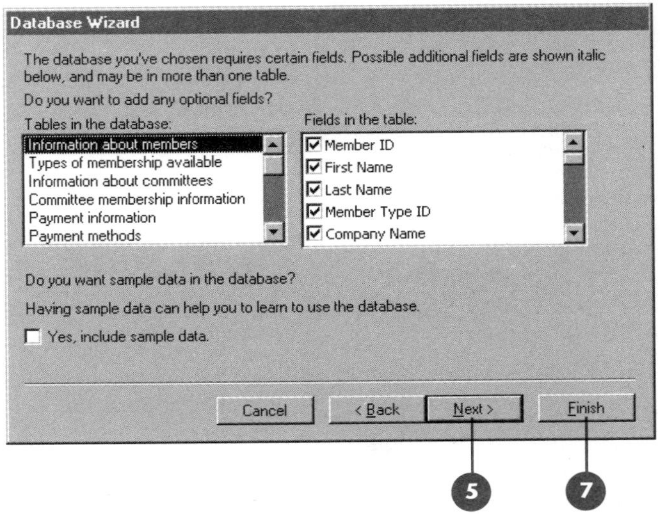

Editing Your Text

You can move (*cut*) or *copy* text within one document or between documents in different programs. In either case, the steps are the same. The text is stored on the *Clipboard*, a temporary storage area, until you cut or copy a new selection. You can also move or copy selected text to a new location without storing it on the Clipboard using a technique called *drag-and-drop editing*.

Cut or Copy and Paste Text

1. Select the text you want to move or copy.
2. Click the Cut or Copy button on the Standard toolbar.
3. Click where you want to insert the text.
4. Click the Paste button on the Standard toolbar.

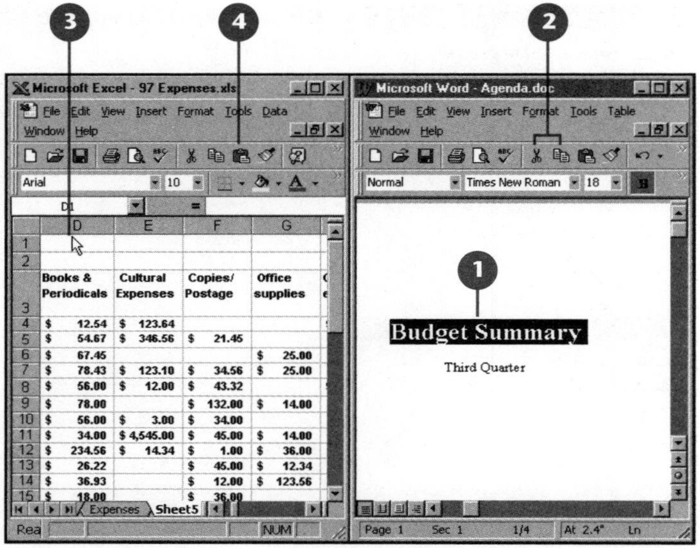

Drag and Drop Text

1. If you want to drag and drop text between programs or documents, display both program or document windows.
2. Select the text you want to move or copy.
3. To move the text to a new location, position the pointer over the selected text, and then press and hold the mouse button.

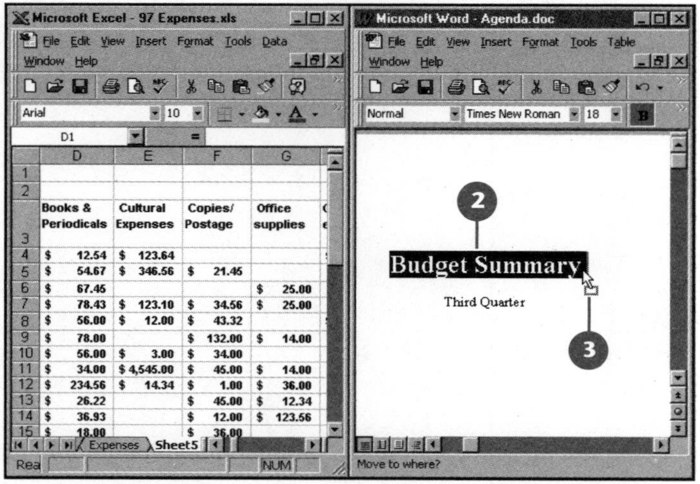

TIP

Use drag-and-drop to copy text. *If you hold down the Ctrl key while you drag your mouse, a plus sign (+) appears in the pointer box, indicating that you are dragging a copy of the selected text.*

SEE ALSO

See "Selecting Text" on page 69 for more information on ways to select text easily and quickly.

SEE ALSO

See "Working with Windows" on page 24 for information on how to open and display multiple windows.

SEE ALSO

See "Selecting, Moving, and Resizing Objects" on page 34 for information on working with objects.

4. To copy the text and paste the copy in a new location, also press and hold the Ctrl key.

5. Drag the pointer to the new location, and then release the mouse button (and the Ctrl key, if necessary).

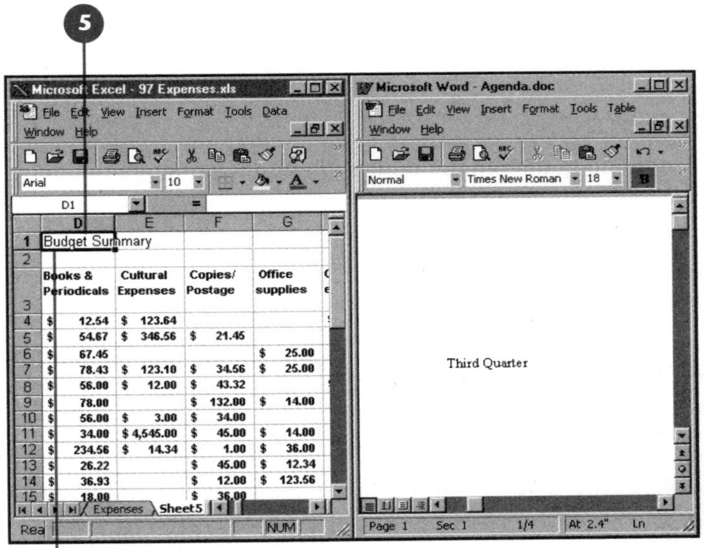

"Budget Summary" dragged from Word document to Excel worksheet

Finding and Replacing Text

The Find and Replace commands make it easy to search for and, if you want, replace specific text or formulas in a document. The Find And Replace dialog boxes vary slightly from one Office program to the next, but the commands all work essentially the same way.

TIP

Things to remember when you search for text. *When you replace text in Word or PowerPoint, a dialog box will notify you when you have reached the end of the document. When you replace text in Excel or Access, a dialog box will notify you when no more matching data is found.*

Find Text

1. Position the cursor (or insertion point) at the beginning of the document.
2. Click the Edit menu, and then click Find.
3. Type the text you want to locate in the Find What box.
4. Click Find Next until the text you want to locate is highlighted.
5. If a dialog box opens when you reach the end of the document, as it does in some Office programs, click OK.
6. When you're finished, click Close.

You might need to drag the dialog box out of the way to see the highlighted text.

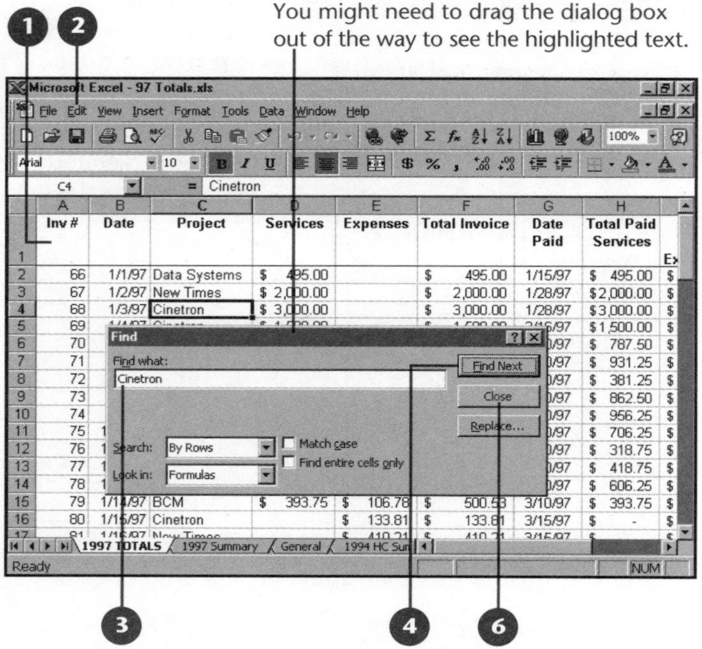

Find and replace special characters and document elements. *In a Word document, you can search for and replace special characters (for example, an em dash) and document elements (for example, a tab character). Click the More button in the Find And Replace dialog box, click Special, and then click the item you want from the popup menu.*

Format text you find and replace. *In a Word document, you can search for and replace text with specific formatting features, such as a font and font size. Click the More button in the Find And Replace dialog box, click Format, click the formatting option you want, and then complete the corresponding dialog box.*

Format your company name for greater impact. *Find the name of your company in your latest marketing document you created in Word. Replace it with a formatted version of the company name (for example, specify a new font and size).*

Replace Text

1 Position the cursor (or insertion point) at the beginning of the document.

2 Click the Edit menu, and then click Replace.

3 Type the text you want to search for in the Find What box.

4 Type the replacement text in the Replace With box.

5 Click Find Next to begin the search and highlight the next instance of the search text.

6 Click Replace to substitute the replacement text and find the next instance of the search text, or click Find Next to locate the next instance of the search text without making a replacement.

7 If a dialog box opens when you reach the end of the document, as it does in some Office programs, click OK.

8 When you're finished, if necessary, click Close.

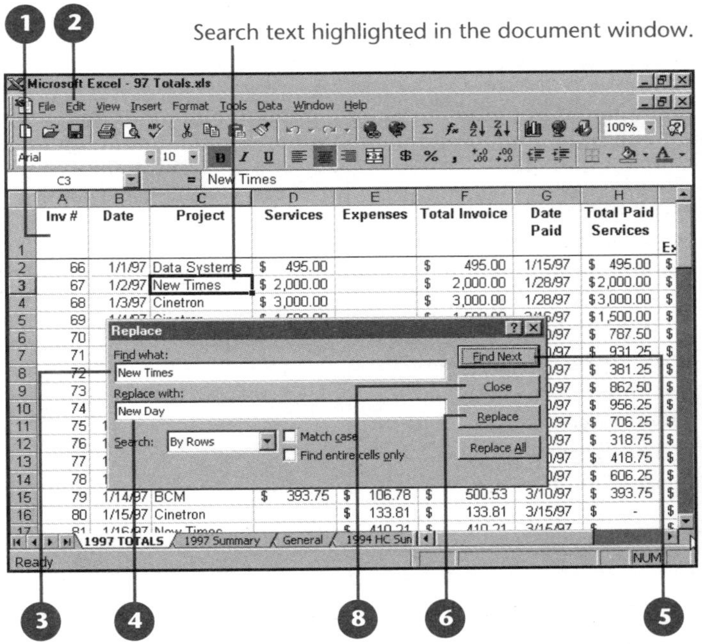

Search text highlighted in the document window.

Auto-Correcting Your Text

Since the dawn of typing, people have mistyped certain words or letter combinations consistently. How many times do you misspell "and" or hold down the Shift key too long? *AutoCorrect* corrects common misspellings and incorrect capitalization as you type. It also replaces typed characters, such as -- (two hyphens), with typographical symbols, such as — (an em dash). What's more, you can add your personal problem words to the AutoCorrect list. In most cases, AutoCorrect won't correct errors until you've pressed the Enter key or the spacebar.

Replace Text as You Type

- To correct incorrect capitalization or spelling errors automatically, continue typing until AutoCorrect makes the required correction.
- To replace two hyphens with an em dash, turn ordinals into superscripts (for example, 1st to 1st), or make a fraction stacked (for example, $^1/_2$) continue typing until AutoCorrect makes the appropriate change.
- To create a bulleted or numbered list, type 1. or * (for a bullet), press the Tab key, type any text, and then press the Enter key. AutoCorrect automatically inserts the next number or bullet. To end the list, quickly press the Enter key twice.

EXAMPLES OF AUTOCORRECT CHANGES

Type of Correction	If You Type	AutoCorrect Inserts
Capitalization	ann marie	Ann Marie
Capitalization	microsoft	Microsoft
Capitalization	thursday	Thursday
Superscript ordinals	2nd	2nd
Stacked fractions	1/2	$^1/_2$
Em dashes	Madison--a small city in southern Wisconsin--is a nice place to live.	Madison—a small city in southern Wisconsin—is a nice place to live.
Common typos	accomodate	accommodate
Common typos	can;t	can't
Common typos	windoes	windows

TIP

Use Undo to change an AutoCorrect change. *To reverse an AutoCorrect change, click the Undo button on the Standard toolbar as soon as AutoCorrect makes the change.*

TIP

You can create exceptions to AutoCorrect. *You can also specify abbreviations and terms that you don't want AutoCorrect to automatically correct by clicking the Exceptions button and adding these items to the list of exceptions.*

TRY THIS

Customize your AutoCorrect list. *Add your commonly mistyped words to the AutoCorrect list. You can also add abbreviations. Type your initials (in lowercase letters preferably) in the Replace box and your full name in the With box. Then try it: type your initials and press the spacebar, and watch AutoCorrect display your name.*

Add AutoCorrect Entries

1. Click the Tools menu, and then click AutoCorrect.
2. If necessary, click the AutoCorrect tab.
3. In the Replace box, type the incorrect text you want AutoCorrect to correct.
4. In the With box, type the text or symbols you want AutoCorrect to use as a replacement.
5. Click Add.
6. In Word, click any of the tabs to display AutoCorrect formatting settings.
7. When you're finished, click OK.

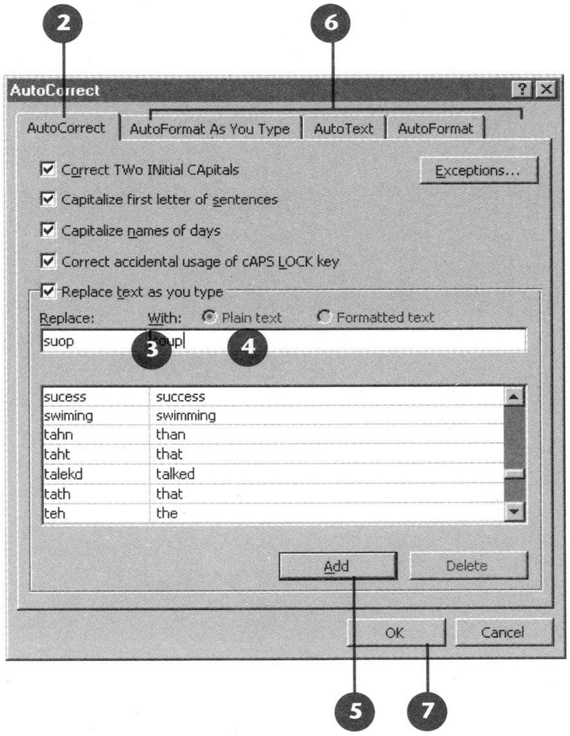

Selecting, Moving, and Resizing Objects

As you learn more about and use each Office 97 product, you will want to enhance your documents with more than just text or numbers. To do so, you can insert an object. An *object* is a picture or graphic image you create with a drawing program or you insert from an existing file of another program. For example, you can insert a company logo that you have drawn yourself, or you can insert a piece of *clip art*—pictures that come with Office 97. To work with an object you need to select it first. Once an object is selected, you can resize or move it with its selection *handles,* the little squares that appear on the edge of the object when you click the object to select it.

Select and Deselect an Object

- ◆ Click an object to display its handles.
- ◆ Click within the document window to deselect a selected object.

Unselected object
This object has no handles, which means it is not selected.

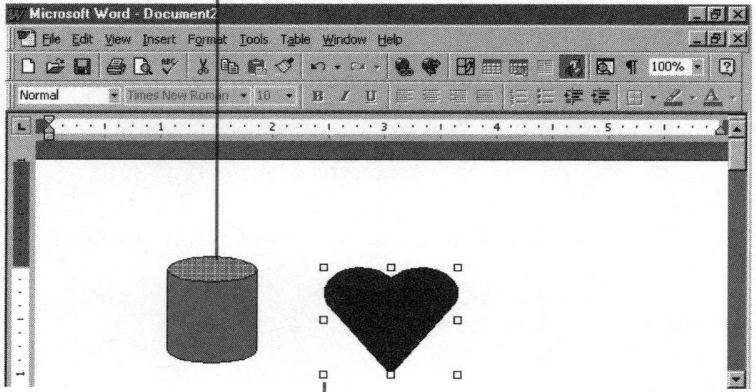

Selected object
Square white handles appear around a selected object.

Move an Object

1. Click an object to select it.
2. Drag the object to a new location as shown by the dotted outline of the object.
3. Release the mouse button to drop the object in the new location.

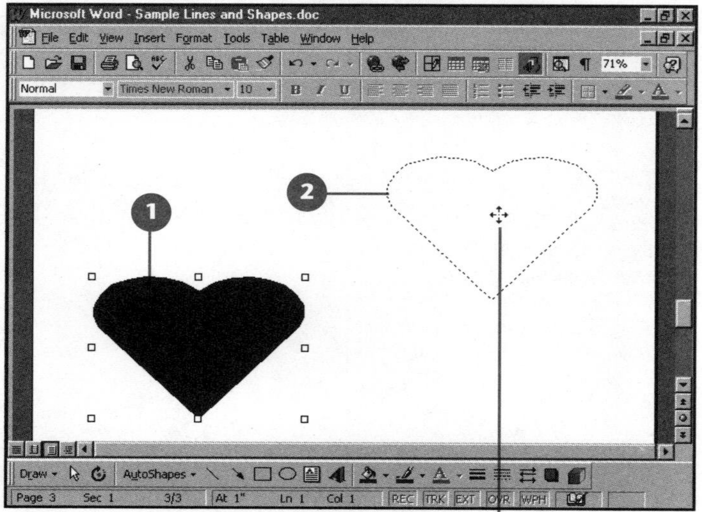

This pointer might look different or not appear at all.

TIP

An Access object. *The word "object" can take on a new meaning with each program. For example, when you create an Access database, all tables, queries, forms, and reports are considered objects.*

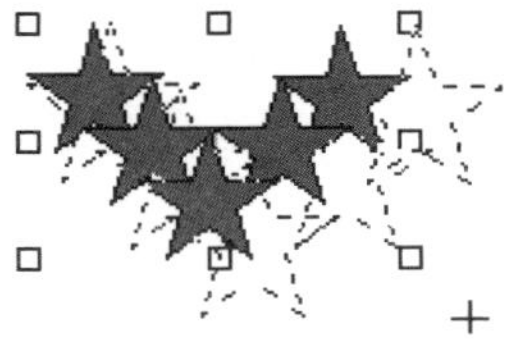

Resize an Object

1. Click the object to be resized.
2. Drag one of the sizing handles:
   - ◆ To resize the object in the vertical or horizontal direction, drag a sizing handle on the side of the selection box.
   - ◆ To resize the object proportionally in both the vertical and horizontal directions, drag a sizing handle on the corner of the selection box.

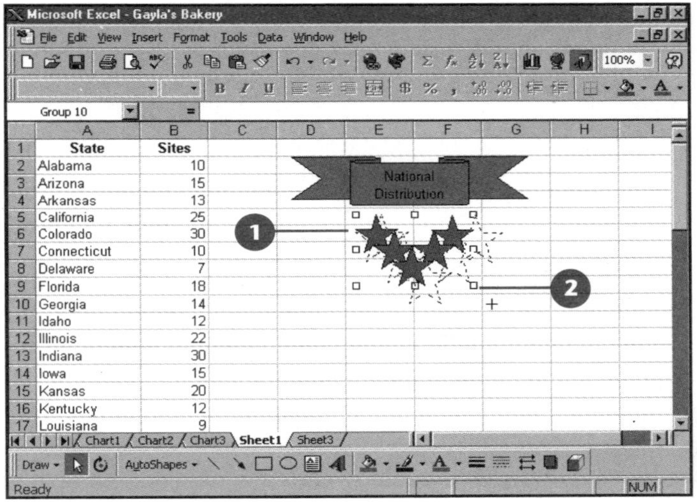

TIP

What is a point? *Points are a measurement unit used to size text and space in a document. One inch equals 72 points. Usually body text is 10 or 12 points. Headings are often 18, 24 or even 36 points. Apply different point sizes to your text to determine which size is best for your document.*

Resize an Object Precisely

1. Click the object to be resized.
2. Click the Format menu, and then click Object, Picture, or AutoShape (depends on the program.)
3. Click the Scale Height and Width spin arrows to resize the object.
4. Click OK.

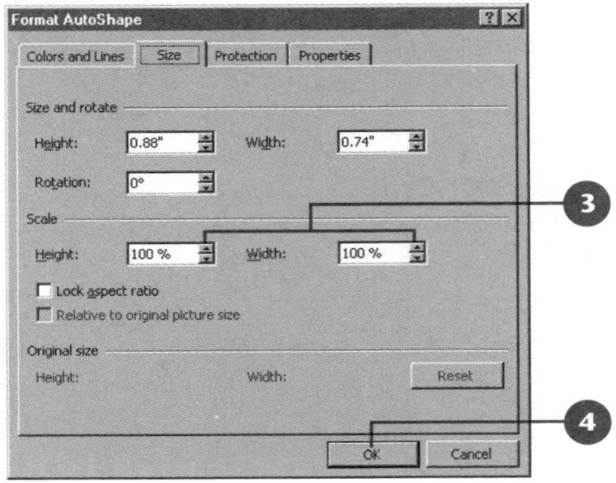

Drawing and Enhancing Objects

Drawn objects, like curved lines, or lightning bolts, can liven up your document or help make your point. Using the options on the Drawing toolbar, you can draw numerous objects without leaving the program you happen to be working in. After you add an object to your document, you can improve on it with a host of colors, and special effects that reflect you, your company, or your organization. Simply select the object you want to enhance, and then select the effect you prefer. To make your documents easy to read, take care not to add too many lines, shapes, or other objects.

Draw Lines and Shapes

1. Right-click any toolbar and then click Drawing.
2. Click the AutoShapes button on the Drawing toolbar, point to Lines or Basic Shapes, and then select the line or shape you want.
3. Click in the document window, drag the pointer until the line or shape is the size you want, and then release the mouse button.
4. If you make a mistake, press the Delete key while the line or shape is still selected, and try again.

2 Click to draw a straight line.

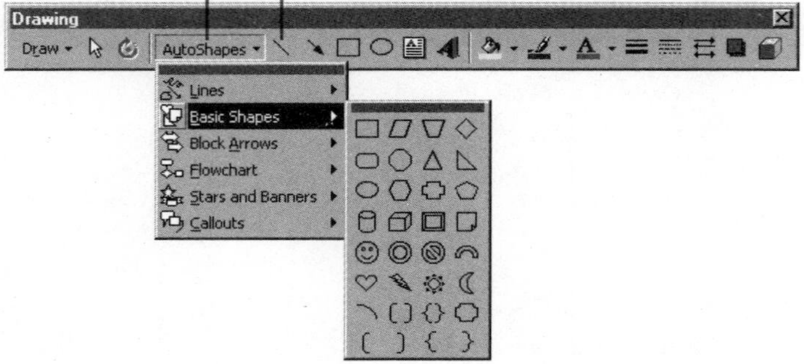

When drawing some curvy lines, you need to click the mouse button once for every curve you want.

Some samples of lines and shapes you can draw

TIP

Use the Drawing toolbar to align, group, or rotate objects. *Click Draw on the Drawing toolbar to use commands to group, reorder, align or distribute, and rotate or flip objects.*

SEE ALSO

See "Selecting, Moving, and Resizing Objects" on page 34 for information on working with objects.

TRY THIS

Create a design or logo to add to all your personal correspondence. *Combine colors and shadows, or colors and 3-D for the most dramatic effects.*

Add Color, Shadows, and 3-D

Before you can add color, shadows, or 3-D effects to an object, you need to open the Drawing toolbar.

- To fill a selected shape with color, click the Fill Color drop-down arrow, and then select the color you want.
- To change the line color of a selected object, click the Line Color drop-down arrow, and then select the color you want.
- To add a shadow to a selected object, click the Shadow button, and then select the shadow you want.
- To add 3-D to a selected object, click the 3-D button, and then select the 3-D effect you want.

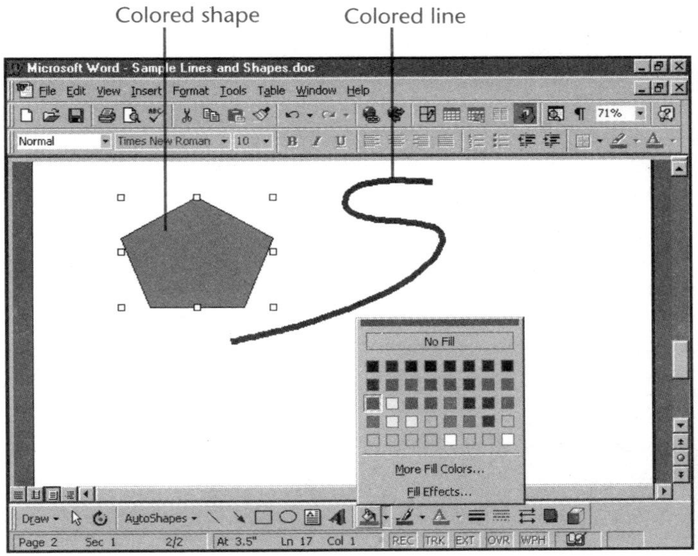

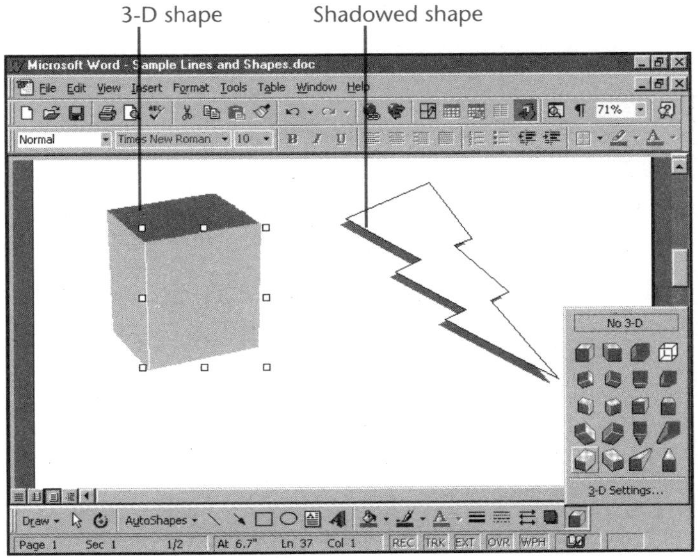

Adding WordArt

To add life to your documents, you can add a WordArt object to your document. *WordArt* is a Microsoft Office program that allows you to add visual enhancements to your text that go beyond changing a font or font size. You can select a WordArt style that stretches your text horizontally, vertically, or diagonally. Like many enhancements you can add to a document, WordArt is an object that you can move and reshape.

Insert WordArt button

Create WordArt

1. Click the Drawing button on the Standard toolbar.
2. Click the WordArt button on the Drawing toolbar.
3. Double-click the style of text you want to insert.
4. Type the text you want in the Edit WordArt Text dialog box.
5. Click the Font drop-down arrow, and then select the font you want.
6. Click the Size drop-down arrow, and then select the font size you want, measured in points.
7. If you want, click the Bold button, the Italic button, or both.
8. Click OK.

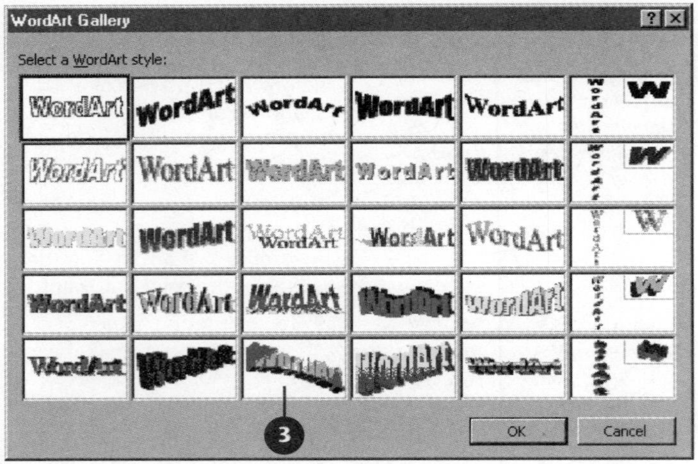

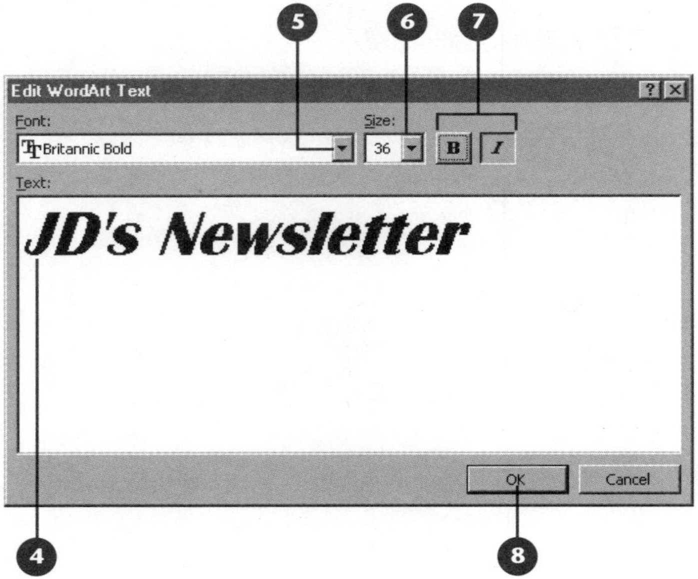

TIP

Use other WordArt toolbar buttons. *Use the WordArt toolbar buttons to rotate your WordArt object, change its alignment, and customize the spacing between each character.*

TIP

Displaying the WordArt toolbar. *When you click a WordArt object, its selection handles and the WordArt toolbar reappear.*

TRY THIS

Create a neighborhood newsletter. *Create a newsletter for your neighborhood's crime-watch group. Use WordArt for the title of the newsletter and some of the article titles.*

TIP

Use the keyboard to delete a WordArt object. *Select the object and then press Delete.*

9. With the WordArt selected, drag any handle to reshape the object until the text is the size you want.
10. Use the WordArt toolbar buttons to format or edit the WordArt even more.
11. Drag the WordArt to the location you want.
12. Click outside the WordArt text to deselect the object and close the toolbar.

USING WORDART TOOLBAR BUTTONS

Icon	Button Name	Description
	Insert WordArt	Create new WordArt
Edit Text...	Edit Text	Edit the existing text in a WordArt object
	WordArt Gallery	Choose a new style for existing WordArt
	Format WordArt	Change the attributes of existing WordArt
	WordArt Shape	Modify the shape of an existing WordArt object
	Free Rotate	Rotate an existing object
	WordArt Same Letter Heights	Makes upper and lowercase letters the same height
	WordArt Vertical	Changes horizontal letters into a text vertical formation
	WordArt Alignment	Allows the alignment of an existing object to be modified
	WordArt Character Spacing	Allows the spacing between characters to be changed

3

Adding and Modifying Media Clips

You can add pictures, sounds, and videos to Office documents. Your company might have a logo that it includes in all Office documents. Or you might want to use *clip art,* copy-right-free graphics, in your document for a special presentation you need to give. A picture is any *graphic object* that you insert as a single unit. You can insert pictures that you've created in a drawing program with extensions, such as .BMP or .TIF, or scanned in, or you can insert clip art. If you have inserted a picture, you can crop, or cut out, an image by hand using the Crop tool on the Picture toolbar. To further modify an image, you can change its color to default colors (automatic), grayscale, black and white, or watermark.

Insert Clip Art from the Clip Gallery

1. Select the position where you want to insert a media clip.
2. Click the Insert menu, point to Picture, and then click Clip Art.
3. Click the tab for the type of clip media you want to insert.
4. Click a category in the list on the left.
5. Click a media clip in the box. If necessary, scroll to see the available media clips.
6. Click Insert.

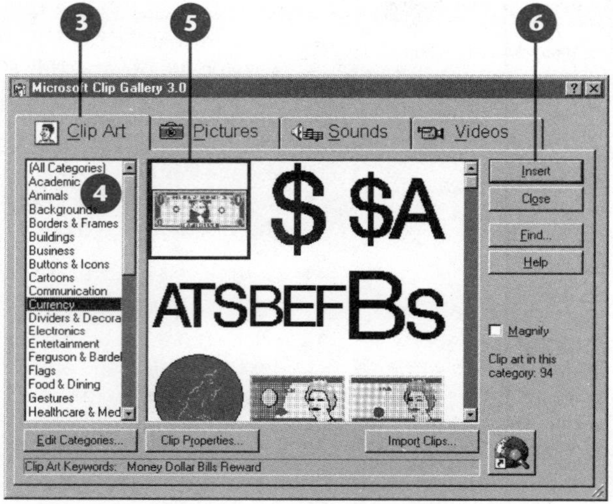

Insert a Picture

1. Click in the document where you want to insert the picture.
2. Click the Insert menu, point to Picture, and then click From File.
3. Open the folder where your picture is stored.
4. Click the image you want to use.
5. Click Insert.

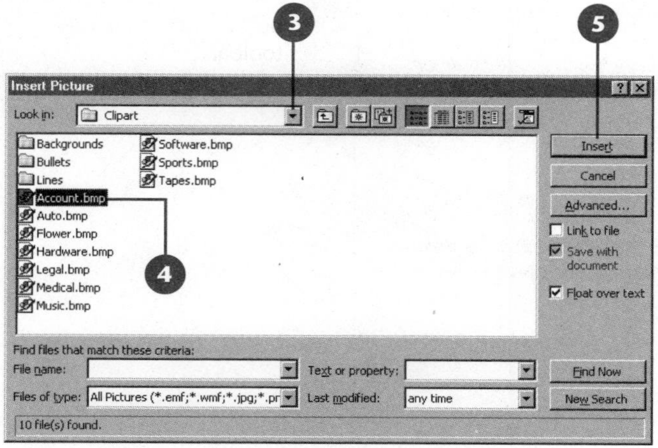

SEE ALSO

See "Enhancing Clip Art" on page 198 for information on modifying clip art and pictures.

Crop button

Crop an Image Quickly

1. Click the image.
2. Click the Crop button on the Picture toolbar.
3. Drag the sizing handles until the borders surround the area you want to crop.

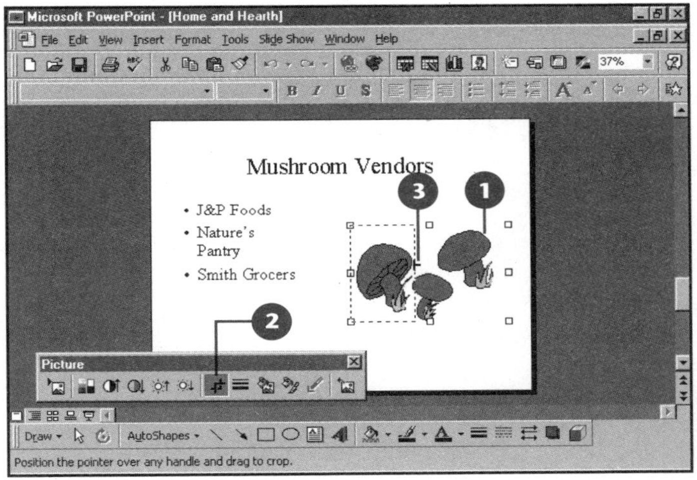

Choose a Color Type

1. Click the object whose color you want to change.
2. Click the Image Control button on the Picture toolbar.
3. Click one of the Image Control options:
   - Automatic (default coloring)
   - Grayscale (whites, blacks, and grays)
   - Black & White (white and black)
   - Watermark (whites and very light colors)

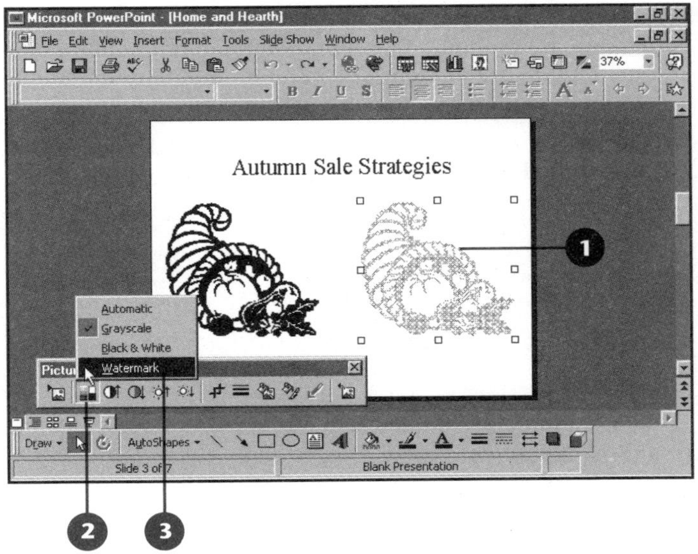

3

Grouping Documents in a Binder

The first step in grouping documents in a binder is either to create a new binder or open an existing one. Then you can add documents (also called *sections*) to it. Sometimes you'll want to add new, blank documents to your binder; other times you'll want to add existing ones.

> **TIP**
>
> **You can change the order of sections in a binder.** *It doesn't matter in which order you add sections to your binder. You can change the order in which the sections appear using the Rearrange Sections dialog box.*

Blank Binder icon

Create a New Binder

1. Click the Start button on the taskbar, and then click New Office Document.
2. Click the General tab.
3. Double-click the Blank Binder icon.

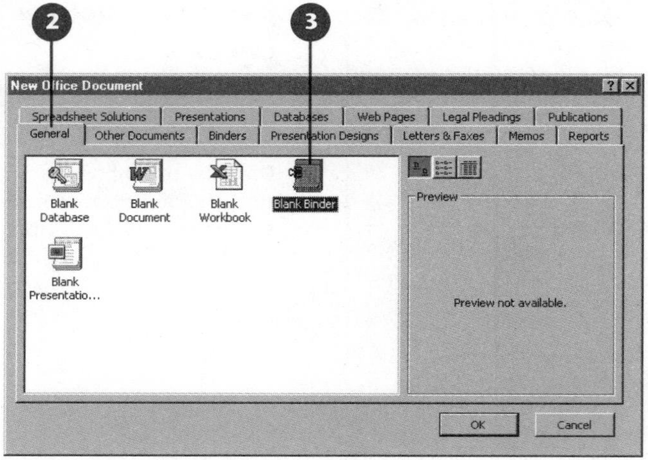

Open an Existing Binder

1. Click the Start button on the taskbar, and then click Open Office Document.
2. Open the folder where your binder is stored.
3. Double-click the binder you want to open.

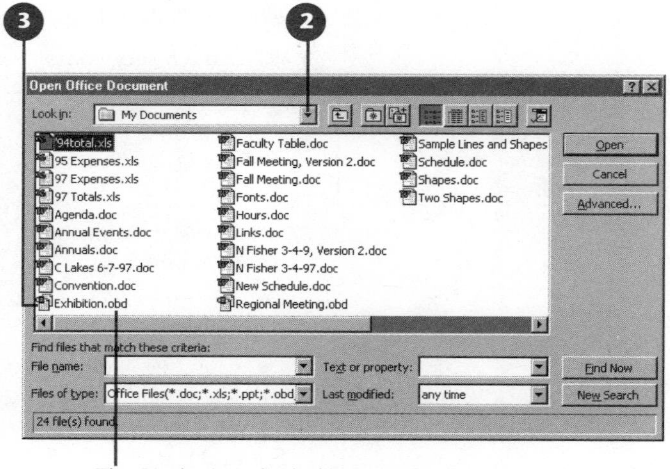

The Binder icon looks like a stack of papers bound together with a metal binder clip.

Add Sections to a Binder

1. Right-click the left pane of an open binder.
2. Click Add or Add From File.
3. Click the General tab in the Add Section dialog box, or open the folder where your document is stored in the Add From File dialog box.
4. Double-click the document you want to add.

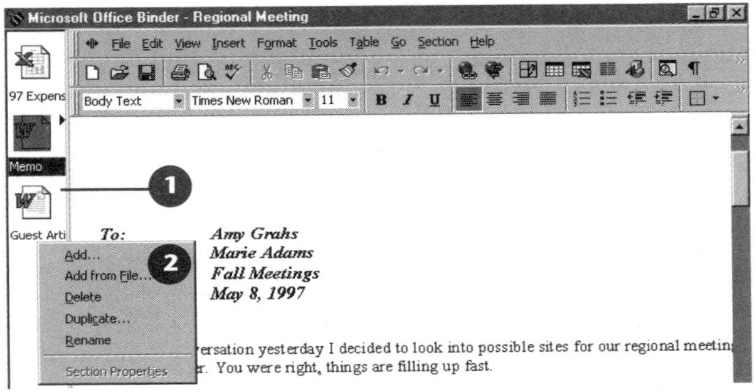

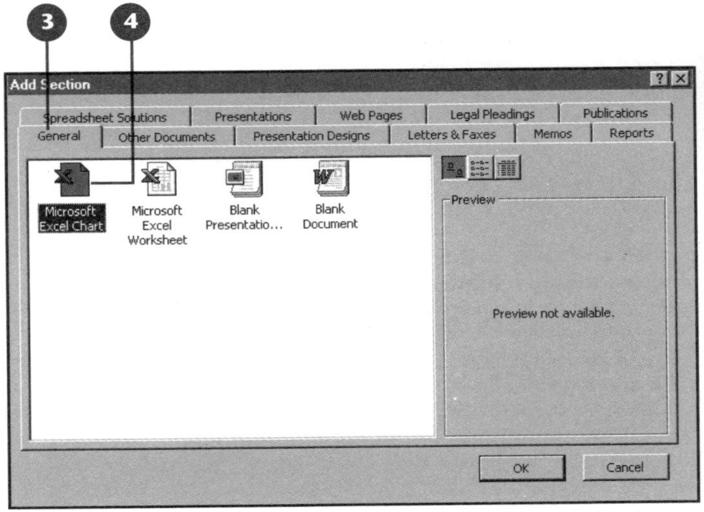

TIP

Original vs. copy. *When you add an existing document to a binder, you're really adding a copy of a document. The original document remains untouched; any changes you make to the binder copy do not affect the original and vice versa. In order to avoid confusion, it's best to rename the binder copy.*

TIP

Save a binder. *When you save a binder you save all the documents that are in it. Saving a binder works the same as saving any other Office document. Click the Save button on the Standard toolbar to save a binder for the first time, or click the File menu, click Save Binder As, and then complete the dialog box to save a copy of the binder with a different name.*

TIP

Print a binder. *You can print a binder the same way you print documents within Office programs. The only difference is that in Binder you can print more than one document at a time. You can print the whole binder, or you can print individual documents within the binder. Click the File menu, click Print Binder, and then click the options you want.*

Making Corrections

Everyone makes mistakes and changes their mind at some point, especially when creating or revising a document. With Office 97 you can instantly correct typing errors by pressing a key. You can also reverse more complicated actions, such as typing an entire word, formatting a paragraph, or creating a chart, with the Undo button. If you change your mind, you can just as easily click the Redo button to restore the action you undid.

TIP

Use Undo or Redo to reverse or repeat an action. *To undo or redo a series of actions, continue clicking either the Undo or Redo button until you've reversed or repeated all the actions in the series.*

TIP

Use the keyboard to quickly undo your last action. *Press Ctrl+Z. To redo your undo, press Ctrl+Y.*

Undo or Redo an Action Using the Standard Toolbar

- Click the Undo button to reverse your most recent action, such as typing a word, formatting a paragraph, or creating a chart.
- Click the Redo button to restore the last action you reversed.
- Click the Undo drop-down arrow, and then select the consecutive actions you want to reverse.
- Click the Redo drop-down arrow, and then select the consecutive actions you want to restore.

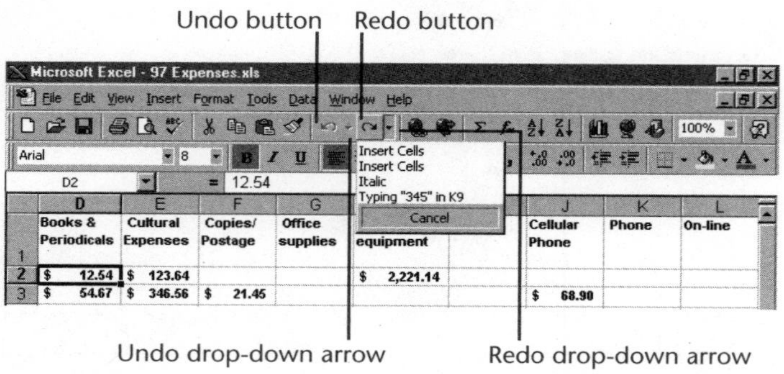

CORRECT TYPING ERRORS USING THE KEYBOARD

To Delete	Press
One character at a time to the left of the insertion point	Backspace
One word at a time to the left of the insertion point	Crtl+Backspace
One character at a time to the right of the insertion point	Delete
One word at a time to the right of the insertion point	Crtl+Delete
Selected text	Backspace or Delete

4

Creating Internet Documents with Office 97

IN THIS SECTION

World Wide Web technology is now available for all your Microsoft Office 97 documents. For better productivity and easier compilation of information, you can add *hyperlinks* (graphic or text objects you click to jump to other Office documents and intranet or Internet pages) within your Office documents. (See "Sharing Information Between Programs" on page 310 for more information about embedding hyperlinks into your document).

Once you click several hyperlinks, perhaps opening Word, Excel, PowerPoint, and even Access in the process, you also need a way to move between these open documents. The Web toolbar makes this simple with its Web-like navigation tools. You can move backward or forward one document at a time or jump to any document with just a couple of mouse clicks.

In fact, whether a document is stored on your computer, network, intranet, or across the globe, you can access it from Office 97. Just display the Web toolbar from within any Office program, and you're ready to jump to any document, no matter where it resides.

Inserting Hyperlinks

Sometimes you'll want to refer to another part of the same document or a file created in a different program. Rather than duplicating the material or adding a footnote, you can create a *hyperlink*, a graphic or colored, underlined text object that you click to move (or *jump*) to a new location. The jump can be within the same document, to a location in another file on your computer or network, or to a Web page on your intranet or the Internet.

Insert Hyperlink button

Insert a Hyperlink Within a Document

1. Choose the location from which you want the hyperlink to jump (a Word bookmark, an Excel named range or cell, or a PowerPoint slide number).
2. Click where you want to insert the hyperlink, type the text you want to use as the hyperlink, and then select it.
3. Click the Insert Hyperlink button on the Standard toolbar.
4. Click the Named Location In File Browse button, and then double-click the name you want to jump to.
5. Click OK.

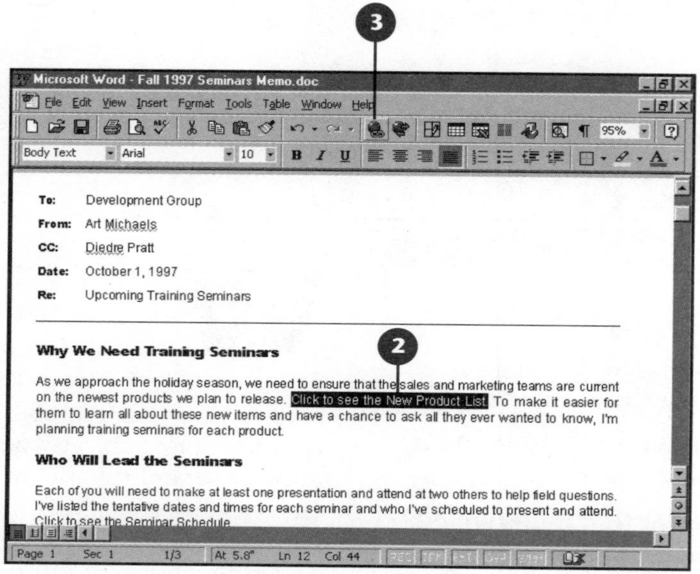
3
Microsoft Word - Fall 1997 Seminars Memo.doc
File Edit View Insert Format Tools Table Window Help
Body Text
Arial
10
To: Development Group
From: Art Michaels
CC: Diedre Pratt
Date: October 1, 1997
Re: Upcoming Training Seminars
2
Why We Need Training Seminars
As we approach the holiday season, we need to ensure that the sales and marketing teams are current on the newest products we plan to release. Click to see the New Product List. To make it easier for them to learn all about these new items and have a chance to ask all they ever wanted to know, I'm planning training seminars for each product.
Who Will Lead the Seminars
Each of you will need to make at least one presentation and attend at two others to help field questions. I've listed the tentative dates and times for each seminar and who I've scheduled to present and attend.
Page 1 Sec 1 1/3 At 5.8" Ln 12 Col 44

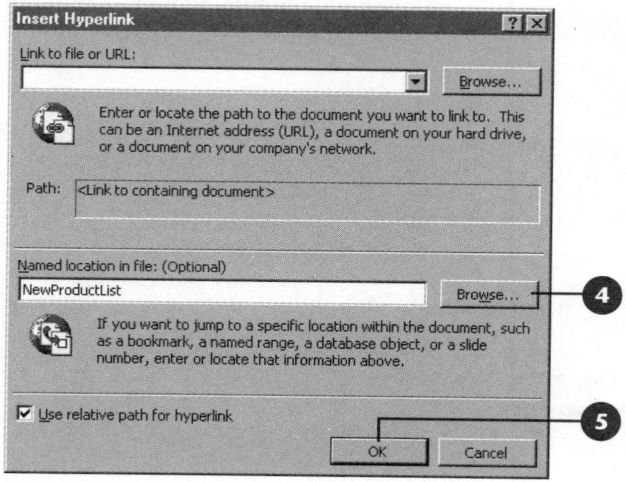
Insert Hyperlink
Link to file or URL:
Browse...
Enter or locate the path to the document you want to link to. This can be an Internet address (URL), a document on your hard drive, or a document on your company's network.
Path: <Link to containing document>
Named location in file: (Optional)
NewProductList
Browse...
4
If you want to jump to a specific location within the document, such as a bookmark, a named range, a database object, or a slide number, enter or locate that information above.
Use relative path for hyperlink
5
OK
Cancel

TRY THIS

Create hyperlinks in a long document. *Try making the main entries of the table of contents in a Word report hyperlinks. This way a reader can click the table of contents entry to jump to that section instead of scrolling to find it.*

TIP

Hyperlinks in Microsoft Access. *When you create a hyperlink in Access, it appears as a label on the form or report. Access uses the Caption property as the display text for the hyperlink.*

Insert a Hyperlink Between Documents

1. Position the insertion point where you want the hyperlink to appear.
2. Type and then select the text you want to use as the hyperlink.
3. Click the Insert Hyperlink button on the Standard toolbar.
4. Click the Link To File Or URL Browse button, and then double-click the file you want to jump to.
5. Click OK.

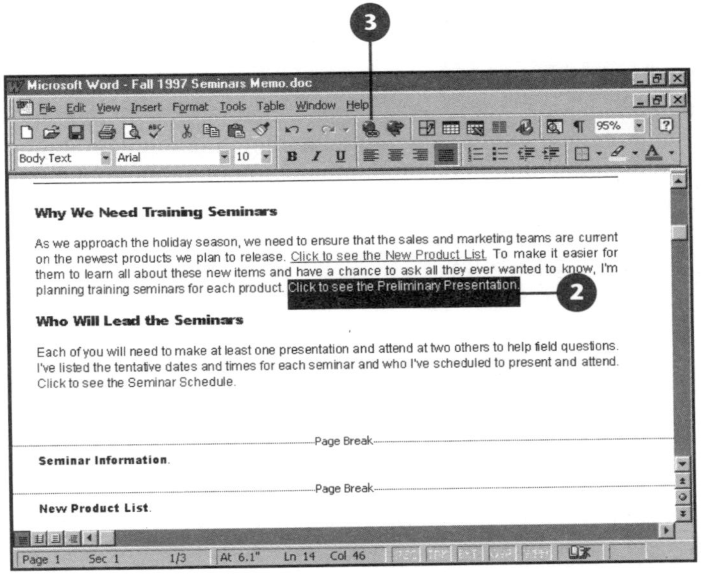

3
Microsoft Word - Fall 1997 Seminars Memo.doc
File Edit View Insert Format Tools Table Window Help
Body Text
Arial
10
95%
Why We Need Training Seminars
As we approach the holiday season, we need to ensure that the sales and marketing teams are current on the newest products we plan to release. Click to see the New Product List. To make it easier for them to learn all about these new items and have a chance to ask all they ever wanted to know, I'm planning training seminars for each product. Click to see the Preliminary Presentation.
2
Who Will Lead the Seminars
Each of you will need to make at least one presentation and attend at two others to help field questions. I've listed the tentative dates and times for each seminar and who I've scheduled to present and attend. Click to see the Seminar Schedule.
Page Break
Seminar Information
Page Break
New Product List
Page 1 Sec 1 1/3 At 6.1" Ln 14 Col 46

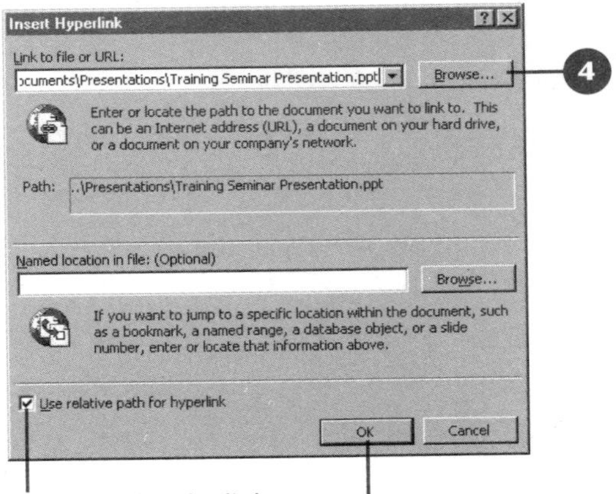

Insert Hyperlink
Link to file or URL:
ocuments\Presentations\Training Seminar Presentation.ppt
Browse...
4
Enter or locate the path to the document you want to link to. This can be an Internet address (URL), a document on your hard drive, or a document on your company's network.
Path: ..\Presentations\Training Seminar Presentation.ppt
Named location in file: (Optional)
Browse...
If you want to jump to a specific location within the document, such as a bookmark, a named range, a database object, or a slide number, enter or locate that information above.
Use relative path for hyperlink
OK
Cancel

This maintains the link even if you move the file.

5

4

Using and Removing Hyperlinks

Hyperlinks extend a document well beyond that one file. Rather than duplicating the important information stored in other documents, you can create hyperlinks to the relevant material. When you click a hyperlink for the first time (during a session), the color of the hyperlink changes color indicating that you have accessed the hyperlink. If a link becomes outdated or unnecessary, you can easily remove it.

SEE ALSO

See "Jumping to Hyperlinked Documents" on page 50 for more information about using hyperlinks.

Use a Hyperlink

1. Position the mouse pointer (which changes to a hand cursor) over any hyperlink.
2. Click the hyperlink. The screen:
   - Jumps to a new location within the same document.
   - Jumps to a location on an Intranet or Internet Web site.
   - Opens a new file and the program in which it was created.

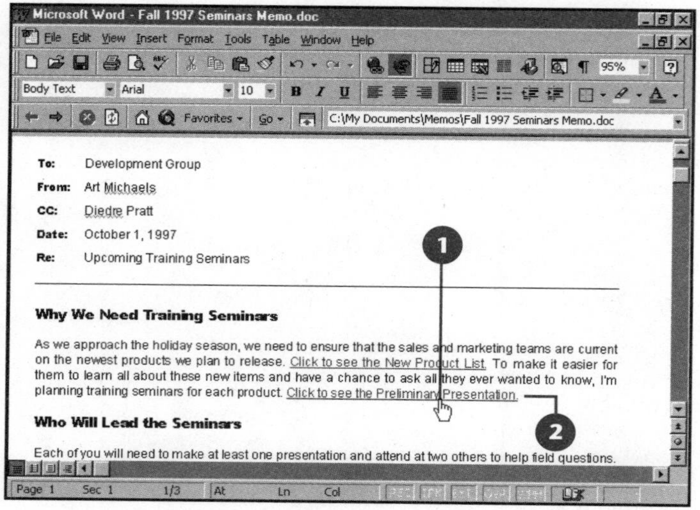
Microsoft Word - Fall 1997 Seminars Memo.doc
File Edit View Insert Format Tools Table Window Help
95%
Body Text
Arial
10
Favorites
Go
C:\My Documents\Memos\Fall 1997 Seminars Memo.doc
To: Development Group
From: Art Michaels
CC: Diedre Pratt
Date: October 1, 1997
Re: Upcoming Training Seminars
Why We Need Training Seminars
As we approach the holiday season, we need to ensure that the sales and marketing teams are current on the newest products we plan to release. Click to see the New Product List. To make it easier for them to learn all about these new items and have a chance to ask all they ever wanted to know, I'm planning training seminars for each product. Click to see the Preliminary Presentation.
Who Will Lead the Seminars
Each of you will need to make at least one presentation and attend at two others to help field questions.
1
2
Page 1 Sec 1 1/3 At Ln Col

TRY THIS

Rename a hyperlink. *Drag the I-beam pointer across an existing hyperlink to select it. Be careful that you don't click it. Type the new text you want to use as the hyperlink to replace the highlighted text.*

Remove a Hyperlink

1. Drag the I-beam pointer across the hyperlink to select it without clicking it.
2. Click the Insert Hyperlink button on the Standard toolbar.
3. Click Remove Link and then click OK.
4. If necessary, delete the text.

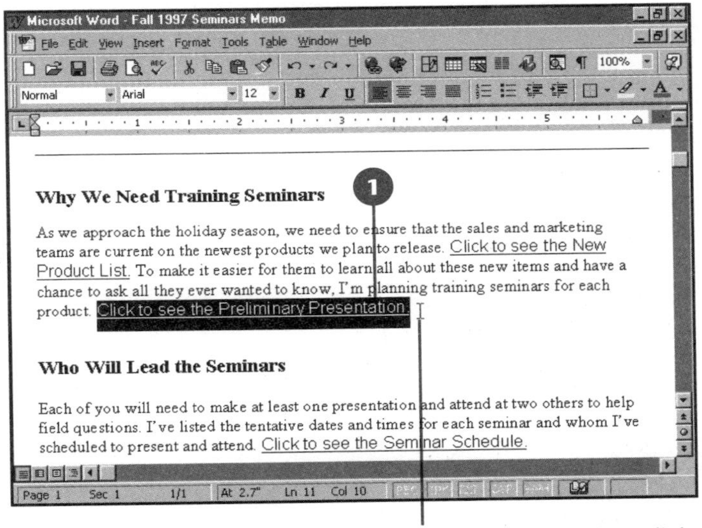

Microsoft Word - Fall 1997 Seminars Memo
File Edit View Insert Format Tools Table Window Help
Normal
Arial
12
100%
1
Why We Need Training Seminars
As we approach the holiday season, we need to ensure that the sales and marketing teams are current on the newest products we plan to release. Click to see the New Product List. To make it easier for them to learn all about these new items and have a chance to ask all they ever wanted to know, I'm planning training seminars for each product. Click to see the Preliminary Presentation.
Who Will Lead the Seminars
Each of you will need to make at least one presentation and attend at two others to help field questions. I've listed the tentative dates and times for each seminar and whom I've scheduled to present and attend. Click to see the Seminar Schedule.
Page 1 Sec 1 1/1 At 2.7" Ln 11 Col 10

Use this pointer to highlight the hyperlink. If you click the hyperlink, you will jump to another location rather than select it.

Jumping to Hyperlinked Documents

You can jump directly to a document on your computer or network, or to a Web page on your intranet or the Internet using the Web toolbar. In the Address box on the Web toolbar, type the address to the document you want to view and press Enter. To jump to a document on your hard drive or network, enter its filename (including its path, for example, C:\My Documents\Memos\To Do List.doc). To jump to a Web document, enter its Internet address (a URL, for example, http://www.microsoft.com).

Jump to a Document Using the Address Box

1. Click the Address box on the Web toolbar to select the current address.
2. Type an address to the document. For example, C:\My Documents \Memos\Fall 1997 Seminars Memo.doc. The address includes:
   - A hard drive (C:\)
   - One or more folders (My Documents \Memos)
   - A filename (Fall 1997 Seminars Memo.doc)
3. Press Enter.

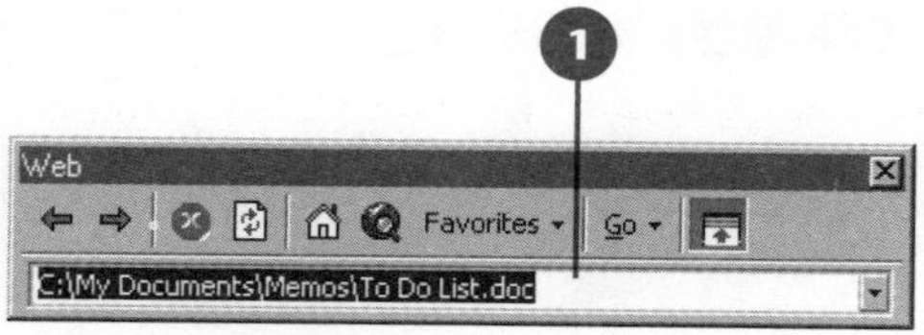
1
Web
Favorites
Go
C:\My Documents\Memos\To Do List.doc

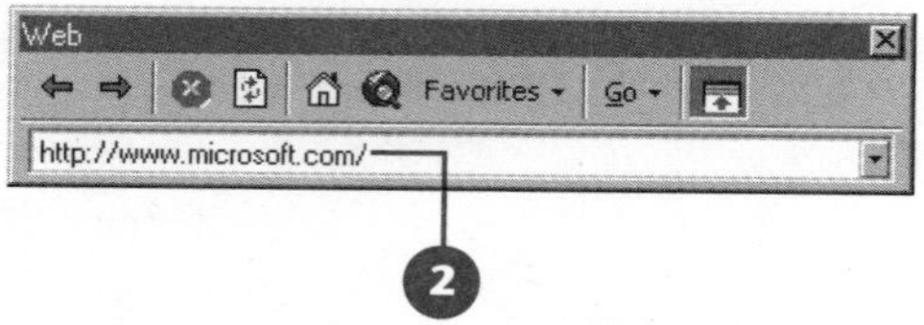
Web
Favorites
Go
http://www.microsoft.com/
2

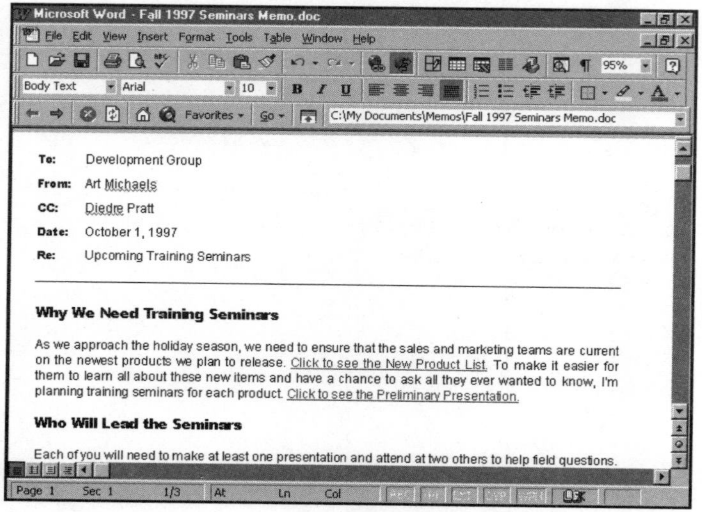
Microsoft Word - Fall 1997 Seminars Memo.doc
File Edit View Insert Format Tools Table Window Help
Body Text
Arial
10
95%
Favorites
Go
C:\My Documents\Memos\Fall 1997 Seminars Memo.doc
To: Development Group
From: Art Michaels
CC: Diedre Pratt
Date: October 1, 1997
Re: Upcoming Training Seminars
Why We Need Training Seminars
As we approach the holiday season, we need to ensure that the sales and marketing teams are current on the newest products we plan to release. Click to see the New Product List. To make it easier for them to learn all about these new items and have a chance to ask all they ever wanted to know, I'm planning training seminars for each product. Click to see the Preliminary Presentation.
Who Will Lead the Seminars
Each of you will need to make at least one presentation and attend at two others to help field questions.
Page 1 Sec 1 1/3 At Ln Col

TIP

Internet Addresses and URLs. *Every Web page has a uniform resource locator (URL), an Internet address in a form your browser program can decipher. Like postal addresses and e-mail addresses, each URL contains specific parts that identify where a Web page is located. For example, the URL for Microsoft's Web page is* ***http://www.microsoft.com/*** *where "http://" shows the address is on the Web and "www.microsoft.com" shows the computer that stores the Web page. As you browse various pages, the URL includes their folders and filenames.*

TRY THIS

Open a Web document. *In the Address box, enter the complete location of the document you want to open, including the computer drive, filename, and file extension. If you have access to the Internet, you can enter a URL for a Web page.*

Jump to a Web Document Using the Address Box

1. Click the Address box on the Web toolbar to select the current address.
2. Type an Internet address. For example, http://www.microsoft.com (Microsoft's Web address).
3. Press Enter.
4. Connect to the Internet through your Internet service provider (ISP) or network. Your Web browser opens (such as Microsoft Internet Explorer).
5. Click any hyperlink to explore the Web site.
6. When you are finished, click the File menu, and then click Close.
7. If necessary, click Yes to disconnect from the Internet.

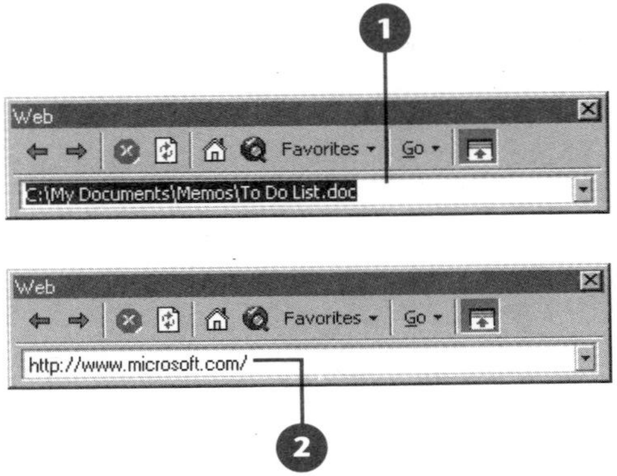

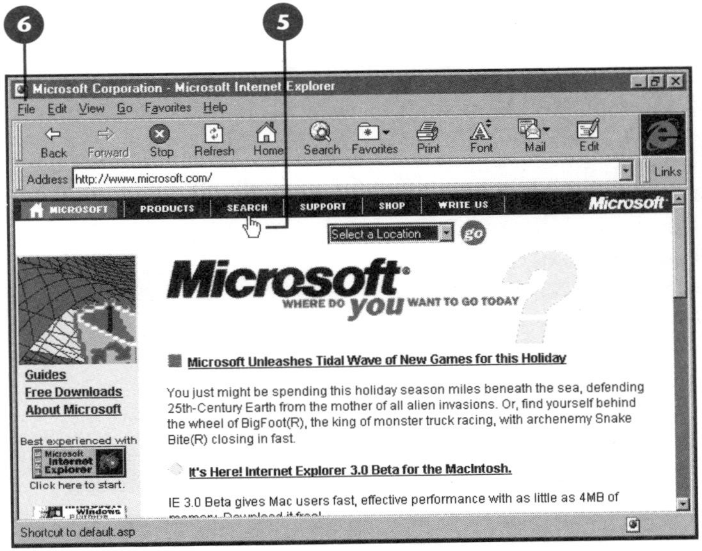

Navigating Hyperlinked Documents

As you explore hyperlinked documents, you might want to retrace your steps and return to a document you've already visited. You can move backward and then forward one document at a time, or you can jump directly to any document from the *Address list*, which shows the last 10 documents you've linked to. This way you can quickly jump to any document without having to click through them one by one. After you start the jump to a document, you can stop the link if the document opens (or *loads*) slowly or you decide not to access it. If a document loads incorrectly or you want to update the information it contains, you can reload, or *refresh*, the page.

Refresh Current Page button

Move Forward and Backward One Document

1. Click the Forward button on the Web toolbar.
2. Click the Back button on the Web toolbar.

The Back button dims when you reach the first document you opened.

Jump to Any Open Hyperlinked Document

1. Click the Address drop-down arrow.
2. Click the document you want.

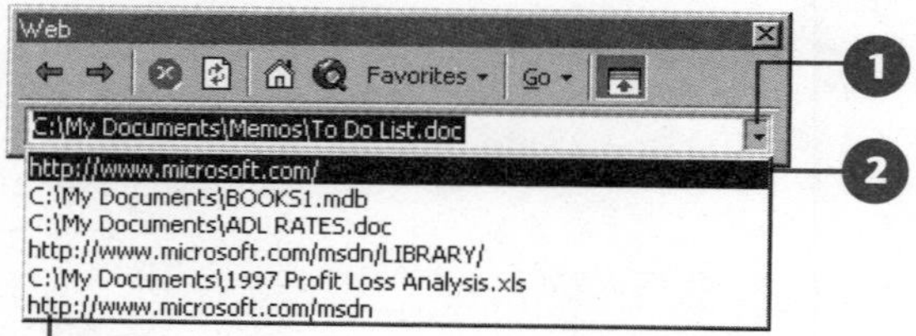

The address list shows all the documents you've opened this session, in the order you opened them.

Stop a Link

1. Click the Stop Current Jump button on the Web toolbar.

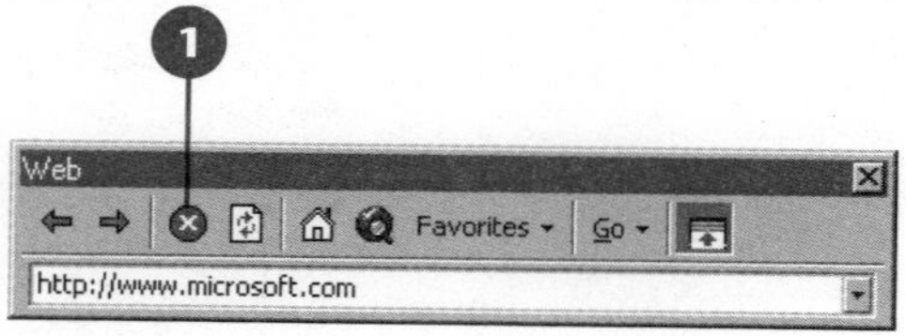

Reload a Document

1. Click the Refresh Current Page button on the Web toolbar.

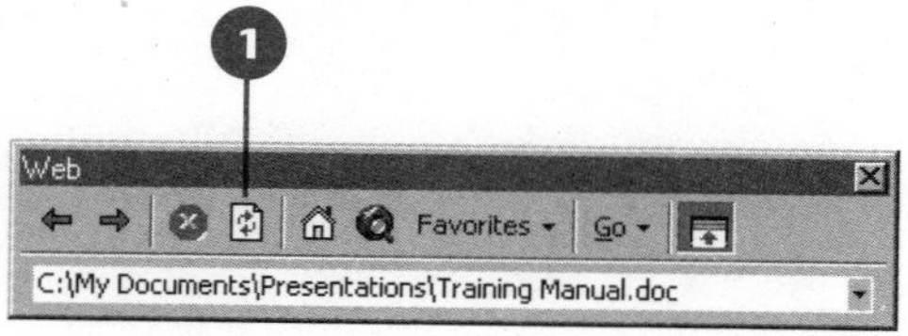

Creating HTML Documents

HyperText Markup Language (HTML) is a simple coding system used to format documents for an intranet or the Internet. A browser program interprets these codes to determine how to display a certain document. You can save any open file as an HTML document ready to publish on the World Wide Web or your Intranet. When you use the Save As HTML command, it starts the Internet Assistant, which converts your Office document to an HTML document. Then you can publish it on the Web or on your Intranet. Be aware that some formatting or other parts of your file might not be available in HTML and therefore might display incorrectly.

Convert Files to HTML

1. Open the document you want to save as HTML.
2. Click the File menu, and then click Save As HTML. (If this command doesn't appear, install Web Authoring Tools from the Office 97 CD-ROM.)
3. A Save As HTML dialog appears (for Word) or an Internet Assistant dialog box appears (for Excel, PowerPoint, and Access).

   For Word, select the drive and folder where you want to store the file, type a name for the file, click Save, and then click Yes to confirm the save.

   For Excel, PowerPoint, and Access, follow the wizard instructions, click Next after you complete each step, and then click Finish.

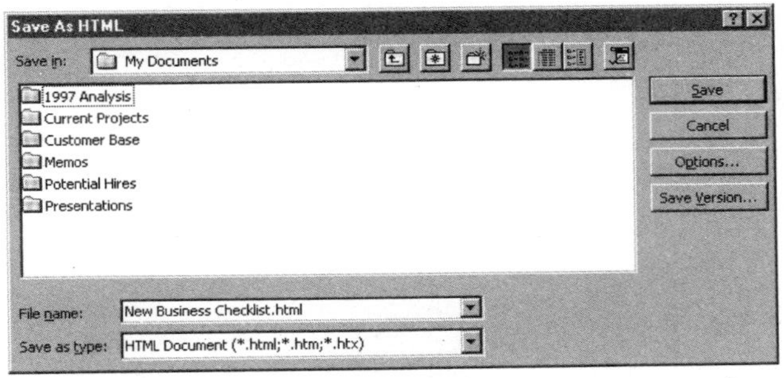

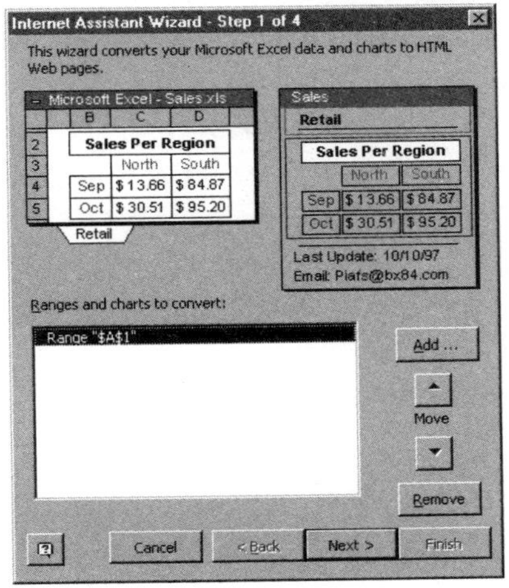

4

Getting Started with the Web Toolbar

The Web toolbar provides an easy way to navigate hyperlinked documents in any Office program. The Web toolbar looks and works the same no matter which Office program you are using. While you're browsing, you can hide all the other toolbars to gain the greatest space available on your screen and improve readability. You can make any document your *start page*, or home base. Set your start page to a document you want to access quickly and frequently.

Web Toolbar button

Display or Hide the Web Toolbar

1. Click the Web Toolbar button on the Standard toolbar. This button toggles on and off to show and hide the Web toolbar.

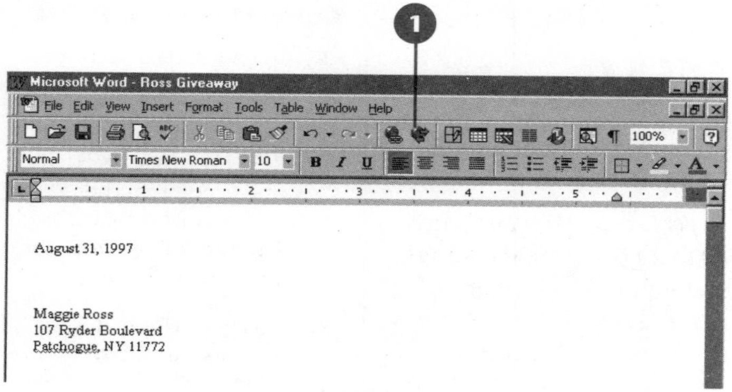

Hide or Display Other Toolbars

1. Click the Show Only Web Toolbar button on the Web toolbar.

1 Click to make any visible toolbars disappear or reappear.

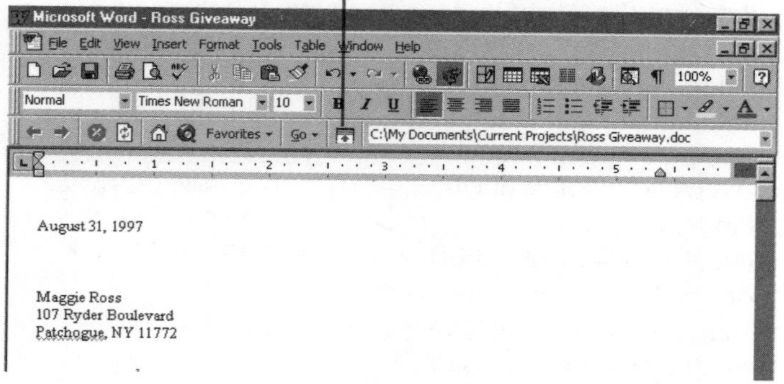

TRY THIS

Change your start page. *If you have Internet access, set your start page to the Web page on your Intranet or the Internet you visit most frequently.*

Jump to Your Start Page

1. Click the Start Page button on the Web toolbar.

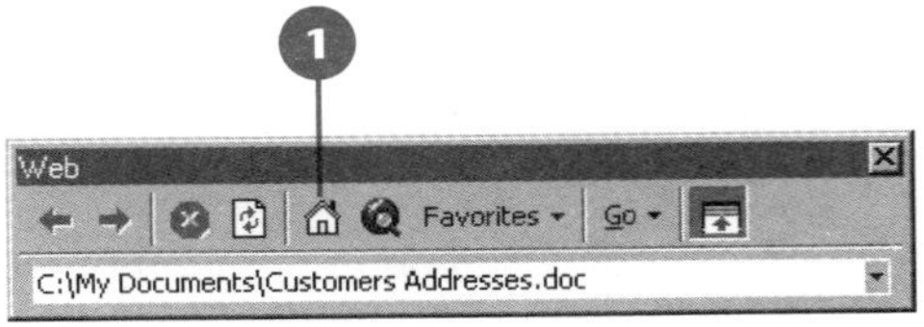

Change Your Start Page

1. Open the document you want as your start page.
2. Click the Go button on the Web toolbar.
3. Click Set Start Page.
4. Click Yes to confirm the new start page.

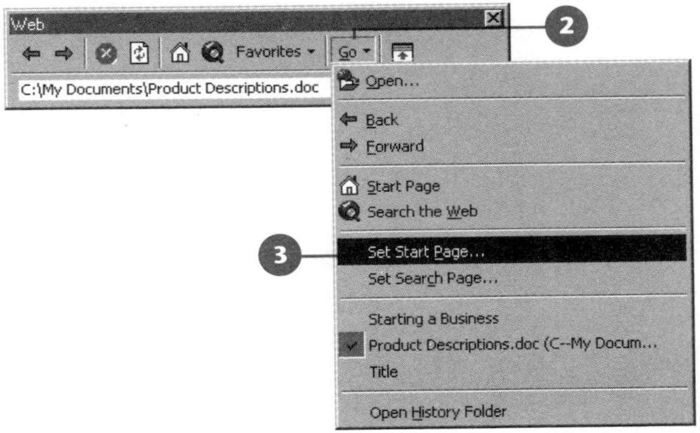

You can use any document, including an intranet or Web page, as your start page.

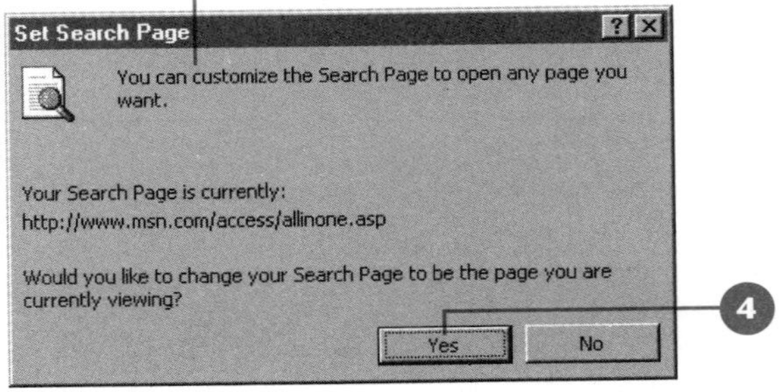

Getting Information from the Web

You can find all kinds of information on the Web. The best way to find information is to use a search engine. A *search engine* allows you to search through a collection of material to find what you are looking for. There are many search engines available on the Web, such as Yahoo! and Excite. You can make any document your *search page*. Set your search page to a reliable search engine you want to access frequently.

Search for Information on the Web

1. Click the Search The Web button on the Web toolbar.
2. Connect to the Internet through your Internet service provider (ISP) or network. Your Web browser opens (such as Microsoft Internet Explorer).
3. Type in a topic you want to search for on the Internet.
4. Select a search engine.
5. Click the Search button to start the search.
6. When you are finished, click the File menu, and then click Close.
7. If necessary, click Yes to disconnect from the Internet.

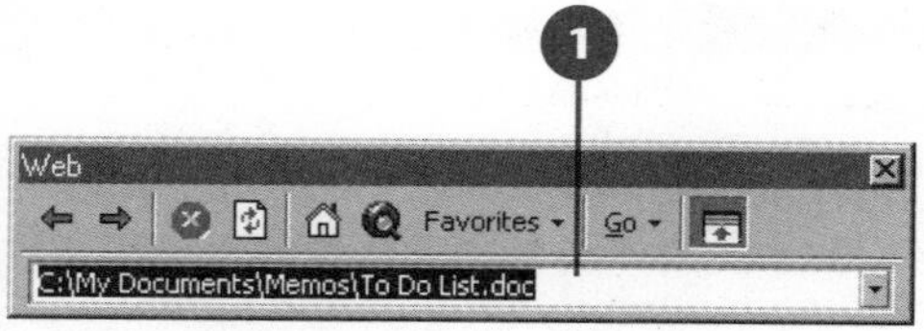

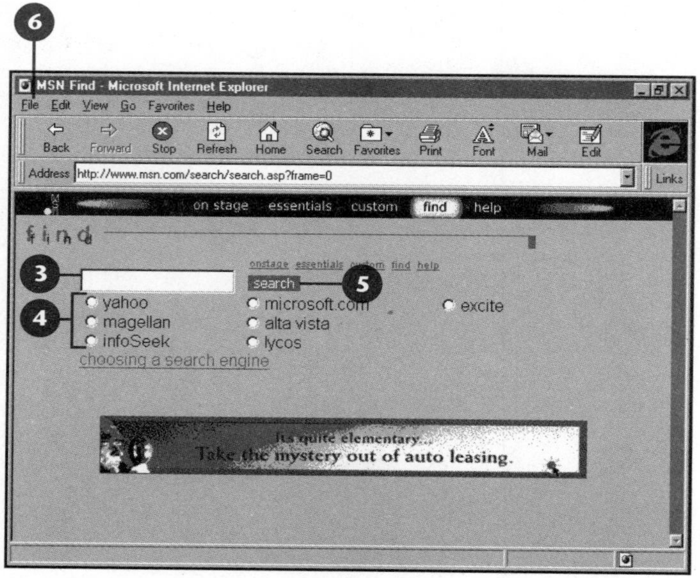

> **TIP**
>
> **Use Office 97 file viewers to display files.** *File viewers allow anyone to view and print documents created in Word, Excel, and PowerPoint just as they would from within the programs even if they don't own the programs. You can download the viewers for free from Microsoft 's Web site located at* ***http://microsoft.com/msoffice/*** *and send them to anyone who needs to look at your Word, Excel, and PowerPoint files.*

Change Your Search Page

1. Open the document you want as your search page.
2. Click the Go button on the Web toolbar.
3. Click Set Search Page.
4. Click Yes to confirm the new search page.

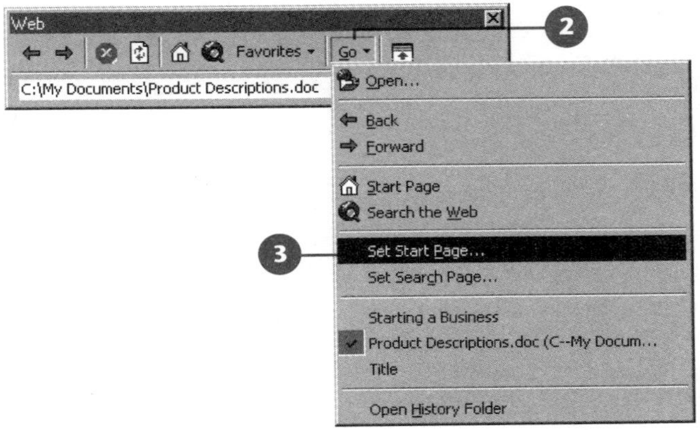

You can use any document, including an intranet or Web page, as your start page.

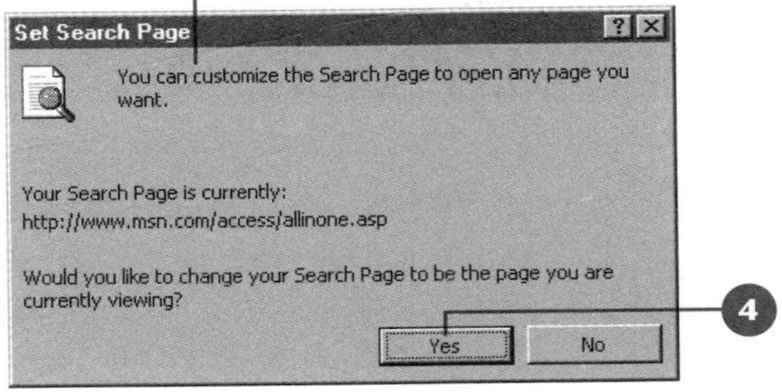

4

Getting Media Clips from the Web

You can find and download additional clip art, pictures, sounds, and videos from the Web into the Microsoft Clip Gallery. With a click of a button, you can connect to the Web (through your browser), find graphic and multimedia files, and then download them into the Microsoft Clip Gallery.

SEE ALSO

See "Adding and Modifying Media Clips" on page 40 for more information about inserting clip art, pictures, sounds, and videos.

Connect To Web For Additional Clips

Get Additional Clips from the Web

1. Click the Insert menu, point to Picture, and then click Clip Art.
2. Click the Connect To Web For Additional Clips button. Your Web browser opens (such as Microsoft Internet Explorer).
3. Connect to the Internet through your Internet service provider (ISP) or network.
4. If necessary, click the Accept button, and then click Browse.
5. Click the media type you want: Clip Art, Pictures, Sounds, or Videos.
6. Click the Select A Category drop-down list arrow, and then click the category you want.
7. Click Go.
8. When you are finished, click the File menu, and then click Close.

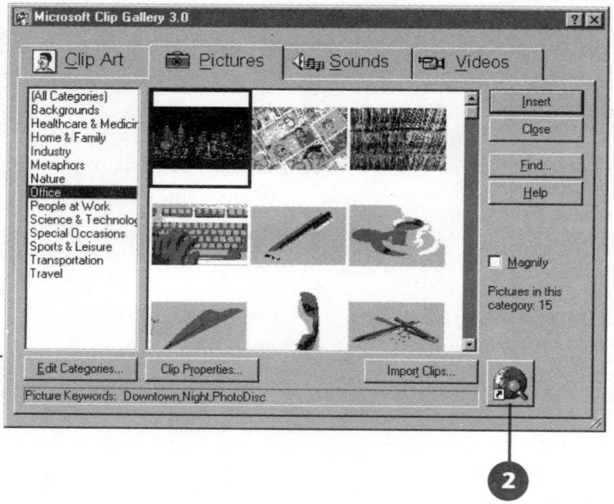

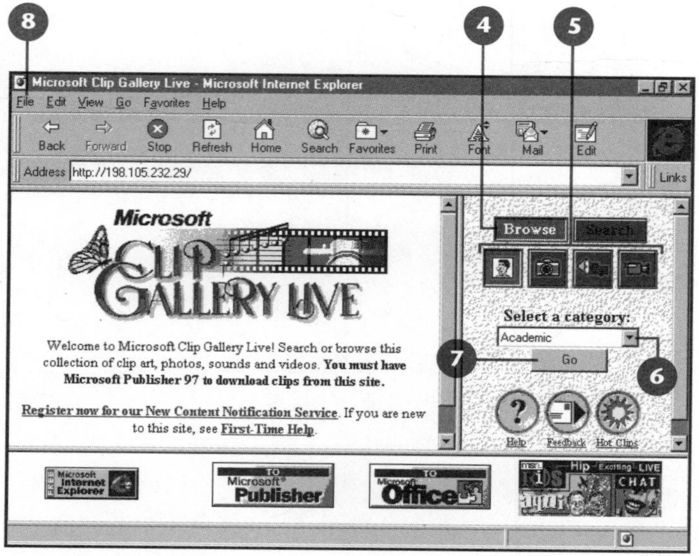

Returning to Favorite Documents

When you have jumped to a document that you would like to return to in the future, you can add the document to a list of favorites. The Favorites button provides shortcuts to files you explore frequently so you won't need to retype long file locations. These shortcuts can open documents on your computer, network, Intranet, and the Internet.

Add a File Shortcut to Your Favorites Folder

1. Open the file you want to access from the Favorites folder.
2. Click the Favorites button on the Web toolbar.
3. Click Add To Favorites.
4. Type a new name if you want.
5. Click Add.

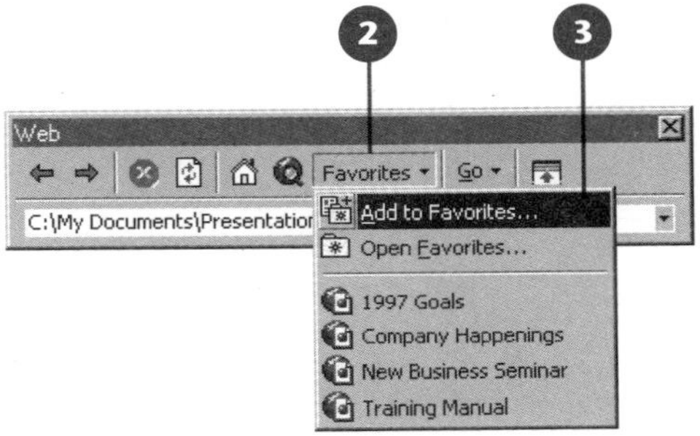

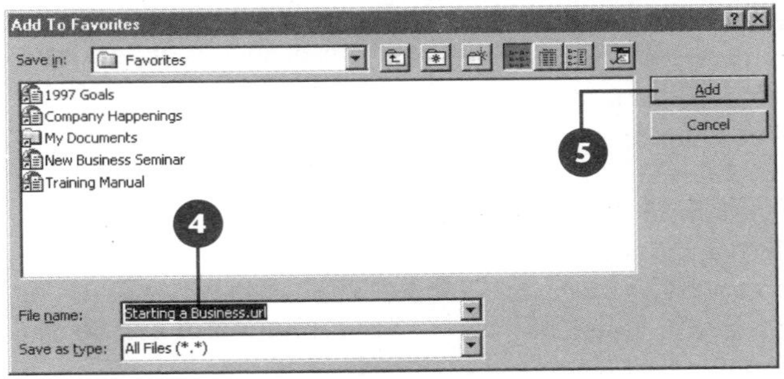

Jump to a Favorite Document

1. Click the Favorites button on the Web toolbar.
2. Click the document you want.

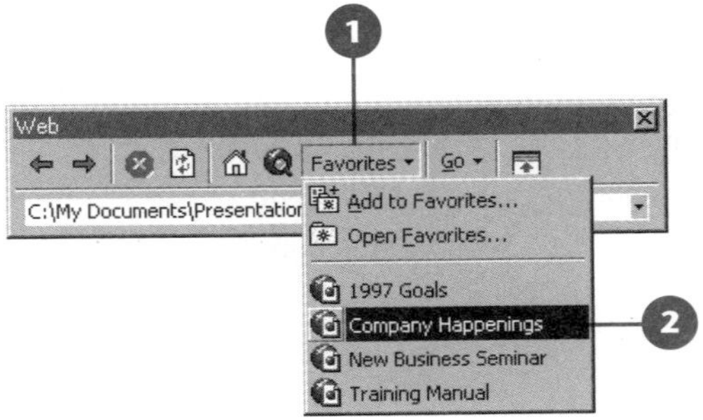

Getting Documents from the Internet

File Transfer Protocol (FTP) is an inexpensive and efficient way to transfer files between your computer and other computers on the Internet. You can *download*, or receive from another computer, any kind of file, including text, graphics, sound, and video files. To download a file, you need to access an FTP site. Whenever you access an FTP site, you need an ID and password to identify who you are. Anonymous FTP sites are open to anyone; they usually use "anonymous" as an ID and your full e-mail address as the password. You can also save the address to an FTP site to revisit the site later.

Access an FTP Site

1. Click the Open button on the Standard toolbar.
2. Click the Look In drop-down arrow.
3. Click the FTP site you want to log into.
4. Select a Log On As option. (Anonymous or User)
5. Enter a password (your e-mail address or personal password).
6. Click OK.

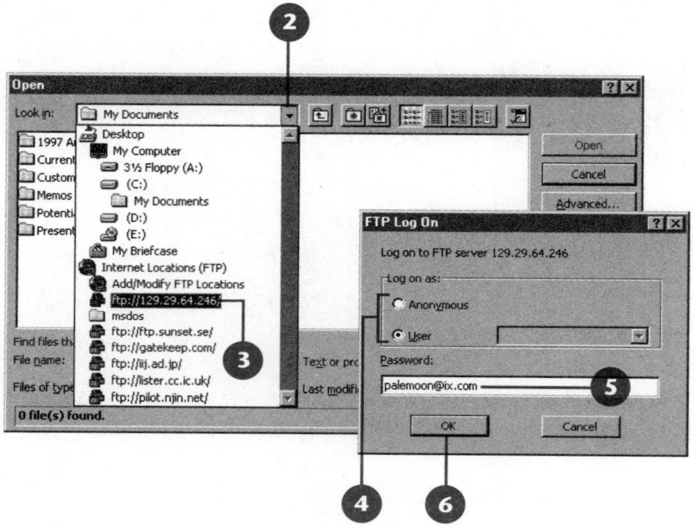

Save the Address to an FTP Site

1. Click the Open button on the Standard toolbar.
2. Click the Look In drop-down arrow.
3. Click Add/Modify FTP Locations.
4. Type the complete URL for an FTP site.
5. Type your e-mail address as the password.
6. Click Add.
7. Click OK.

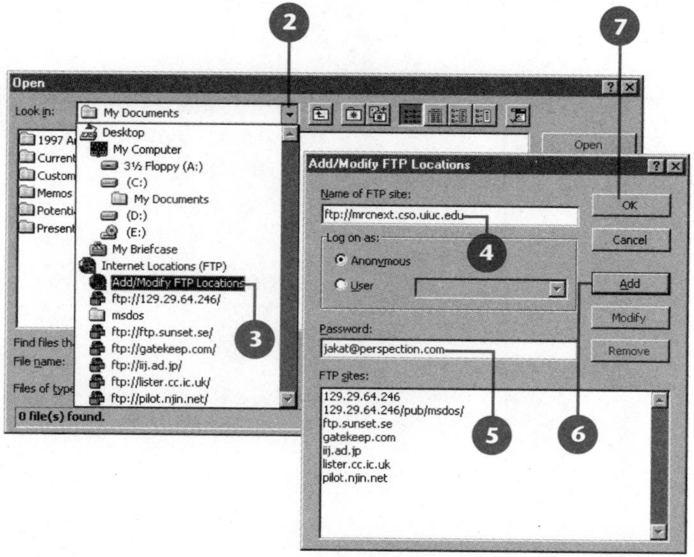

5

Creating a Document with Word 97

IN THIS SECTION

Welcome to Microsoft Word 97. This section will familiarize you with this program's many features to help you produce professional looking documents. You'll learn the most efficient methods to complete the tasks involved in creating documents.

Introducing Word

Microsoft Word, a *word processing program*, is designed to help you create and edit letters, reports, mailing lists, and tables as easily as possible. The files you create and save in Word are known as *documents*. Documents usually include not only text, but also graphics, bulleted lists, and various desktop publishing elements such as drop caps and headlines.

For most people, the real beauty of Word is its editing capabilities. For example, if you don't like where a paragraph is located in a document, you can cut it out and paste it in a new location just by clicking a couple of buttons on the toolbar. Then you can quickly add formatting elements like boldface and special fonts to make your documents look professional and up-to-date.

Viewing the Word Window

Menu bar
The nine menus give you access to all Word options. Simply click a menu name to display a list of related menu commands, and then click the command you want to issue.

Title bar
Microsoft Word and the name of the document appear in the title bar. "Document1" is a temporary name Word uses until you assign a new one.

Standard and Formatting toolbars
These and other toolbars contain buttons that give you quick access to a variety of Word commands and features. If you're not sure what a specific tool does, move the mouse pointer over it to display the name of the toolbar button.

Insertion point
The blinking insertion point (also called a cursor) shows you where the next character you type will appear.

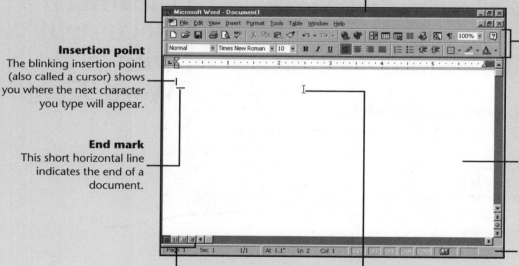

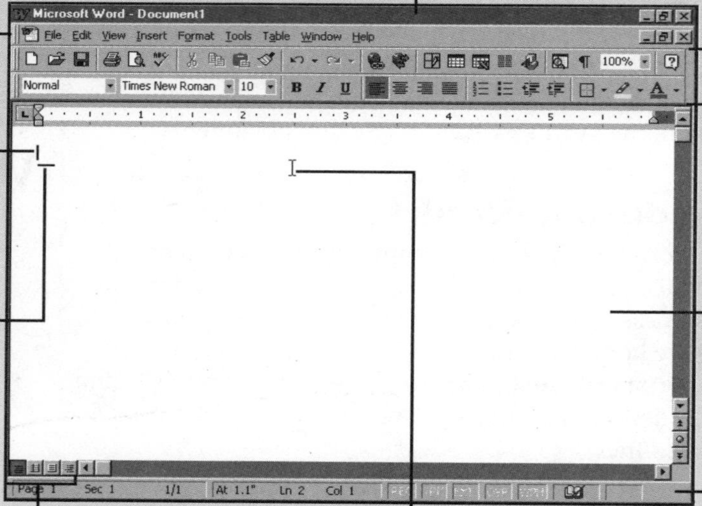

End mark
This short horizontal line indicates the end of a document.

Document window
You enter text and graphics here. As with all Windows applications, the document window can be maximized or minimized independently of the program window.

Status bar
The status bar tells you the location of the insertion point in a document and provides information about current settings and commands.

Document view buttons
Click to see your document in different ways. Normal view is best for typing and editing. Online layout view shows your document as it will appear on the World Wide Web. Switch to page layout view to see how the printed page will look. Use outline view to create a document outline.

Mouse pointer
In the document window, the mouse pointer appears as an I-beam. The pointer shape changes depending on where you point in the Word window.

Changing Document Views

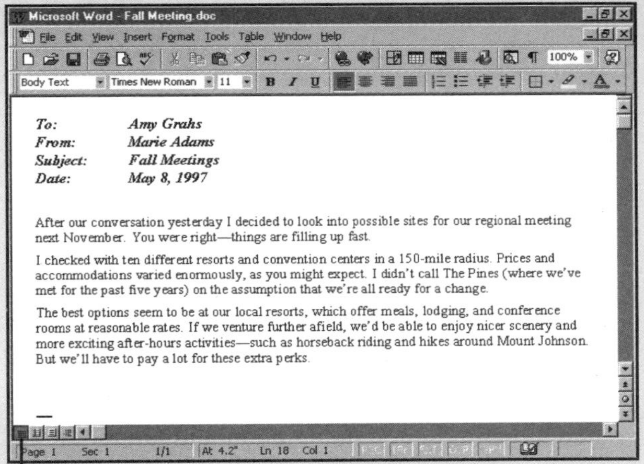
Microsoft Word - Fall Meeting.doc
To: Amy Grahs
From: Marie Adams
Subject: Fall Meetings
Date: May 8, 1997
After our conversation yesterday I decided to look into possible sites for our regional meeting next November. You were right—things are filling up fast.
I checked with ten different resorts and convention centers in a 150-mile radius. Prices and accommodations varied enormously, as you might expect. I didn't call The Pines (where we've met for the past five years) on the assumption that we're all ready for a change.
The best options seem to be at our local resorts, which offer meals, lodging, and conference rooms at reasonable rates. If we venture further afield, we'd be able to enjoy nicer scenery and more exciting after-hours activities—such as horseback riding and hikes around Mount Johnson. But we'll have to pay a lot for these extra perks.

Normal View button

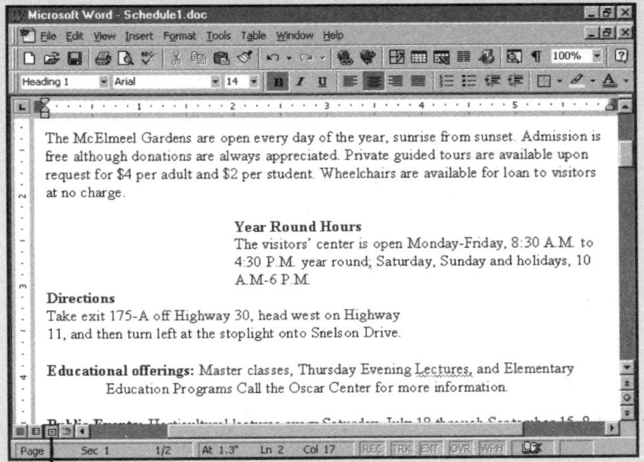
Microsoft Word - Schedule1.doc
The McElmeel Gardens are open every day of the year, sunrise from sunset. Admission is free although donations are always appreciated. Private guided tours are available upon request for $4 per adult and $2 per student. Wheelchairs are available for loan to visitors at no charge.
Year Round Hours
The visitors' center is open Monday-Friday, 8:30 A.M. to 4:30 P.M. year round; Saturday, Sunday and holidays, 10 A.M.-6 P.M.
Directions
Take exit 175-A off Highway 30, head west on Highway 11, and then turn left at the stoplight onto Snelson Drive.
Educational offerings: Master classes, Thursday Evening Lectures, and Elementary Education Programs Call the Oscar Center for more information.

Page Layout View button

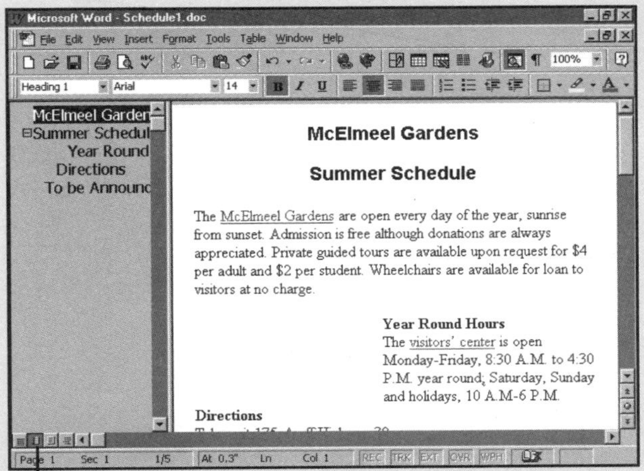
Microsoft Word - Schedule1.doc
McElmeel Garden
Summer Schedul
Year Round
Directions
To be Announc
McElmeel Gardens
Summer Schedule
The McElmeel Gardens are open every day of the year, sunrise from sunset. Admission is free although donations are always appreciated. Private guided tours are available upon request for $4 per adult and $2 per student. Wheelchairs are available for loan to visitors at no charge.
Year Round Hours
The visitors' center is open Monday-Friday, 8:30 A.M. to 4:30 P.M. year round; Saturday, Sunday and holidays, 10 A.M.-6 P.M.
Directions

Online Layout View button

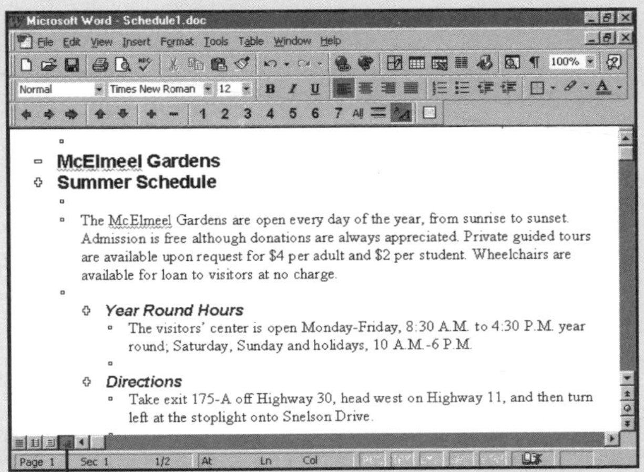
Microsoft Word - Schedule1.doc
McElmeel Gardens
Summer Schedule
The McElmeel Gardens are open every day of the year, from sunrise to sunset. Admission is free although donations are always appreciated. Private guided tours are available upon request for $4 per adult and $2 per student. Wheelchairs are available for loan to visitors at no charge.
Year Round Hours
The visitors' center is open Monday-Friday, 8:30 A.M. to 4:30 P.M. year round; Saturday, Sunday and holidays, 10 A.M.-6 P.M.
Directions
Take exit 175-A off Highway 30, head west on Highway 11, and then turn left at the stoplight onto Snelson Drive.

Outline View button

Creating a Document

After starting Word, you'll see a new, blank document in the document window, ready for you to begin entering text. You can open and work on as many new documents as you'd like. As you type text, Word moves, or *wraps*, the insertion point to a new line when the previous one is full. You can move the insertion point anywhere within the document either by clicking in the desired location or by pressing a key.

TIP

Use Word's nonprinting symbols to manage document format. *To hide them, click the Show/Hide button on the Standard toolbar.*

SEE ALSO

See "Changing Document Views" on page 63 for information about changing the way the document appears on the screen.

Enter and Delete Text in a Document

1. Click where you want to insert or delete text.
2. Begin typing.
3. Press Enter when you want to begin a new paragraph or insert a blank line.
4. Press Backspace to delete text to the left of the insertion point, or press Delete to delete text to the right of the insertion point.

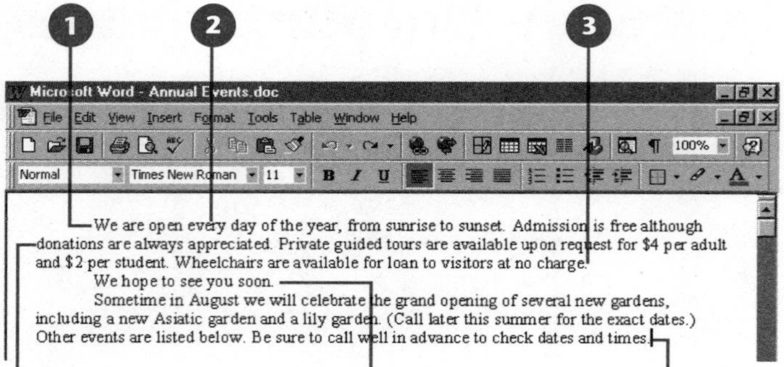
1
2
3
Microsoft Word - Annual Events.doc
File Edit View Insert Format Tools Table Window Help
Normal
Times New Roman
11
100%
We are open every day of the year, from sunrise to sunset. Admission is free although donations are always appreciated. Private guided tours are available upon request for $4 per adult and $2 per student. Wheelchairs are available for loan to visitors at no charge.
We hope to see you soon.
Sometime in August we will celebrate the grand opening of several new gardens, including a new Asiatic garden and a lily garden. (Call later this summer for the exact dates.) Other events are listed below. Be sure to call well in advance to check dates and times.

Characters automatically wrap to next line within a paragraph.

Press Enter to begin a new paragraph.

The characters you type appear at the location of the insertion point.

Open a New Document

1. Click the New button on the Standard toolbar.

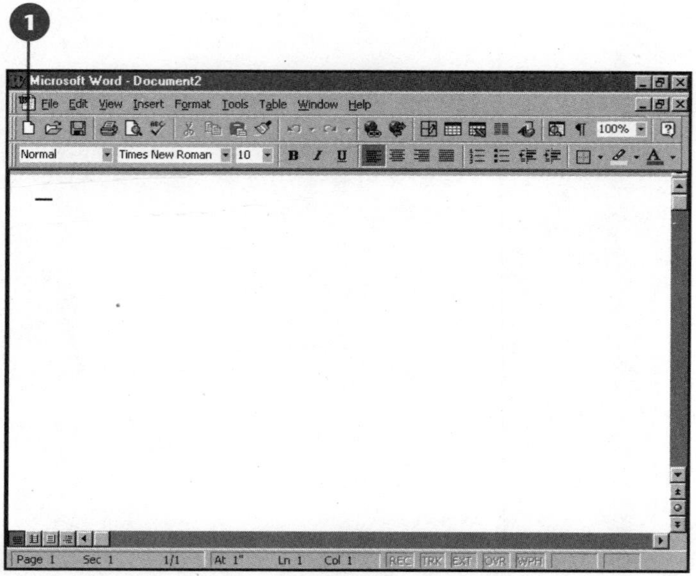
1
Microsoft Word - Document2
File Edit View Insert Format Tools Table Window Help
Normal
Times New Roman
10
100%
Page 1
Sec 1
1/1
At 1"
Ln 1
Col 1
REC
TRK
EXT
OVR
WPH

Moving Around in a Document

As your document gets longer, some of your work will shift out of sight. You can easily move any part of a document back into view by *scrolling, paging,* or *browsing*. Sometimes you'll want to switch views for easier editing and to see how your printed document will look. In all four document views, you can use the tools described here to move around your document.

SEE ALSO

See "Finding and Replacing Text and Formatting" on page 72 for information about locating specific text and formatting.

Scroll, Page, and Browse Through a Document

- To scroll through the document one line at a time, click the up or down scroll arrow on the vertical scroll bar.
- To scroll quickly through an entire document, click and hold the up or down scroll arrow on the vertical scroll bar.
- To scroll to a specific page in the document, click and drag the scroll box on the vertical scroll bar until the page number you want appears in the yellow box.

  To page through the document one page at a time, press PgUp or PgDn on the keyboard.
- To browse by page, edits, headings, or other items, click the Browse button and then click the item you want to browse by. If a dialog box opens, enter the page or item you want to find, and then click the Up and Down Browse Arrow buttons to move from one item to the next.

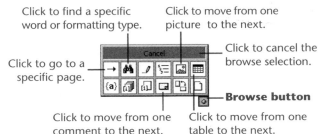

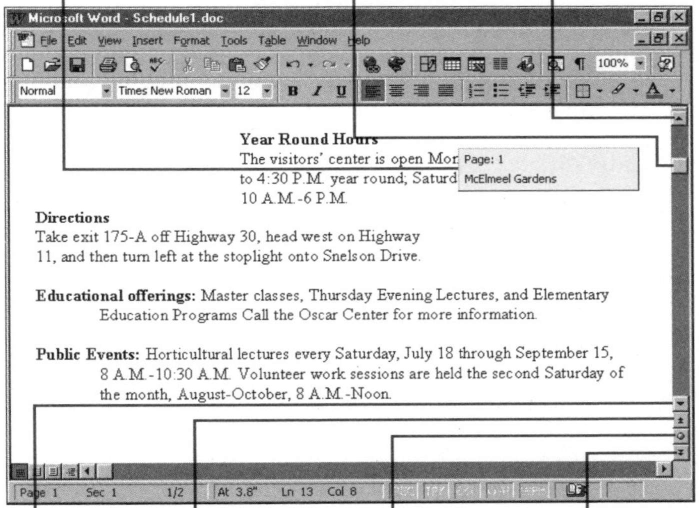
The current page appears here when you click the vertical scroll box.
Vertical scroll box
Up scroll arrow
Microsoft Word - Schedule1.doc
Year Round Hours
The visitors' center is open Mon
to 4:30 P.M. year round; Saturd
10 A.M.-6 P.M.
Page: 1
McElmeel Gardens
Directions
Take exit 175-A off Highway 30, head west on Highway 11, and then turn left at the stoplight onto Snelson Drive.
Educational offerings: Master classes, Thursday Evening Lectures, and Elementary Education Programs Call the Oscar Center for more information.
Public Events: Horticultural lectures every Saturday, July 18 through September 15, 8 A.M.-10:30 A.M. Volunteer work sessions are held the second Saturday of the month, August-October, 8 A.M.-Noon.
Down scroll arrow
Previous Page button
Browse button
Next Page button

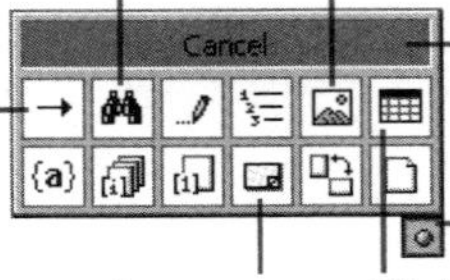
Click to find a specific word or formatting type.
Click to move from one picture to the next.
Cancel
Click to cancel the browse selection.
Click to go to a specific page.
Browse button
Click to move from one comment to the next.
Click to move from one table to the next.

Working with Multiple Documents

The only difference between working with one open document and working with multiple open documents is that you need to make a document active before you can edit it. The same is true when you view different parts of the same document in two windows simultaneously. No matter how you display a document or documents, Word's commands and toolbar buttons work the same as usual.

Switch Between Open Documents

1. Click the Window menu.
2. Click the document you want to work on next.

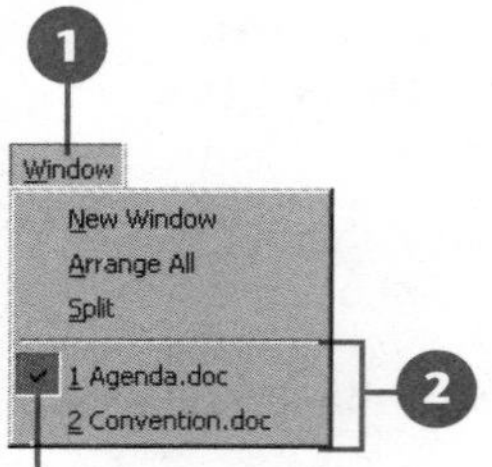

View All Open Documents Simultaneously

1. Click the Window menu, and then click Arrange All.
   - ◆ Each document has its own title bar, ruler, and vertical scroll bar.
2. Click in the window of the document you want to work on (becomes the active document), and then edit the document as usual.
3. To display only one document again, click the Maximize button in the active document window.

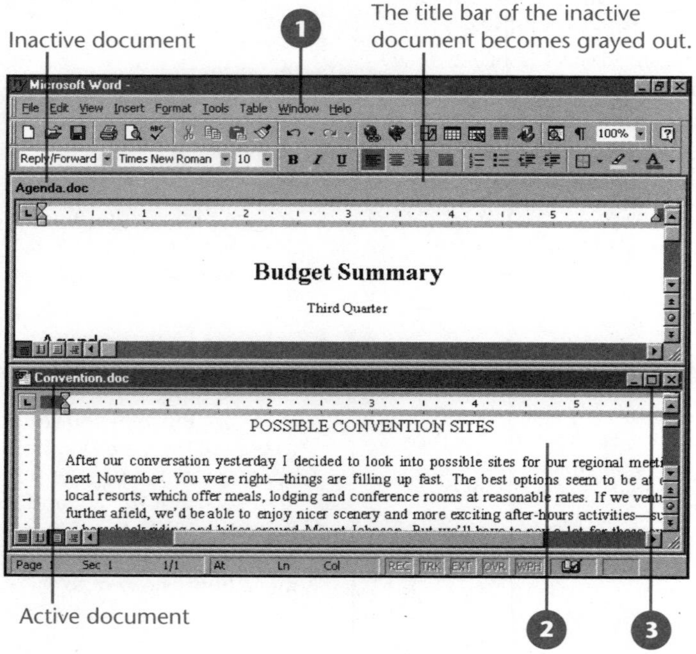

> **TIP**
>
> **View all open windows to move or copy text between documents.** *You can cut, copy, and paste text or drag and drop text between two open windows or panes.*

> **SEE ALSO**
>
> *See "Editing Your Text" on page 28 for more information on moving text between documents.*

Work on Two Parts of the Same Document

1. Click the Window menu, and then click Split.
2. Drag the split bar until the two window panes are the sizes you want.
3. Click in the document window to set the split and display a vertical scroll bar and rulers for each pane.
4. Click in each pane and scroll to the parts of the document you want to work on. Each pane scrolls independently.
5. Click in the pane you want to work in, and edit the text as usual.
6. To return to a single pane, click the Window menu, and then click Remove Split.

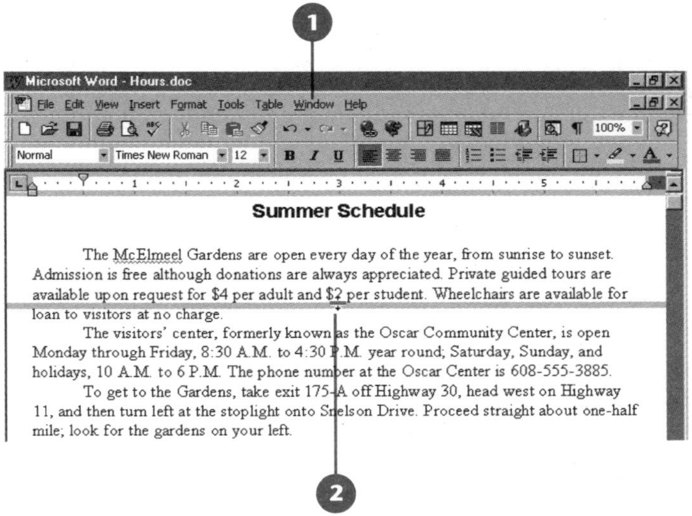
1
Microsoft Word - Hours.doc
File Edit View Insert Format Tools Table Window Help
Normal
Times New Roman
12
100%
Summer Schedule
The McElmeel Gardens are open every day of the year, from sunrise to sunset. Admission is free although donations are always appreciated. Private guided tours are available upon request for $4 per adult and $2 per student. Wheelchairs are available for loan to visitors at no charge.
The visitors' center, formerly known as the Oscar Community Center, is open Monday through Friday, 8:30 A.M. to 4:30 P.M. year round; Saturday, Sunday, and holidays, 10 A.M. to 6 P.M. The phone number at the Oscar Center is 608-555-3885.
To get to the Gardens, take exit 175-A off Highway 30, head west on Highway 11, and then turn left at the stoplight onto Snelson Drive. Proceed straight about one-half mile; look for the gardens on your left.
2

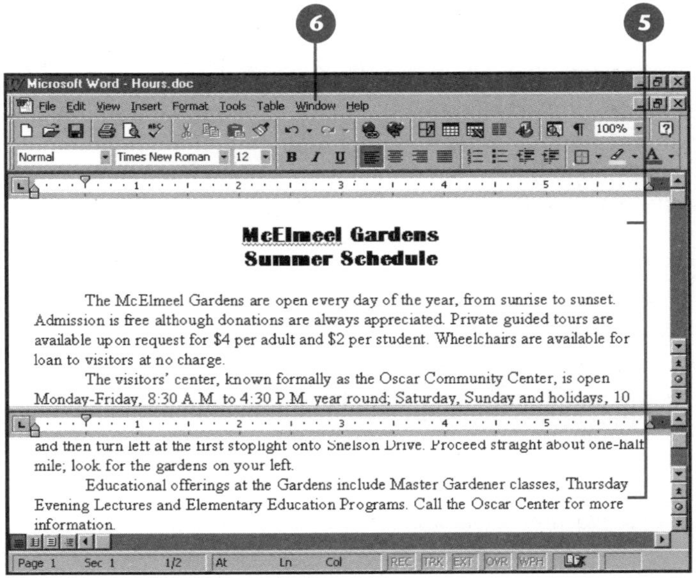
6
5
Microsoft Word - Hours.doc
File Edit View Insert Format Tools Table Window Help
Normal
Times New Roman
12
100%
McElmeel Gardens
Summer Schedule
The McElmeel Gardens are open every day of the year, from sunrise to sunset. Admission is free although donations are always appreciated. Private guided tours are available upon request for $4 per adult and $2 per student. Wheelchairs are available for loan to visitors at no charge.
The visitors' center, known formally as the Oscar Community Center, is open Monday-Friday, 8:30 A.M. to 4:30 P.M. year round; Saturday, Sunday and holidays, 10
and then turn left at the first stoplight onto Snelson Drive. Proceed straight about one-half mile; look for the gardens on your left.
Educational offerings at the Gardens include Master Gardener classes, Thursday Evening Lectures and Elementary Education Programs. Call the Oscar Center for more information.
Page 1 Sec 1 1/2 At Ln Col REC TRK EXT OVR WPH

5

Setting Up the Page

Every document you produce and print might need a different look. To specify how the printed page appears, use the Page Setup dialog box, which, among other things, allows you to specify paper size and *Portrait* (vertical) or *Landscape* (horizontal) orientation. After making any change, it's a good idea to preview the document before you print. The Print button on the Standard toolbar prints one copy of your document using the current settings. If you need more options, use the Print command on the File menu.

TIP

Use Page Setup to set advanced print options. *The Layout tab in the Page Setup dialog box contains more advanced word processing options, such as dividing a document into sections and printing headers and footers.*

Set Up the Page

1. Click the File menu, and then click Page Setup.
2. Click the Paper Size tab.
3. If necessary, specify the size of the paper in your printer.
4. If necessary, change the page orientation.
5. In the Apply To box, select This Section, This Point Forward, or Whole Document.
6. Preview the sample page with your selections.
7. To make your changes the default settings for all new documents, click Default and then click Yes.
8. Click OK.

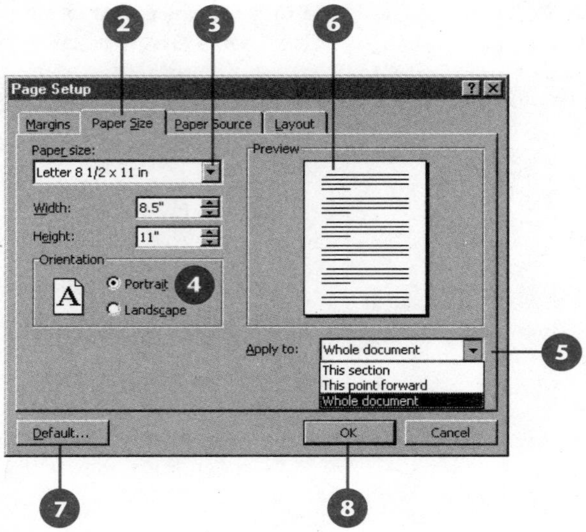

Selecting Text

The first step in working with text is to highlight, or *select*, the text you want to work with. Once you've selected it, you can copy, move, format, and delete words, sentences, and paragraphs. You can even align text easily by first selecting the text you want to adjust. If you finish with or decide not to use a selection, you can click anywhere in the document to *deselect* it.

TIP

Use Undo to restore deleted text. *If, after you select text, you accidentally press Enter and delete the text by mistake, click the Undo button on the Standard toolbar to reverse your action.*

SEE ALSO

See "Moving and Copying Text" on page 70, and "Formatting Text for Emphasis" on page 80 for more information on the various tasks you can perform with selected text.

Select Text

1. Position the pointer in the word, paragraph, line, or part of the document you want to select.
2. Choose the method that accomplishes the task you want to complete in the easiest way. Refer to the table for methods to select text.

SELECTING TEXT

To select	Do this
A single word	Double-click the word.
A single paragraph	Triple-click a word within the paragraph.
A single line	Click in the left margin next to the line.
Any part of a document	Click at the beginning of the text you want to highlight, and then drag to the end of the section you want to highlight.
The entire document	Triple-click in the left margin.

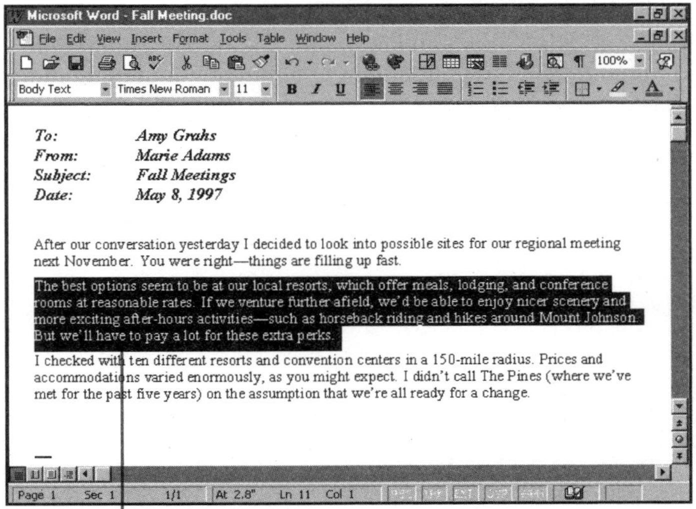
Microsoft Word - Fall Meeting.doc
File Edit View Insert Format Tools Table Window Help
Body Text
Times New Roman
11
100%
To: Amy Grahs
From: Marie Adams
Subject: Fall Meetings
Date: May 8, 1997
After our conversation yesterday I decided to look into possible sites for our regional meeting next November. You were right—things are filling up fast.
The best options seem to be at our local resorts, which offer meals, lodging, and conference rooms at reasonable rates. If we venture further afield, we'd be able to enjoy nicer scenery and more exciting after-hours activities—such as horseback riding and hikes around Mount Johnson. But we'll have to pay a lot for these extra perks.
I checked with ten different resorts and convention centers in a 150-mile radius. Prices and accommodations varied enormously, as you might expect. I didn't call The Pines (where we've met for the past five years) on the assumption that we're all ready for a change.
Page 1 Sec 1 1/1 At 2.8" Ln 11 Col 1

Black highlighting indicates this text is selected.

Moving and Copying Text

You can move selected text by cutting and then pasting it in a new location. Or you can copy it and then paste the copy in a different location. You can paste multiple copies of text into your document from the *Clipboard*, a temporary storage area that holds your copies until they are replaced by new cut or copied text.

TIP

Go to a specific location. *If you want to move or copy selected text in a location that isn't on your screen, press F5 to display the Go To tab in the Find and Replace dialog box, and then specify the page, section, bookmark, comment or other location you want to go to.*

Move or Copy Using the Standard Toolbar

1. Select the text you want to move or copy.
2. Click the Cut or Copy button on the Standard toolbar.
3. Click in the new location.
4. Click the Paste button on the Standard toolbar.

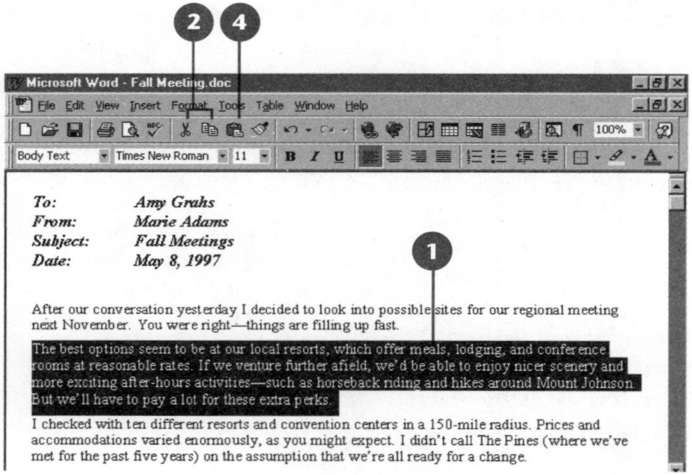

2
4
Microsoft Word - Fall Meeting.doc
File Edit View Insert Format Tools Table Window Help
Body Text
Times New Roman
11
100%
To: Amy Grahs
From: Marie Adams
Subject: Fall Meetings
Date: May 8, 1997
1
After our conversation yesterday I decided to look into possible sites for our regional meeting next November. You were right—things are filling up fast.
The best options seem to be at our local resorts, which offer meals, lodging, and conference rooms at reasonable rates. If we venture further afield, we'd be able to enjoy nicer scenery and more exciting after-hours activities—such as horseback riding and hikes around Mount Johnson. But we'll have to pay a lot for these extra perks.
I checked with ten different resorts and convention centers in a 150-mile radius. Prices and accommodations varied enormously, as you might expect. I didn't call The Pines (where we've met for the past five years) on the assumption that we're all ready for a change.

Move or Copy Text by Dragging It

1. Select the text you want to move or copy.
2. Move the pointer over the selected text.
3. To move the text to a new location, click and hold the mouse button. To copy the text to a new location, also press and hold the Ctrl key.

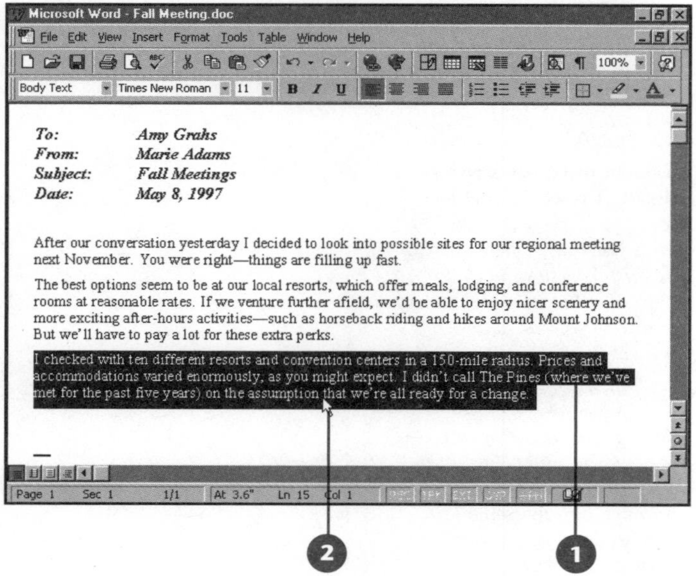

Microsoft Word - Fall Meeting.doc
File Edit View Insert Format Tools Table Window Help
Body Text
Times New Roman
11
100%
To: Amy Grahs
From: Marie Adams
Subject: Fall Meetings
Date: May 8, 1997
After our conversation yesterday I decided to look into possible sites for our regional meeting next November. You were right—things are filling up fast.
The best options seem to be at our local resorts, which offer meals, lodging, and conference rooms at reasonable rates. If we venture further afield, we'd be able to enjoy nicer scenery and more exciting after-hours activities—such as horseback riding and hikes around Mount Johnson. But we'll have to pay a lot for these extra perks.
I checked with ten different resorts and convention centers in a 150-mile radius. Prices and accommodations varied enormously, as you might expect. I didn't call The Pines (where we've met for the past five years) on the assumption that we're all ready for a change.
Page 1 Sec 1 1/1 At 3.6" Ln 15 Col 1
2
1

TRY THIS

Move and copy text between documents. *With two or more documents open, select and cut or copy a paragraph from one document. Use the Window menu to display the second document and then paste the text into it.*

SEE ALSO

See "Working with Windows" on page 24 for information about displaying multiple document windows.

TIP

Copy text to another part of the document. *If you want to copy text to another part of the document, select the text, copy it, move to the new location, right-click the mouse button, and then click Paste.*

4. Drag the mouse pointer to the new location, and release the button (and the Ctrl key, if necessary).

5. Click anywhere in the document to deselect the text.

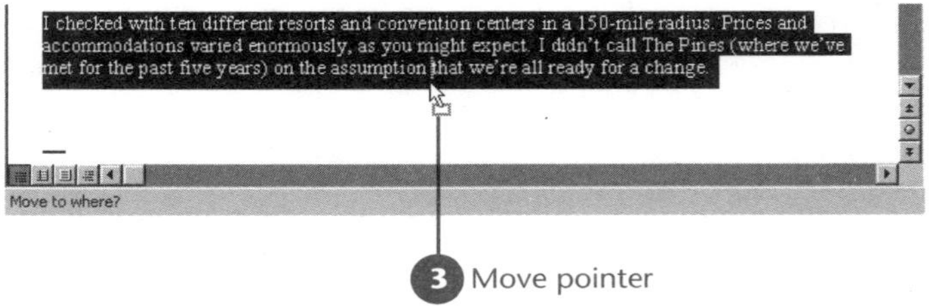
I checked with ten different resorts and convention centers in a 150-mile radius. Prices and accommodations varied enormously, as you might expect. I didn't call The Pines (where we've met for the past five years) on the assumption that we're all ready for a change.
Move to where?
3 Move pointer

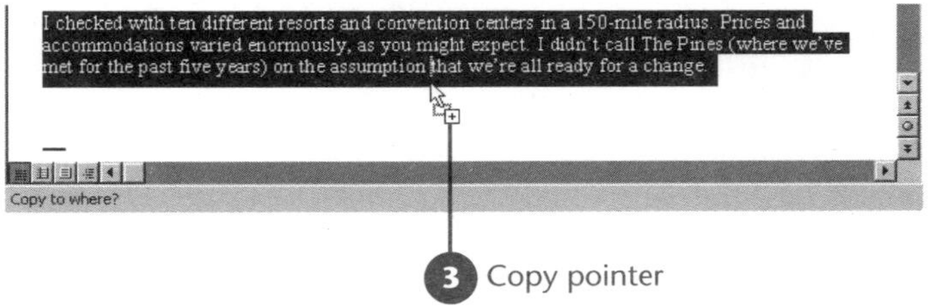
I checked with ten different resorts and convention centers in a 150-mile radius. Prices and accommodations varied enormously, as you might expect. I didn't call The Pines (where we've met for the past five years) on the assumption that we're all ready for a change.
Copy to where?
3 Copy pointer

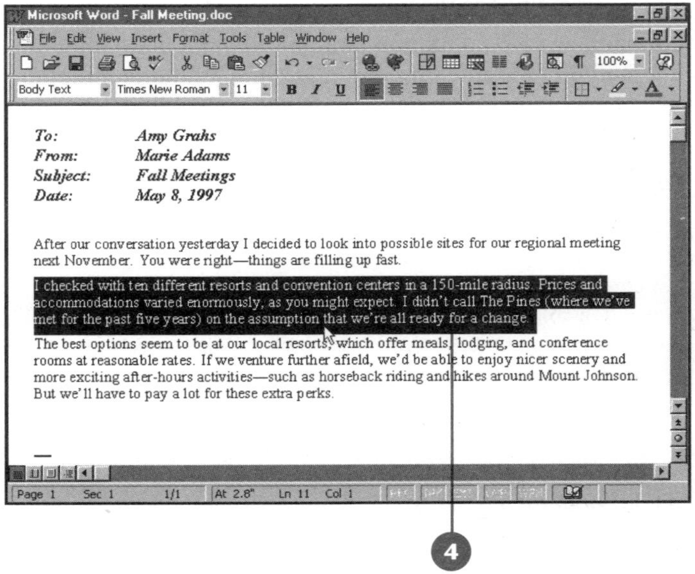
Microsoft Word - Fall Meeting.doc
File Edit View Insert Format Tools Table Window Help
Body Text
Times New Roman
11
100%
To: Amy Grahs
From: Marie Adams
Subject: Fall Meetings
Date: May 8, 1997
After our conversation yesterday I decided to look into possible sites for our regional meeting next November. You were right—things are filling up fast.
I checked with ten different resorts and convention centers in a 150-mile radius. Prices and accommodations varied enormously, as you might expect. I didn't call The Pines (where we've met for the past five years) on the assumption that we're all ready for a change.
The best options seem to be at our local resorts, which offer meals, lodging, and conference rooms at reasonable rates. If we venture further afield, we'd be able to enjoy nicer scenery and more exciting after-hours activities—such as horseback riding and hikes around Mount Johnson. But we'll have to pay a lot for these extra perks.
Page 1 Sec 1 1/1 At 2.8" Ln 11 Col 1
4

5

Finding and Replacing Text and Formatting

The Find command makes it easy to locate specific text and formatting in a long document. You can use the Replace command to substitute different text and formatting instantly. The Find and Replace dialog box provides many options that help you find and replace exactly what you want. To fine-tune a search, the Match Case option will enable you to find words that begin with an uppercase letter or that are set in all lowercase or uppercase letters. You can even use a wildcard to find series of words. For example, the search text "ran*" will find "ranch," "ranger," rank," "ransom," and so on. The Go To tab helps you move quickly to a specific location in your document.

Find Text and Formatting

1. Click the Edit menu, and then click Find.
2. Type the text you want to locate in the Find What box.
3. Click the More button, and then select the formatting and search options you want to use.
4. Click Find Next repeatedly to locate each instance of the specified criteria.
5. When you see a message that Word has finished searching the document, click OK.
6. Click Cancel.

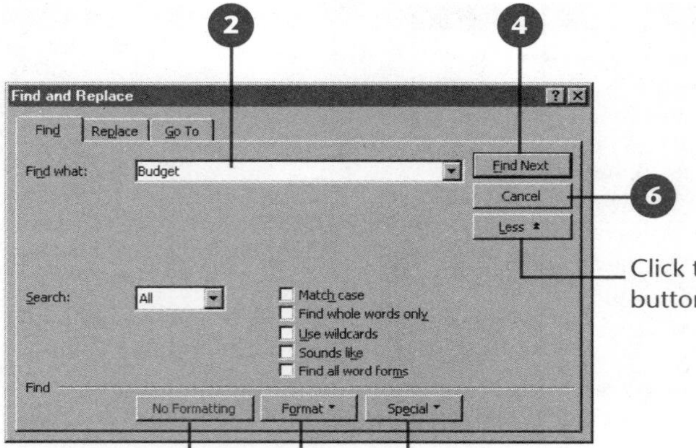

Click to change the button to More.

Click to remove any formatting settings from the search text.

Click to select special characters and symbols you want to search for, such as paragraph marks, page breaks, and em dashes.

Click to open dialog boxes in which you can specify formatting you want to locate.

Find Information by Type

1. Press the F5 key.
2. In the Go To What box, click the type of location or information you want to move to.
3. Enter the item number (or bookmark name) in the Enter box.
4. Click Go To.
5. Click Close.

This setting tells Word to search for the third page break.

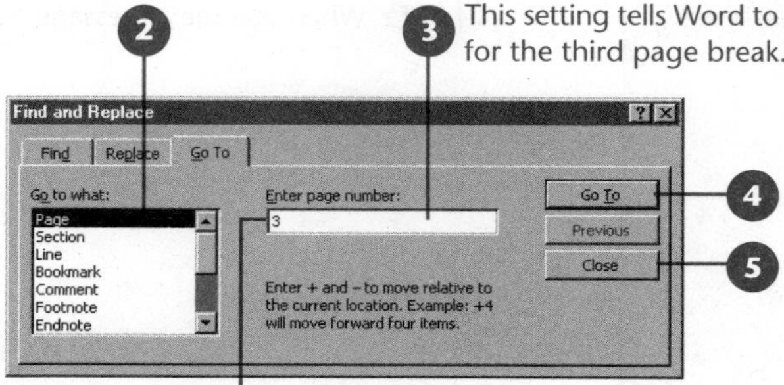

To find all instances of the selected item, leave the Enter box empty.

TIP

Use wildcards to help you search. *When the Use Wildcard option is selected, the Special pop-up menu displays the available wildcards you can use. To enter a wildcard in the Find What or Replace What box, click Special, and then click a wildcard. For example, the search text "ran*" will find "ranch," "ranger," and so on.*

TIP

Use the Less and More buttons to display options. *In the Find and Replace dialog box, the Less and More buttons interchange with each other. If your search is a simple one, click Less to decrease the size of the dialog box. If your search is a more complex one, click More to increase the number of available options.*

SEE ALSO

See "Moving Around in a Document" on page 65 for information about scrolling, paging, and browsing through a document.

Replace Text and Formatting

1. Click the Edit menu, and then click Replace.
2. Type the text you want to locate in the Find What box.
3. Click the More button and then select the formatting you want to locate, if any, and the search options you want to use.
4. Type the text you want to substitute in the Replace With box.
5. Select the formatting, if any, you want to substitute.
6. Click the Find Next, Replace, or Replace All button.
7. When you see a message that Word has finished searching the document, click OK.
8. Click Cancel.

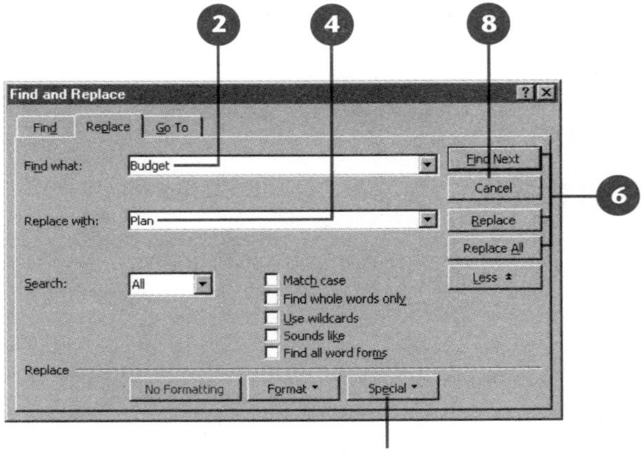

Click to select special characters and symbols you want to locate or to use to replace search text.

5

Checking Your Spelling and Grammar

As you type, Word inserts a wavy red line under words it can't find in its dictionary (such as misspellings or names) or duplicated words (for example, the the). You can correct these errors as they arise or after you finish the entire document. Before you print your final document, it's a good idea to check for grammatical errors using the spelling and grammar checker.

TIP

Use AutoCorrect to correct spelling as you type. *AutoCorrect automatically corrects common misspellings, as well as other mistakes (such as the accidental usage of the Caps Lock key).*

SEE ALSO

See "AutoCorrecting Your Text" on page 32 for more information on correcting misspelled words as you type.

Correct a Misspelled Word as You Type

1. Right-click any word with a red wavy underline to display the Spelling shortcut menu.
2. Click a suggested substitution, or tell Word to ignore all instances of the word.

If you have a lot of spelling errors, it's easier to use the Spelling And Grammar Checker to find and correct them.

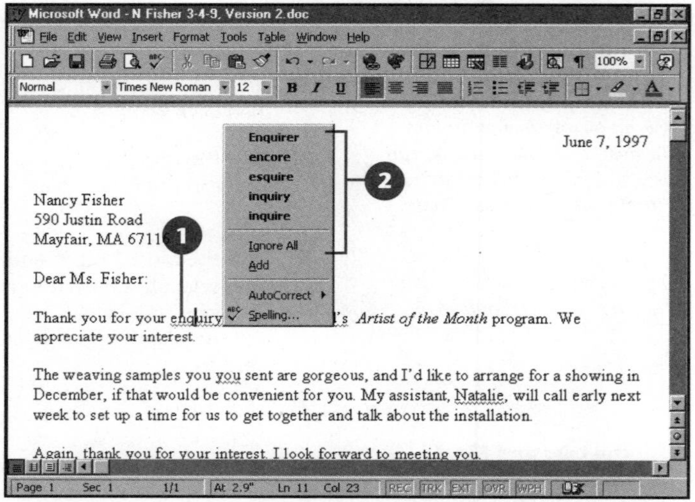
Microsoft Word - N Fisher 3-4-9, Version 2.doc
File Edit View Insert Format Tools Table Window Help
Normal
Times New Roman
12
100%
Enquirer
encore
esquire
inquiry
inquire
Ignore All
Add
AutoCorrect
Spelling...
2
1
June 7, 1997
Nancy Fisher
590 Justin Road
Mayfair, MA 6711
Dear Ms. Fisher:
Thank you for your enquiry
's Artist of the Month program. We
appreciate your interest.
The weaving samples you you sent are gorgeous, and I'd like to arrange for a showing in
December, if that would be convenient for you. My assistant, Natalie, will call early next
week to set up a time for us to get together and talk about the installation.
Again, thank you for your interest. I look forward to meeting you.
Page 1 Sec 1 1/1 At 2.9" Ln 11 Col 23 REC TRK EXT OVR WPH

TRY THIS

Add your name to the dictionary. *Add your own first and last name to Word's dictionary so your name will never be flagged as a misspelling.*

TIP

Select text to check a specific part of a document. *You can check spelling, grammar, or usage in part of a document by first selecting the text you want to check. Then follow the steps for checking the entire document.*

TIP

Check just spelling. *If you want to just check your spelling, clear the Check Grammar check box in the Spelling And Grammar dialog box.*

Spelling and Grammar button

Correct Grammar and Spelling

1. Click at the beginning of the document, and then click the Spelling And Grammar button on the Standard toolbar.
2. As it checks each sentence in the document, Word highlights misspelled words in the Not In Dictionary box or problematic sentences in the Sentence box, and an appropriate alternative in the Suggestions box.
3. You can select any of the suggestions, and then click the Change button to make a substitution.
4. You can click the Ignore button to skip the word or rule, or the Ignore All button to skip every instance of the word or rule.
5. If none of Word's suggestions seem appropriate, you can click in the document and edit it yourself. Click the Resume button to continue.
6. When the grammar check is complete, Word displays a list of readability statistics. Click OK to return to the document.

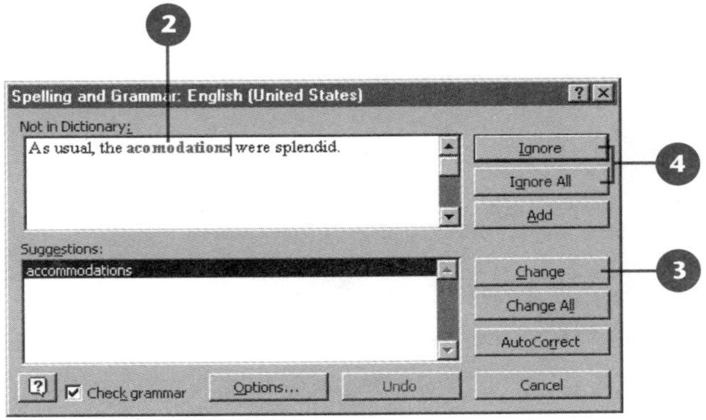

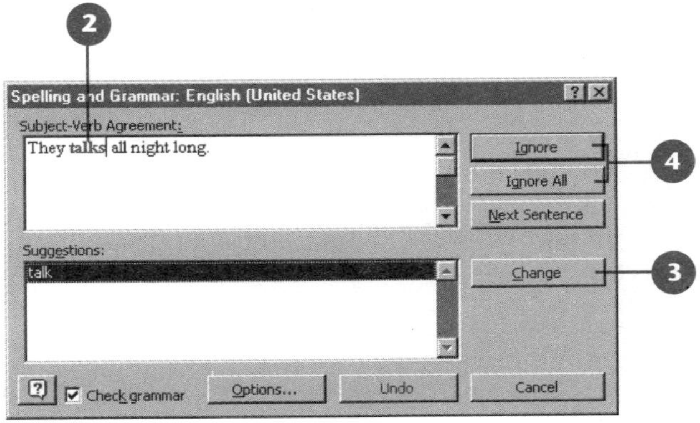

Checking Your Word Usage

Using the same word over and over in a document can sometimes take away from your message's effectiveness. If you need help finding exactly the right word, check Word's Thesaurus. Using this feature can save you time and improve the quality and level of readability of your document.

SEE ALSO

See "Checking Your Spelling and Grammar" on page 74 for information on spell checking.

Use the Thesaurus

1. Select or type the word in the document you want to look up.
2. Click the Tools menu, point to Language, and then click Thesaurus.
3. Click a word in the Meanings box to display its synonyms in the Replace With Synonym box.
4. If you want to see more choices or words with opposite meanings, click Related Words or Antonyms in the Meanings box. (These options are not available for every word.)
5. If you want to continue looking up synonyms, click a word in the Replace With box for which you want to find synonyms, antonyms, or related words, and then click Look Up.
6. When you find the word you want to use, click it, and then click Replace.
7. If you can't find a replacement word, click Cancel.

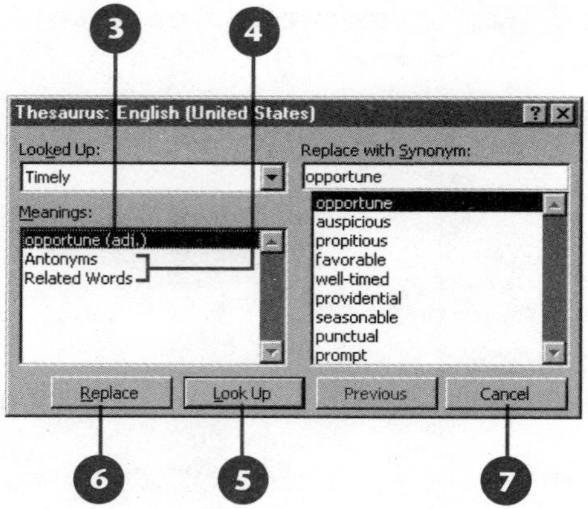

Previewing a Document

If you preview your document before you print, you will save yourself time and money. *Print Preview* shows you exactly how your text will fit on each printed page. This is especially helpful when you have a multiple page document divided into sections with different headers and footers for each section. The Print Preview toolbar provides the tools you need to better analyze how the text is presented on each page.

SEE ALSO

See "Setting Margins" on page 88 for information on adjusting the space between the edge of a page and the text in a header or footer.

Print Preview button

Preview a Document

1. Click the Print Preview button on the Standard toolbar.
   - ◆ View one page

     Click the One Page button to view one page at a time.
   - ◆ View multiple pages

     Click the Multiple Pages button to view more than one page at a time.
   - ◆ Change view size

     Click the Zoom drop-down arrow to select a screen display magnification.
   - ◆ Shrink to fit page

     Click the Shrink To Fit button to shrink the document by one page.
   - ◆ Display full screen

     Click the Full Screen button to display the document with only the toolbar visible.
2. When you're done, click the Close button on the Print Preview toolbar.

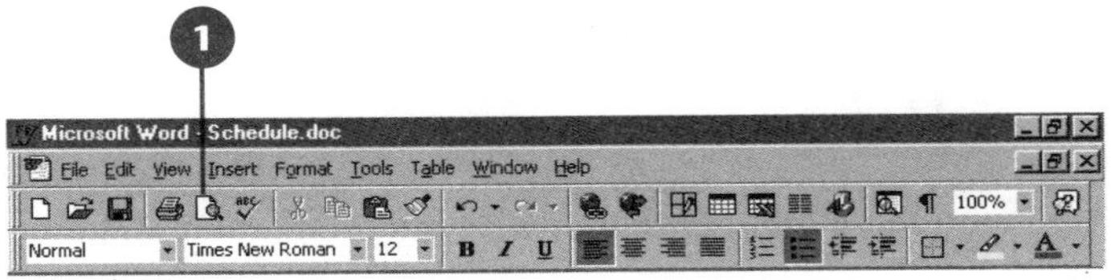

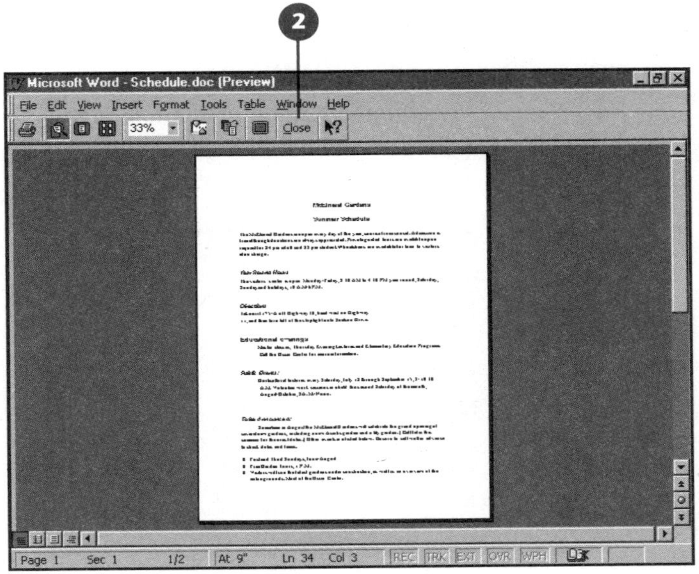

Printing a Document

Printing is one of the most essential tasks you need to master. Word makes printing easy, and its options give you the flexibility to print your document just as you want it. You can select any printer that is available to you. The Print What option lets you print more than just your document. You can choose to print your annotations, a list of styles used in the document, and AutoText entries, just to name a few. You can specify specific pages to print, as well as the number of copies you want to print.

Print button

Print a Document Quickly

1. Click the Print button on either the Standard toolbar or the Print Preview toolbar.

Print a Page with Options

1. Click the File menu, and then click Print.
2. Make sure the active printer appears in the Printer Name box.
3. Select a Page Range option:
   - All. Prints the entire document
   - Current Page. Prints the page in which the insertion point is currently located
   - Selection. Prints a highlighted block of text
   - Pages. Prints only specified pages
4. Type the number of copies you want to print, and select whether to collate the copies.
5. Click OK.

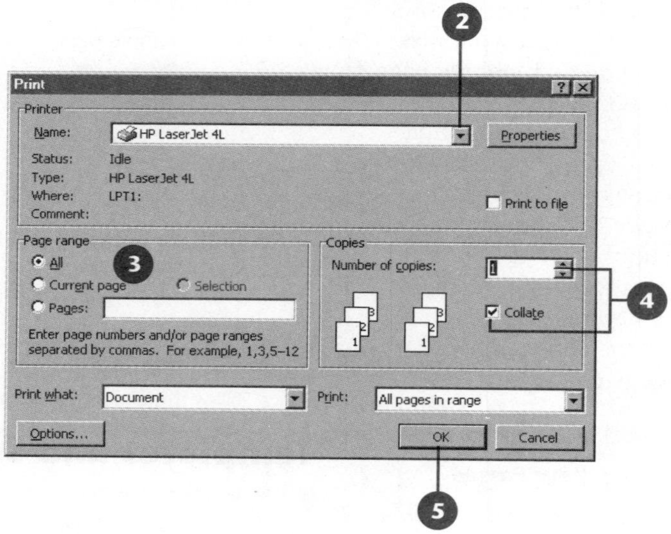

6

Formatting a Document with Word 97

IN THIS SECTION

As you become more comfortable with Microsoft Word 97, you will want to use its extensive word processing and desktop publishing features to format the information in your documents. To make sure the document looks professional, you will set tabs, create indents, adjust line and paragraph spacing, and format text for emphasis with italics, boldface, and underline, just to name a few. You may also want to know how to create bulleted and numbered lists. Each and every one of these tasks is made easy with Word.

Templates and Styles

Word documents are based on templates, which are predesigned and preformatted files that serve as the basis of a variety of Word documents. For example, Word provides templates for memos, reports, cover pages for faxes, and so on. Each template is made up of styles that have common design elements, such as coordinated fonts and sizes, colors, and page layout designs. In a template, you can have styles for headings, bulleted and numbered lists, body text, and headers and footers, which you apply to the text in your documents. You can also modify a template or style, or create one of your own to better suit your needs.

Formatting Text for Emphasis

You'll often want to *format*, or change the style, of certain words or phrases to add emphasis to parts of a document. **Boldface**, *italics*, underlines, highlights, and other text effects are *toggle switches*, which means you simply click to turn them on and off. For special emphasis you can combine formats, such as bold and italics. Using one *font*, or letter design, for headings and another for main text, adds a professional look to your document.

TRY THIS

Color your text. *Try brightening up a document by using the Color box in the Font dialog box to change selected text to a color of your choice. Of course, unless you have a color printer, colored text (as well as highlighting) will print in shades of gray.*

Format Existing Text Quickly

1. Select the text you want to emphasize.
2. Click the Bold, Italic, Underline, or Highlight button on the Formatting toolbar.
   - Remember that you can add more than one formatting option at a time. For example, this text uses both boldface and italics.
3. Click anywhere in the document to deselect the formatted text.

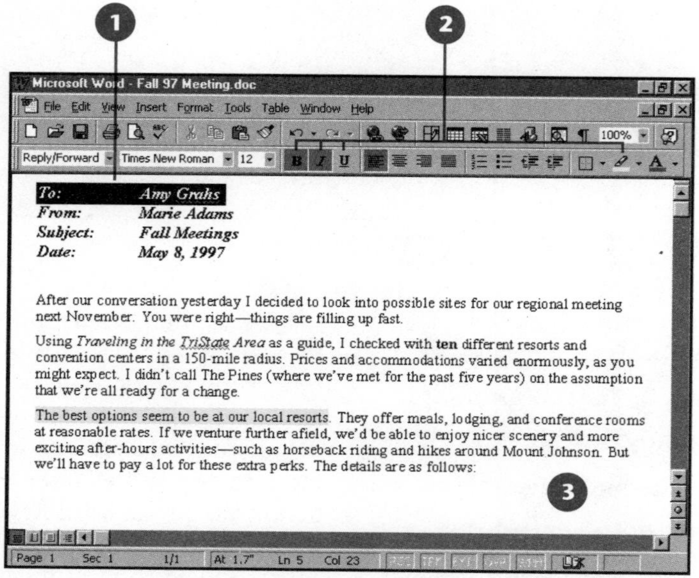
1
2
3
Microsoft Word - Fall 97 Meeting.doc
File Edit View Insert Format Tools Table Window Help
Reply/Forward
Times New Roman
12
100%
To: Amy Grahs
From: Marie Adams
Subject: Fall Meetings
Date: May 8, 1997
After our conversation yesterday I decided to look into possible sites for our regional meeting next November. You were right—things are filling up fast.
Using Traveling in the TriState Area as a guide, I checked with ten different resorts and convention centers in a 150-mile radius. Prices and accommodations varied enormously, as you might expect. I didn't call The Pines (where we've met for the past five years) on the assumption that we're all ready for a change.
The best options seem to be at our local resorts. They offer meals, lodging, and conference rooms at reasonable rates. If we venture further afield, we'd be able to enjoy nicer scenery and more exciting after-hours activities—such as horseback riding and hikes around Mount Johnson. But we'll have to pay a lot for these extra perks. The details are as follows:
Page 1 Sec 1 1/1 At 1.7" Ln 5 Col 23

Change the Font or Size of Existing Text Quickly

1. Select the text you want to format.
2. Click the Font or Font Size drop-down arrow on the Formatting toolbar.
3. Click a new font or a new point size.

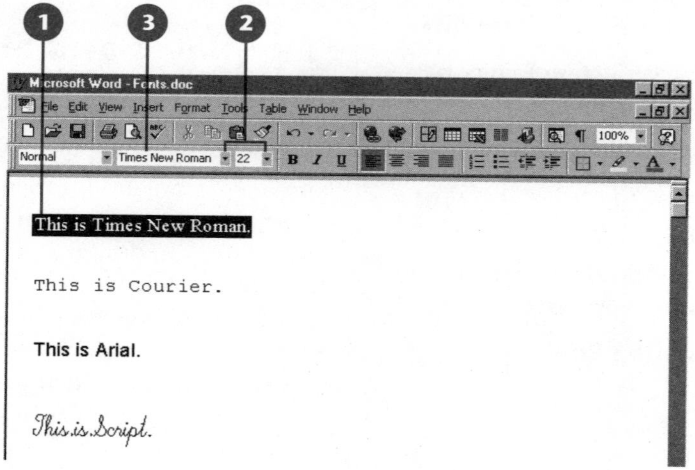
1
3
2
Microsoft Word - Fonts.doc
File Edit View Insert Format Tools Table Window Help
Normal
Times New Roman
22
100%
This is Times New Roman.
This is Courier.
This is Arial.
This is Script.

TIP

Format text as you type. *You can add most formatting options to text as you type. First select the formatting options or changes you want, and then type the text. If necessary, turn off the formatting options when you're done.*

TRY THIS

Highlight key points in a memo. *Open an existing memo, and then use the Highlight button to highlight key points in your memo with a bright yellow color.*

SEE ALSO

See "Creating and Modifying a Style" on page 94 for information about using Word styles to format text consistently throughout a document.

Apply Formatting Effects to Text

1. Select the text you want to format.
2. Click the Format menu, and then click Font.
3. Click the Font tab.
   - ◆ To change character spacing settings, click the Character Spacing tab.
   - ◆ To add animation effects, click the Animation tab.
4. Click the formatting options you want.
5. In the Effects area, click the options you want.
6. Check the results in the Preview box.
7. To make the new formatting options the default for all new Word documents, click Default, and then click Yes.
8. Click OK.

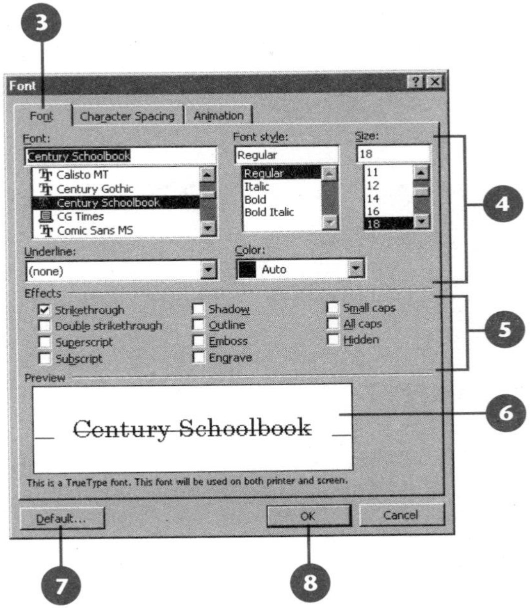

6

Setting Text Alignment

Word documents by default are aligned on the left, with the text uneven, or *ragged*, on the right margin. Left aligned text works well for most documents, but you can easily change the alignment of selected paragraphs. *Right-aligned text*, which lines up smoothly along the right margin and is ragged along the left margin, is good for adding a date to a letter. *Justified text* spreads out evenly between the two margins, creating a clean, professional look. *Centered text* is useful for titles and headings.

Left or Right Align Text

1. Select at least one line in each paragraph you want to align.
2. Click the Align Left or Align Right button on the Formatting toolbar.

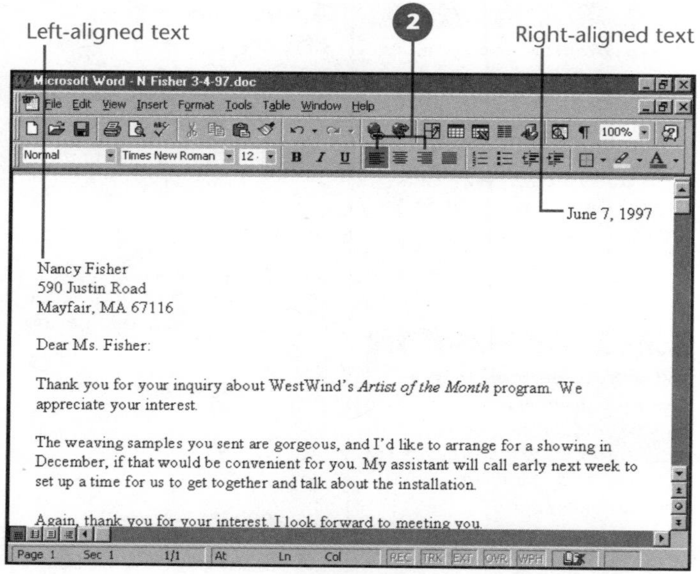
Left-aligned text
2
Right-aligned text
Microsoft Word - N Fisher 3-4-97.doc
File Edit View Insert Format Tools Table Window Help
Normal
Times New Roman
12
June 7, 1997
Nancy Fisher
590 Justin Road
Mayfair, MA 67116
Dear Ms. Fisher:
Thank you for your inquiry about WestWind's Artist of the Month program. We appreciate your interest.
The weaving samples you sent are gorgeous, and I'd like to arrange for a showing in December, if that would be convenient for you. My assistant will call early next week to set up a time for us to get together and talk about the installation.
Again, thank you for your interest. I look forward to meeting you.
Page 1 Sec 1 1/1 At Ln Col REC TRK EXT OVR WPH

Center or Justify Text

1. Select at least one line in each paragraph you want to align.
2. Click the Center or Justify button on the Formatting toolbar.

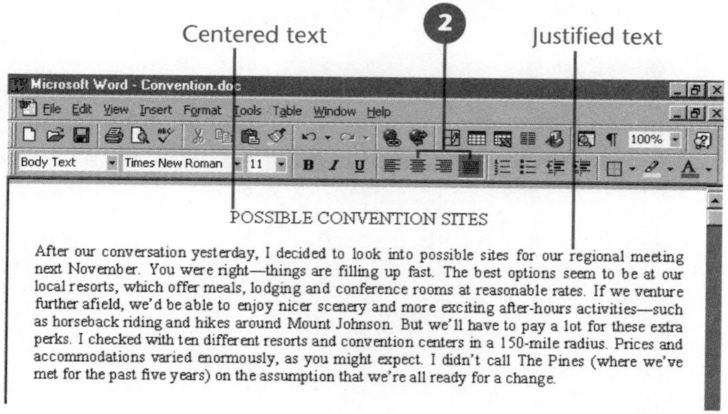
Centered text
2
Justified text
Microsoft Word - Convention.doc
File Edit View Insert Format Tools Table Window Help
Body Text
Times New Roman
11
POSSIBLE CONVENTION SITES
After our conversation yesterday, I decided to look into possible sites for our regional meeting next November. You were right—things are filling up fast. The best options seem to be at our local resorts, which offer meals, lodging and conference rooms at reasonable rates. If we venture further afield, we'd be able to enjoy nicer scenery and more exciting after-hours activities—such as horseback riding and hikes around Mount Johnson. But we'll have to pay a lot for these extra perks. I checked with ten different resorts and convention centers in a 150-mile radius. Prices and accommodations varied enormously, as you might expect. I didn't call The Pines (where we've met for the past five years) on the assumption that we're all ready for a change.

TIP

Set text alignment before you type. *You can also set the text alignment before you type. Just click the appropriate alignment button on the Formatting toolbar, and then type the text you want.*

Setting Line Spacing

The lines in all Word documents are single-spaced by default, which is appropriate for letters and most documents. But you can easily change your document to double or one-and-half-spaced lines to allow extra space between every line. This is useful when you want to make notes on a printed document. Sometimes, you'll want to add space above and below certain paragraphs, such as for headlines or indented quotations to help set off the text.

TIP

Use shortcut keys to set line spacing. *You can quickly change line spacing for selected text or new paragraphs to single, 1.5, and double-spaced by pressing Ctrl+1 for single-spaced lines; Ctrl+5 for 1.5 spaced lines; or Ctrl+2 for double-spaced lines.*

Change Line Spacing

1. Select the paragraph or paragraphs that you want to change.
2. Click the Format menu, click Paragraph, and then click the Indents And Spacing tab.
3. Click the Line Spacing drop-down arrow, and then click the option you want.
4. If necessary, type the precise line spacing you want in the At box.
5. Click OK.

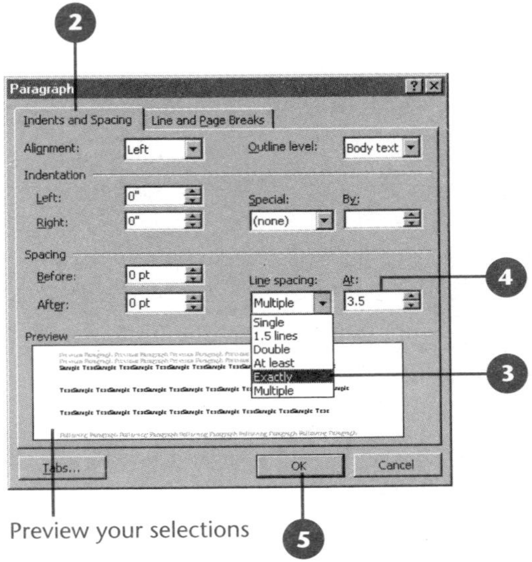

Change Paragraph Spacing

1. Select the paragraph you want to change.
2. Click the Format menu, click Paragraph, and then click the Indents And Spacing tab.
3. To add space above each selected paragraph, type a measurement (in points) in the Before box.
4. To add space below each selected paragraph, enter a measurement (in points) in the After box.
5. Click OK.

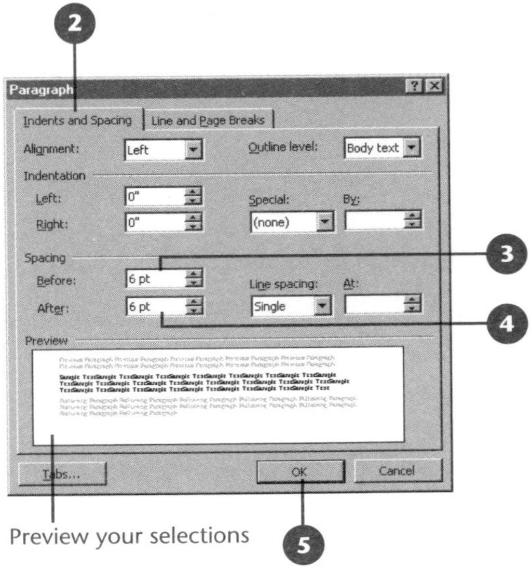

6

Displaying Rulers

There are two rulers that appear in the Word document window: the horizontal ruler and the vertical ruler. The horizontal ruler appears across the top of the document window and shows the length of the typing line. You use the horizontal ruler to adjust margins and indents quickly, set tabs, and adjust column widths. The vertical ruler appears along the left edge of the document window and allows you to adjust top and bottom margins of the document page and the row height in tables. Word automatically displays the horizontal ruler in normal view, and both rulers in page layout view; however, you can choose to hide the rulers if you want.

Show and Hide the Rulers

1. Click the View menu, and then click Ruler.
   - To display the horizontal ruler, click the Normal View button.
   - To display both rulers, click the Page Layout View button.

Normal view shows only the horizontal ruler.

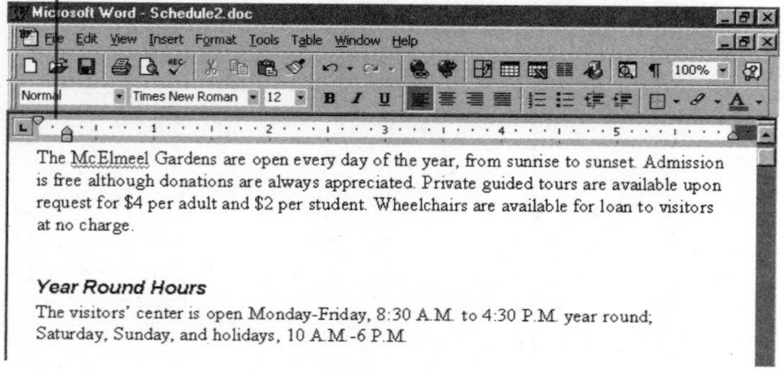
Microsoft Word - Schedule2.doc
File Edit View Insert Format Tools Table Window Help
Normal
Times New Roman
12
100%
The McElmeel Gardens are open every day of the year, from sunrise to sunset. Admission is free although donations are always appreciated. Private guided tours are available upon request for $4 per adult and $2 per student. Wheelchairs are available for loan to visitors at no charge.
Year Round Hours
The visitors' center is open Monday-Friday, 8:30 A.M. to 4:30 P.M. year round; Saturday, Sunday, and holidays, 10 A.M.-6 P.M.

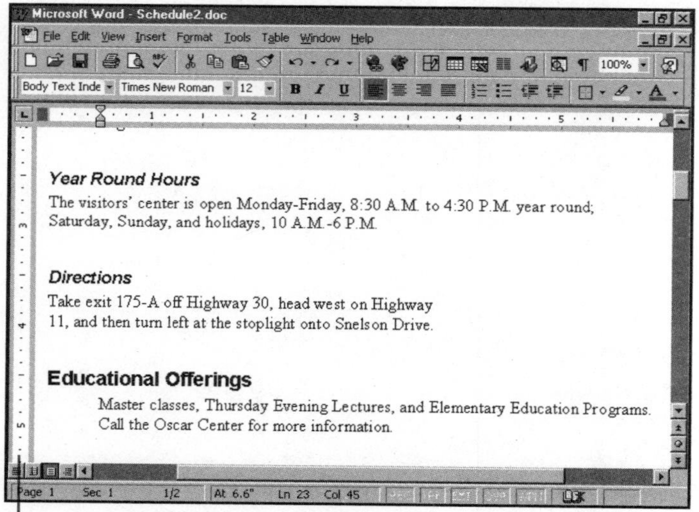
Microsoft Word - Schedule2.doc
File Edit View Insert Format Tools Table Window Help
Body Text Inde
Times New Roman
12
100%
Year Round Hours
The visitors' center is open Monday-Friday, 8:30 A.M. to 4:30 P.M. year round; Saturday, Sunday, and holidays, 10 A.M.-6 P.M.
Directions
Take exit 175-A off Highway 30, head west on Highway 11, and then turn left at the stoplight onto Snelson Drive.
Educational Offerings
Master classes, Thursday Evening Lectures, and Elementary Education Programs. Call the Oscar Center for more information.
Page 1 Sec 1 1/2 At 6.6" Ln 23 Col 45

Page Layout view shows both the horizontal and the vertical ruler.

Setting Paragraph Tabs

You can use tabs in your document to adjust how text or numerical data aligns in relation to the document margins. A *tab stop* is a predefined stopping position along the document's typing line. Word's default tab stops are set every half inch, and you can set more than one tab per paragraph. There are four tab stops you can use to align your text: left, right, center, and decimal (for numerical data).

TIP

Display tab characters on the screen. *A tab character, which displays as an arrow pointing to the right, appears on the screen when you press the Tab key and click the Show/Hide button on the Standard toolbar to show nonprinting symbols.*

Create and Clear a Tab Stop

1. Select the paragraph(s) for which you want to set a tab stop.
2. Click the Tab button on the horizontal ruler until it shows the type of tab stop you want.
3. Click on the ruler where you want to set the tab stop.
4. If necessary, drag the tab stop to position it exactly where you want.
5. To clear a tab stop, drag it off the ruler.

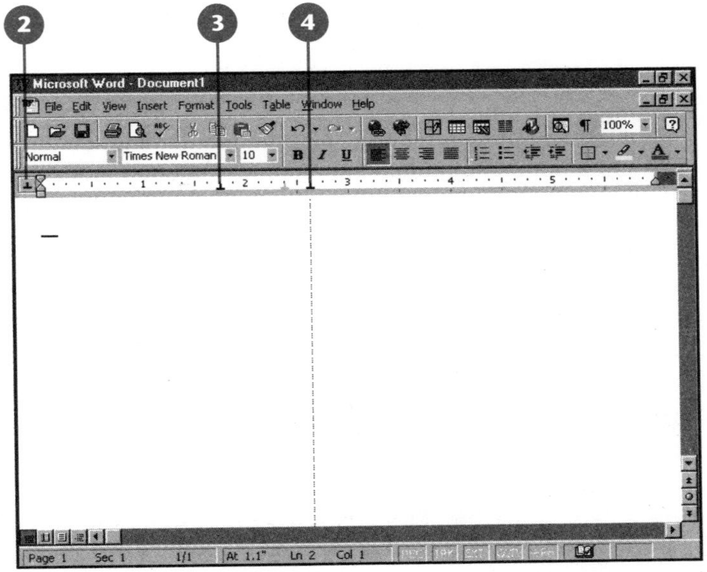

USING THE KEYBOARD FOR LAYOUT	
Tab Stop	**Purpose**
	Aligns text to the left of the tab stop
	Aligns text to the right of the tab stop
	Centers text on the tab stop
	Aligns numbers on the decimal point

Setting Paragraph Indents

The horizontal ruler makes it easy to indent entire paragraphs from the right or left margin. If you prefer to use the Increase Indent button on the Formatting toolbar, keep in mind that it indents text according to Word's default tab stops, which occur every half inch across the width of the document. In addition, you can indent just the first line or just the second and subsequent lines of a paragraph from the left margin.

TIP

Use the Tab key to quickly indent a line. *You can quickly indent the first line of a paragraph by pressing the Tab key.*

SEE ALSO

See "Creating Bulleted and Numbered Lists" on page 96 for information on aligning and indenting text using lists.

Indent a Paragraph Using the Ruler

Position the pointer in the paragraph you want to indent, or press Enter to begin a new paragraph. Use one of the following indent markers on the ruler:

- To change the left indent of the first line of text, drag the First Line Indent marker at the top of the ruler.
- To change the indent of the second line of text, drag the Hanging Indent marker.
- To change the left indent for all lines of text within a paragraph, drag the Left Indent marker.
- To change the right indent for all lines of text, drag the Right Indent marker.

As you drag an indent marker, a dotted guideline appears on the screen to help you position the indent accurately.

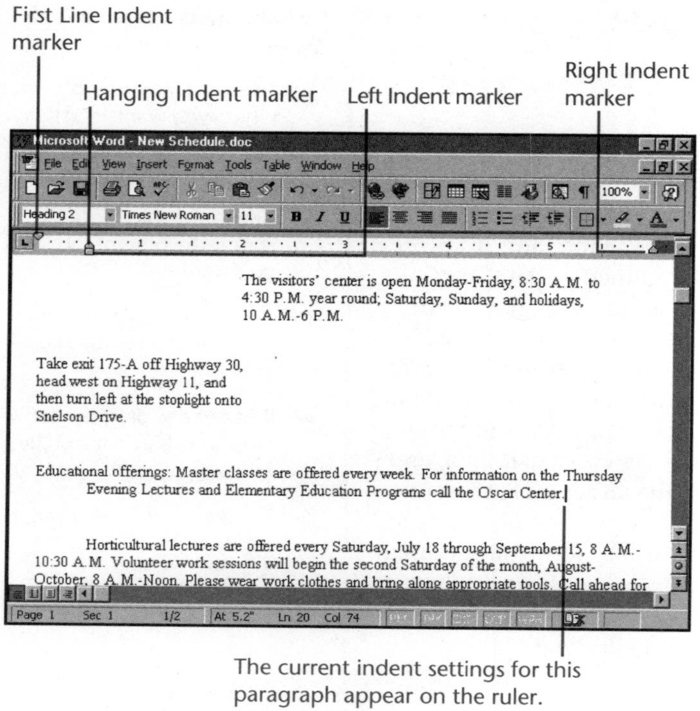
First Line Indent marker
Hanging Indent marker
Left Indent marker
Right Indent marker
Microsoft Word - New Schedule.doc
The visitors' center is open Monday-Friday, 8:30 A.M. to 4:30 P.M. year round; Saturday, Sunday, and holidays, 10 A.M.-6 P.M.
Take exit 175-A off Highway 30, head west on Highway 11, and then turn left at the stoplight onto Snelson Drive.
Educational offerings: Master classes are offered every week. For information on the Thursday Evening Lectures and Elementary Education Programs call the Oscar Center.
Horticultural lectures are offered every Saturday, July 18 through September 15, 8 A.M.-10:30 A.M. Volunteer work sessions will begin the second Saturday of the month, August-October, 8 A.M.-Noon. Please wear work clothes and bring along appropriate tools. Call ahead for
The current indent settings for this paragraph appear on the ruler.

SEE ALSO

See "Displaying Rulers" on page 84 for information about displaying and hiding the horizontal and vertical rulers.

Indent a Paragraph Using the Formatting Toolbar

Select at least one line in each paragraph you want to indent, and then on the Formatting toolbar click the:

- Increase Indent button to move the entire paragraph to the right one half inch at a time.
- Decrease Indent button to move the entire paragraph to the left one half inch at a time.

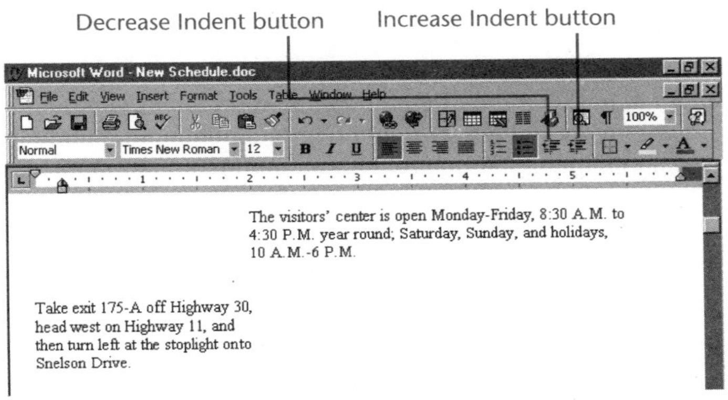

TIP

Use the Paragraph dialog box to adjust line spacing. *You can select from Single, 1.5 lines, and Double line spacing, or choose to customize the line spacing even more by selecting the At Least, Exactly, or Multiple option and entering a value in the At box.*

Indent a Paragraph Using a Dialog Box

1. Select at least one line in each paragraph you want to indent.
2. Click the Format menu, click Paragraph, and then click the Indents And Spacing tab.
3. Type the desired left and right indents (in inches) in the Left and Right boxes.
4. If necessary, click First Line or Hanging in the Special list box.
5. Type the amount of first line or hanging indent (in inches) in the By box.
6. Click OK.

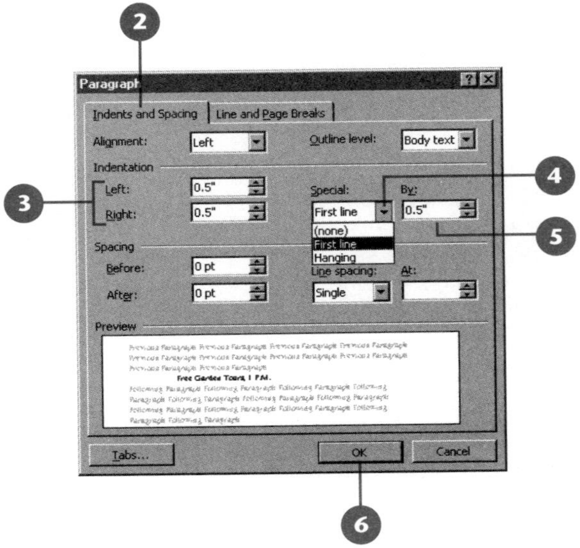

Setting Margins

Margins are the blank space between the edge of a page and the text. The default setting for Word documents is 1.25 inches on the left and right, and 1 inch on the top and bottom. You can set new margins for an entire section or document by dragging the margin boundaries on the rulers. To set new margins for the document from the current location of the insertion point forward, use the Page Setup dialog box.

SEE ALSO

See "Displaying Rulers" on page 84 for information about displaying and hiding the horizontal and vertical rulers.

Set Margins Using the Horizontal or Vertical Rulers

1. Click the Page Layout View button or the Normal View button.
2. Position the pointer over a margin boundary on the horizontal or vertical ruler.
3. Drag the left, right, top, or bottom margin boundary to a new position.
4. If desired, press and hold the Alt key while dragging the margin boundary to display the measurement of the text area.

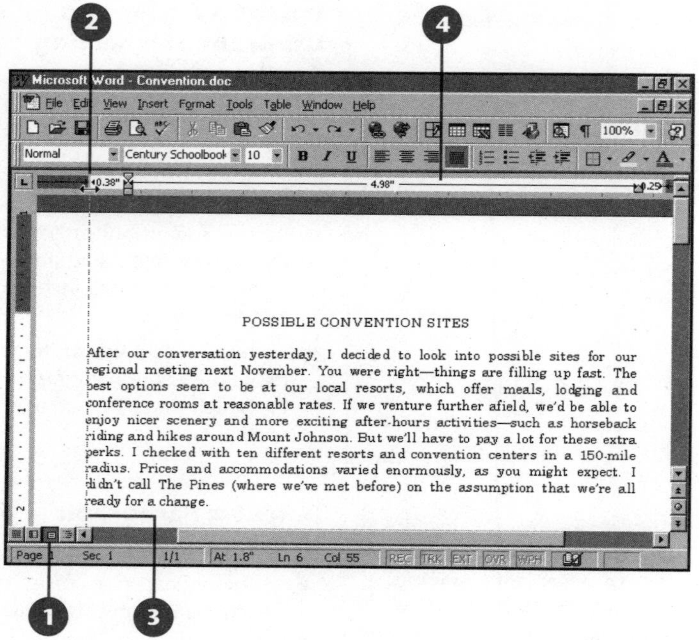
2
4
Microsoft Word - Convention.doc
File Edit View Insert Format Tools Table Window Help
Normal
Century Schoolbook
10
100%
0.38"
4.98"
0.25"
POSSIBLE CONVENTION SITES
After our conversation yesterday, I decided to look into possible sites for our regional meeting next November. You were right—things are filling up fast. The best options seem to be at our local resorts, which offer meals, lodging and conference rooms at reasonable rates. If we venture further afield, we'd be able to enjoy nicer scenery and more exciting after-hours activities—such as horseback riding and hikes around Mount Johnson. But we'll have to pay a lot for these extra perks. I checked with ten different resorts and convention centers in a 150-mile radius. Prices and accommodations varied enormously, as you might expect. I didn't call The Pines (where we've met before) on the assumption that we're all ready for a change.
Page 1
Sec 1
1/1
At 1.8"
Ln 6
Col 55
REC
TRK
EXT
OVR
WPH
1
3

TIP

Mirror margins. *The Mirror Margins option allows you to adjust the left and right margins, so that, when you print on both sides of a page, the inside margins of facing pages are the same width and the outside margins are the same width.*

TIP

Margins for headers and footers. *Word measures the distance from the top and bottom of the page to the header or footer. Preview your document to make sure there is enough room to print the header text on the page; if not, adjust the margins here.*

SEE ALSO

See "Inserting New Pages and Sections" on page 92 for information about dividing your document into sections.

Set Margins Using a Dialog Box

1. If you want to change margins for only part of the document, click in the paragraph where you want the new margins to begin. (When changing margins for the entire document, it doesn't matter where the insertion point is located.)
2. Click the File menu, click Page Setup, and then click the Margins tab.
3. Type new margin measurements (in inches) in the Top, Bottom, Left or Right boxes.
4. Check your changes in the Preview box.
5. Click the Apply To drop-down arrow, and then select Whole Document or This Point Forward.
6. To make the new margin settings the default for all new Word documents, click Default, and then click Yes.
7. Click OK.

You don't have to type the inch (") symbol.

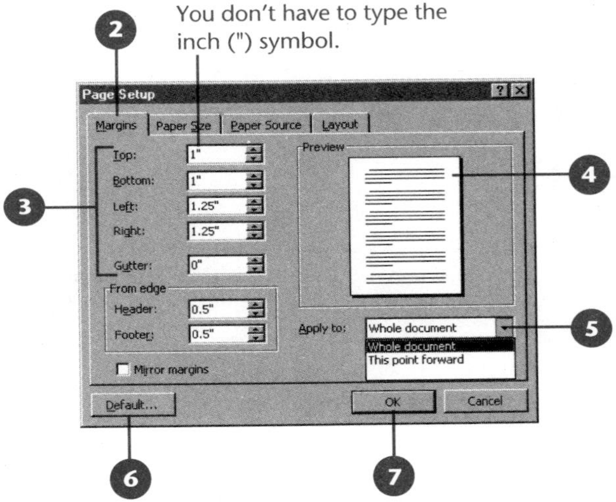

6

Working with Templates

A *template* is a special document in which you can store styles, text and formatting to use in other documents. You can use your own or any of Word's predefined templates as the basis of a new document, or attach template styles to the current document. When you attach a template to an existing document, you make the template styles available to only that document.

TIP

You are probably using the Normal template. *By default, all Word documents use the Normal template, which automatically formats text in 10-point Times New Roman, and offers three different heading styles.*

SEE ALSO

See "Creating and Modifying a Style" on page 94 for information on creating styles.

Save a Document as a Template

1. Open a new or existing document.
2. Add the text, graphics, and formatting you want to appear in all new documents based on this template. Adjust margin settings and page size, and create new styles as necessary.
3. Click the File menu, and then click Save As.
4. Click the Save As Type drop-down arrow, and then click Document Template.
5. Make sure the Templates folder (usually located in the Microsoft Office folder within the Programs folder) or one of its subfolders appears in the Save In box.
6. Type a name for the new template in the File Name box.
7. Click Save. You can open the template, and make and save other changes just as you would any other document.

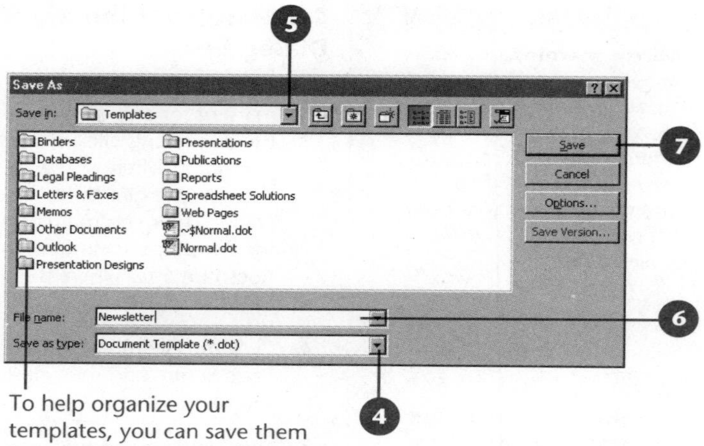

To help organize your templates, you can save them in any of the specialized folders within the Templates folder.

TIP

Copy template text and graphics. *If you want to add template text or graphics to an existing document, open the template, and then cut and paste the text or graphics you want to your document.*

SEE ALSO

See "Choosing Templates and Wizards" on page 26 for information about choosing a template to create a document from the Office Shortcut Bar.

Create a New Document from a Template

1. Click the File menu, and then click New.
2. Click the tab for the type of template you want.
3. Double-click the icon for the template you want.
4. Edit the template to create a new document.
5. Click the Save button on the Standard toolbar and save your document.

If you save a template in the Templates folder, you'll find its icon on the General tab.

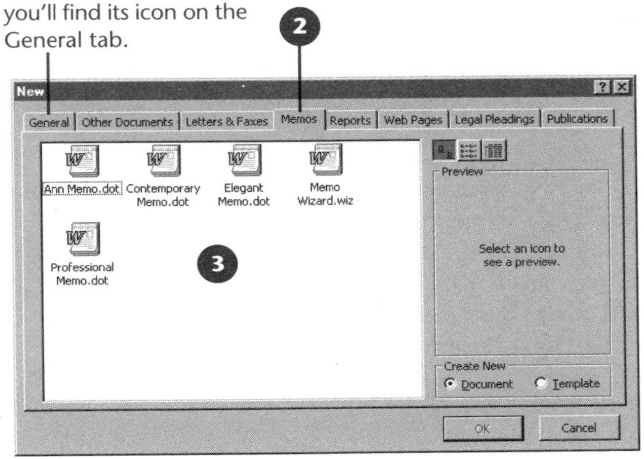

Apply a Template to an Existing Document

1. Open the document to which you want to apply a new template.
2. Click the Format menu, and then click Style Gallery.
3. Click a template name to preview it.
4. Click OK to add the template styles to the document.

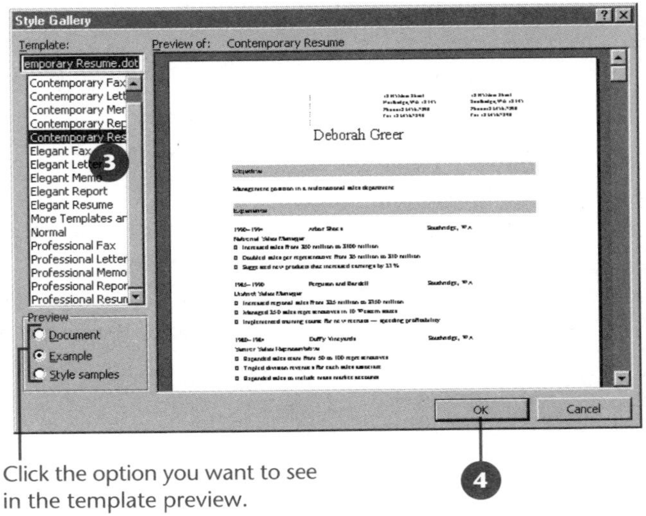

Click the option you want to see in the template preview.

Inserting New Pages and Sections

When you fill a page, Word automatically inserts a page break and begins a new page. As you add or delete text, this *soft page break* will move. To start a new page before you reach the end of the current one, you need to manually insert a page break (called a *hard page break* because it doesn't shift as you edit text). A *section* is a mini-document within a document; you can format it with different margins, page orientation, and so on, no matter how the rest of the document looks.

TRY THIS

Work with a section. *Open or create a multipage document, add a section break in the middle, and then format each section differently. Then use different margins and line spacing for each section, and print the results.*

Insert and Delete a Page Break

1. Click where you want to insert a hard page break.
2. Press Ctrl+Enter to insert a hard page break.
3. Click the page break and then press Backspace or Delete to delete it.

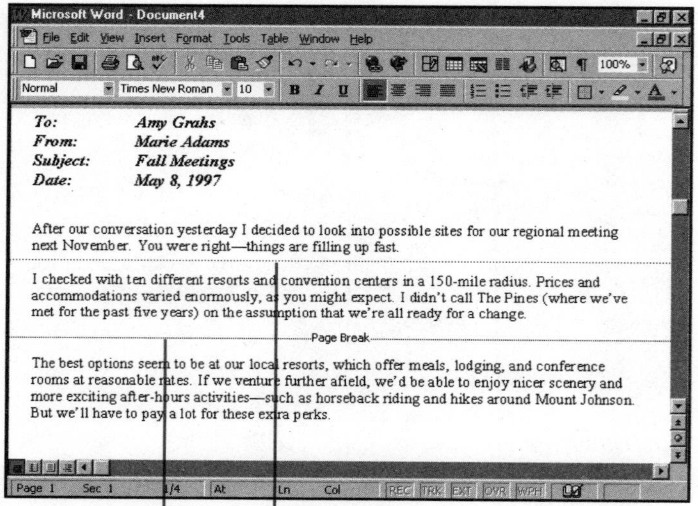

Microsoft Word - Document4
File Edit View Insert Format Tools Table Window Help
Normal
Times New Roman
10
100%
To: Amy Grahs
From: Marie Adams
Subject: Fall Meetings
Date: May 8, 1997
After our conversation yesterday I decided to look into possible sites for our regional meeting next November. You were right—things are filling up fast.
I checked with ten different resorts and convention centers in a 150-mile radius. Prices and accommodations varied enormously, as you might expect. I didn't call The Pines (where we've met for the past five years) on the assumption that we're all ready for a change.
Page Break
The best options seem to be at our local resorts, which offer meals, lodging, and conference rooms at reasonable rates. If we venture further afield, we'd be able to enjoy nicer scenery and more exciting after-hours activities—such as horseback riding and hikes around Mount Johnson. But we'll have to pay a lot for these extra perks.
Page 1 Sec 1 1/4 At Ln Col REC TRK EXT OVR WPH

2

Soft page break

Insert and Delete a Section Break

1. Click where you want to insert a section break.
2. Click the Insert menu, and then click Break.
3. Under Section Breaks, click the break option you want.
4. Click OK.
5. Click the section break and then press Backspace or Delete to delete it.

Starts the section start on new page

Starts the section wherever the insertion point is located

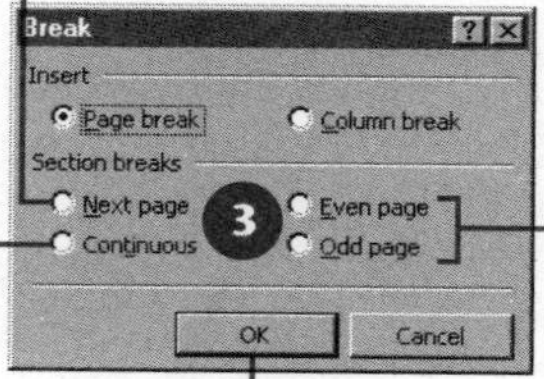

Break
Insert
Page break
Column break
Section breaks
Next page
Continuous
Even page
Odd page
OK
Cancel

3

Starts the section on the next even or odd page

4

Applying a Style

A *style* is a collection of formatting settings you can apply to selected text. You can copy styles from selected text and apply them elsewhere in your document with the Format Painter. But the easiest way to use a style is to save it as part of a document or template. The document or template. The style's name will then appear in the Style list box on the Formatting toolbar, ready for you to use whenever you like.

TIP

Paint a format in multiple locations. *Select the formatting you want to copy. Double-click the Format Painter button, and then drag the pointer over the text you want to format in each location. Click the Format Painter button again when you are finished.*

SEE ALSO

See "Working with Templates" on page 90 for information on applying predefined template styles to a document.

Copy a Style with the Format Painter

1. Select the text with the formatting style you want to copy.
2. Click the Format Painter button on the Standard toolbar.
3. Select the text you want to format with the Format Painter pointer.

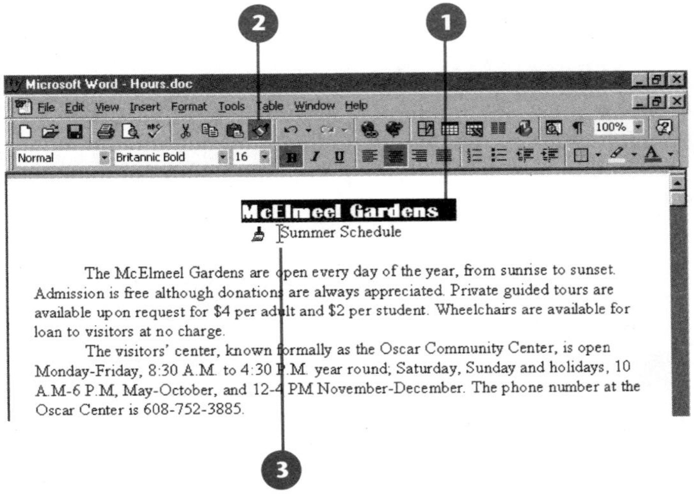
2
1
Microsoft Word - Hours.doc
File Edit View Insert Format Tools Table Window Help
Normal
Britannic Bold
16
100%
McElmeel Gardens
Summer Schedule
The McElmeel Gardens are open every day of the year, from sunrise to sunset. Admission is free although donations are always appreciated. Private guided tours are available upon request for $4 per adult and $2 per student. Wheelchairs are available for loan to visitors at no charge.
The visitors' center, known formally as the Oscar Community Center, is open Monday-Friday, 8:30 A.M. to 4:30 P.M. year round; Saturday, Sunday and holidays, 10 A.M-6 P.M, May-October, and 12-4 PM November-December. The phone number at the Oscar Center is 608-752-3885.
3

Change a Style Using the Style List Box

1. Make sure the template with the styles you want is attached to the current document.
2. Select the text you want to format.
3. Click the Style drop-down arrow on the Formatting toolbar.
4. Click the style you want to use.

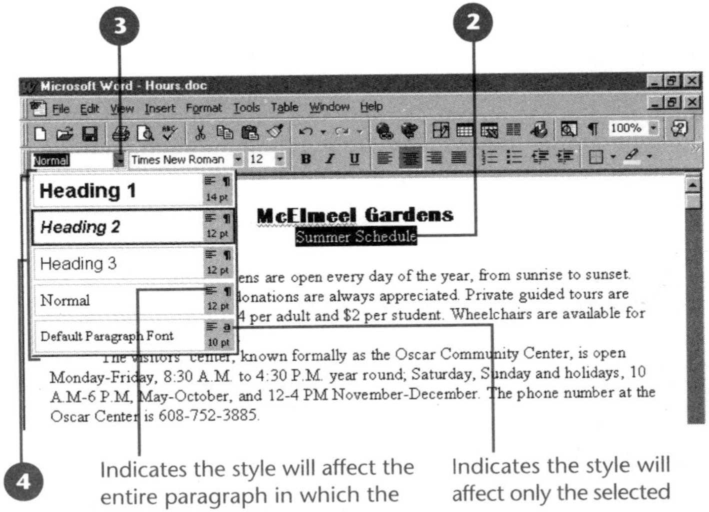
3
2
Microsoft Word - Hours.doc
File Edit View Insert Format Tools Table Window Help
Normal
Times New Roman
12
100%
Heading 1
14 pt
Heading 2
12 pt
Heading 3
12 pt
Normal
12 pt
Default Paragraph Font
10 pt
McElmeel Gardens
Summer Schedule
4

Indicates the style will affect the entire paragraph in which the insertion point is located

Indicates the style will affect only the selected text

6

Creating and Modifying a Style

Even though Word provides a variety of styles to choose from, you can create a new style or modify an existing style to better fit your needs. When you create a new style, you need to specify if the style applies to paragraphs or characters. Also, make sure you give the style a name that indicates the purpose of it. When you modify a style, you simply make adjustments to an existing one.

TIP

Use the List box to change style settings. *The List box in the Style dialog box provides three options: Styles In Use, All Styles, and User-Defined Styles. The styles listed in the Styles list box are based on the List option you choose.*

Create a New Style

1. Select the text whose formatting you want to save as a style.
2. Click the Format menu, click Style, and then click New.
3. Type a short, descriptive name that describes the style's purpose.
4. Click the Style Type drop-down arrow, and then click Paragraph if you want the style to include the line spacing and margins of the selected text, or click Character if you want the style to include only formatting, such as font type, bold, and so on.
5. Click the Add To Template check box to add the new style to the current template.
6. Click OK.
7. Click Apply or click Close.

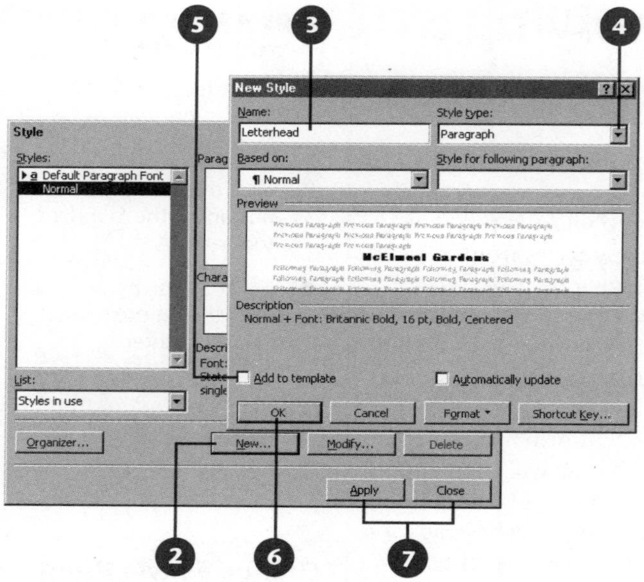

Modify a Style

1. Click the Format menu, and then click Style.
2. In the Styles list box, click the style you want to modify.
3. Click Modify.
4. Click the Format menu, and then select the type of formatting you want to modify. To change character formatting, such as font type and bold face, click Font. To change line spacing and indents, click Paragraph.
5. In the next dialog box, select the formatting options you want, and then click OK.
6. Review the description of the style, and make other formatting changes as necessary.
7. Click OK.
8. Click Apply or click Close.

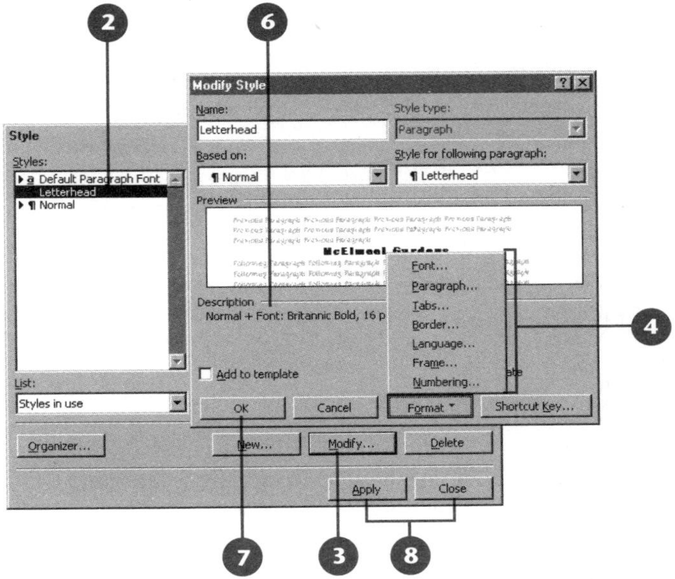

TRY THIS

Modify a style quickly. *Add italics to your text formatted with the Title style. Select the title text, click the Italic button on the formatting toolbar, click the Style drop-down arrow, click Title, click the Update The Style To Reflect Recent Changes option button, and then click OK.*

TRY THIS

Create a style quickly. *Try creating a heading style that centers and bolds text. Select the text, and then click the Center button and the Bold button on the Formatting toolbar. Then highlight the style name in the Style box on the Formatting toolbar. Type a short, descriptive name, such as Titles, and then press Enter. The style is now available for your document.*

SEE ALSO

See "Working with Templates" on page 90 for information about applying predefined template styles to a document.

Creating Bulleted and Numbered Lists

The best way to draw attention to a list is to format it with bullets or numbers, a task Word can perform for you. Once you've created a bulleted or numbered list, you can change its character or number default style to one of Word's numerous predefined formats. For example, you can change a numerical list to an alphabetical list. If you move, insert, or delete items in a numbered list, Word will renumber the list sequentially for you.

Bullets button

Create a Bulleted List

1. Type an asterisk (*) at the beginning of a new paragraph, and then press Tab.
2. Type the first item in your list, and then press Enter to convert the asterisk to a bullet.
3. For each additional item in your list, type the item and press Enter to insert a new bullet.
4. When you finish your list, press Enter twice to return to normal text.

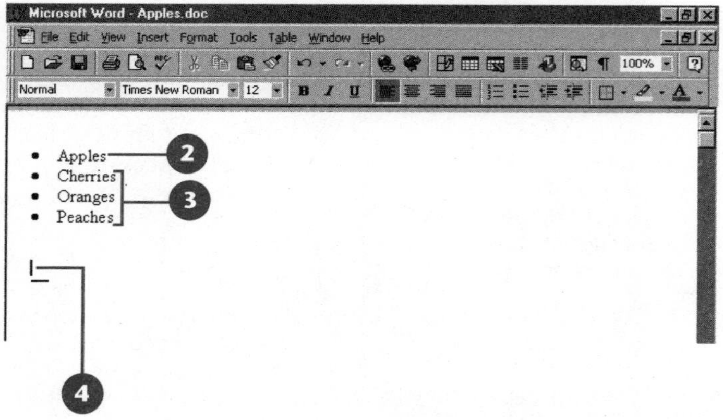

Create a Numbered List

1. Type 1 followed by a period (1.) at the beginning of a new paragraph, and then press Tab.
2. Type the first item in your list, and then press Enter to format the number.
3. For each additional item in your list, type the item and press Enter to insert sequential numbers.
4. When you finish your list, press Enter twice to return to normal text.

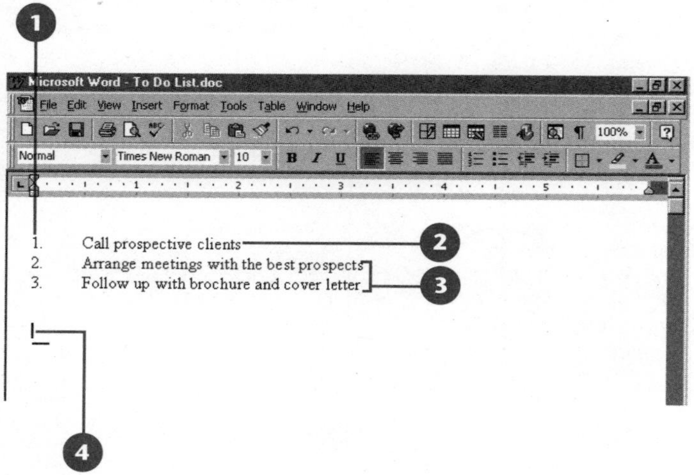

SEE ALSO

See "Setting Paragraph Indents" on page 86 for information on using the Increase Indent and Decrease Indent buttons.

TIP

Change spacing between character and text. *You can change the amount of space between the bullet or number and the text. Click Customize in the Bullets and Numbering dialog box, and then change the Bullet (or Number) Position and Text Position options to specify where you want the bullet (or number) to appear and how much to indent the text.*

Switch Between a Bulleted List and a Numbered List

1. Select the list.
2. Click the Bullets or Numbering button on the Formatting toolbar.

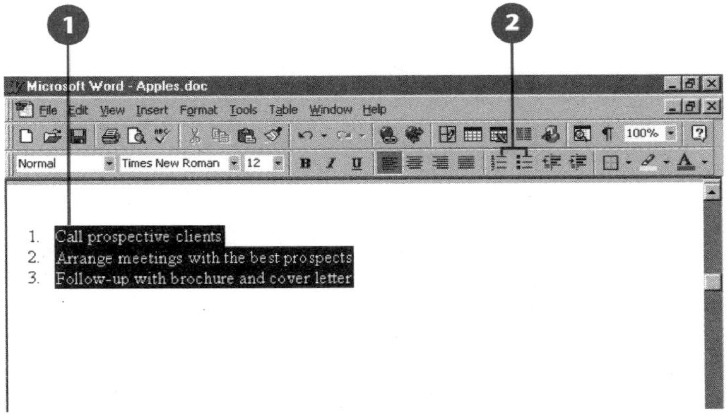

Change Bullet or Numbering Styles

1. Select the bulleted or numbered list.
2. Click the Format menu, and then click Bullets And Numbering.
3. Click either the Bulleted tab or the Numbered tab.
4. Click a predefined format.
5. If necessary, click Customize and change the predefined format style and position settings.
6. Click OK.

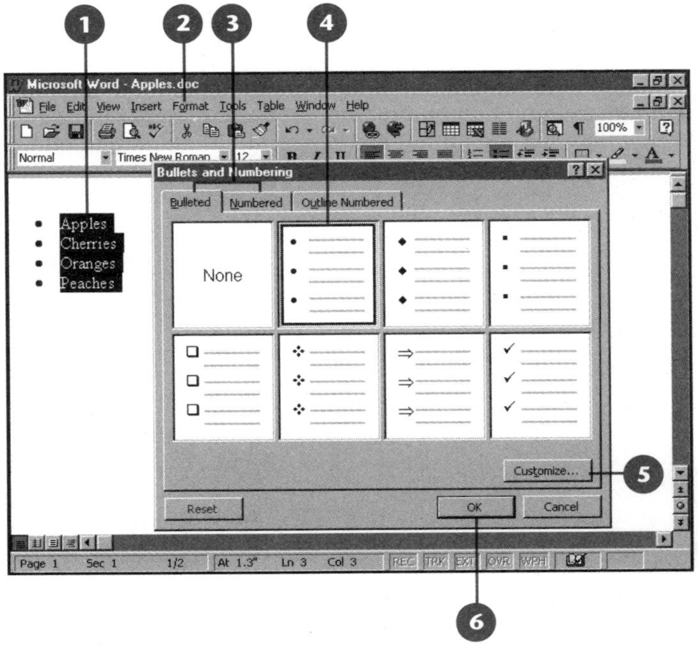

Creating Bookmarks

A *bookmark* is a location or selection of text that you name for reference purposes. Word marks the location with the name you specify. Bookmarks are more than placeholders; for example, you can use them to create and number cross-references.

Tag a Location with a Bookmark

1. Click in the document where you want to insert a bookmark.
2. Click the Insert menu, and then click Bookmark.
3. Type a descriptive name (fewer than 40 characters) in the Bookmark Name box.
4. Click Add.

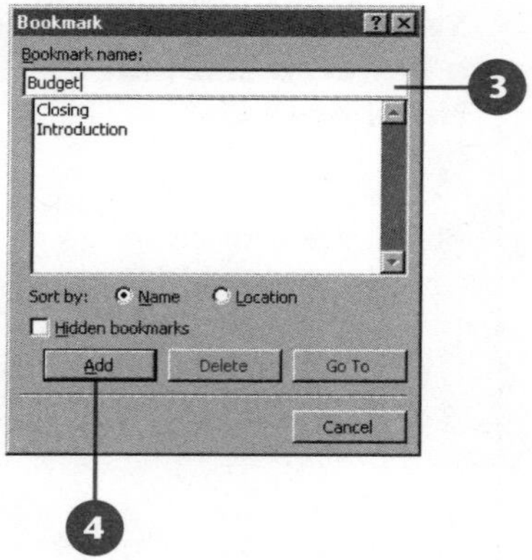

Go to a Bookmark Location

1. Click the Edit menu, and then click Go To.
2. Click Bookmark in the Go To What list box.
3. Click the Enter Bookmark Name drop-down arrow, and then click the bookmark you want to move to.
4. Click Go To.
5. Choose another bookmark if you want.
6. Click Close.

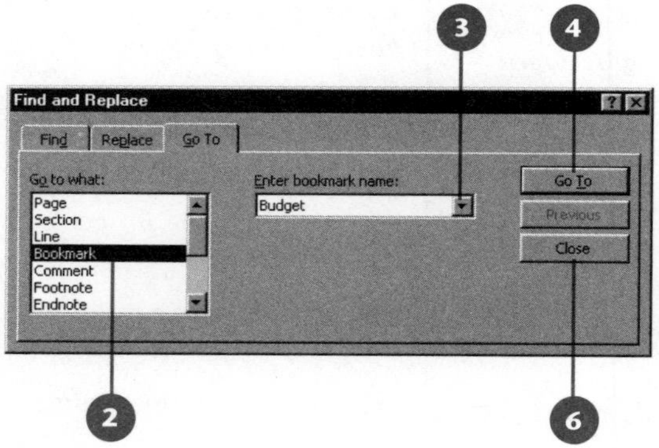

7

Enhancing a Document with Word 97

IN THIS SECTION

Once you've mastered the basics of word processing with Microsoft Word 97, you can try some of the more advanced features. In most cases, there's more than one way to perform tasks such as creating tables or adding clip art. To save you time, this book focuses on the fastest and easiest methods.

Enhancing Your Document

After you've created your basic document, take a moment to consider how you can enhance its appearance and communicate its message more effectively. For example, you could draw attention to important text and data or clarify the details of a complicated paragraph by using a table. If your document is a brochure or newsletter, you'll probably want to take advantage of Word's desktop publishing features, which allow you to format text in columns, as well as add headlines instantly.

Several Word features—among them, templates, styles, and the Find and Replace commands—are designed to help you work faster and more efficiently. You can use any of Word's predefined templates and styles, or create your own, to serve as the foundation for your routine documents.

Creating Headers and Footers

A *header* is text that is printed in the top margin of every page. *Footer* text is printed in the bottom margin. Common information to put in headers and footers includes your name, the name of your document, the date the document is printed, and page numbers. If you've divided your document into sections, you can create different headers and footers for each section.

TIP

Use Alignment buttons to change text placement. *Instead of using the default tab stops, you can use the Alignment buttons on the Formatting toolbar. For example, you might want just your company name aligned on the right margin of the header.*

Create and Edit Headers and Footers

1. Click the View menu, and then click Header And Footer.

   Word switches to page layout view to display the header text area.

2. If necessary, click the Switch Between Header And Footer button on the Header And Footer toolbar to display the footer text area.
3. Click in the header or footer area, and then type the text you want.
4. To insert common phrases, click the Insert AutoText button on the Header And Footer toolbar, point to Footer or Header, and then click the text you want.
5. Edit and format the existing header or footer text as you would any other text.
6. When you're finished, click the Close button on the Header And Footer toolbar.

Document text appears in light gray, indicating that it is not available for editing.

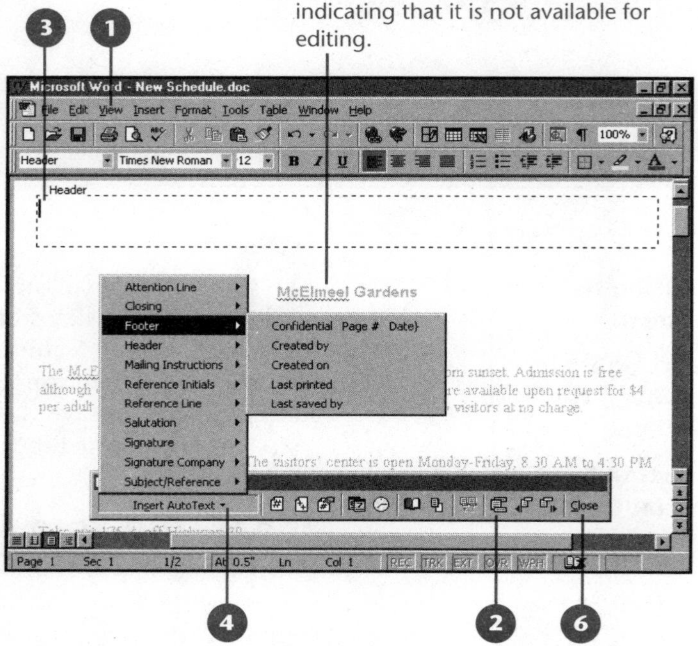

TIP

Use Default tab stops to adjust header and footer text. *Headers and footers have three default tab stops. The first, on the far left, aligns text on the left margin. The second, in the middle, centers text. The third, on the far right, aligns text on the right margin.*

TRY THIS

Create section headers and footers. *Divide a multipage document into sections, and then create different headers and footers for each section.*

SEE ALSO

See "Settings Margins" on page 88 for information about setting margins for headers and footers.

Create Different Headers and Footers for Different Pages

1. Click the View menu, and then click Header And Footer.
2. Click the Page Setup button on the Header And Footer toolbar.
3. Click the Layout tab, if necessary.
4. To create a unique header or footer for the first page of the document, click the Different First Page check box. To create different headers or footers for odd and even pages, click the Different Odd And Even check box.
5. Click OK.
6. Click the Show Previous button and Show Next button to move from one header to the next, and enter and format the text you want in the remaining headers and footers.

   To move between the header and footer, click the Switch Between Header And Footer button.
7. Click the Close button on the Header And Footer toolbar.

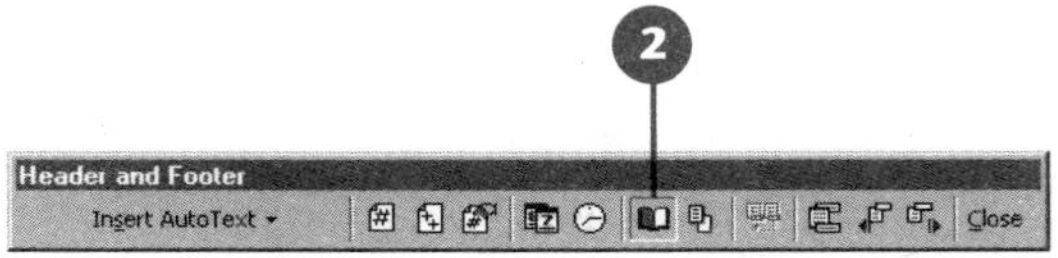

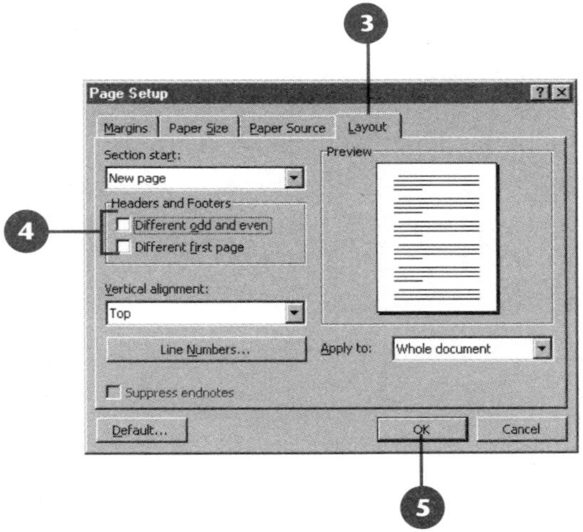

Inserting Page Numbers, the Date, and Time

To better document your work, you can have every page in the document numbered. Inserting this information in a header or footer is a standard way of keeping track of your work. When you insert the date and time, Word uses your computer's internal calendar and clock as its source. Numbering the pages in a document is also an important tracking tool, even if the document is only a few pages. You can insert the total number of pages in a document as well as the individual page numbers.

SEE ALSO

See "Creating Headers and Footers" on page 100 for information on headers and footers.

Insert Page Numbers, the Date or Time

1. Click the View menu, and then click Header And Footer.
2. Click in the header or footer where you want to insert. Remember to use the Tab key to move to the next tab stop.
3. Click the appropriate button or buttons on the Header And Footer toolbar.

   You can enter text along with the header and footer information. For example, you can type the word "Page."
4. If necessary, select the date, time, or page number, and then format it as you would any other text.
5. To delete any item, select it, and then press Delete.
6. When you're done, click the Close button on the Header And Footer toolbar.

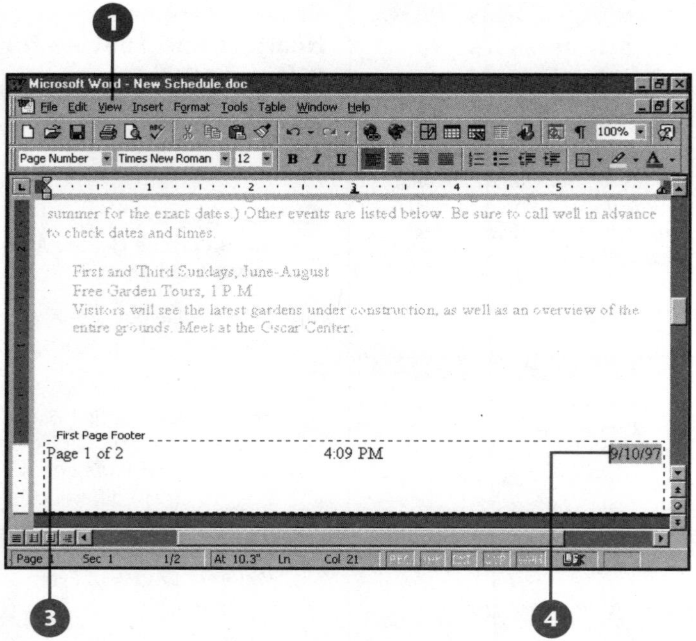

Insert Page Number button
Click to insert the correct page number on each page.

Insert Date button
Click to insert the current date from your computer's calendar.

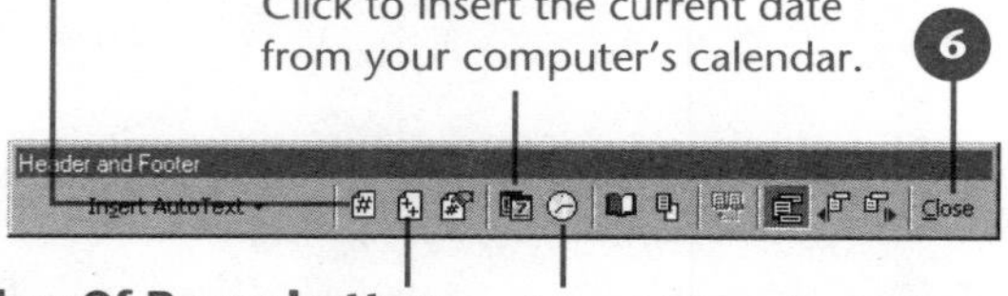

Insert Number Of Pages button
Click to insert total number of pages in the document.

Insert Time button
Click to insert the current time from your computer's clock.

Inserting Symbols and Special Characters

Being able to insert just the right symbol or character in your document is a good example of Word's extensive desktop publishing capabilities. Your document's professional appearance will not be compromised by having to pencil in an arrow or a mathematical symbol (Ü). Inserting a symbol or special character is easy; position the pointer where you want to insert the symbol or character, choose the Symbol command and select a symbol or character.

TIP

Create a shortcut key to insert symbols and special characters. *If you use a symbol or character repeatedly, you can assign it a keyboard combination. Select the symbol or special character you want, click Shortcut Key, and then complete the Customize Keyboard dialog box.*

Insert Symbols and Special Characters

1. Click in the document where you want to insert a symbol or character.
2. Click the Insert menu, and then click Symbol.
3. Click the either the Symbols tab or the Special Characters tab.
4. If you don't see the symbol you want on the Symbols tab, select a new font in the Font list box.
5. Click the symbol or character you want.
6. Click Insert.
7. Click Close.

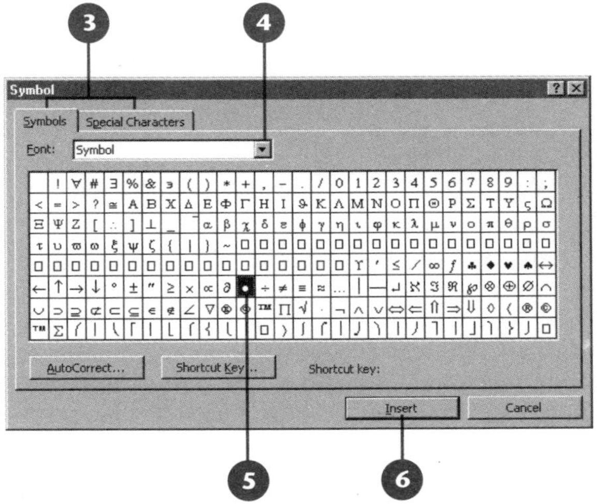

Creating a Table

A *table* organizes information neatly into rows and columns. The intersection of a row and column is called a *cell*. You enter text into cells just as you would anywhere else in a document, except that pressing the Tab key moves you from one cell to the next. You can also create a table from existing text. If, for example, you have aligned related information using tabs and you then decide to use a table to present the information more efficiently, you can convert the text to a table. If you decide not to use the table, you can convert a table to text just as easily.

SEE ALSO

See "Modifying a Table" on page 106 and "Formatting a Table" on page 110 for information on changing the appearance of your table.

Create a Table Quickly

1. Move the insertion point to the beginning of a new paragraph.
2. Click the Insert Table button on the Standard toolbar.
3. Drag to select the appropriate number of rows and columns.
4. Release the mouse button to insert a blank grid in the document. The insertion point is in the first cell, ready for you to begin typing.

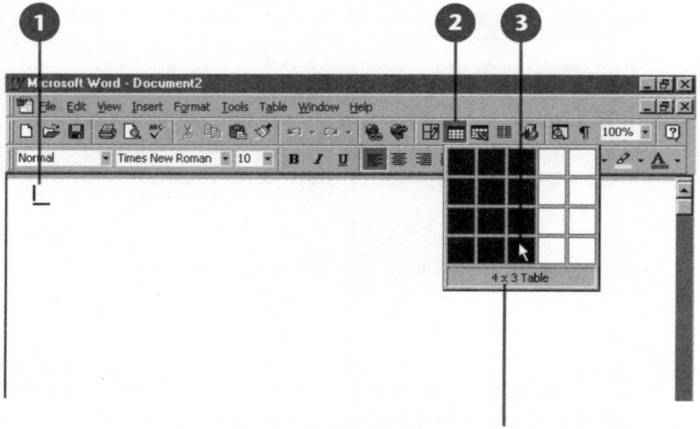

The first number indicates the number of rows, the second the number of columns. This 4x3 table will have four rows and three columns.

Convert a Table to Text

1. Click anywhere within the table, click the Table menu, and then click Select Table.
2. Click the Table menu, and then click Convert Table To Text.
3. Select the symbol you want to separate the text in each cell.
4. Click OK.

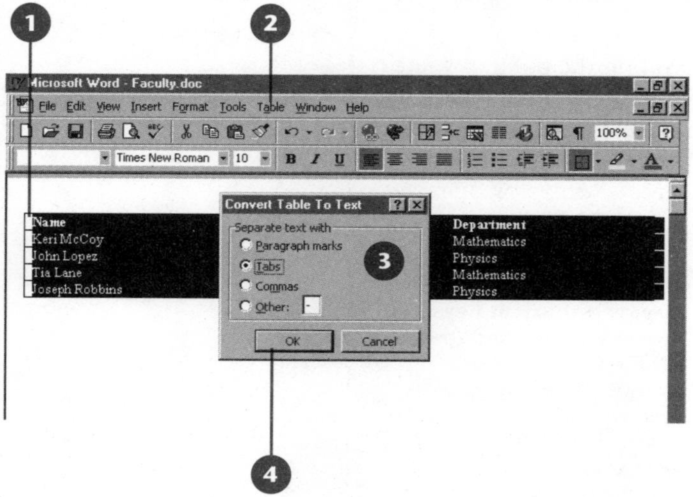

Entering Text in a Table

Once you create your table or convert text to a table, you need to enter (or add) text in each cell. You will probably use the first row in the table for your column headings, or list the headings down the first column on the left. You also need to know how to move around the table to make entering text easy. Knowing how to select the rows and columns of a table is also essential to working with the table itself.

TIP

Expand the row height as you type. *As you type in a cell, the text will wrap to the next line according to the width of the column; in other words, the height of a row expands as you enter text that is greater than the width of the column.*

SEE ALSO

See "Modifying a Table" on page 106 and "Formatting a Table" on page 110 for information on changing the appearance of your table.

Enter Text and Move Around a Table

The insertion point shows where text you type will appear in a table. After you type text in a cell:

- Press Enter to start a new paragraph within that cell.
- Press Tab to move the insertion point to the next cell to the right (or to the first cell in the next row).
- Use the arrow keys or click anywhere in the table to move the insertion point to a new location.

Type and format text in a cell just as you would anywhere else in a document.

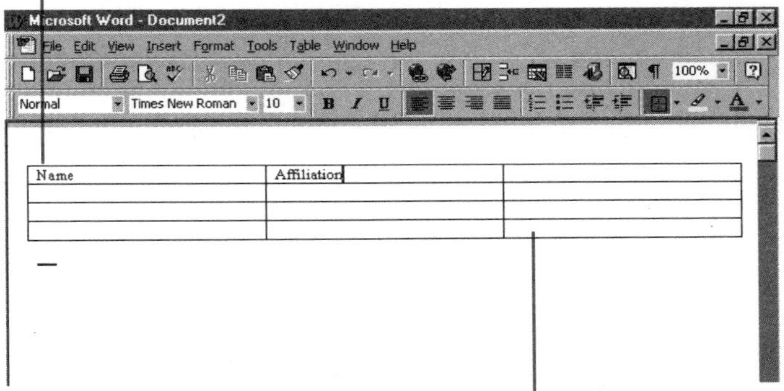

With the insertion point in the lower right cell, press the Tab key to add a new row to the table.

Modifying a Table

After you create a table or begin to enter text in one, you might want to add more rows or columns to accommodate the text you are entering in the table. When you add a row, you select the row above which you want the new, blank row to appear. When you add a column, you select the column to the left of which you want the new, blank column to appear. When you want to insert more than one row or column, select that number of rows and columns first. For example, if you want to insert two rows, select two rows first. When you delete rows and columns from a table, the table aligns itself.

Select Table Elements

Refer to the table for methods to select table elements, including:

- One or more cells
- One or more rows and columns
- The entire table

SELECTING TABLE ELEMENTS

To Select	Do This
The entire table	Click anywhere in the table, click the Table menu, and then click Select Table.
One or more rows	Click in the left margin next to the first row you want to select, and then drag to select as many rows as you want.
One or more columns	Click just above the first column you want to select, and then drag to select as many columns as you want.
The row or column where	Click the Table menu, and then the insertion point is located click either Select Row or Select Column.
A single cell	Triple-click a cell.
More than one cell	Triple-click one cell, and then drag the I-beam pointer to select others.

Insert Additional Rows

1. Select the row above which you want the new rows to appear.
2. Drag down to select the number of rows you want to insert.
3. Click the Insert Rows button on the Standard toolbar.

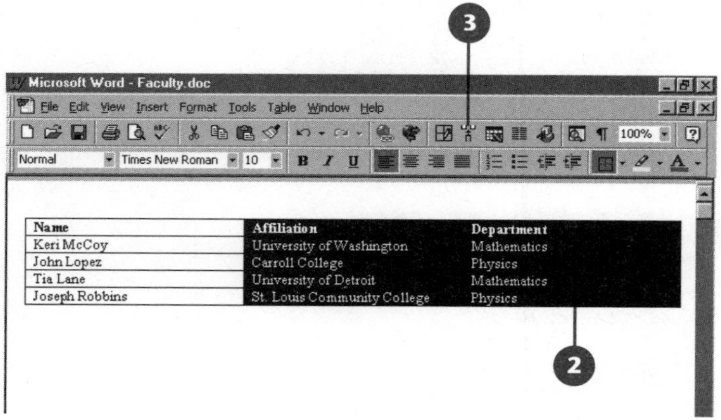

TIP

Arrange rows and columns. *You can arrange the position of a row or column easily. Select the row or column you want to move, and then position the pointer over it until the pointer changes to a move pointer. Then drag the selected row or column to a new position in the table.*

SEE ALSO

See "Entering Text in a Table" on page 105 for information on moving between rows and columns.

Insert Columns button

7

Insert Additional Columns

1. Select the column to the left of which you want the new columns to appear.
2. Drag right to select the number of columns you want to insert.
3. Click the Insert Columns button on the Standard toolbar.

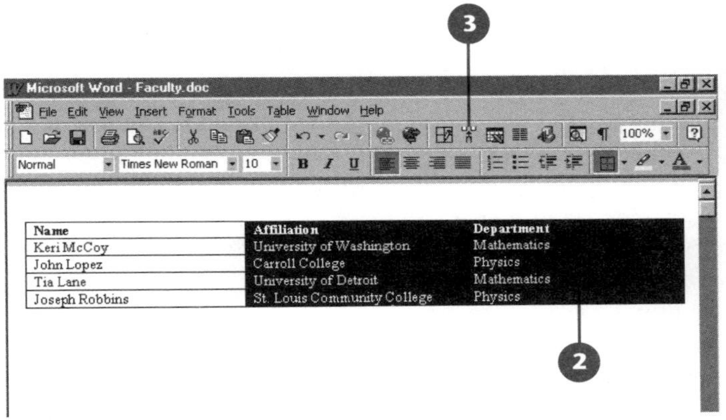

Delete Rows and Columns

1. Select the rows or columns you want to delete.
2. Right-click the selected rows or columns.
3. Click Delete Rows or Delete Columns.

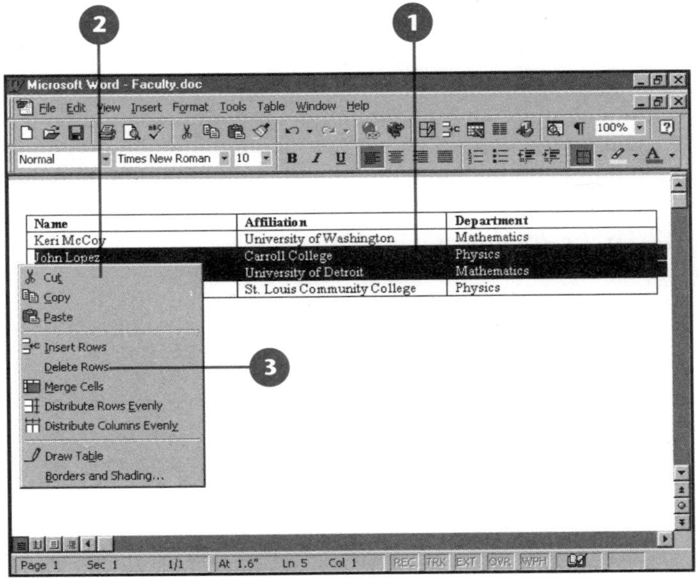

Adjusting Table Elements

Often there is more to modifying a table than adding or deleting rows or columns; you need to make each row or column just the right size to accommodate the text you are entering in the table. For example, you might have a title in the first row of a table that is longer than the first cell in that row. To spread the title across the top of the table, you can merge (combine) the cells together to form one long cell. Sometimes to indicate a division in a topic, you will also need to split (or divide) a cell into two. Moreover, the width of a column and height of a row can also be modified to better suit your needs.

Merge and Split Table Cells

- To combine (or *merge*) two or more cells into a single cell, select the cells you want to merge, right-click, and then click Merge Cells.
- To divide (or *split*) a cell into multiple cells, right-click the cell you want to split, and then click Split Cells. Type the number of rows or columns (or both) you want to split the selected cell into, and then click OK.

Before merging cells
The three cells in this row will be combined into one.

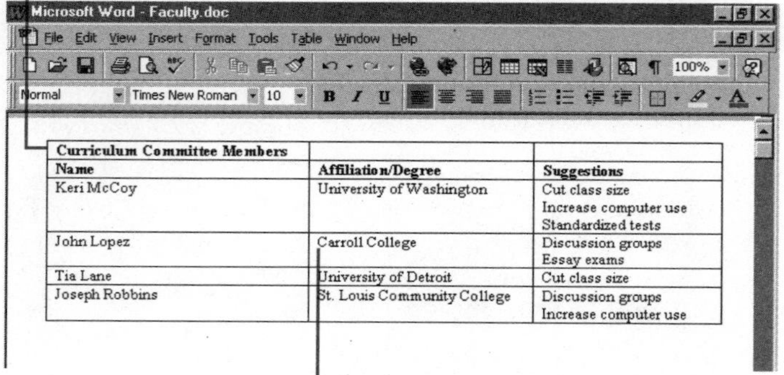

Before splitting a cell
This cell will be divided into two cells.

Three cells merged into one.

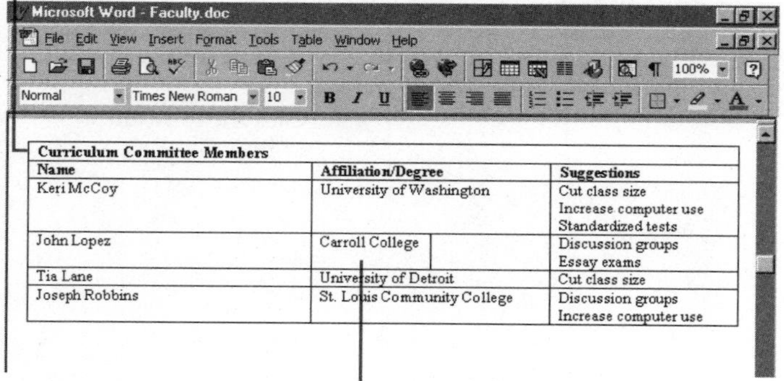

Single cell splits into two

TIP

Adjust column text with AutoFit. *If you can't decide the appropriate widths for the columns in your table, click the AutoFit button, and Word will adjust the columns to fit the longest entry in each column.*

TIP

Adjust column widths individually. *To adjust each column width separately, click the Previous Column or Next Column button on the Column tab in the Cell Height And Column dialog box.*

SEE ALSO

See "Formatting a Table" on page 110 for information on changing the look of a table.

Adjust Column Widths

1. Select the columns you want to change.
2. Click the Table menu, then click Cell Height And Width.
3. Click the Column tab.
4. To specify an exact width, enter an inch measurement in the Width Of Column box.
5. Click OK.

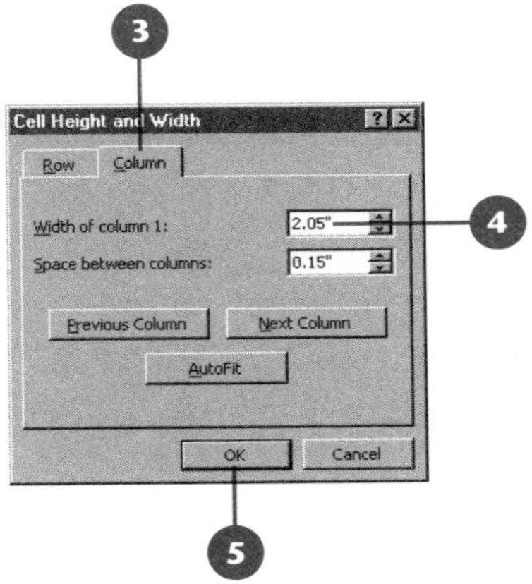

Adjust Row Heights

1. Select the rows you want to change.
2. Click the Table menu, and click Cell Height And Width.
3. Click the Row tab.
4. Click Exactly or At Least in the Height Of Rows box.
5. Enter an inch measurement in the At box.
6. Click OK.

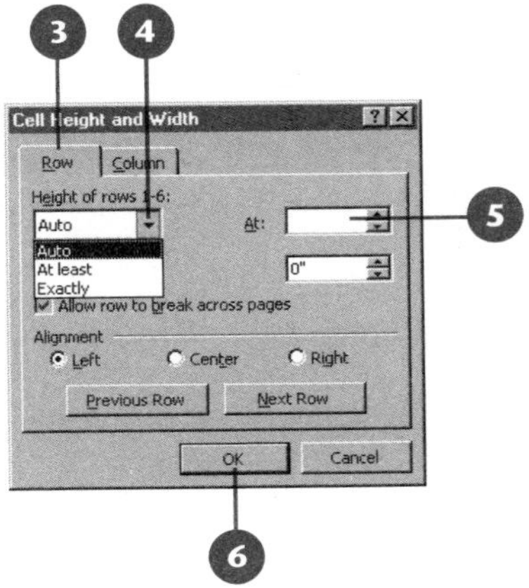

Formatting a Table

Word makes it easy for you to format your table. You can change the alignment of the text in the cells (by default, text aligns on the left of a cell and numbers align on the right). If changing the alignment isn't enough, you can use the Table AutoFormat dialog box to format your table. This dialog box provides a variety of predesigned table formats that you can apply to a selected table. If the AutoFormat offerings don't suit your needs, you can choose to add borders and shading manually. Borders and shading help to make printed tables easier to read and more attractive.

SEE ALSO

See "Adding Desktop Publishing Effects" on page 114 for information about manually adding borders and shading.

Format a Table Automatically

1. Right-click the table, and then click Table AutoFormat.
2. Select a format from the Formats list.
3. Preview the results in the Preview box.
4. When you find a format you like, click OK.

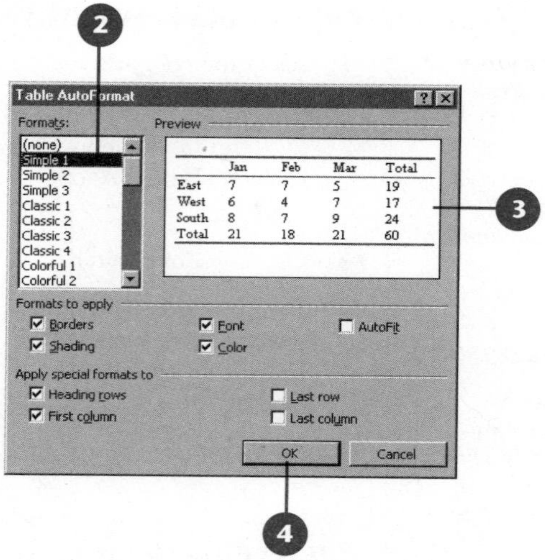

Align Text Within Cells

1. Select the cells, rows, or columns you want to align.
2. Click the Align Left, Center, Align Right, or Justify button on the Formatting toolbar.

Centered text
Center column headings to make them stand out.

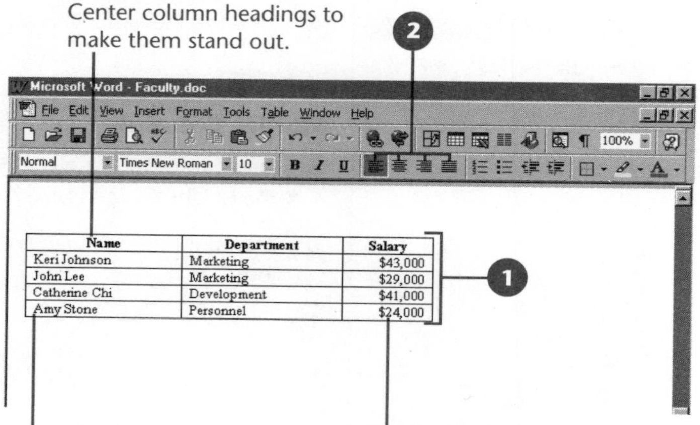

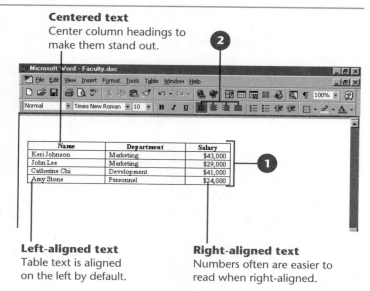

Left-aligned text
Table text is aligned on the left by default.

Right-aligned text
Numbers often are easier to read when right-aligned.

Arranging Text in Columns

Newspaper style columns can give newsletters and brochures a more polished look. Begin by using the Columns button to create the columns. Then choose among several column options to improve their appearance. Keep in mind that you can format an entire document or individual sections in columns. You must switch to page layout view to view the columns side-by-side on the screen.

TIP

Use the Formatting toolbar to align text in a column. *Select the columns you want to format, then click the Align Left, Center, Align Right, or Justify button on the Formatting toolbar.*

Create Columns

1. Switch to page layout view.
2. Select the text you want to arrange in columns.
3. Click the Columns button on the Standard toolbar.
4. Drag to select the number of columns you want.

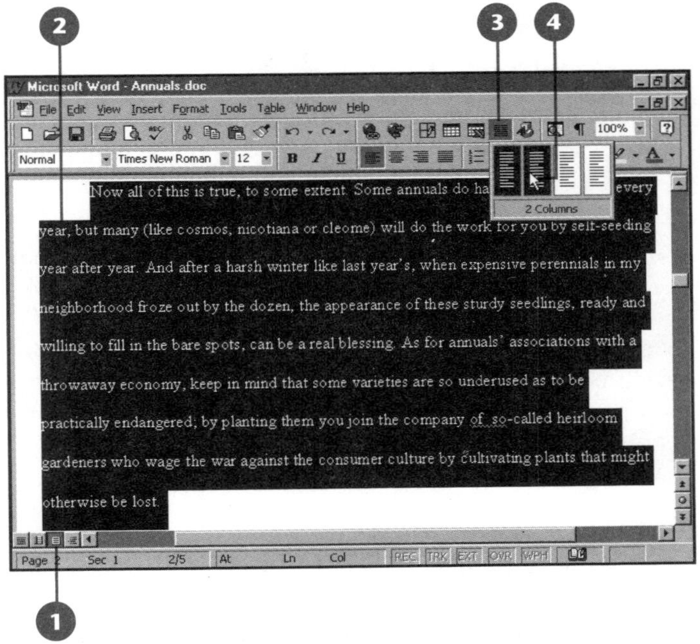

Microsoft Word - Annuals.doc
File Edit View Insert Format Tools Table Window Help
Normal
Times New Roman
12
100%
2 Columns
Now all of this is true, to some extent. Some annuals do ha every
year, but many (like cosmos, nicotiana or cleome) will do the work for you by self-seeding
year after year. And after a harsh winter like last year's, when expensive perennials in my
neighborhood froze out by the dozen, the appearance of these sturdy seedlings, ready and
willing to fill in the bare spots, can be a real blessing. As for annuals' associations with a
throwaway economy, keep in mind that some varieties are so underused as to be
practically endangered; by planting them you join the company of so-called heirloom
gardeners who wage the war against the consumer culture by cultivating plants that might
otherwise be lost.
Page 2 Sec 1 2/5 At Ln Col
REC TRK EXT OVR WPH
2
3
4
1

Modify Columns

1. Switch to page layout view.
2. Click the Format menu, and then click Columns.
3. Select the column options you want.
4. Click OK.

If you prefer, choose any of these commonly used column formats.

Click to separate columns with a thin vertical line.

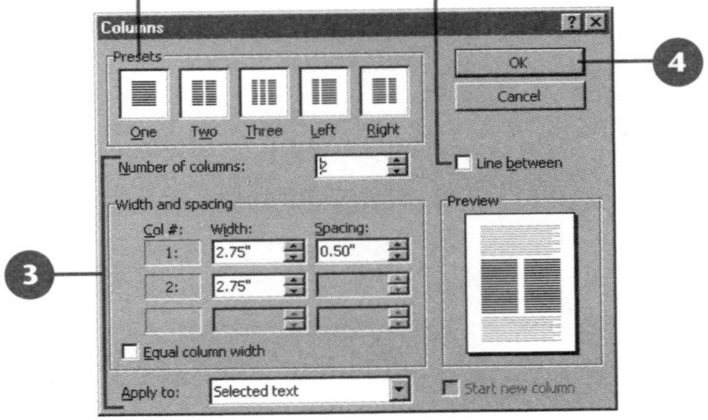

Columns
Presets
One
Two
Three
Left
Right
OK
Cancel
Number of columns:
Line between
Width and spacing
Col #:
Width:
Spacing:
1:
2.75"
0.50"
2:
2.75"
Preview
Equal column width
Apply to:
Selected text
Start new column
3
4

Inserting Comments and Summaries

Comments in a document are like electronic adhesive notes. You can use them to get feedback from other readers before finalizing a document, or to remind yourself of revisions and changes you plan to make to the document in the future. If you need feedback on the basic ideas in a document, compile the main points of your document in a *summary*, which you can distribute to your colleagues, instead of the entire document.

Next Comment button

Insert a Comment

1. Click in the document where you want to insert a comment.
2. Click the Insert menu, and then click Comment to open the comment pane.
3. Click the Comments From drop-down arrow to view the comments made by you or other reviewers.
4. Type your comment in the comment pane next to the code.
5. Click Close.

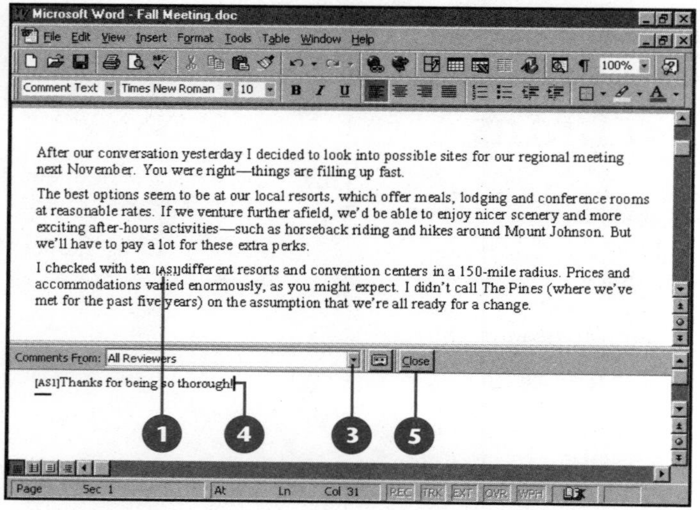
Microsoft Word - Fall Meeting.doc
File Edit View Insert Format Tools Table Window Help
Comment Text
Times New Roman
10
100%
After our conversation yesterday I decided to look into possible sites for our regional meeting next November. You were right—things are filling up fast.
The best options seem to be at our local resorts, which offer meals, lodging and conference rooms at reasonable rates. If we venture further afield, we'd be able to enjoy nicer scenery and more exciting after-hours activities—such as horseback riding and hikes around Mount Johnson. But we'll have to pay a lot for these extra perks.
I checked with ten [AS1]different resorts and convention centers in a 150-mile radius. Prices and accommodations varied enormously, as you might expect. I didn't call The Pines (where we've met for the past five years) on the assumption that we're all ready for a change.
Comments From: All Reviewers
Close
[AS1]Thanks for being so thorough!
1
4
3
5
Page
Sec 1
At
Ln
Col 31
REC TRK EXT OVR WPH

Read a Comment

1. Click the View menu, and then click Comments.
2. In the comment pane, read the comment associated with the first code in the document window.
3. Click the Next Comment button on the Comment toolbar to display the next code in the document window.
4. Click Close when you are finished reading comments.

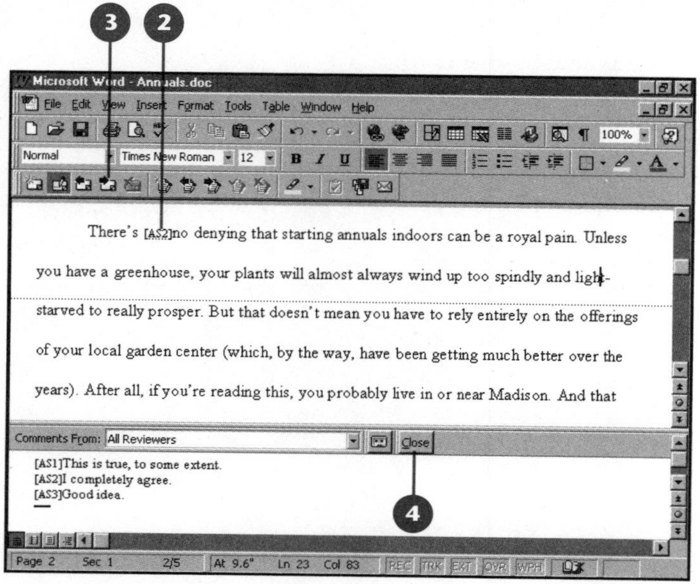
3
2
Microsoft Word - Annuals.doc
File Edit View Insert Format Tools Table Window Help
Normal
Times New Roman
12
100%
There's [AS2]no denying that starting annuals indoors can be a royal pain. Unless you have a greenhouse, your plants will almost always wind up too spindly and light-starved to really prosper. But that doesn't mean you have to rely entirely on the offerings of your local garden center (which, by the way, have been getting much better over the years). After all, if you're reading this, you probably live in or near Madison. And that
Comments From: All Reviewers
Close
[AS1]This is true, to some extent.
[AS2]I completely agree.
[AS3]Good idea.
4
Page 2
Sec 1
2/5
At 9.6"
Ln 23
Col 83
REC TRK EXT OVR WPH

TIP

Use the Show/Hide button to display comment code. *If you can't see a comment code in the document without the comment pane open, click the Show/Hide button on the Standard toolbar.*

Delete a Comment

1. Right-click the comment code in the document window.
2. Click Delete Comment.

   After you delete a comment, Word renumbers the remaining comments to keep them sequential.

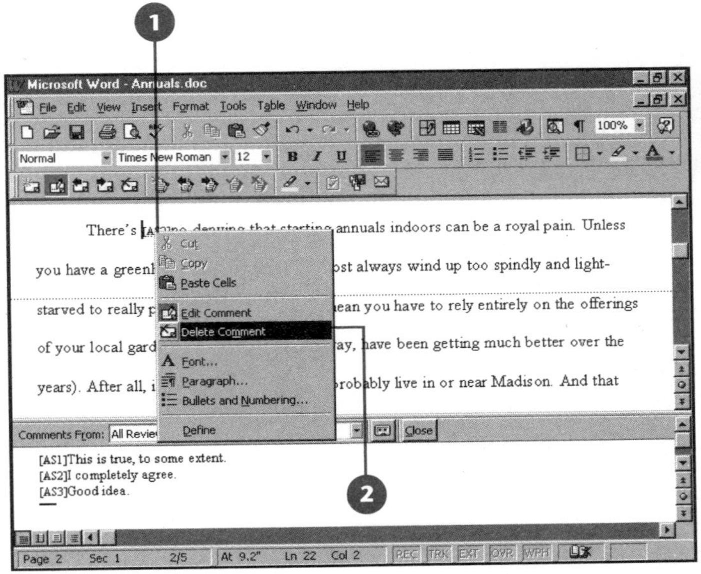

Summarize Your Document

1. Click the Tools menu, then click AutoSummarize.
2. Choose the type of summary option you want.
3. Click the Percent Of Original drop-down arrow, and click the best length for your summary.
4. Click OK.
5. Read your summary carefully and edit it as necessary.

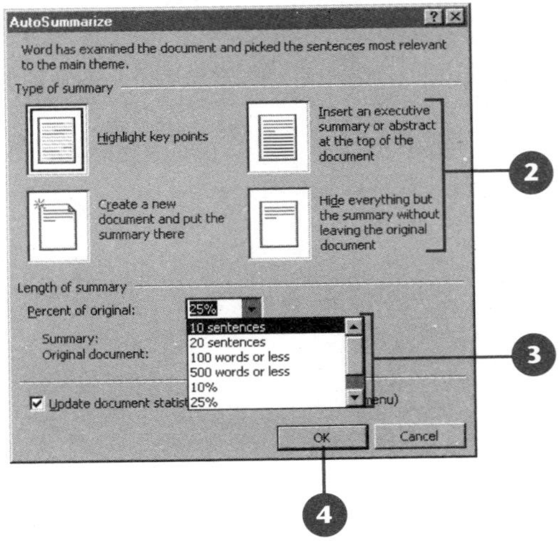

Adding Desktop Publishing Effects

A few simple desktop publishing elements, such as drop caps and borders, can help you create newsletters and brochures that look like they've been professionally produced. These special elements look especially good when combined with pictures and text arranged in column format.

TIP

Add a border quickly to text. *Select the text you want to put a border around, and then click the Tables And Borders button on the Standard toolbar. Use the Tables and Borders toolbar to apply the options you want.*

Add a Drop Cap to Text

1. Switch to page layout view.
2. Click in the paragraph where you want to create a drop cap.
3. Click the Format menu, and then click Drop Cap.
4. Click the Dropped icon to flow text around the drop cap or the In Margin icon to move the drop cap to the left margin.
5. If you want, select a different font for the drop cap, change the height for the drop cap, or change the distance of the drop cap from the paragraph text.
6. Click OK.

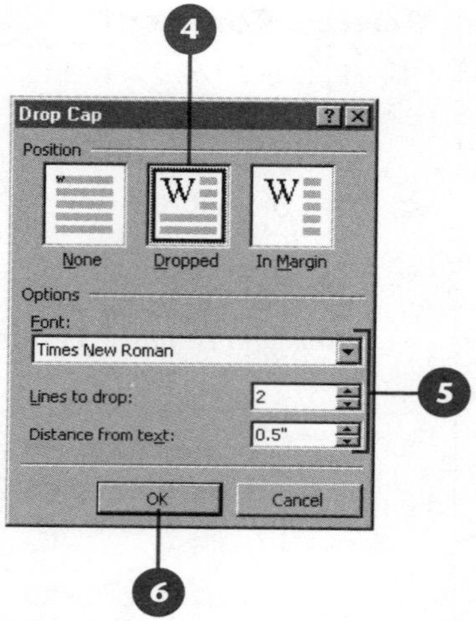

8

Creating a Worksheet with Excel 97

IN THIS SECTION

If you're spending too much time number-crunching, rewriting financial reports, drawing charts, and searching for your calculator, you're probably eager to start using Microsoft Excel 97. This book teaches you to use Excel's most popular features so you can become productive immediately.

Microsoft Excel is a *spreadsheet program,* which is designed to help you record, analyze, and present quantitative information. Excel makes it easy to track and analyze sales, organize finances, create budgets, and accomplish a variety of business tasks in a fraction of the time it would take using pen and paper.

The file you create and save in Excel is called a *workbook*. It contains a collection of worksheets, which look similar to an accountant's ledger sheets, but you can use Excel to perform calculations and other tasks automatically.

Using Excel, you can create a variety of documents that can be used for analysis and record keeping, such as:

- Monthly sales and expense reports
- Charts displaying annual sales data
- An inventory of products
- A payment schedule for an equipment purchase

Viewing the Excel Window

When you start Excel, the Excel program windows opens with a blank workbook—ready for you to use. The Excel window contains everything you need to work with your Excel workbook.

The *title bar* contains the name of the active workbook.

Any data contained in the active cell appears on the *formula bar.*

All Excel commands are organized in menus on the *menu bar.*

The address of the currently selected (or active) cell appears in the *Name box.*

The *active cell* is the currently selected cell (its address appears in the name box); you enter data in the active cell.

The *mouse pointer* takes this shape when Excel is ready to perform a new task. The mouse pointer is context-sensitive; its shape changes depending on the action you are performing.

The *status bar* shows information about selected commands or procedures.

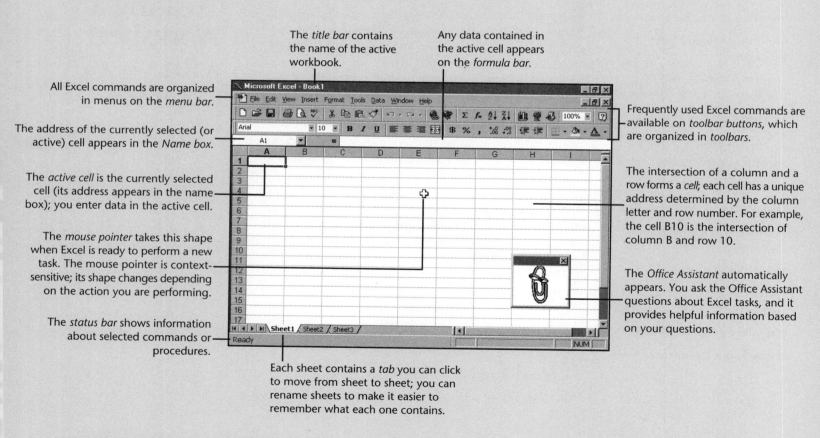

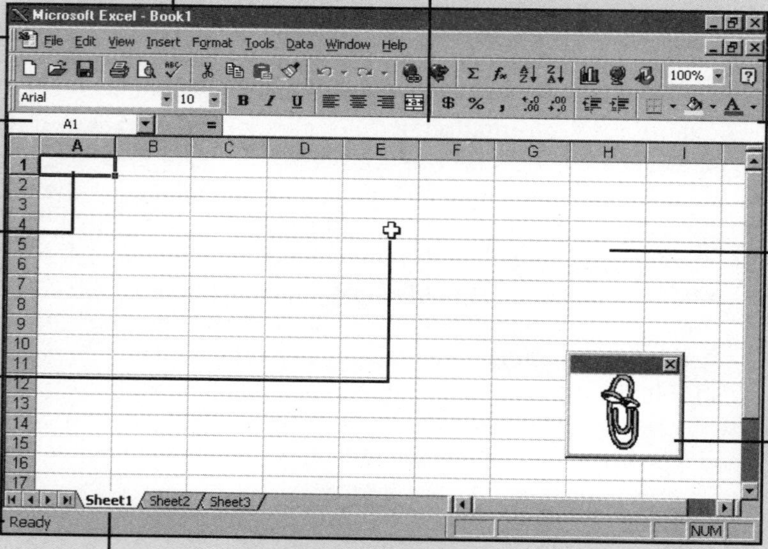

Frequently used Excel commands are available on *toolbar buttons*, which are organized in *toolbars*.

The intersection of a column and a row forms a *cell*; each cell has a unique address determined by the column letter and row number. For example, the cell B10 is the intersection of column B and row 10.

The *Office Assistant* automatically appears. You ask the Office Assistant questions about Excel tasks, and it provides helpful information based on your questions.

Each sheet contains a *tab* you can click to move from sheet to sheet; you can rename sheets to make it easier to remember what each one contains.

Moving Around the Workbook

You can move around a worksheet or workbook using your mouse or the keyboard. You might find that using your mouse to move from cell to cell is most convenient, while using various keyboard combinations is easier for covering large areas of a worksheet quickly. However, there is no one right way; whichever method feels the most comfortable is the one you should use. If you have the new Microsoft Mouse—with the wheel button in between the left and right buttons—you can click the wheel button and move the mouse in any direction to move quickly through the worksheet.

Use the Mouse to Navigate

Using the mouse, you can navigate to:

- Another cell
- Another part of a worksheet
- Another worksheet

To move from one cell to another, point to the cell you want to move to, and then click.

The wheel button looks like this when clicked. Drag the pointer in any direction to move to a new location quickly.

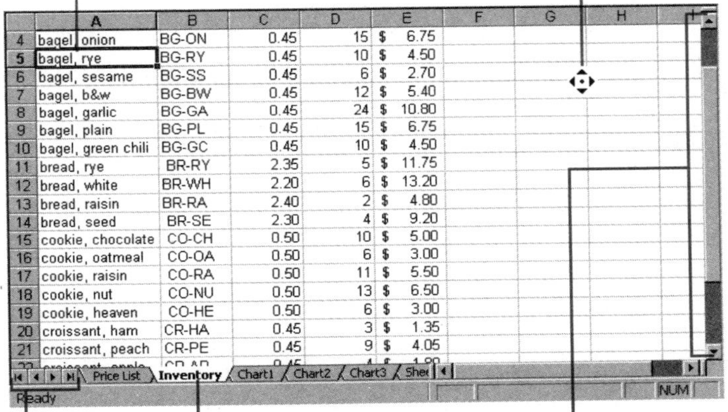

To see more sheet tabs *without* changing the active sheet, click a sheet scroll button.

To move from one worksheet to another, click the tab of the sheet you want to see.

To see other parts of the worksheet *without* changing the location of the active cell, click the horizontal and vertical scroll bars, or drag the scroll buttons.

Entering Labels and Numbers in a Worksheet

Labels turn a worksheet full of numbers into a meaningful report by clarifying the relationship between the numbers. You use labels to identify the data in the worksheet columns and rows. To help keep your labels consistent, Excel's PickList features automatically complete your entries based on labels you have entered previously. To enter a number as a label, for example, the year 1997, you type an apostrophe (') before the number. Then Excel does not use the number in its calculations. You can enter values as whole numbers, decimals, percentages, or dates. You can enter values using the numbers on the top row of your keyboard, or the numeric keypad on the right.

Enter a Text Label

1. Click the cell where you want to enter a label.
2. Type a label. A label can include uppercase and lowercase letters, spaces, punctuation, and numbers.
3. Click the Enter button on the formula bar, or press Enter.

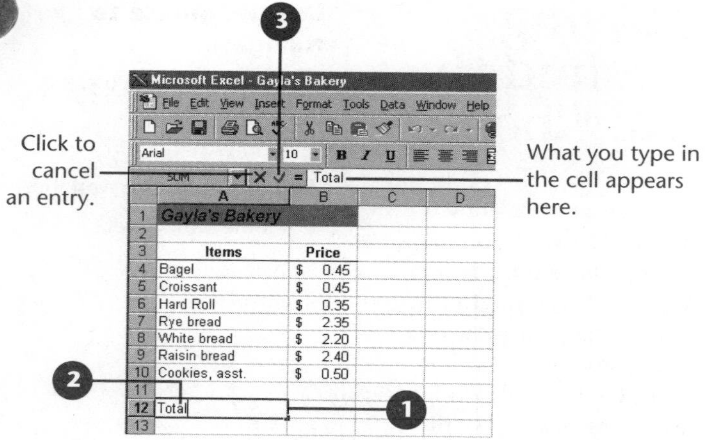

Enter a Number as a Label

1. Click the cell where you want to enter a number as a label.
2. Type ' (an apostrophe). The apostrophe is a *label prefix* and does not appear in the worksheet.
3. Type a number value. Examples of numbers that you might use as labels include a year, a social security number, or a telephone number.
4. Click the Enter button on the formula bar, or press Enter.

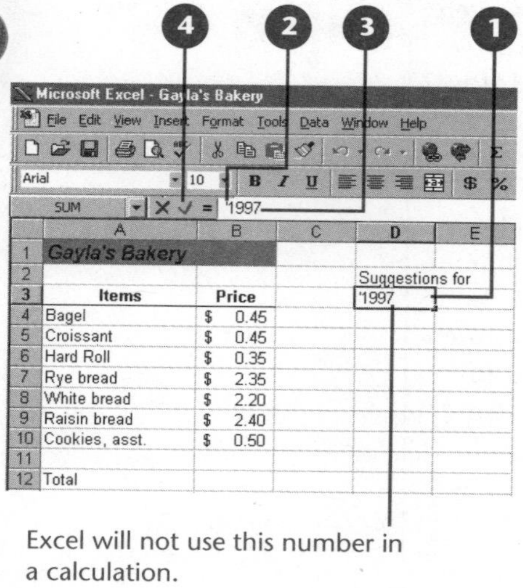

TIP

Use AutoComplete to help enter labels. *Type the first few characters of a label. If Excel recognizes the entry, AutoComplete completes it, and then you press Enter or click the Enter button on the formula bar. If Excel does not recognize the entry, AutoComplete is not activated, so you can continue typing the entry, and then press Enter or click the Enter button on the formula bar.*

TIP

Long labels might appear truncated. *When you enter a label that is wider than the cell it occupies, the excess text appears to spill into the next cell to the right—unless there is data in the adjacent cell. If the adjacent cell contains data, the label will appear truncated—you'll only see the portion of the label that fits in the cell's current width.*

Enter a Label Using the PickList

1. Right-click the cell where you want to enter a label, and then click Pick From List.
2. Click an entry from the drop-down list.

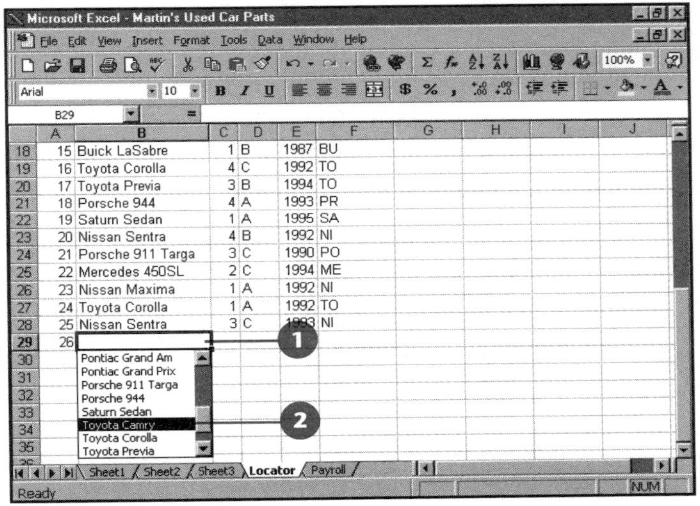

Enter a Value

1. Click the cell where you want to enter a value.
2. Type a value. To simplify your data entry, type the values without commas and dollar signs and apply a numeric format to them later.
3. Press Enter, or click the Enter button on the formula bar.

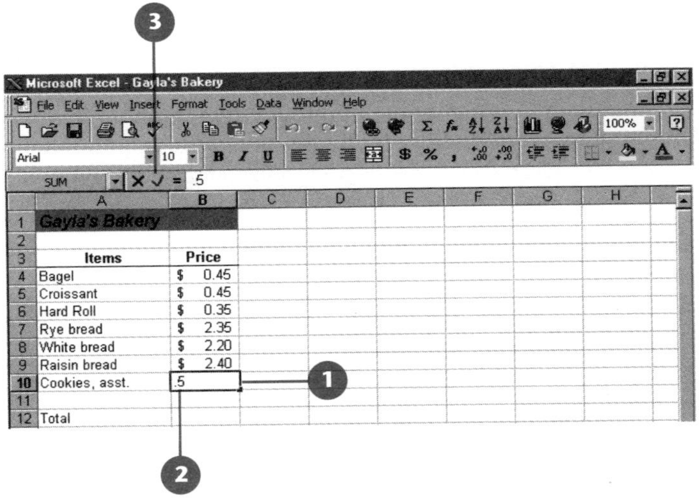

Editing Cell Contents

No matter how much you plan, you can count on having to make changes in a worksheet. Sometimes it's because you want to correct an error; other times you might want to incorporate new information, or see how your worksheet results would be affected by different conditions, such as higher sales, fewer units produced, or other variables. You edit data just as easily as you enter it, using the formula bar or directly editing the active cell.

Edit Cell Content Using the Formula Bar

1. Click the cell you want to edit.
2. Press F2 to change to the Edit mode. (The status bar now displays Edit instead of Ready in the lower left corner.)
3. If necessary, use the mouse pointer or the Home, End, and arrow keys to position the insertion point in the cell.
4. If necessary, use any combination of the Backspace and Delete keys to erase unwanted characters.
5. If necessary, type new characters.
6. Click the Enter button on the formula bar to accept the edit, or click the Cancel button to cancel it.

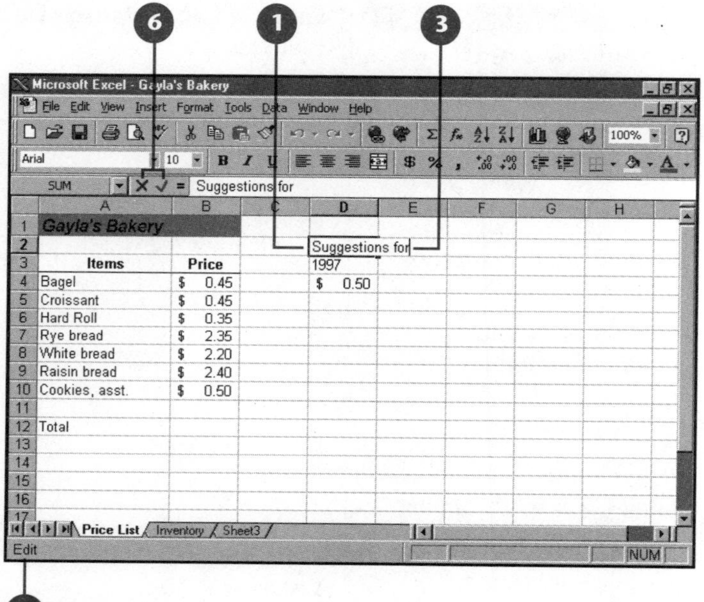

2 The mode indicator changes to Edit.

SEE ALSO

See "Working with Cells" on page 124 for information on inserting and deleting a cell.

Edit Cell Content In-Cell

1. Double-click the cell you want to edit. The insertion point appears within the cell.
2. If necessary, use the mouse pointer or the Home, End, and arrow keys to position the insertion point where you want it.
3. If necessary, use any combination of the Backspace and Delete keys to erase unwanted characters.
4. If necessary, type new characters.
5. Click the Enter button on the formula bar to accept the edit, or click the Cancel button to cancel it.

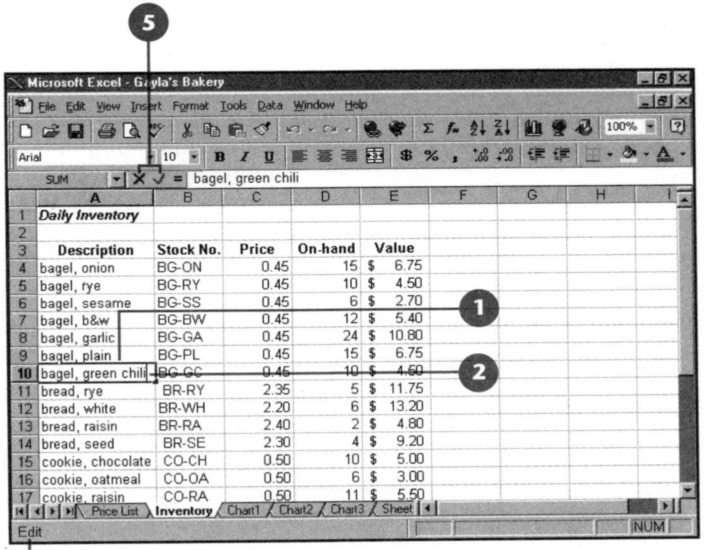

The mode indicator changes to Edit.

8

Selecting Multiple Cells

A *range* is one or more selected cells that you can edit, delete, format, print, or use as an argument in a formula just as you would a single cell. A range can consist of *contiguous* cells (where all the selected cells are adjacent to each other) or *noncontiguous* cells (where all the cells are not adjacent to each other). A range reference begins with the top leftmost cell in the range, followed by a colon (:), and ends with the cell address of the bottom rightmost cell in the range. To make working with ranges easier, Excel allows you to name them. The name "Sales," for example, is easier to remember than the coordinates B4:D10.

Select a Range

1. Click the first cell you want to include in the range.
2. Drag the mouse diagonally to the last cell you want to include the range. When a range is selected, the top leftmost cell is surrounded by the active cell border while the additional cells are highlighted in black.

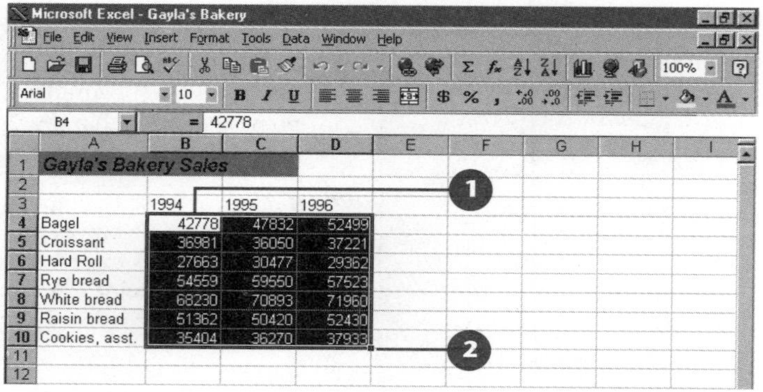

Select a Non-contiguous Range

1. Click the first cell you want to include in the range.
2. Drag the mouse diagonally to the last contiguous cell.
3. Press and hold the Ctrl key and drag the mouse over the next group of cells you want in the range.
4. Repeat steps 3 and 4 until all the cells are selected.

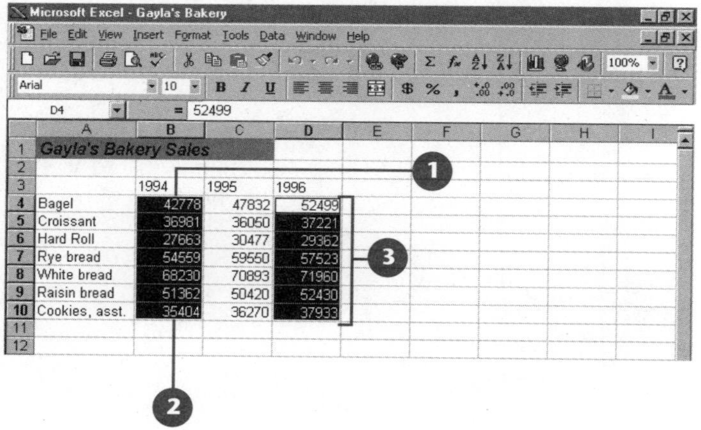

SEE ALSO

See "Using Ranges in Formulas" on page 128 for information on creating formulas using range names.

Name a Range

1. Select a range you want to name.
2. Click the Name box on the formula bar.
3. Type a name for the range. A range name can include uppercase or lowercase letters, numbers, and punctuation. Try to use a simple name that reflects the type of information in the range, such as "Sales94."
4. Press Enter. The range name will appear in the Name box whenever you select the range.

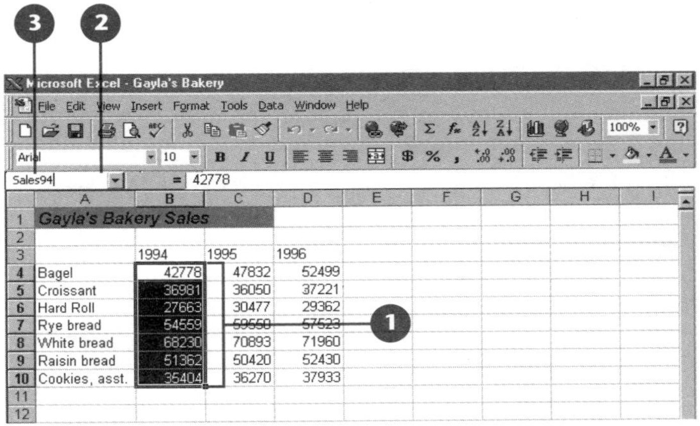

8

TRY THIS

Go to a named range in a worksheet. *Press the F5 key to see a list of named ranges. Click the name of the range you want to go to, and then click OK.*

Select a Named Range

1. Click the Name box drop-down arrow on the formula bar.
2. Click the name of the range you want to select. The range name appears in the Name box, and all cells included in the range are highlighted in the worksheet.

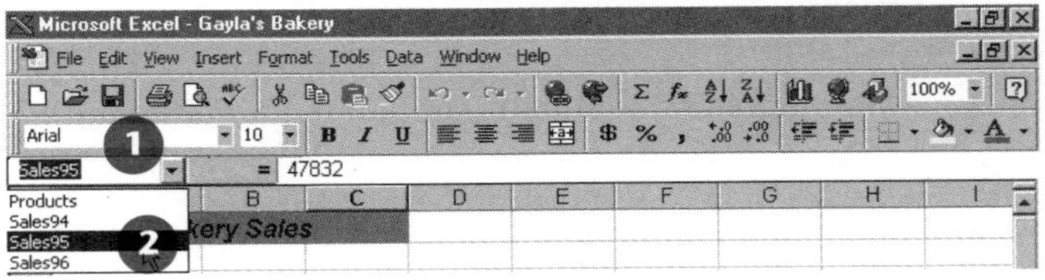

Working with Cells

You can insert new, blank cells anywhere in the worksheet, so you can enter new data or data you forgot to enter earlier, exactly where you want it. Inserting cells moves the remaining cells in the column or row in the direction of your choice and adjusts any formulas so they refer to the correct cells. You can also delete cells if you find you don't need them; deleting cells shifts the remaining cells to the left or up—just the opposite of inserting cells. When you delete a cell, Excel removes the actual cell from the worksheet.

SEE ALSO

See "Selecting Multiple Cells" on page 122 for information on selecting cells to edit a worksheet.

Insert a Cell

1. Select the cell or cells where you want to insert the new cell(s). For example, to insert two blank cells at the position of C10 and C11, select cells C10 and C11.
2. Click the Insert menu, and then click Cells.
3. Click the option you want. If you want the contents of cells C10 and C11 to move to cells D10 and D11, click the Shift Cells Right option button, or if you want the contents of cells C10 and C11 to move to cells C12 and C13, click the Shift Cells Down option button. Either way, two blank cells are now at the position of C10 and C11.
4. Click OK.

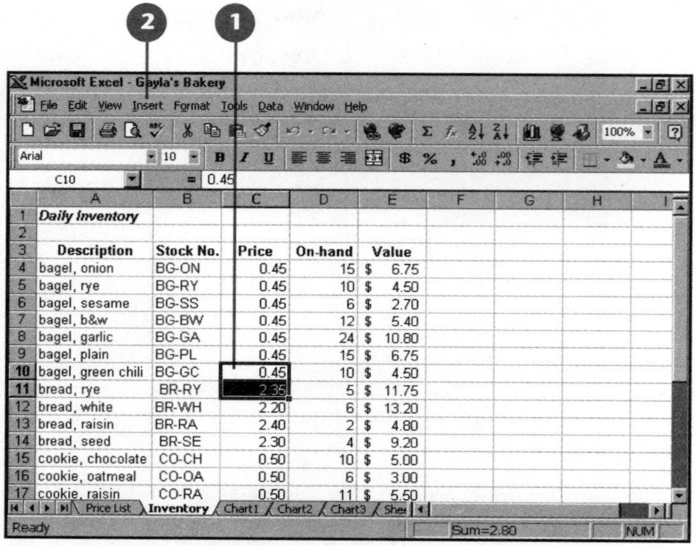

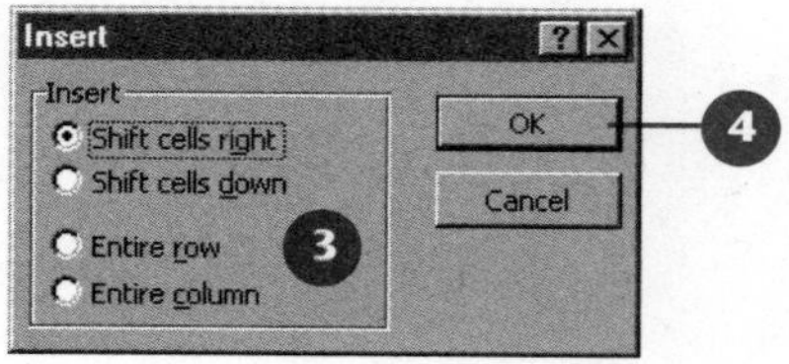

TIP

Deleting a cell vs. clearing a cell. *Deleting a cell is different from clearing a cell; deleting removes the cells from the worksheet, and clearing removes only the cell content or format or both.*

Delete a Cell

1. Select the cell or cells you want to delete.
2. Click the Edit menu, and then click Delete.
3. Click the option you want. If you want the remaining cells to move left, click the Shift Cells Left option button, or if you want the remaining cells to move up, click the Shift Cells Up option button.
4. Click OK.

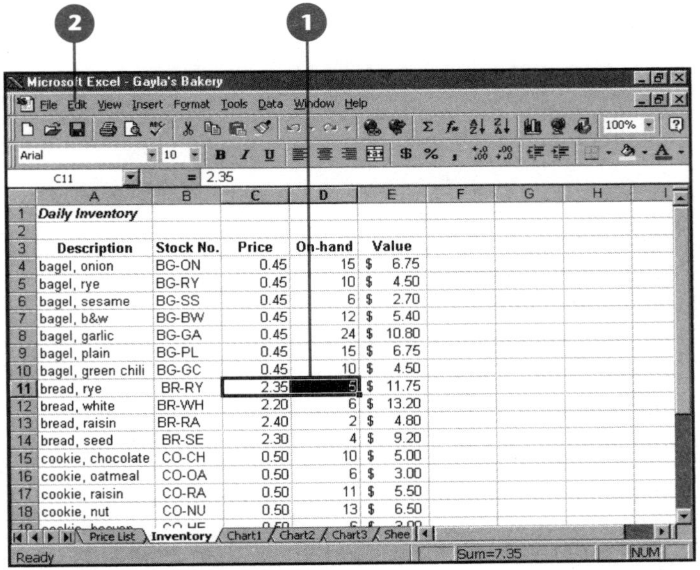

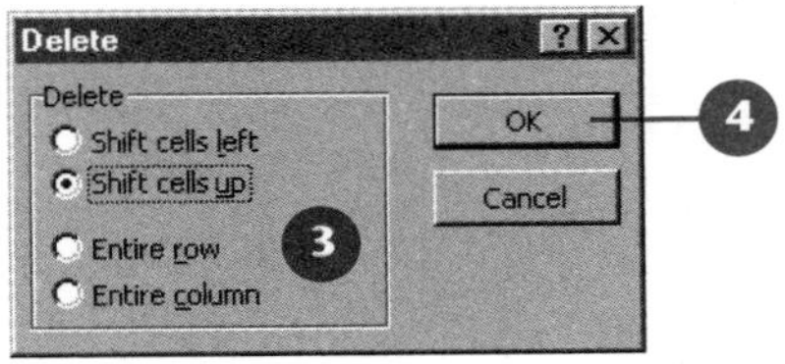

Creating a Formula

A *formula* calculates values to return a result. In an Excel worksheet, you use values (such as *147* or *$10.00)*, arithmetic operators (shown in the table), and cell references to create formulas. An Excel formula always begins with the equal sign (=). Although the formulas in the worksheet cells don't display, by default, you can change the view of the worksheet to display them.

TIP

Select a cell to enter its address to avoid careless typing mistakes. *Click a cell to insert its cell reference in a formula rather than typing its address.*

Enter a Formula

1. Click a cell where you want to enter a formula.
2. Type = (an equal sign) to begin the formula. If you do not begin a formula with an equal sign, Excel will display the information you type; it will not calculate it.
3. Enter the first argument. An *argument* can be a number or a cell reference. If it is a cell reference, you can type the reference or click the cell in the worksheet.
4. Enter an arithmetic operator.
5. Enter the next argument.
6. Repeat steps 4 and 5 to add to the formula.
7. Click the Enter button on the formula bar, or press Enter. Notice that the result of the formula appears in the cell and the formula appears in the formula bar.

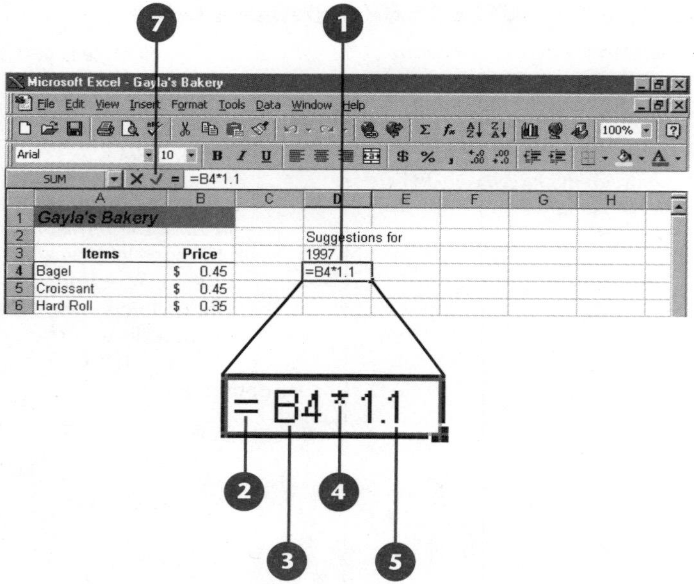

ARITHMETIC OPERATORS		
Symbol	**Operation**	**Example**
+	addition	=E3+F3
-	subtraction	=E3-F3
*	multiplication	=E3*F3
/	division	=E3/F3

TIP

Use the order of precedence to create correct formulas. *Formulas containing more than one arithmetic operator follow the order of precedence. Excel performs its calculations based on the following order: exponentiation, multiplication and division, and finally, addition and subtraction. For example, in the formula 5 + 2 * 3, Excel performs multiplication first (2*3) and addition after (5+6) for a result of 11. To change the order of precedence, use parentheses in a formula—Excel will calculate operations within parentheses first. Using parentheses, the result of (5 + 2) * 3 is 21.*

Display Formulas

1. Click the Tools menu, and then click Options.
2. Click the View tab.
3. Click to select the Formulas check box.
4. Click OK.

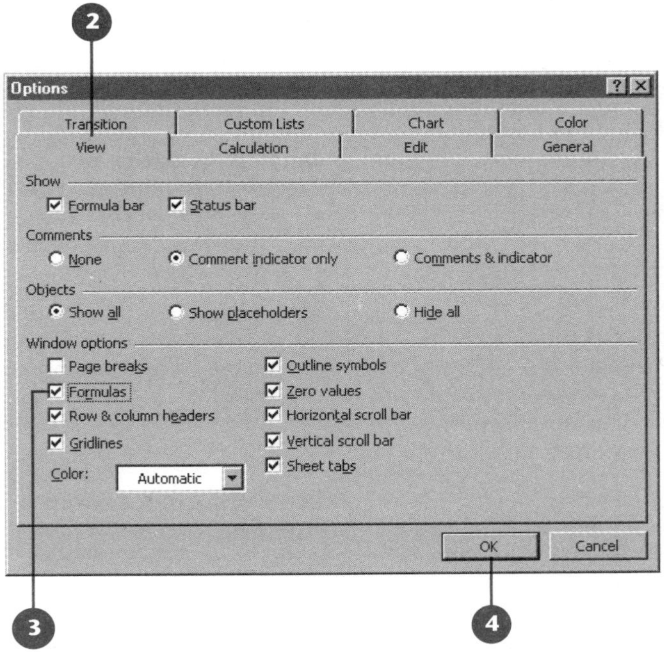

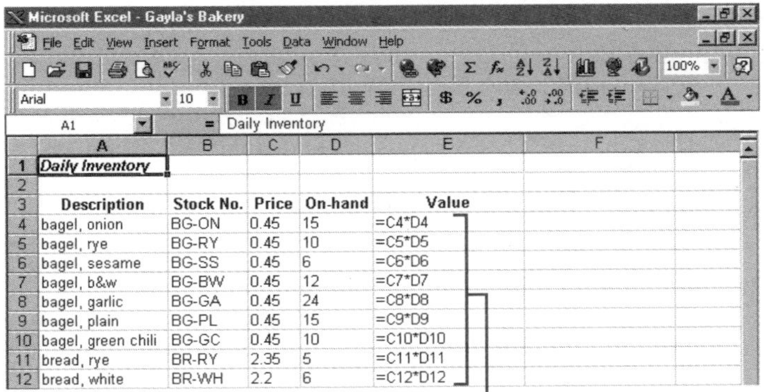

The formulas appear here

8

Using Ranges in Formulas

You can simplify formulas by using ranges and range names. For example, if 12 cells in your worksheet contain monthly budget amounts, and you want to multiply each amount by 10%, you can insert one range address in a formula instead of inserting 12 different cell addresses, or you can insert a range name. Using a range name in a formula helps to identify what the formula does; the formula =1997 SALES * .10, for example, is more meaningful than =D7:O7*.10.

> **TIP**
>
> **Use the Paste Function button to help you create a function.** *Click the Paste Function button on the Standard toolbar, click a function, and then enter or select a range.*

Use a Range in a Formula

1. Type an equal sign (=) to begin the formula.
2. Click the first cell of the range, and then drag to select the last cell in the range. Excel enters the range address for you.
3. Complete the formula, and then click the Enter button on the formula bar or press Enter.

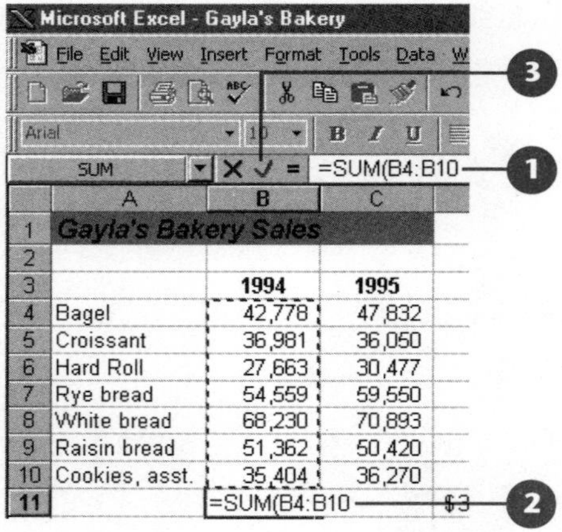

Use a Range Name in a Formula

1. Type an equal sign (=) to begin the formula.
2. Press F3 to display a list of named ranges.
3. Click the name of the range you want to insert.
4. Click OK in the Paste Name dialog box.
5. Complete the formula, and then click the Enter button on the formula bar or press Enter.

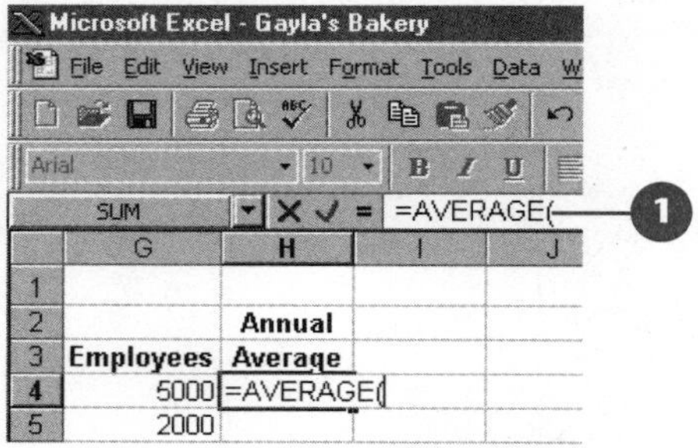

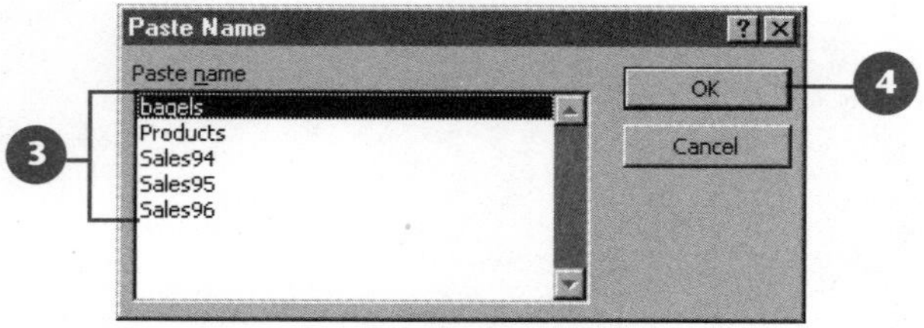

Performing Calculations Using Functions

Functions are predesigned formulas that save you the time and trouble of creating commonly used equations. Excel includes hundreds of functions that you can use alone or in combination with other formulas or functions. Functions perform a variety of tasks from adding, averaging, and counting to more complicated tasks, such as calculating the monthly payment amount of a loan. You can enter a function manually if you know its name and all the required arguments, or you can easily insert a function using the Paste Function.

Enter a Function

1. Click the cell where you want to enter the function.
2. Type = (an equal sign), type the name of the function, and then type (, an opening parenthesis. For example, to insert the SUM function, type =SUM(.
3. Type the argument or click the cell or range you want to insert in the function.
4. Click the Enter button on the formula bar or press Enter. Excel will automatically add the closing parenthesis to complete the function.

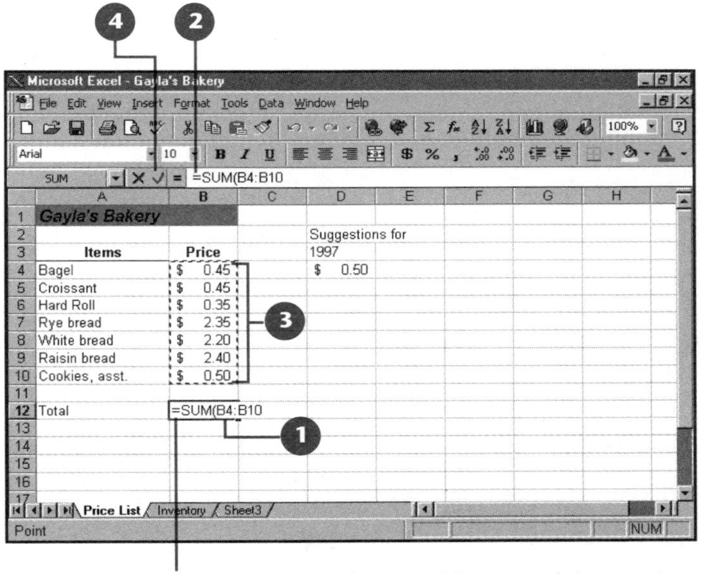

A function always begins with an equal sign.

COMMONLY USED EXCEL FUNCTIONS		
Function	**Description**	**Sample**
SUM	Displays the sum of the argument	=SUM(*argument*)
AVERAGE	Displays the average value in the argument	=AVERAGE(*argument*)
COUNT	Calculates the number of values in the argument	=COUNT(*argument*)
MAX	Determines the largest value in the argument	=MAX(*argument*)
MIN	Determines the smallest value in the argument	=MIN(*argument*)
PMT	Determines the monthly payment in a loan	=PMT(*argument*)

Worksheet Basics

Each new workbook you open has three workbook sheets. You can switch from sheet to sheet by clicking the sheet tab. Clicking the sheet tab makes that sheet *active*. Each of the sheets is named consecutively—Sheet1, Sheet2, and Sheet3. You can give a sheet a more meaningful name, and the size of the sheet tab automatically accommodates the name's length. You can add or delete sheets in a workbook. If you were working on a project that involved more than three worksheets, you could add sheets to a workbook rather than use multiple workbooks. That way, all your related information would be in one file. Deleting unused sheets saves disk space.

Select a Sheet

1. Click the sheet tab to make it the active worksheet.

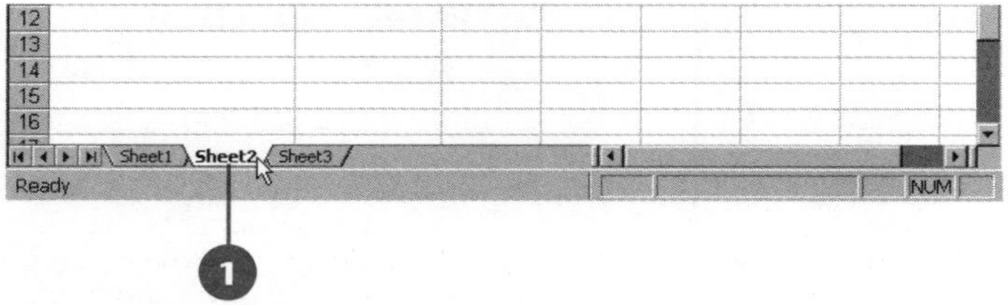

Name a Sheet

1. Double-click the sheet tab you want to name.
2. Type a new name. The current name, which is selected, is automatically replaced when you begin typing.
3. Press Enter.

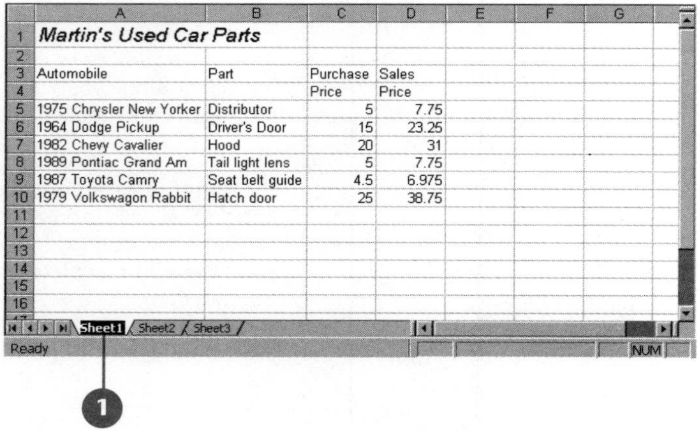

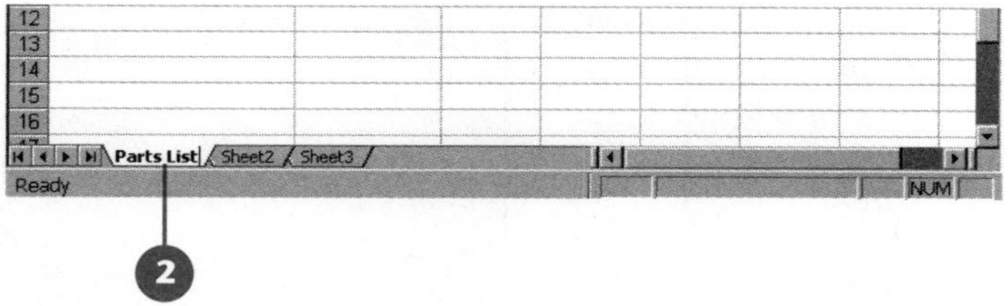

TIP

Use short sheet tab names to save screen space. *Because the size of a sheet tab enlarges to accommodate a longer name, using short names means more sheet tabs will be visible. This is especially important if a workbook contains several worksheets.*

Insert a Worksheet

1. Click the sheet tab (or select any cell in a worksheet) to the right, or *in front of,* where you want to insert the new sheet.
2. Click the Insert menu, and then click Worksheet. A new worksheet will be inserted to the left of, or *behind,* the selected worksheet.

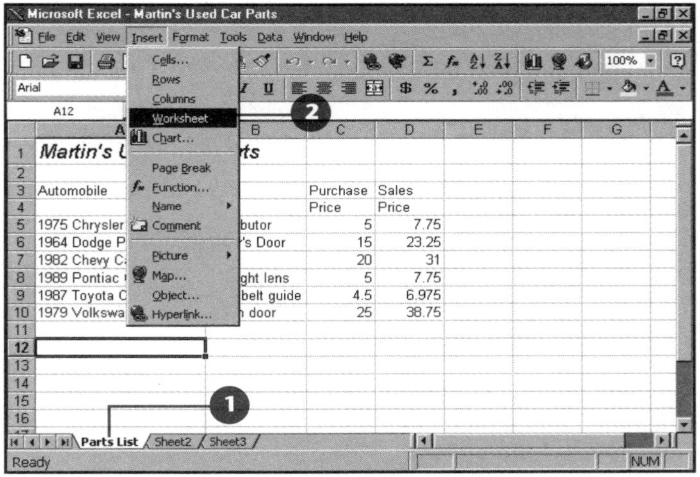

SEE ALSO

See "Moving and Copying a Worksheet" on page 132 for information on reorganizing sheets in a worksheet.

Delete a Worksheet

1. Select any cell in the worksheet you want to delete.
2. Click the Edit menu, and then click Delete Sheet.
3. Click OK to confirm the deletion.

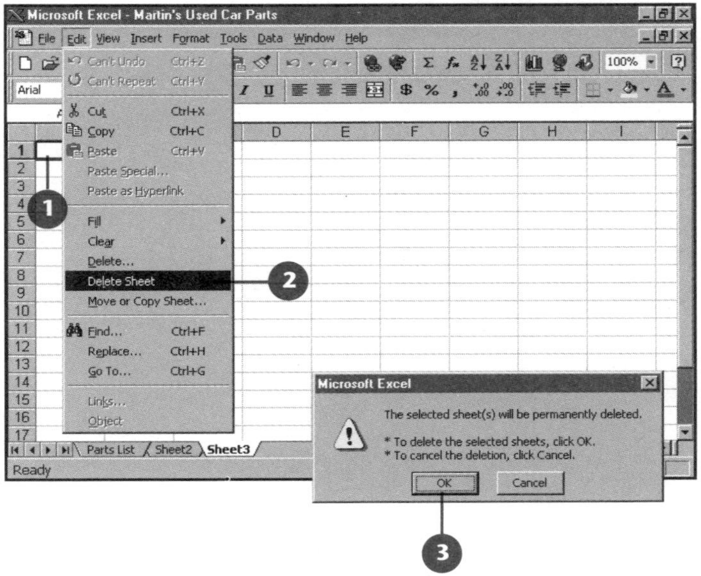

Moving and Copying a Worksheet

After adding several sheets to a workbook, you might want to reorganize them. You can easily move a sheet within a workbook or to another workbook by dragging it to a new location. You can also copy a worksheet within a workbook or to another workbook. Copying a worksheet is easier and often more convenient than having to reenter similar information in a new sheet. The ability to move and copy whole worksheets means you can have your workbooks set up exactly the way you want them, without having to do a lot of needless typing.

Move a Sheet

1. Click the sheet tab of the worksheet you want to move, and then press and hold the mouse button. The mouse pointer changes to a small sheet.
2. Drag the pointer to the right or in front of the sheet tab where you want to move the worksheet.
3. Release the mouse button.

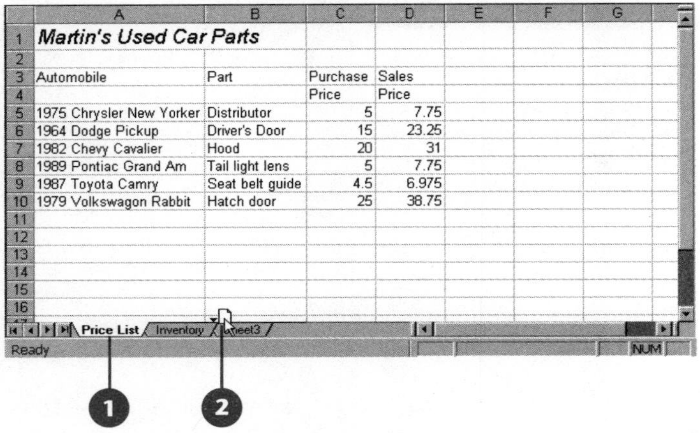

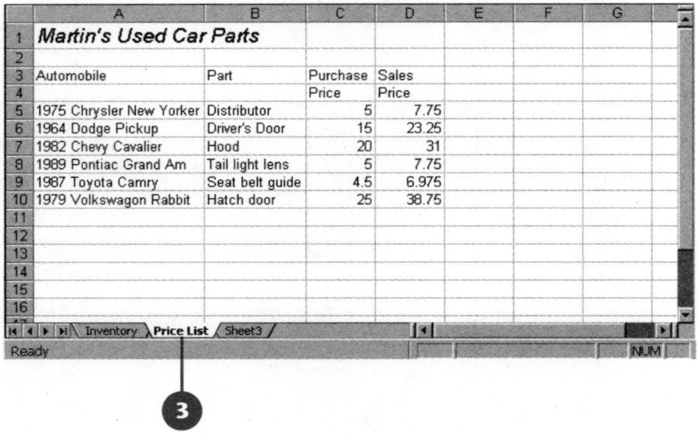

TIP

Use the Create A Copy check box to move a worksheet. *Deselect the Create A Copy checkbox in the Move or Copy dialog box to move a worksheet.*

Copy a Sheet

1. Click the sheet tab of the worksheet you want to copy.
2. Click the Edit menu, and then click Move Or Copy Sheet.
3. If you want to copy the sheet to another workbook, click the To Book drop-down arrow, and select that workbook. The sheets of the selected workbook appear in the Before Sheet box.
4. Click a sheet name in the Before Sheet list. The copy will be inserted before this sheet.
5. Click the Create A Copy check box.
6. Click OK.

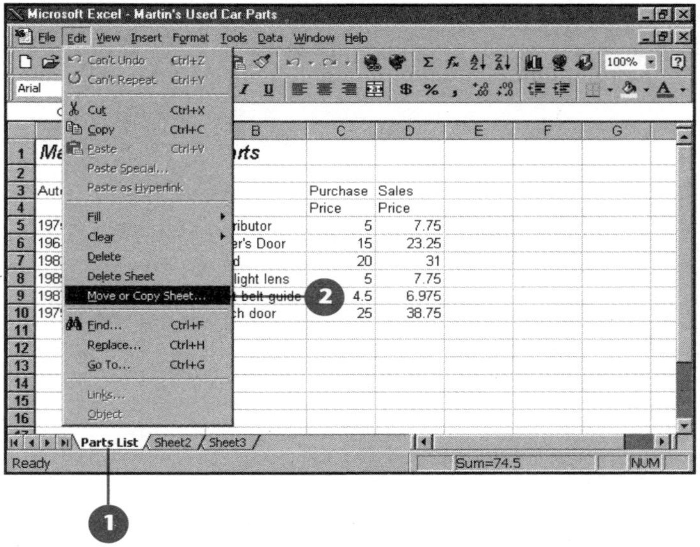

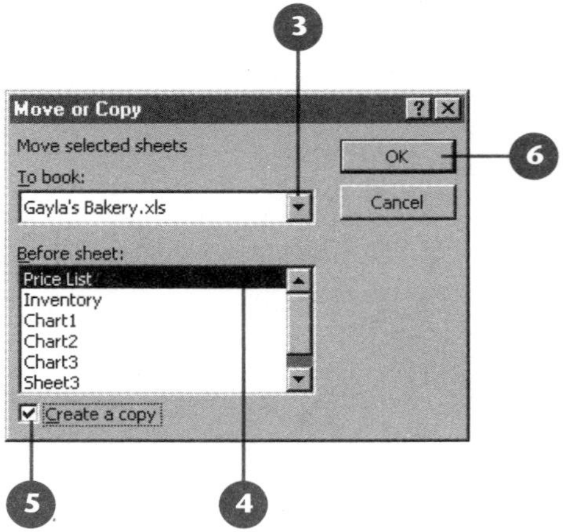

8

Printing a Worksheet

At some point you'll want to print out your work so you can distribute it to others or use it for other purposes. You can print all or part of any worksheet and control the appearance of many features, such as the gridlines that display on the screen, whether the column letters and row numbers display, or whether some columns and rows are repeated on each page.

Specify Print Options Using the Print Dialog Box

1. Click the File menu, and then click Print.
2. If necessary click the Printer drop-down arrow, and then click the printer you want to use.
3. In the Print Range area, click the All or Pages option button.
4. In the Print What area, click the option you want.
5. Click OK.

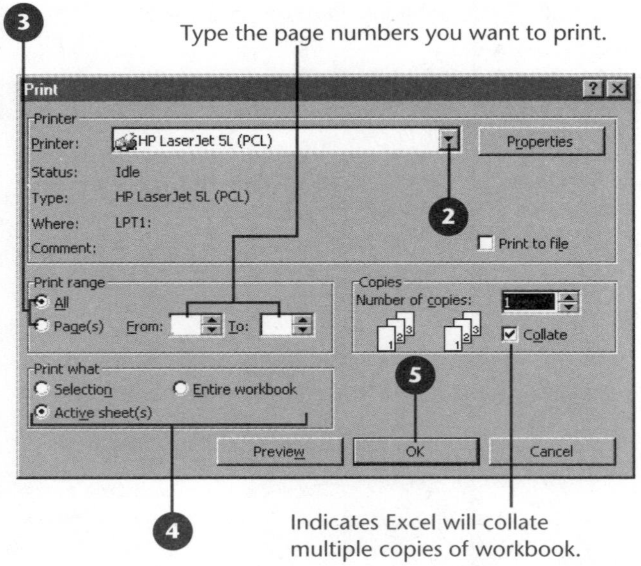

TIP

Print a worksheet quickly. *Click the Print button on the Standard toolbar to print the active worksheet with the current print settings.*

Print Part of a Worksheet

1. Click the File menu, and click Page Setup.
2. Click the Sheet tab.
3. Click in the Print Area text box, and then type the range you want to print, or click the Collapse dialog button, drag the mouse over the cells you want to print, and then click the Collapse dialog button again.
4. Click OK.

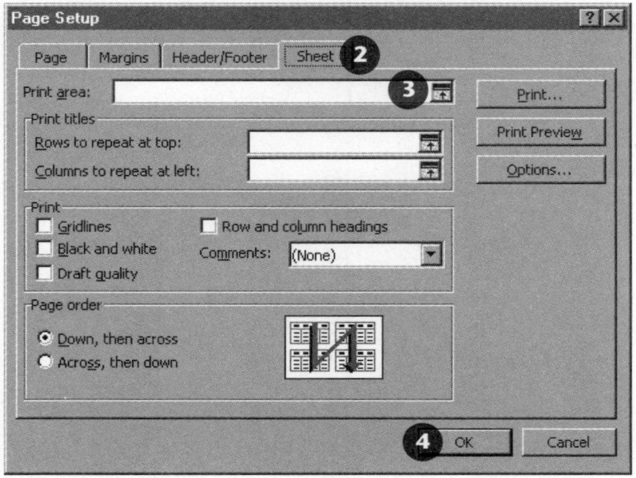

> **TIP**
>
> **The print area should not include any columns or rows you want printed on every page.** *Including this data in the print area will cause that data to print twice on the first page. Instead, use the Print Titles option.*

Print Row and Column Titles on Each Page

1. Click the File menu, and click Page Setup.
2. Click the Sheet tab.
3. In the Print Titles area, enter the number of the row or letter of the column letter that contains the titles, or click the appropriate Collapse Dialog button, select the row or column with the mouse, then click the Collapse Dialog button again to restore the dialog box.
4. Click OK.

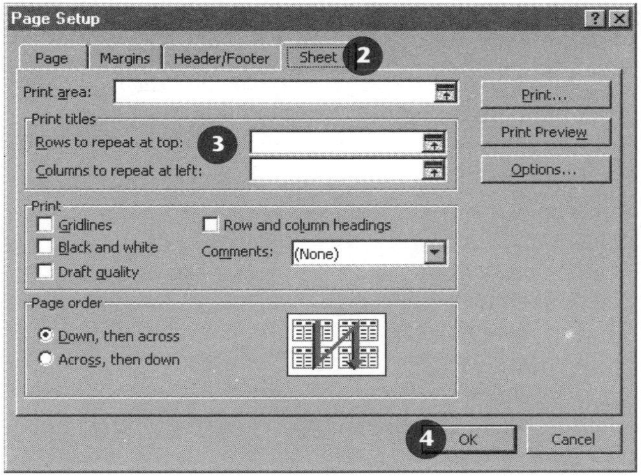

8

> **TIP**
>
> **You can reduce or enlarge the size of the printed characters.** *On the Page tab click the Adjust To up or down arrow to set the percentage size of the printed characters. Click the Fit To up or down arrow to set the specified number of pages you want to fit the printed characters.*

Print Gridlines, Column Letters, and Row Numbers

1. Click the File menu, and click Page Setup.
2. Click the Sheet tab.
3. Click to select the Gridlines check box.
4. Click to select the Row and Column Headings check box.
5. Click OK.

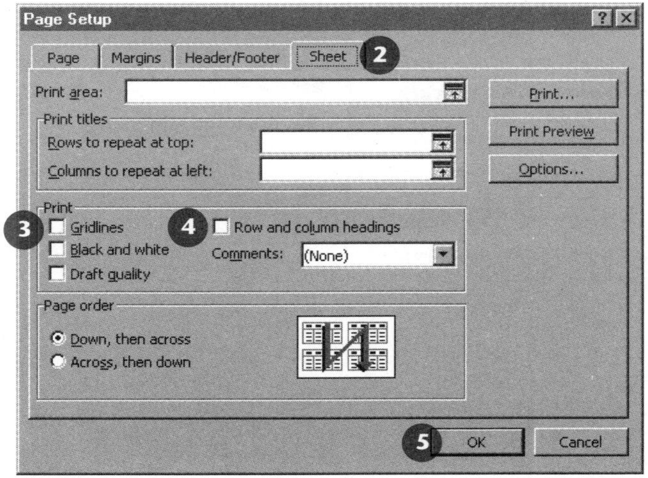

Inserting a Column or Row

You can insert blank columns and rows in a worksheet between columns or rows that are already filled without deleting and retyping anything. When you insert one or more columns, they are inserted to the left of the selected column. When you add one or more rows, they are inserted above the selected row. Excel repositions existing cells to accommodate the new columns and rows and adjusts any existing formulas so that they refer to the correct cells.

> **TIP**
>
> **The Insert menu changes depending on what you select.** *Clicking a column indicator button selects an entire column; then only the Columns command is available on the Insert menu. Clicking a row selector button selects an entire row; then only the Rows command is available on the Insert menu.*

Insert a Column

1. Click anywhere in the column to the right of the location of the new column you want to insert.
2. Click the Insert menu, and then click Columns.

   A column inserts to the left of the selected cell or column.

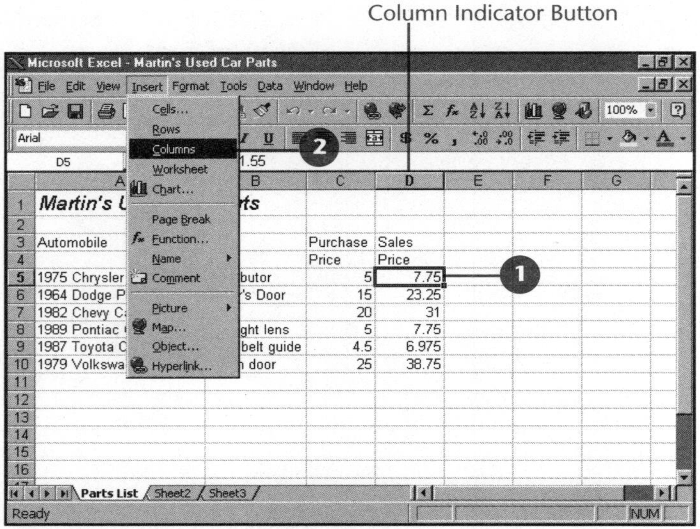

Insert a Row

1. Click anywhere in the row immediately below the location of the row you want to insert.
2. Click the Insert menu, and then click Rows.

   A row inserts above the selected cell or row.

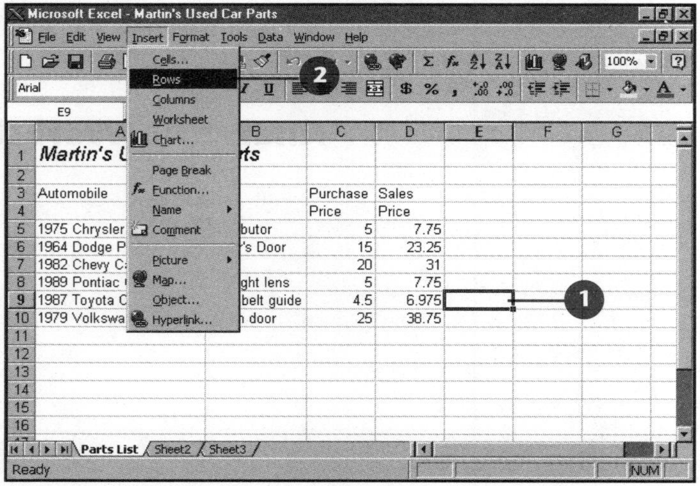

9

Designing a Worksheet with Excel 97

IN THIS SECTION

In addition to using a worksheet to calculate values, you can also use it to manage a list of information, sometimes called a *database*. You can use a Microsoft Excel 97 worksheet to keep an inventory list, a school grade book, or a customer database. Excel provides a variety of tools that make it easy to keep lists up to date and analyze them to get the information you want quickly. For example, you can use these tools to find out how many inventory items are out of stock, which students are earning an A average, or which product is the best selling item.

Analyzing Worksheet Data

Excel's data analysis tools include alphanumeric organizing (called *sorting*), displaying information that meets specific criteria (called *filtering*), and summarizing of data within a table (called a *PivotTable*).

You can analyze data directly in a worksheet, or use a feature called a *Data Form*, an on-screen data entry tool similar to a paper form. A Data Form lets you easily enter data by filling in blank text boxes, and then it adds the information to the bottom of the list. This tool makes entering information in a lengthy list a snap!

Designing Conditional Formatting

You can make your worksheets more powerful by setting up conditional formatting. *Conditional formatting* enables you to determine the formatting of cells based on their contents. For example, you might want this year's sales information to display in red and italics if it's lower than last years sales, but in green and bold if it's higher.

To establish conditional formatting, click the Format menu, and then click Conditional Formatting to open the Conditional Formatting dialog box.

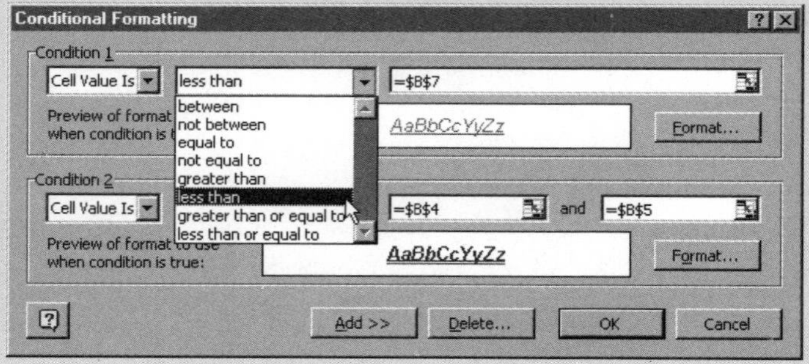

When the dialog box opens, you see option boxes for establishing one condition, a button for opening the Formatting dialog box, and a Preview box showing how the formatting will look if this condition is true. To establish a condition, you select whether to test a cell value or a formula, and the cell or formula against which to test it. If you choose to test a cell value, you also specify a comparison operator to use in the test. Use the Format button to change the formatting that will be applied. You can establish up to two additional conditions by clicking the Add button. When you add a condition, the dialog box expands to display more option boxes, a Format button, and another Preview box.

You can also delete conditions you no longer want by clicking the Delete button.

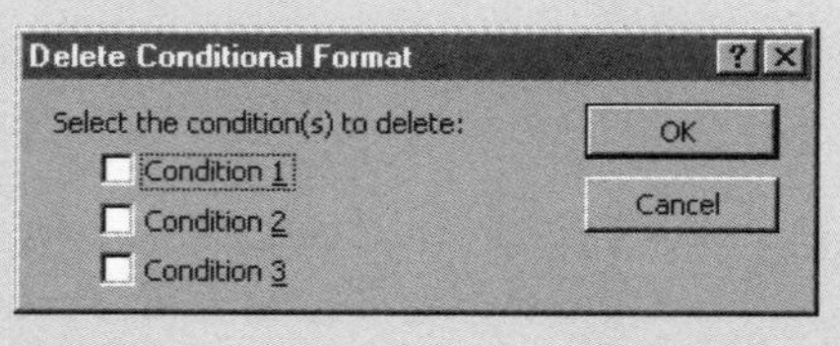

When the Delete Conditional Format dialog box opens, click to select the check box next to the conditions you want to delete.

Controlling Text Flow

The length of a label might not always fit within the width you've chosen for a column. If the cell to the right is empty, a label spills over into it, but if that cell contains data, the label will be truncated (that is, cut off). You can format the cell to automatically wrap text to multiple lines so you don't have to widen the column. For example, you might want a label that says "1997 Division 1 Sales" to fit in a column that is only as wide as "Sales." The contents of cells can also be modified to fit within the space available in a cell or to be combined with the contents of other cells.

Control the Flow of Text in a Cell

1. Select a cell or range that contains the text you want to wrap.
2. Right-click the mouse button, and then select Format Cells.
3. Click the Alignment tab, if necessary.
4. Click one or more Text Control check boxes.
   - Wrap Text wraps text to multiple lines within a cell.
   - Shrink To Fit reduces character size to fit text within a cell.
   - Merge Cells combines selected cells into a single cell.
5. Click OK.

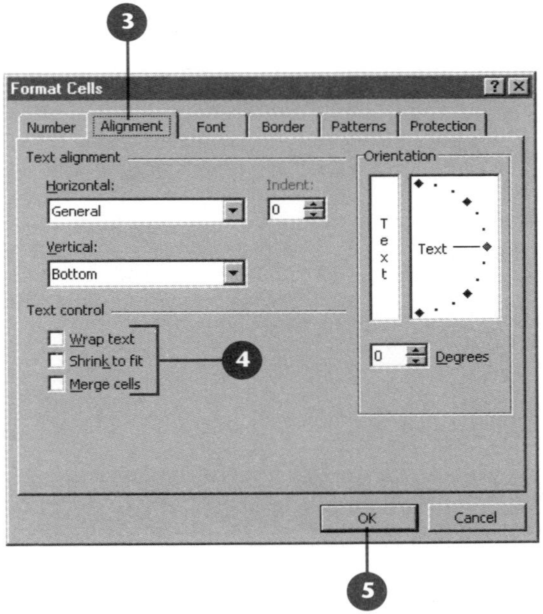

9

Creating a Chart

You have many choices to make when you create a chart, from choosing the chart type you want to use to choosing the objects you want to include and the formatting you want to apply. Excel simplifies the chart-making process with a feature called the Chart Wizard. The *Chart Wizard* is a series of dialog boxes that leads you through all the steps necessary to create an effective chart. You pick and choose from different chart types and styles and select any options you might want to apply while the Chart Wizard is open. Any options you don't add while the Chart Wizard is open can always be added later.

Chart Wizard button

Create a Chart Using the Chart Wizard

1. Select the data range you want to chart. Make sure you include the data you want to chart *and* the column and row labels in the range. The Chart Wizard expects to find this information and automatically incorporates it in your chart.
2. Click the Chart Wizard button on the Standard toolbar.
3. Select a chart type.
4. Select a chart sub-type.
5. Click the Press And Hold To View Sample button to preview your selection.
6. Click Next.
7. Make sure the correct data range is selected.
8. Select the appropriate option button to plot the data series in rows or in columns.
9. Click Next.

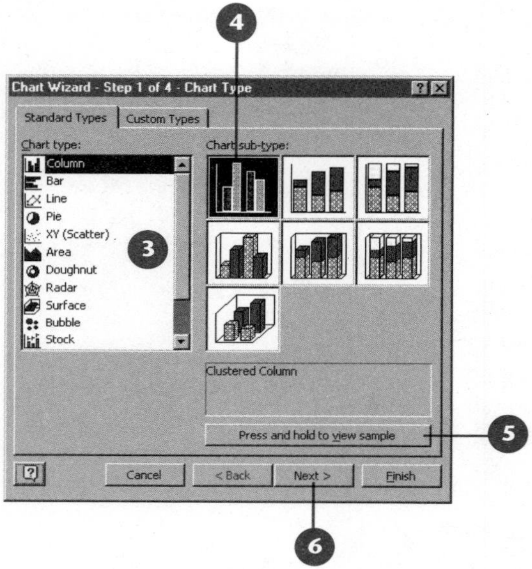

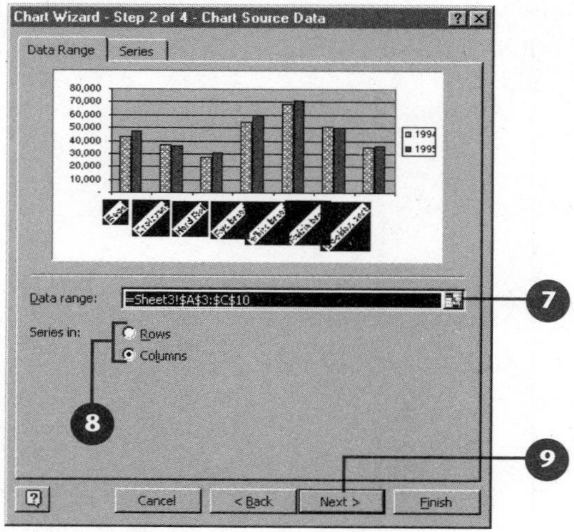

TIP

You can make changes while using the Chart Wizard. *Click the Back button to make changes before clicking the Finish button.*

Place Chart As Object

Place Chart As Sheet

SEE ALSO

See "Inserting a Graph Chart in a Slide" on page 182 for more information about charting.

SEE ALSO

See "Embedding and Linking Information" on page 314 for more information on embedding a chart.

10 To identify the data in the chart, type the titles in the appropriate text boxes.

11 Click Next.

12 Select the option you want to place the chart on a new sheet or on an existing sheet. If you choose to place the chart on an existing sheet rather than on a new sheet, the chart is called an *embedded object*.

13 Click Finish.

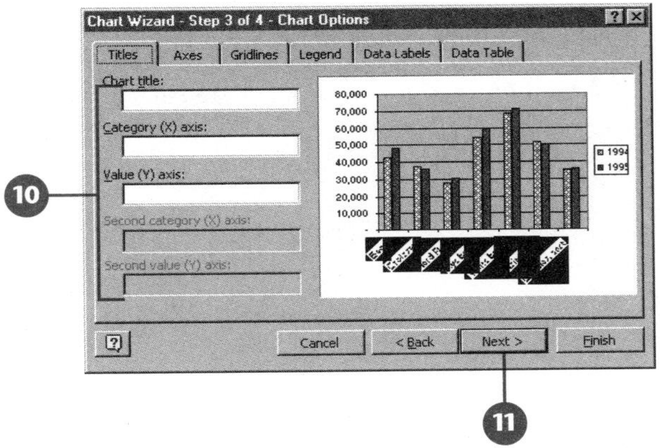

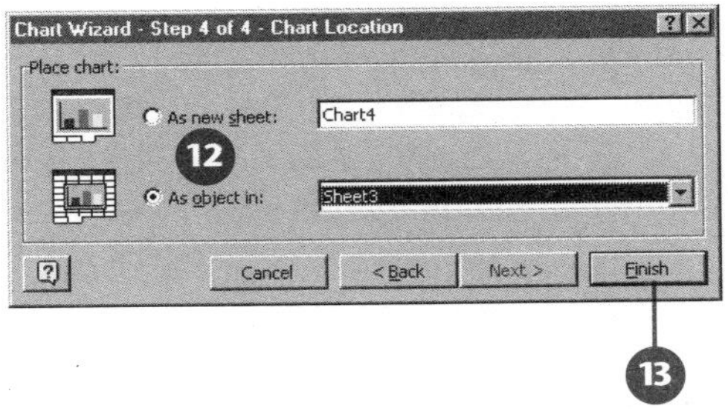

9

Adding and Deleting a Data Series

Each range of data that comprises a bar, column, or pie slice is called a *data series;* each value in a data series is called a *data point.* The data series is defined when you select a range and then open the Chart Wizard. But what happens if you want to add a data series once a chart is complete? Using Excel, you can add a data series by changing the data range information in the Chart Wizard, by using the Chart menu, or by dragging a new data series into an existing chart.

As you create and modify more charts, you might also find it necessary to delete one or more data series. You can easily delete a data series by selecting the series and pressing the Delete key.

Add a Data Series to a Chart Quickly

1. Select the range that contains the data series you want to add to your chart.
2. Drag the range into the existing chart.
3. Release the mouse button.

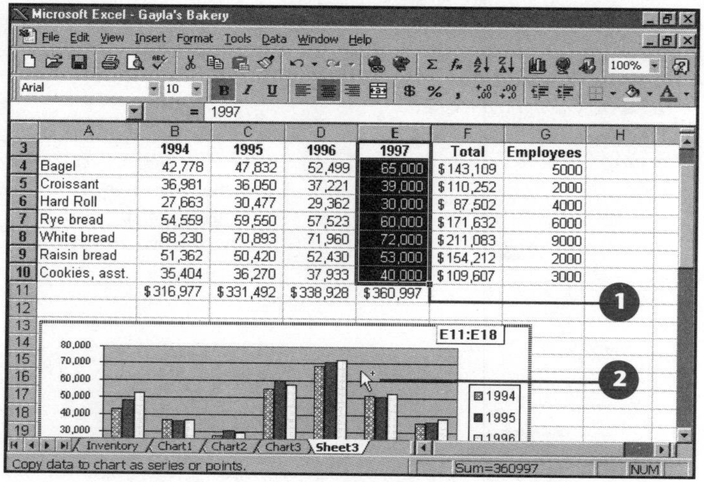

Add a Data Series Using the Add Data Dialog Box

1. Select the chart to which you want to add a data series.
2. Click the Chart menu, and then click Add Data.
3. Type the range in the Range box, or click the Collapse Dialog button, and then drag the pointer over the new range you want to add. When you release the mouse button, the Add Data dialog box reappears.
4. Click OK.

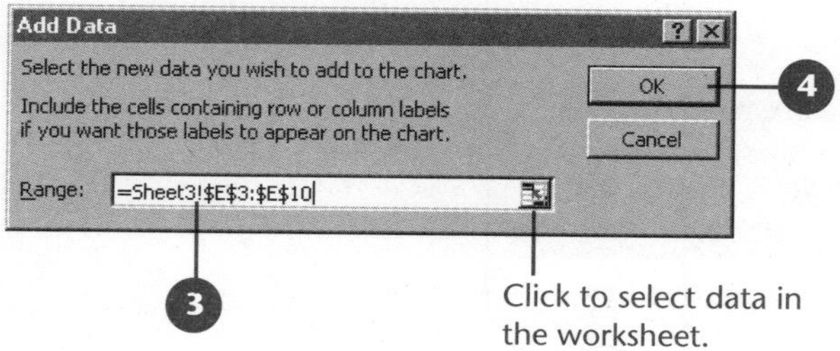

Click to select data in the worksheet.

TIP

You can choose to delete one data point in a chart. *To delete one data point but keep the rest of the series in the chart, click the data point twice so that it is the only point selected, and then press the Delete key.*

TIP

Use the Undo button to reverse a deletion. *Click the Undo button on the Standard toolbar to restore the deleted data series or data point to the chart.*

SEE ALSO

See "Enhancing a Chart" on page 144 for more information on how to customize your chart(s) to fit your needs.

Delete a Data Series

1. Select the chart that contains the data series you want to delete.
2. Click any data point in the data series.
3. Press Delete.

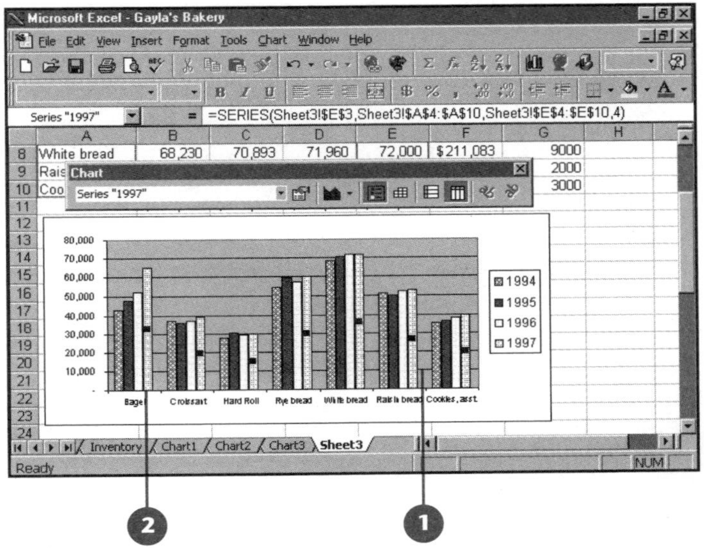

9

Enhancing a Chart

You can add *chart objects,* such as titles, legends, and text annotations, and *chart options* such as gridlines to a chart to enhance the appearance of the chart and increase its overall effectiveness. A *chart title* helps to identify the primary purpose of the chart and a title for each axis further clarifies the data that is plotted. Titles can be more than one line and formatted just like other worksheet text. You can also add a *text annotation,* additional text not attached to a specific axis or data point, to call attention to a trend or some other area of interest. A *legend* helps the reader connect the colors and patterns in a chart with the data they represent.

Gridlines are horizontal and vertical lines you can add to help the reader determine data point values in a chart that without the gridlines would be difficult to read.

Add a Title

1. Select a chart to which you want to add a title or titles.
2. Click the Chart menu, and then click Chart Options.
3. Click the Titles tab.
4. Type the text you want for the title of the chart.
5. To add a title for the x-axis, press Tab and type the text.
6. To add a title for the y-axis, press Tab and type the text.
7. If you want a second line for the x- or y-axis, press Tab to move to the Second Category or Value box, and then type the title text (if available).
8. Preview the title(s) you are adding.
9. Click OK.

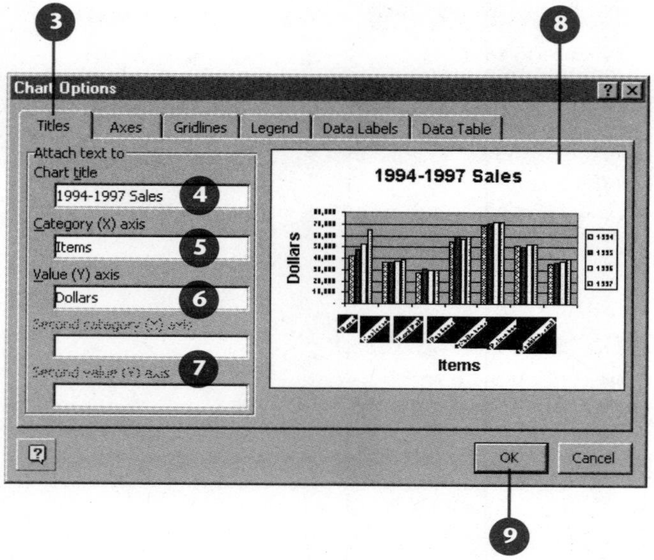

Add or Delete a Legend

1. Select the chart to which you want to add or delete a legend.
2. Click the Legend button on the Chart toolbar. You can drag the legend to move it to a new location.

TIP

Resize the text box to create a multiple line title. *Type the title text, and then resize the text box.*

Add a Text Annotation

1. Select a chart to which you want to add a text annotation.
2. Type the text for the annotation.
3. When you're finished, press Enter and the text annotation appears in a text box within the plot area. Then position the mouse pointer over the text box until the pointer changes shape.
4. Drag the selected text box to a new location.
5. Press Esc to deselect the text box.

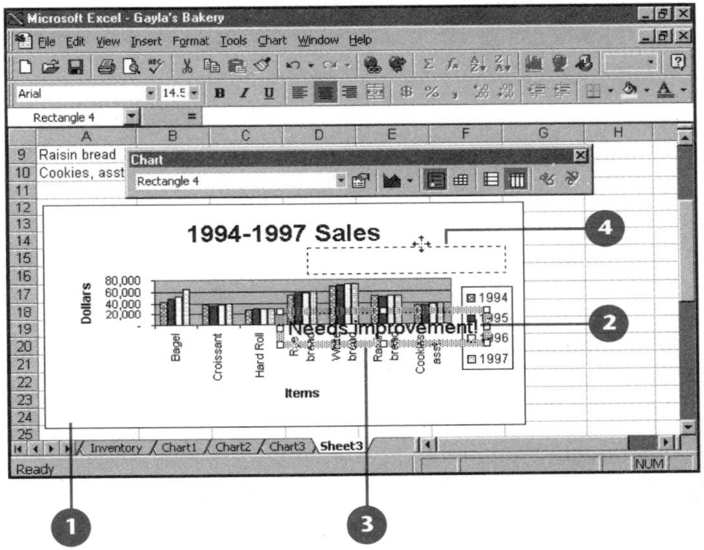

TIP

Major gridlines vs. minor gridlines. *Major gridlines occur at each value on an axis; minor gridlines occur between values on an axis. Use gridlines sparingly and only when they improve the readability of a chart.*

Add Gridlines

1. Select a chart to which you want to add gridlines.
2. Click the Chart menu, and then click Chart Options.
3. Click the Gridlines tab.
4. Select the type of gridlines you want for the x-axis (vertical) and y-axis (horizontal).
5. Click

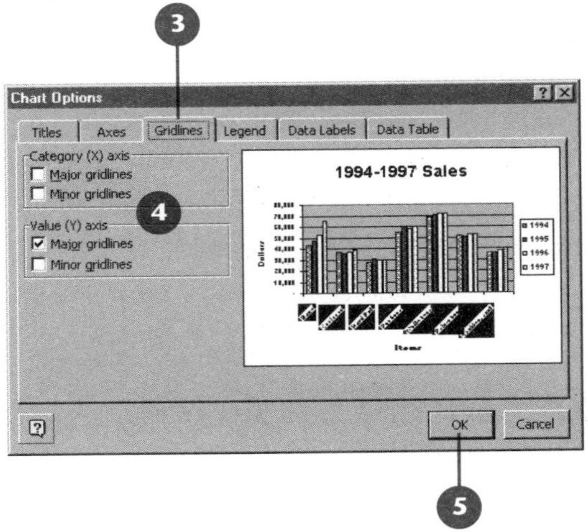

Creating a Map

Data for geographic locations can be charted using any existing chart type, but you can add real impact by using Excel's special mapping feature. This mapping feature analyzes and charts your data in an actual geographic map containing countries or states and helps readers understand the relationship of geographic data when viewed within a map. For example, seeing population data displayed within a map of the United States would probably have more meaning for you than to see the same information displayed in a column chart.

SEE ALSO

See "Modifying a Map" on page 147 for more information on about changing a map.

Map button

Create a Geographic Map

1. Select a range that contains the geographic data you want to map.
2. Click the Map button on the Standard toolbar.
3. Select the map you want to use.
4. Click OK.
5. Press Esc to deselect the map.

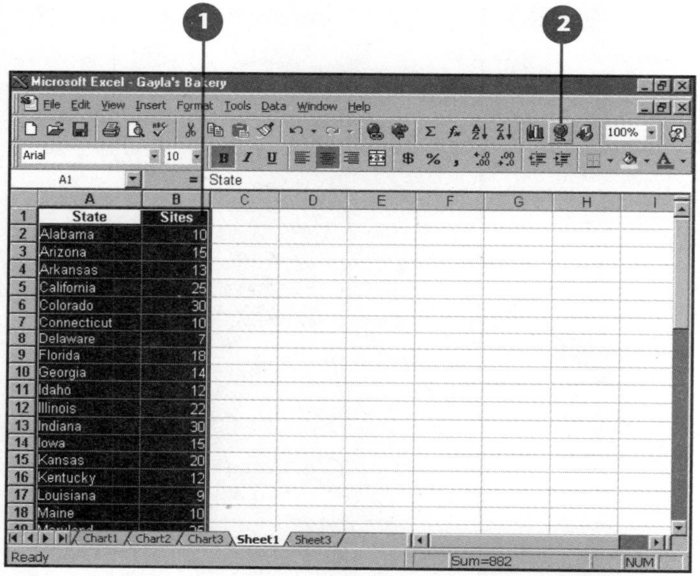

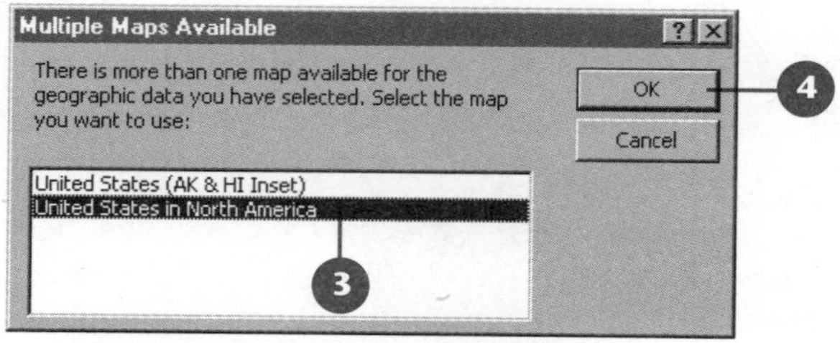

Modifying a Map

An existing geographic map can be modified to reflect updated data. You must update the geographic map when you change the data. In addition, the colors and patterns used to display the data within the map can also be changed.

TIP

Always refresh a map after changing worksheet data. *Unlike chart data, Excel does not automatically update map data whenever the worksheet data changes.*

Map Refresh button

Modify a Geographic Map

1. Make the necessary changes to the worksheet data that is used in your geographic map.
2. Double-click the map.
3. If necessary, click the Map Refresh button on the Microsoft Map toolbar.
4. Change data and the way it is displayed in the map using buttons in the Microsoft Map Control dialog box.
5. Press Esc to deselect the map.

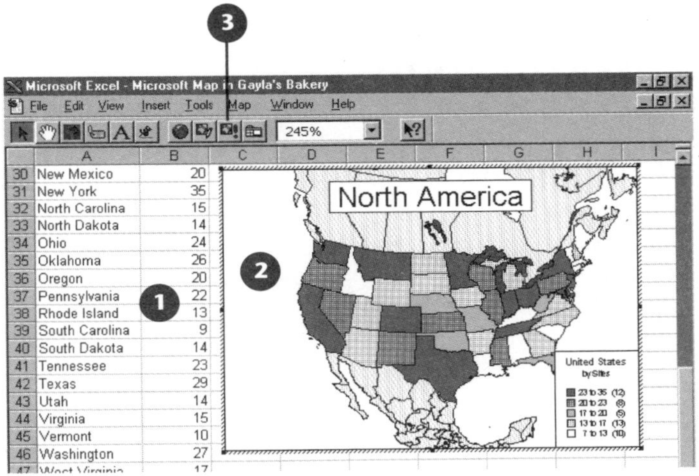

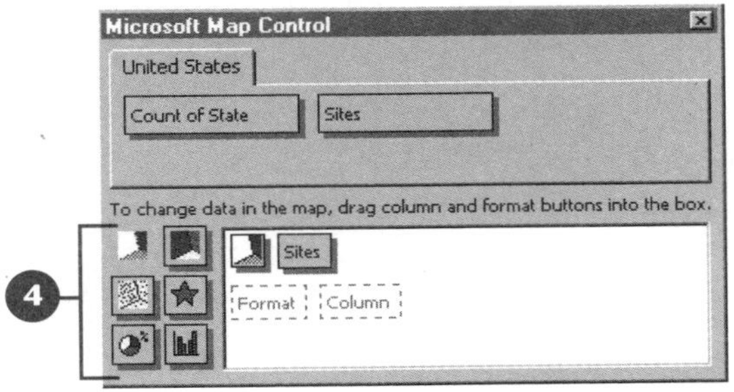

9

Understanding List Terminology

A database is a collection of related records. Examples of databases are an address book, a list of customers or products, or a telephone directory. In Excel, a database is referred to as *list.*

Record
One set of related fields, such as all the fields pertaining to one customer or one product. In a worksheet, each row represents a unique record.

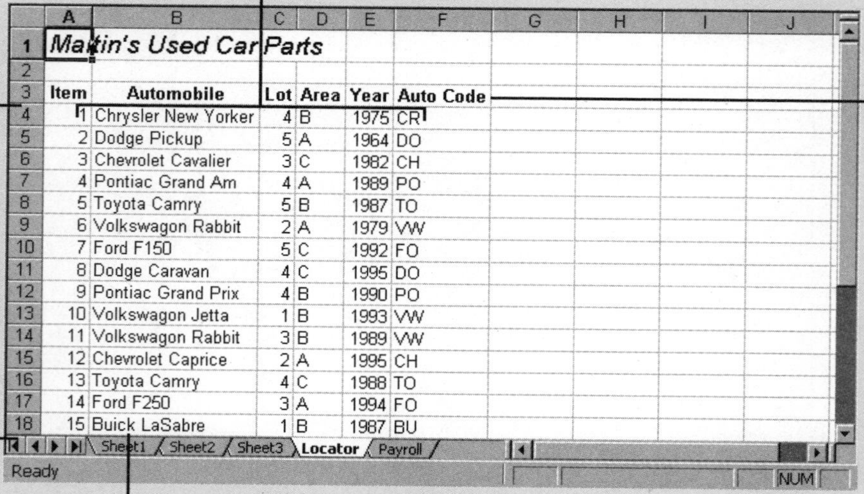

	A	B	C	D	E	F
1	Martin's Used Car Parts					
2						
3	Item	Automobile	Lot	Area	Year	Auto Code
4	1	Chrysler New Yorker	4	B	1975	CR
5	2	Dodge Pickup	5	A	1964	DO
6	3	Chevrolet Cavalier	3	C	1982	CH
7	4	Pontiac Grand Am	4	A	1989	PO
8	5	Toyota Camry	5	B	1987	TO
9	6	Volkswagon Rabbit	2	A	1979	VW
10	7	Ford F150	5	C	1992	FO
11	8	Dodge Caravan	4	C	1995	DO
12	9	Pontiac Grand Prix	4	B	1990	PO
13	10	Volkswagon Jetta	1	B	1993	VW
14	11	Volkswagon Rabbit	3	B	1989	VW
15	12	Chevrolet Caprice	2	A	1995	CH
16	13	Toyota Camry	4	C	1988	TO
17	14	Ford F250	3	A	1994	FO
18	15	Buick LaSabre	1	B	1987	BU

List range
The block of cells that contains the list or part of the list you want to analyze, but that can occupy no more than one worksheet.

Field name
The title given to a field. In an Excel list, the first row contains the names of each field. Each field name's maximum length is 255 characters, including upper and lowercase letters and spaces.

Field
One piece of information, such as customer's last name, or an item's code number. In a worksheet, each column represents a field.

Creating a List

To create a list in Excel, you can enter data in worksheet cells, just as you do any other worksheet data, but the placement of the field names and list range must follow these rules:

- Field names must occupy a single row and be the first row in the list.
- Enter each record in a single row, with each field in the column corresponding to the correct field name.
- Do not include any blank rows within the list range.
- Do not use more than one worksheet for a single list range.

Don't worry about entering records in any particular order; Excel offers several tools for organizing an existing list alphabetically, by date, or in almost any order you can imagine.

Create a List

1. Open a blank worksheet, or use a worksheet that has enough empty columns and rows for the list.
2. Enter a name for each field in adjacent columns across the first row of the list.
3. Enter the field information for each record in a separate row, starting with the row directly beneath the field names. Take advantage of features, such as AutoComplete, that make data entry easier.

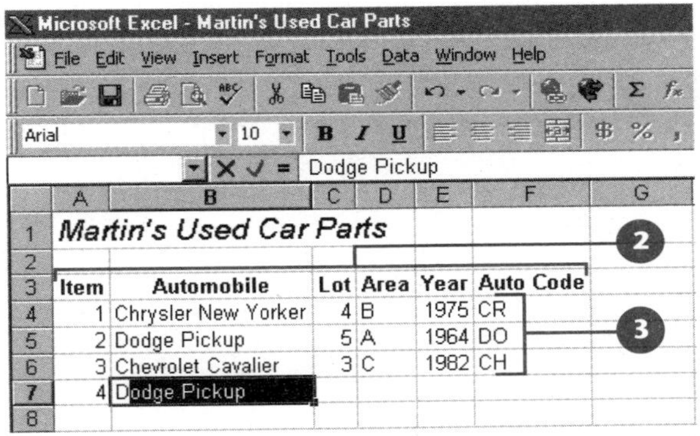

9

Sorting Data in a List

Once you enter records in a list, you can reorganize the information by *sorting* the records. Sometimes, you might want to sort records in a client list alphabetically by last name or numerically by date of their last invoice. You can sort a list alphabetically or numerically, in ascending or descending order using a field or fields you choose as the basis for the sort. You can sort a list on one field using the Standard toolbar or on multiple fields using the Data menu. A simple sort—such as organizing a telephone directory alphabetically by last name—can be made complex by adding more than one *sort field* (a field used to sort the list).

Sort Data Quickly

1. Click a field name you want to sort on.
2. Click the Sort Ascending or the Sort Descending button on the Standard toolbar.

In a list sorted in ascending order, records beginning with a number in the sort field are listed before records beginning with a letter (0-9, A-Z).

In a list sorted in descending order, records beginning with a letter in the sort field appear first (Z-A, 9-0).

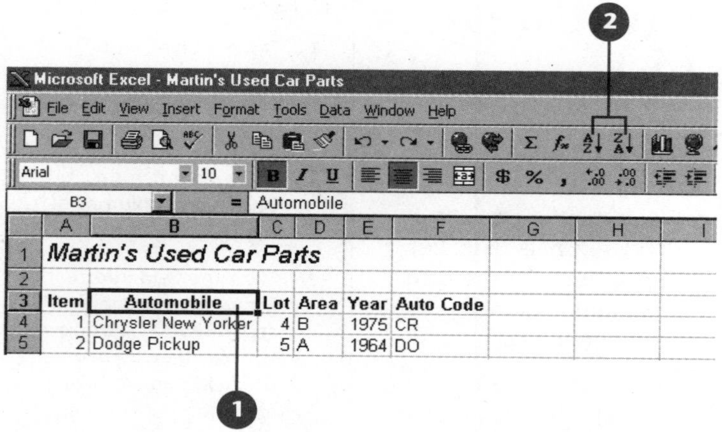

TIP

Protect your original list order with an index field. *Before sorting a list for the first time, try to include an index field, a field that contains ascending consecutive numbers (1, 2, 3, etc.). That way, you'll always be able to restore the original order of the list.*

TIP

You can sort data in rows. *If the data you want to sort is listed across a row instead of down a column, click the Options button in the Sort dialog box, and then click the Sort Left To Right option button in the Sort Options dialog box.*

Sort a List Using More than One Field

1. Click anywhere within the list range.
2. Click the Data menu, and then click Sort.
3. Click the Sort By drop-down arrow, and then click the field on which the sort will be based (the *primary sort field*).
4. Click the Ascending or Descending option button on the Standard toolbar.
5. Click the first Then By drop-down arrow, and then click the Ascending or Descending option button.
6. If necessary, click the second Then By drop-down arrow, and then click the Ascending or Descending option button.
7. Click the Header Row option button to *exclude* the field names (in the first row) from the sort, or click the No Header Row option button to *include* the field names (in the first row) in the sort.
8. Click OK.

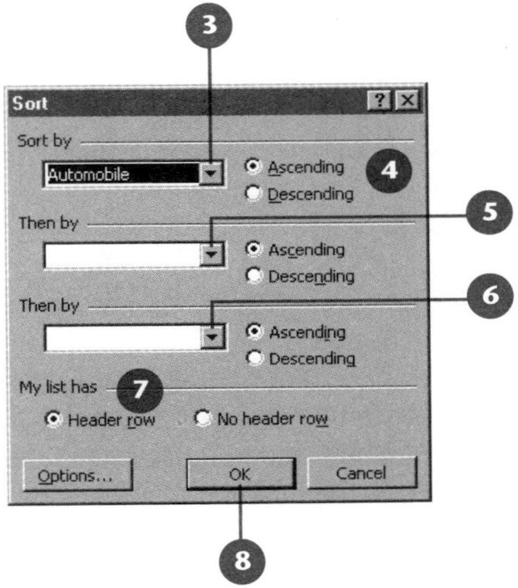

Analyzing Data Using a PivotTable

When you want to summarize information in a lengthy list using complex criteria, use the PivotTable to simplify your task. Without the PivotTable, you would have to manually count or create a formula to calculate which records met certain criteria, and then create a table to display that information for a report or presentation. Once you determine what fields and criteria you want to use to summarize the data, and how you want the resulting table to look, the PivotTable Wizard does the rest.

TIP

Use the Office Assistant to get help. *Click the Office Assistant button in the lower left corner of the dialog box for help using the PivotTable Wizard.*

Create a PivotTable

1. Click any cell within the list range.
2. Click the Data menu, and then click PivotTable Report.
3. If using the list range, make sure the Microsoft Excel List Or Database option button is selected.
4. Click Next.
5. If the range you want is "Database" (the active list range), then skip to step 8.
6. If the range does not include the correct data, click the Collapse Dialog button.
7. Drag the pointer over the list range, including the field names, to select a new range, and then click the Expand Dialog button.
8. Click Next.
9. Drag field name(s) to the ROW and COLUMN and DATA areas.
10. Click Next.
11. Specify the location of the worksheet you want to use in the text box, and then click Finish.

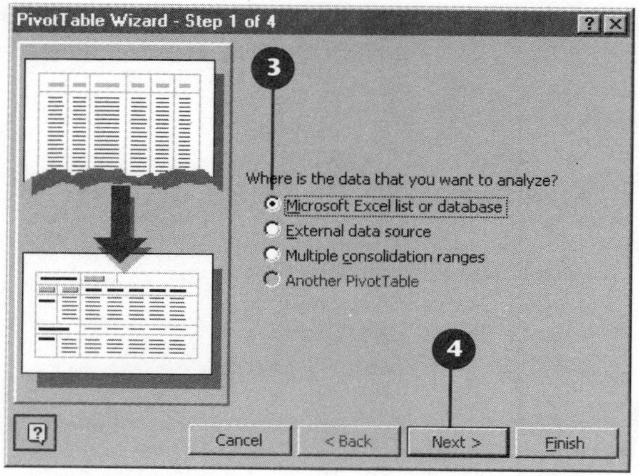

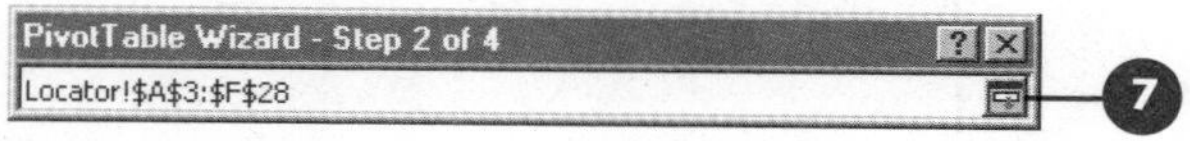

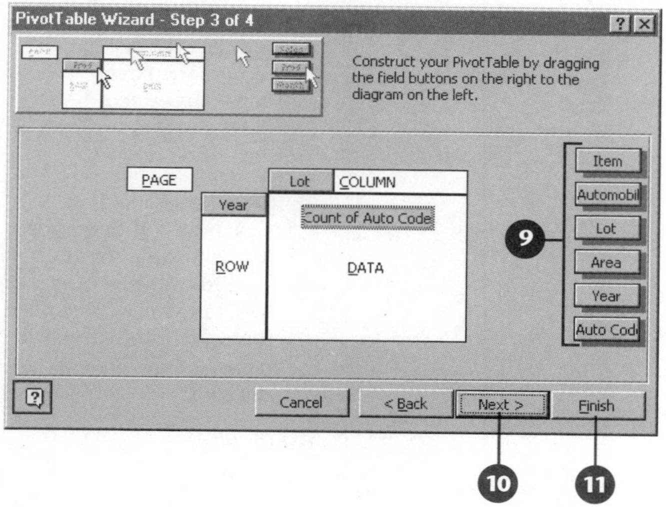

Charting a PivotTable

Data summarized in a PivotTable is an ideal candidate for a chart, since the table itself represents an overwhelming amount of difficult-to-read data. Once you select data within the PivotTable (using buttons on the PivotTable toolbar), then you can chart it like any other worksheet data using the Chart Wizard.

SEE ALSO

See "Creating a Chart" on page 140 for more information about using the Chart Wizard.

Create a Chart from a PivotTable

1. Click the Select Label And Data button on the PivotTable toolbar, or click the PivotTable drop-down arrow on the PivotTable toolbar, point to Select, and then click Label And Data.
2. Click the Chart Wizard button on the Standard toolbar.
3. Make selections from each of the four Chart Wizard dialog boxes.
4. Click Finish.

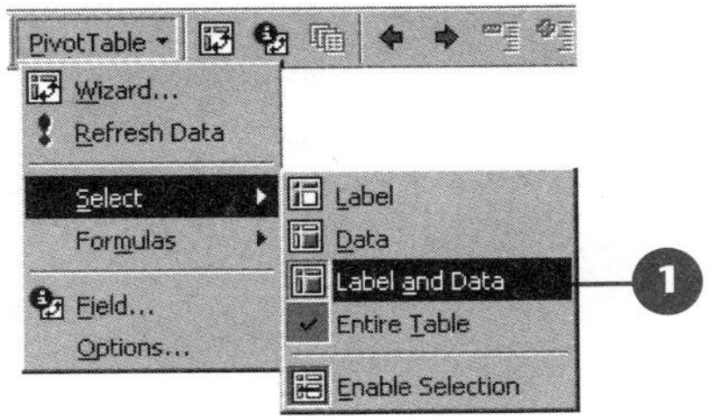

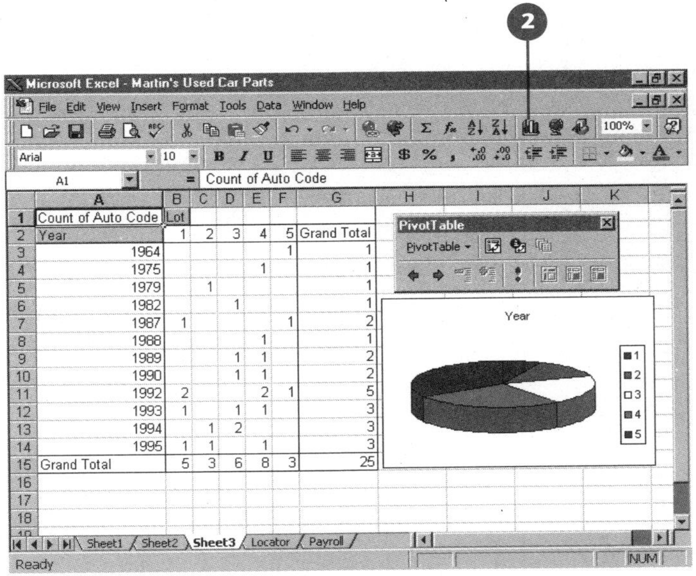

Tracking Changes in a Worksheet

As you build and fine tune a worksheet—particularly if you are sharing workbooks with co-workers—you can keep track of all the changes that are made at each stage in the process. The Track Changes feature makes it easy to know who has made what changes and when the changes were made. To take full advantage of this feature, turn it on the first time you or a co-worker edit a workbook. Then when it's time to review the workbook, all the changes will be recorded. Cells containing changes are surrounded by a blue border, and the changes made can be viewed instantly by moving your mouse pointer over any outlined cell. When you're ready to finalize the workbook, you can review it and either accept or reject the changes.

Turn On the Track Changes Feature

1. Click the Tools menu, point to Track Changes, and then click Highlight Changes.
2. Click the Track Changes While Editing check box.
3. Click OK.
4. Click OK to save the workbook.

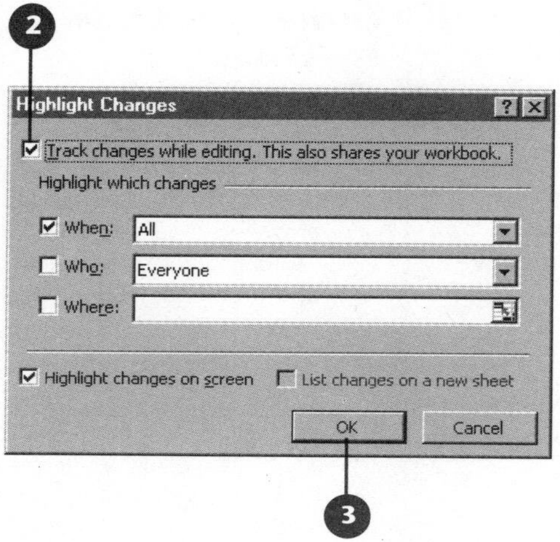

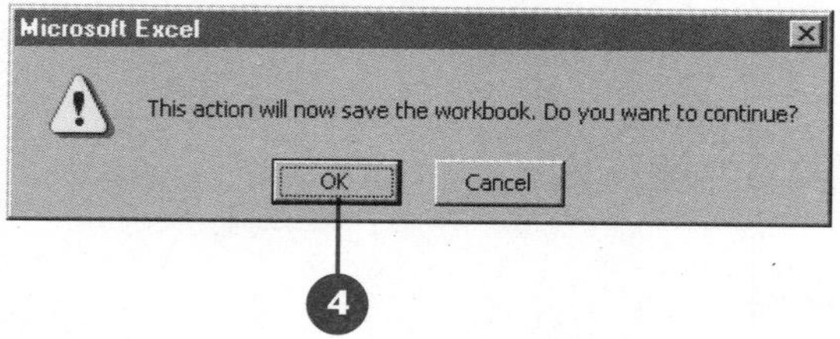

View Changes That Are Tracked

1. Position the mouse pointer over an edited cell.

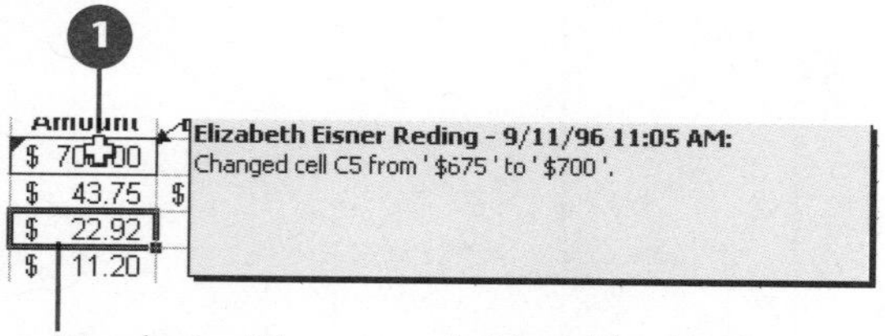

A tracked cell is surrounded by a blue border.

TIP

Title bar changes to alert you of shared status. *When you or another user apply the Track Changes command to a workbook, the message "[Shared]" appears in the title bar of the workbook to alert you that this feature is active.*

SEE ALSO

See "Editing Cell Contents" on page 120 for more information about changing the contents of a cell.

Accept or Reject Tracked Changes

1. Click the Tools menu, point to Track Changes, and then click Accept Or Reject Changes. If necessary, click OK in the message box.
2. Click OK to begin reviewing changes.
3. If necessary, scroll to review all the changes, and then click:
   - Accept to make the selected change to the worksheet.
   - Reject to remove the selected change from the worksheet.
   - Accept All to make all the changes to the worksheet after you have reviewed them.
   - Reject All to remove all the changes to the worksheet after you have reviewed them.
4. Click Close.

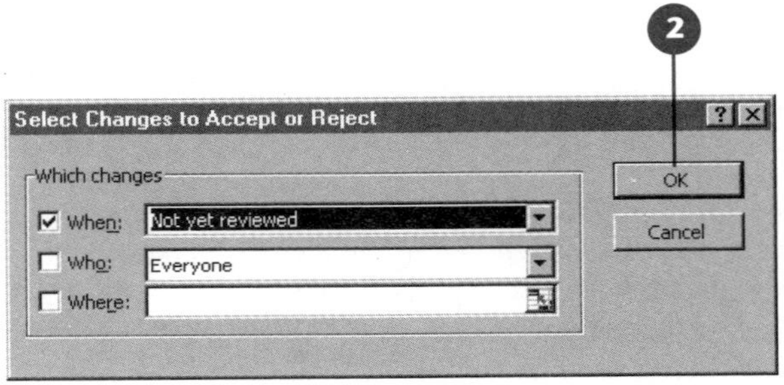

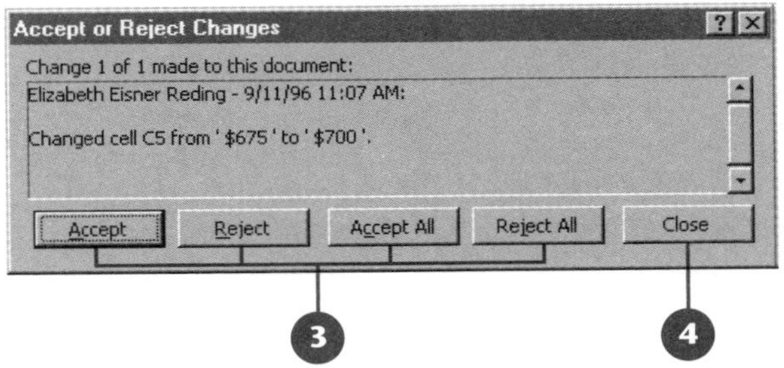

Protecting Your Data

You work very hard creating and entering information in a workbook. To preserve all your work—particularly if your files are being used by others—you can password protect its contents. You can protect a sheet or an entire workbook. In each case, you'll be asked to supply a password, and then enter it again when you want to work on the file.

TIP

Protect your password. *Make sure you keep your password in a safe place. Also, try to avoid obvious passwords like your name or your company.*

TIP

You need your password to unprotect a worksheet. *Turn off protection by clicking the Tools menu, point to Protection, and then click Unprotect Sheet. Enter the password, and then click OK.*

Protect Your Worksheet

1. Click the Tools menu, point to Protection, and then click Protect Sheet. Using the Tools menu, you can protect an individual sheet, the entire workbook, or you can protect and share a workbook. The steps for all are similar.
2. Click the check boxes for the options you want protected in the sheet.
3. Type a password. A password can contain any combination of letters, numbers, spaces, and symbols. Excel passwords are case sensitive so you must type upper and lowercase letters correctly when you enter passwords.
4. Click OK.
5. Retype the password.
6. Click OK.

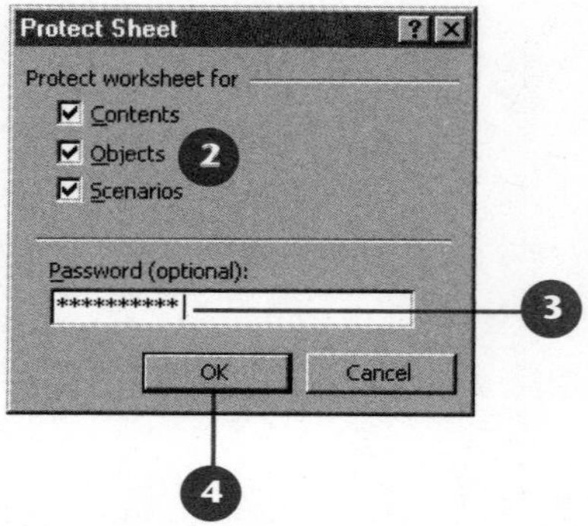
Protect Sheet
Protect worksheet for
Contents
Objects
Scenarios
Password (optional):
OK
Cancel
2
3
4

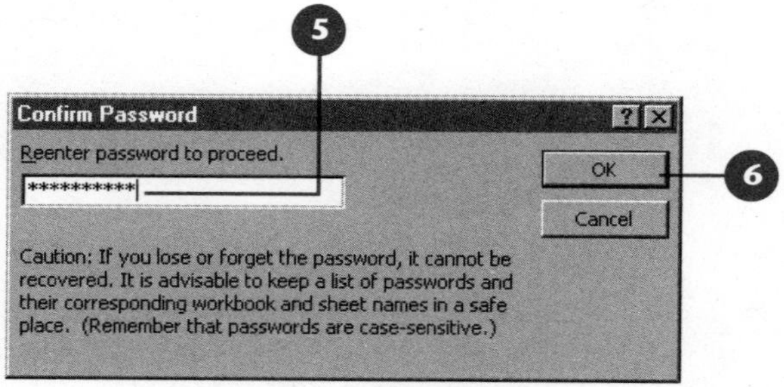
Confirm Password
Reenter password to proceed.
OK
Cancel
Caution: If you lose or forget the password, it cannot be recovered. It is advisable to keep a list of passwords and their corresponding workbook and sheet names in a safe place. (Remember that passwords are case-sensitive.)
5
6

10

Creating a Presentation with PowerPoint 97

IN THIS SECTION

Whether you need to put together a quick presentation of sales figures for your management team or create a polished slide show for your company's stockholders, Microsoft PowerPoint 97 can help you present your information efficiently and professionally.

Introducing PowerPoint

PowerPoint is a *presentation graphics program*: software that helps you create a slide show presentation. PowerPoint makes it easy to generate and organize ideas. It provides tools you can use to create the objects that make up an effective slide show—charts, graphs, bulleted lists, eye-catching text, multimedia video and sound clips, and more. PowerPoint also makes it easy to create slide show supplements, such as handouts, speaker's notes, and transparencies.

When you're ready, you can share your presentation with others, regardless of whether they have installed PowerPoint—in the office or on the Internet, where you can take instant advantage of the power of the World Wide Web from your planning stages right up to showing your presentation. PowerPoint also includes powerful slide show management tools that give you complete control of your online presentation.

Creating a New Presentation

When you first start PowerPoint, a dialog box opens that provides several presentation type options; the option you choose depends on the requirements of your presentation. You can click the Cancel button to close the dialog box without making a selection. You can also create a new presentation once PowerPoint has started by using the File menu.

TIP

You can have more than one presentation open at a time. *This is an especially useful feature when you want to copy slides from one presentation into another. To switch between open presentations, click the Window menu, and then click the presentation you want to switch to.*

Start a New Presentation

1. Start PowerPoint.
2. Click the option button you want to use to begin your presentation.
3. Click OK.
4. Follow the instructions that appear. These will vary, depending on the presentation type you chose.

Helps you generate presentation content

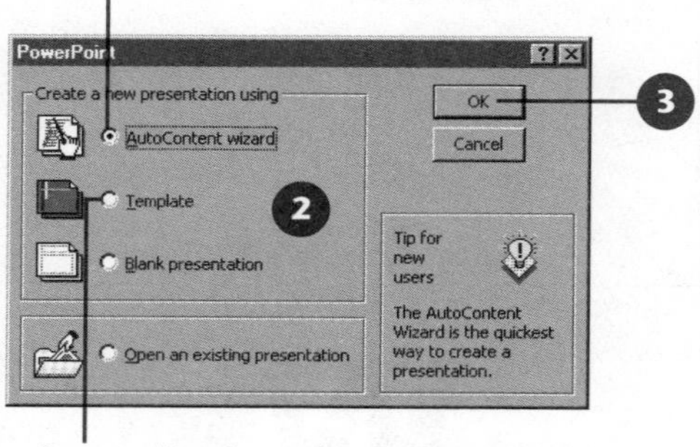

Opens a list of templates, or visual slide designs, from which you preview and then select the icon representing the design you want.

Start a New Presentation Within PowerPoint

1. Click the File menu, and then click New.
2. Click the tab to display the options you want to use to begin your presentation.
3. Click the icon you want to use as the basis of your presentation.
4. Click OK.

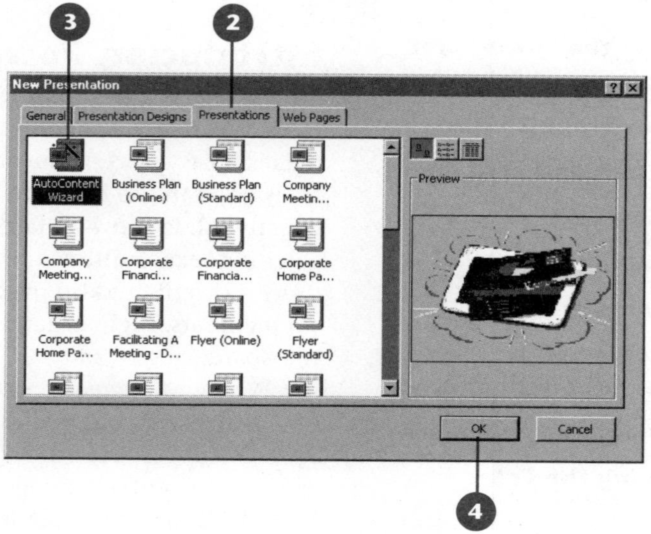

Generating Ideas Using AutoContent Wizard

Often the most difficult part of creating a presentation is knowing where to start. PowerPoint's AutoContent Wizard can help you develop presentation content on a variety of business and personal topics. An AutoContent presentation usually contains 5–10 slides that follow an organized progression of ideas. You edit the text as necessary to meet your needs. Many of the AutoContent presentations are available in Standard or Online formats.

TIP

You can use the AutoContent Wizard from the File menu. *Anytime during a PowerPoint session, click the File menu, click New, click the Presentations tab, click the AutoContent Wizard icon, and then click OK.*

Generate a Presentation Using the AutoContent Wizard

1. Start PowerPoint, click the AutoContent Wizard option button in the PowerPoint dialog box, and then click OK.
2. Read the first wizard dialog box, and then click Next.
3. Click the presentation type you want to use; or to focus on just one set of presentations, click the category button you want, and then click the presentation you want.
4. Click Next.
5. Choose the applicable presentation output, and then click Next.
6. Click the presentation style option button you want to use, and then click Next.
7. Enter information for your title slide, and then click Next.
8. Read the last wizard dialog box, and then click Finish.

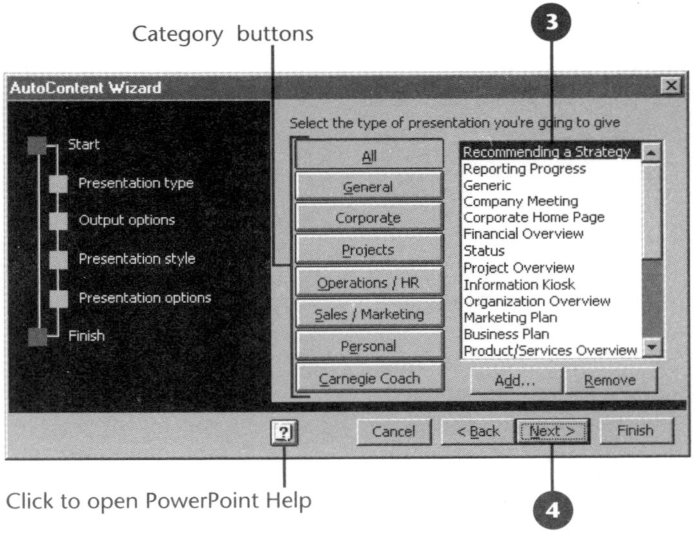

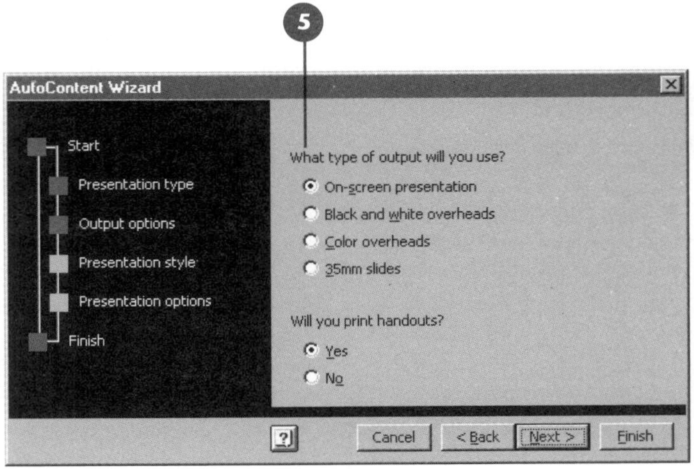

Choosing a Template Design

PowerPoint provides a collection of professionally designed templates that you can use to create effective presentations. Each template provides a format and color scheme to which you need only add text. You can choose a new template for your presentation at any point: when you first start your presentation or after you've developed the content.

TIP

Use a template to create a new presentation. *Create a new presentation with a template anytime during a PowerPoint session, click the File menu, click New, click the Presentation Designs tab, click the presentation design you want to use, and then click OK.*

Create a Presentation with a Template

1. Start PowerPoint, click the Template option button on the PowerPoint dialog box, and then click OK.
2. Click the Presentation Designs tab.
3. Click a presentation design icon you want to use.
4. Click OK.

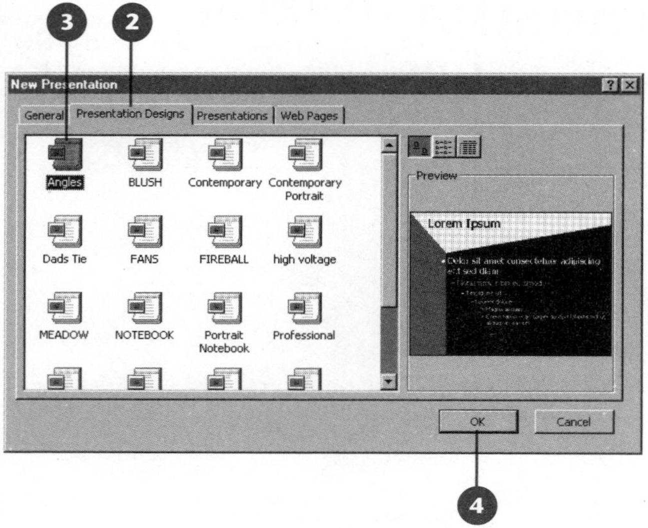

Apply a Template to an Existing Presentation

1. Click the Format menu.
2. Click Apply Design.
3. Click the template you want to apply to your slides.
4. Click Apply.

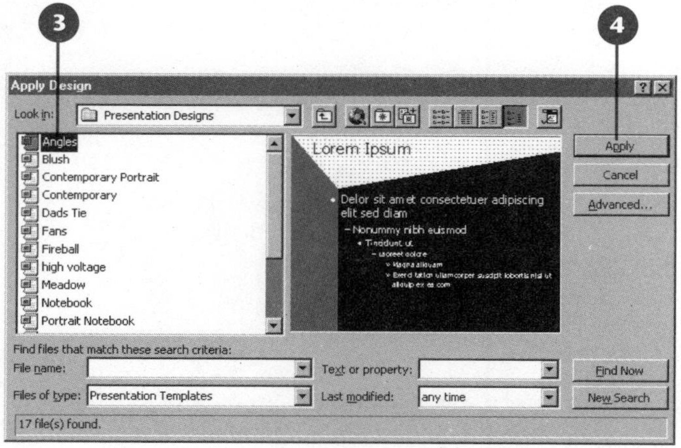

Viewing the PowerPoint Window

The *title bar* displays the program name, Microsoft PowerPoint. If you have a presentation open and maximized, the name of the presentation appears too.

The *Minimize button* shrinks the program window to a button on the taskbar.

The *Maximize button* expands the program window so it fills the entire screen. When you click this button, a Restore button appears in its place that you can click to restore the window to its original size.

The *menu bar* contains the names of the PowerPoint menus that are available. The menus change depending on the task at hand.

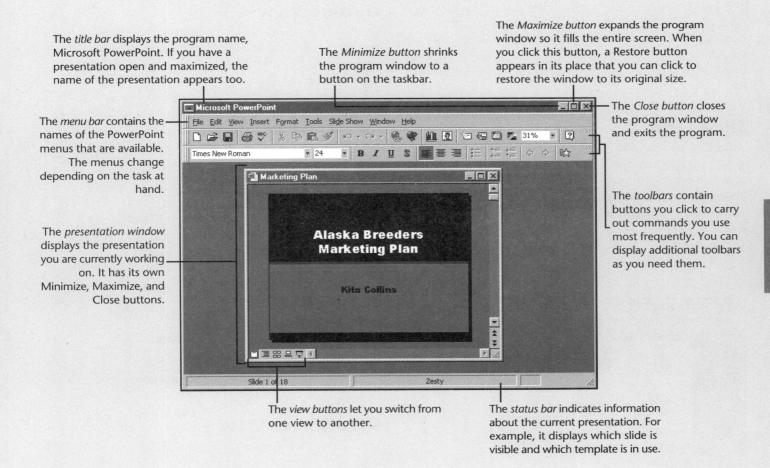

The *Close button* closes the program window and exits the program.

The *toolbars* contain buttons you click to carry out commands you use most frequently. You can display additional toolbars as you need them.

The *presentation window* displays the presentation you are currently working on. It has its own Minimize, Maximize, and Close buttons.

The *view buttons* let you switch from one view to another.

The *status bar* indicates information about the current presentation. For example, it displays which slide is visible and which template is in use.

The PowerPoint Views

To help you during all aspects of developing a presentation, PowerPoint provides five different views: Slide, Outline, Slide Sorter, Notes Page, and Slide Show. You can switch from one view to another with a single click of one of the view buttons, located next to the horizontal scroll bar.

Slide View

Slide view displays one slide at a time. Use this view to modify individual slides. You can move easily through your slides using the scroll bars or the Previous and Next Slide buttons located at the bottom of the vertical scroll bar. When you drag the scroll box up or down the vertical scroll bar, a label appears that indicates which slide will appear if you release the mouse button.

Slide View

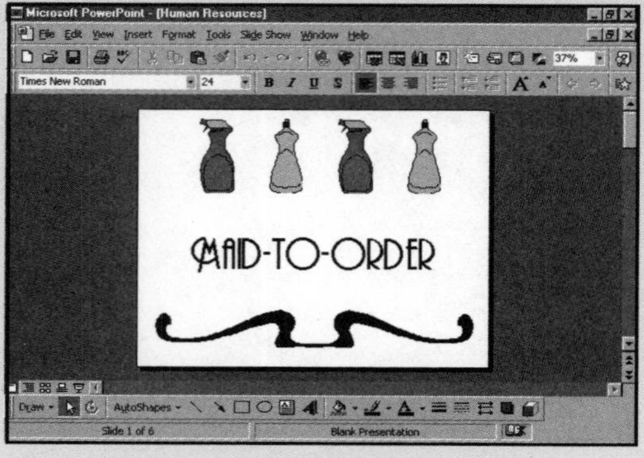
Microsoft PowerPoint - [Human Resources]
File Edit View Insert Format Tools Slide Show Window Help
Times New Roman
24
37%
MAID-TO-ORDER
Draw
AutoShapes
Slide 1 of 6
Blank Presentation

Outline View

Outline view displays a list of the slide titles and their contents in outline format. Use this view to develop your presentation's content. In Outline view, a special toolbar appears that helps you organize and enter your outline. A "thumbnail" or miniature of the active slide appears in a corner to give you an idea of its appearance. Individual slides are numbered. A slide icon appears for each slide. Icons for slides featuring shapes or pictures have small graphics on them.

Outline View

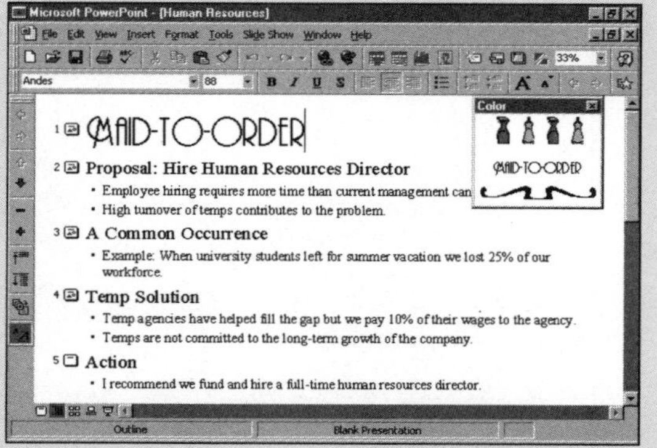
Microsoft PowerPoint - [Human Resources]
File Edit View Insert Format Tools Slide Show Window Help
33%
Andes
88
Color
1 MAID-TO-ORDER
MAID-TO-ORDER
2 Proposal: Hire Human Resources Director
• Employee hiring requires more time than current management can
• High turnover of temps contributes to the problem.
3 A Common Occurrence
• Example: When university students left for summer vacation we lost 25% of our workforce.
4 Temp Solution
• Temp agencies have helped fill the gap but we pay 10% of their wages to the agency.
• Temps are not committed to the long-term growth of the company.
5 Action
• I recommend we fund and hire a full-time human resources director.
Outline
Blank Presentation

Slide Sorter View

Slide Sorter view displays a thumbnail of each slide in the same window, in the order in which the slides appear in your presentation. Use this view to organize your slides, add

Slide Sorter View

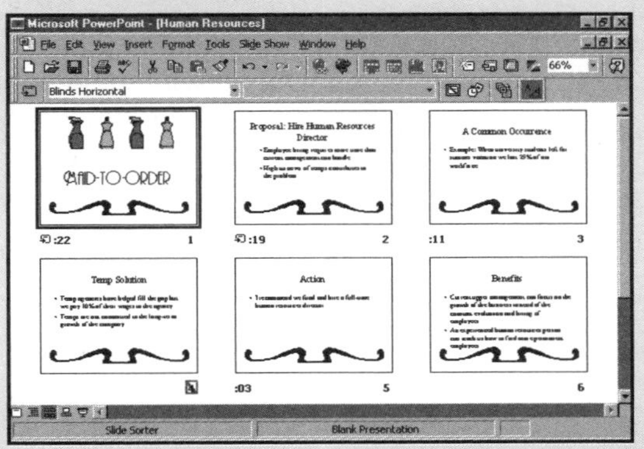

Notes Page View

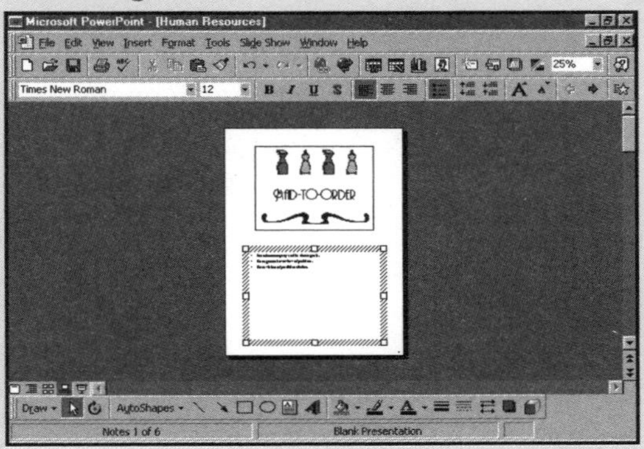

actions between slides, called *slide transitions,* and other effects to your slide show. In Slide Sorter view, a special toolbar appears that helps you add slide transitions and control other aspects of your presentation. When you add a slide transition, a small icon appears that indicates an action will take place as one slide replaces the previous slide during a show. If you hide a slide, a small icon appears that indicates the slide will not show during the presentation.

Notes Page View

Notes Page view displays a reduced view of a single slide along with a large text box in which you can type notes. You can use these notes as you give your presentation. When you work in Notes Page view, you will probably need to use the Zoom drop-down arrow to increase the magnification so you can type more easily. Click the Zoom drop-down arrow, and then click the magnification you want.

Slide Show View

Slide Show view presents your slides, one slide at a time. Use this view when you're ready to give your presentation. In Slide Show view, you can click the screen repeatedly or press Enter to move through the show until you've shown all the slides. You can exit Slide Show View at any time by pressing the Esc key and return to the previous view.

Creating Consistent Slides

For a presentation to be understandable, the objects on its slides need to be arranged in a visually meaningful way. PowerPoint's *AutoLayout* feature helps you arrange objects on your slide in a consistent manner. There are 24 AutoLayouts that are designed to accommodate the most common slide arrangements. When you create a new slide, you apply an AutoLayout to the slide. Placeholders for text or objects on the AutoLayout appear automatically. You can also apply an AutoLayout to an existing slide at any time.

Insert New Slide button

Insert a New Slide

1. Click the Insert New Slide button on the Standard toolbar.
2. Click the AutoLayout that provides the layout you need.
3. Click OK.

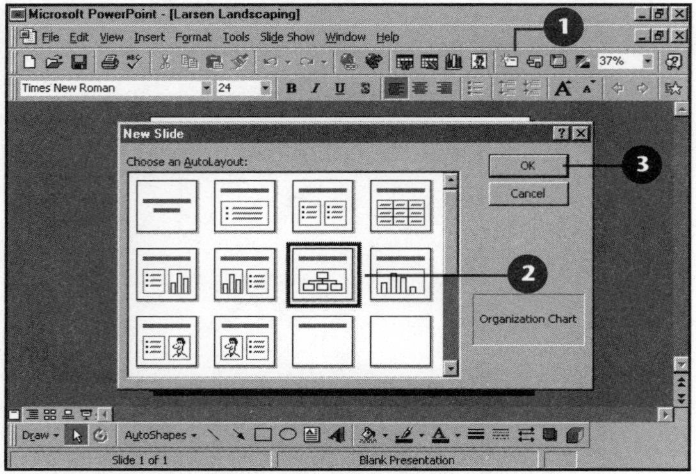

Apply an AutoLayout to an Existing Slide

1. In Slide view, display the slide you want to change.
2. Click the Slide Layout button on the Standard toolbar.
3. Click the AutoLayout you want to apply.
4. Click Apply.

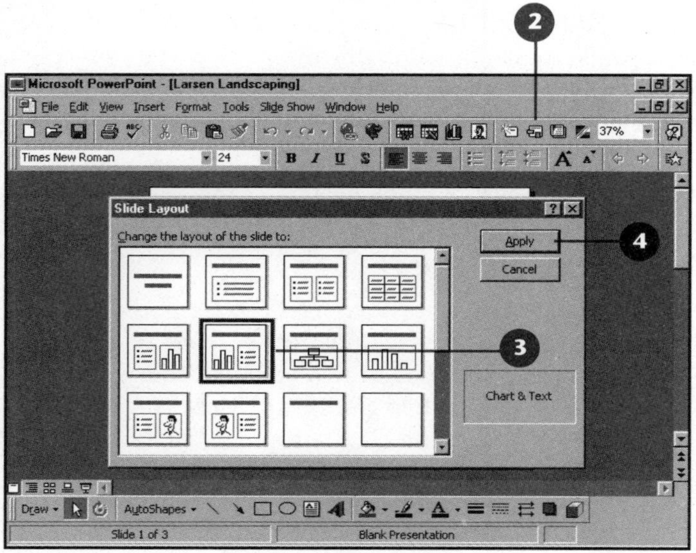

TIP

Use AutoLayout to create placeholders. *When you apply an AutoLayout to a slide, an arranged group of placeholders appears—one placeholder for each object on the slide. The placeholders include instructions for entering object contents.*

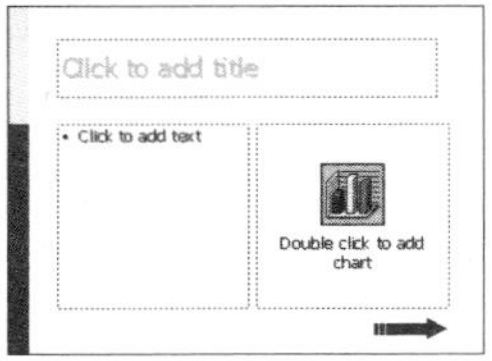

Enter Information into a Placeholder

1. For text placeholders, click the placeholder and type the necessary text.
   - ◆ For other objects, double-click the placeholder and work with whatever accessory PowerPoint starts.

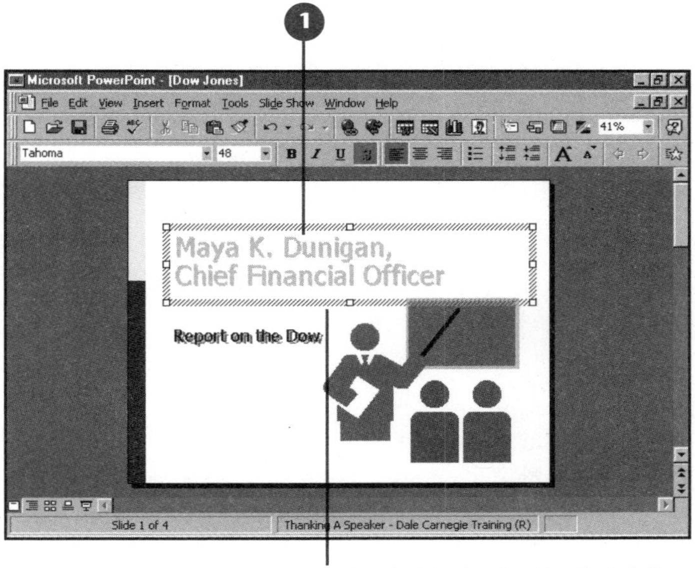

A placeholder is a border that defines the size and location of an object.

10

AUTOLAYOUT PLACEHOLDERS	
Placeholder	**Description**
Bulleted List	Displays a short list of related points
Clip Art	Inserts a picture
Chart	Inserts a chart
Organization Chart	Insert an organizational chart
Table	Inserts a table from Microsoft Word
Media Clip	Inserts a music, sound, or video clip
Object	Inserts an object created in another program, such as an Excel spreadsheet or WordArt object

Entering Text

In Slide view, you type text directly into the text placeholders. If you type more text than fits in the placeholder, you might need to adjust the font size of the text you are typing or resize the selection box. You can also increase or decrease the vertical distance between two lines of text. The *insertion point* indicates where text will appear when you type. To place the insertion point into your text, move the pointer arrow over the text—the pointer changes to an I-beam to indicate that you could click and then type.

TRY THIS

Enter symbols. *You can enter symbols into your text, such as © and ®, or foreign or accented characters, such as Ô, depending on the fonts installed on your computer. Click the Insert menu, click Symbol, in the Symbol dialog box click the Font drop-down arrow, click the font you want, click the symbol you want in the grid, and then click Insert. Click Close when you are done.*

Enter Text into a Placeholder

1. In Slide view, click the text placeholder if it isn't already selected.
2. Type the text you want to enter.
3. Click outside the text object to deselect the object.

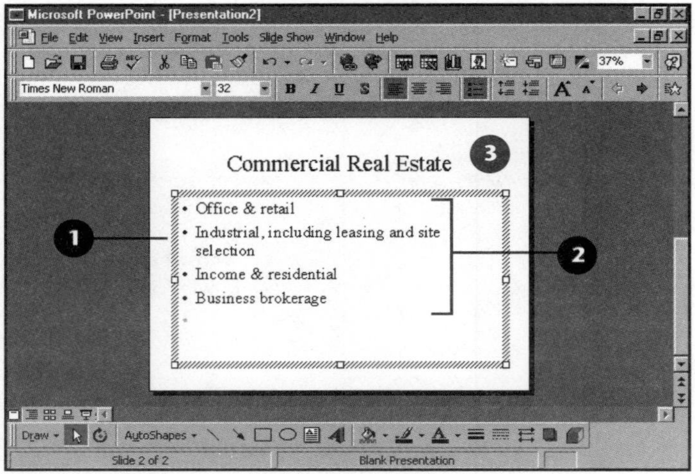

Insert Text

1. To insert text between two existing words, click between the words.
2. Type the text.

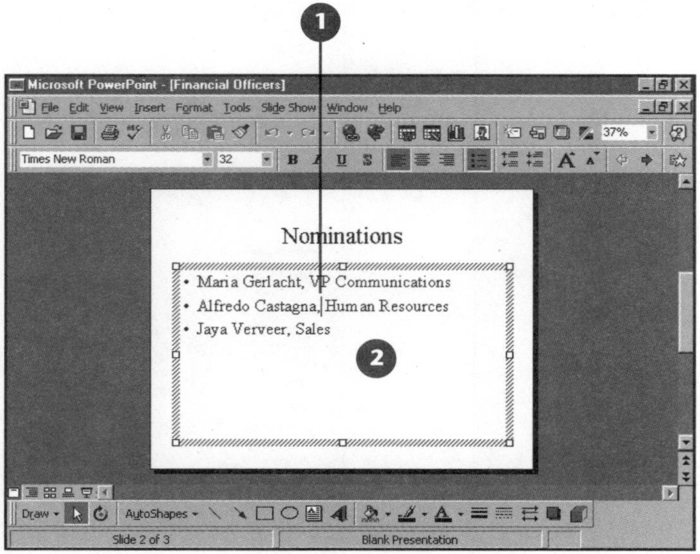

TIP

Use the keyboard to enter bulleted text quickly. *When entering bulleted text, be sure the insertion point is at the beginning of the line, press Tab to indent a level and press Shift+Tab to move back out a level.*

TRY THIS

Expand a bulleted list into a set of slides. *If you decide that the bulleted items in a bulleted list should be separate slides, you can click the bulleted list object, click Tools, and then click Expand Slide. PowerPoint automatically creates new slides whose titles correspond to the items in the first level of the bulleted list.*

TIP

Check your paragraph adjustment. *When you decrease paragraph spacing, make sure you leave enough space for the height of each entire letter, including extenders such as the bottom of "p" and the top of "b."*

Enter Bulleted Text

1. In Slide view, click the bulleted text placeholder.
2. Type the first bulleted item.
3. Press Enter. PowerPoint automatically bullets the next line.
4. Type the next bulleted item, and continue until you have completed the list.

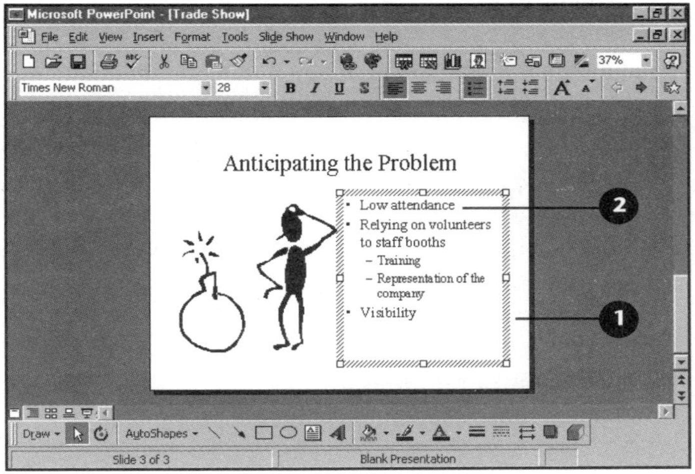

Adjust Paragraph Spacing

1. Click anywhere in the paragraph you want to adjust.
2. Click the Increase Paragraph Spacing or the Decrease Paragraph Spacing button on the Formatting toolbar to increase or decrease the vertical distance between paragraphs.

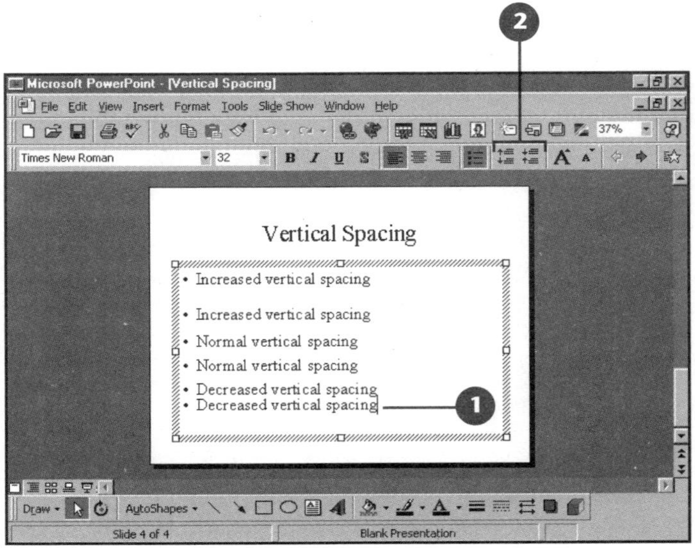

10

Developing an Outline

If you created your presentation using one of the AutoContent Wizards, PowerPoint generates an outline automatically. If you prefer to develop your own outline, you can create a blank presentation, and then switch to Outline view and type in your outline from scratch. If you want to use an existing outline from another document, such as a Microsoft Word document, make sure it is set up using outline heading styles. You can then bring the outline into PowerPoint, and PowerPoint creates slide titles, subtitles, and bulleted lists based on those styles.

Outline View button

Enter Text in Outline View

1. In Outline view, click to position the insertion point where you want the text to appear.
2. Type the text you want to enter, pressing Enter after each line.

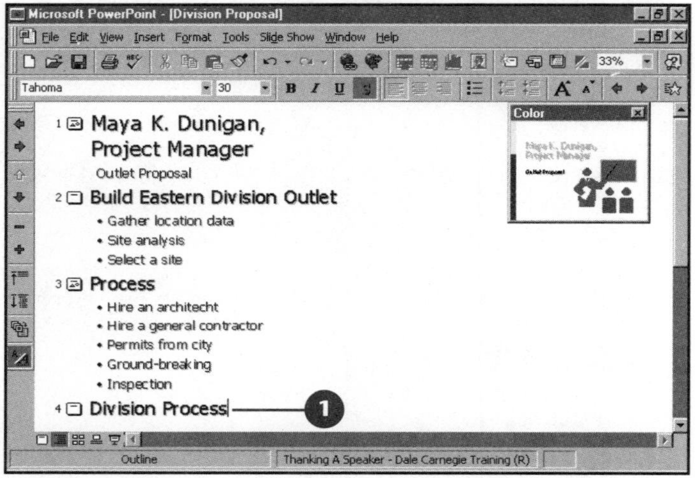

Add a Slide in Outline View

1. In Outline view, click at the end of the previous slide text.
2. Click the Insert New Slide button on the Standard toolbar, or press Ctrl+Enter to insert a slide using the existing slide layout.

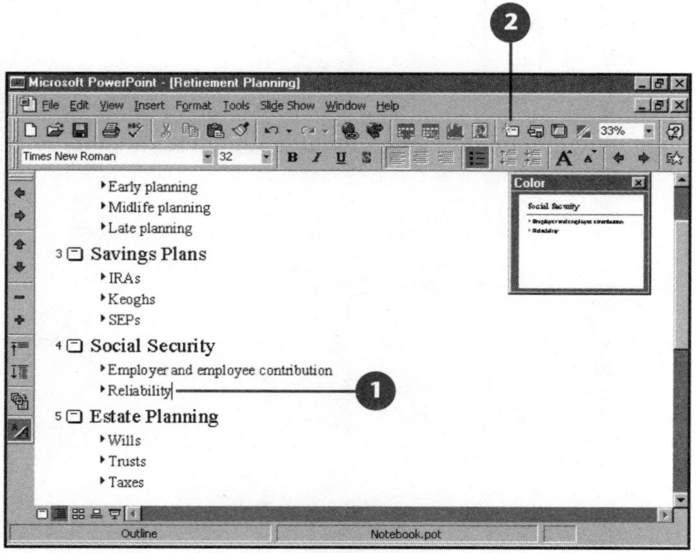

TIP

Different ways to delete a Slide. *In Outline or Slide Sorter view, click the slide you want to delete, and then press Delete. In Slide view, move to the slide you want to delete, click the Edit menu, and then click Delete Slide.*

Duplicate a Slide

1. Click the slide you want to duplicate.
2. Click the Insert menu.
3. Click Duplicate Slide.

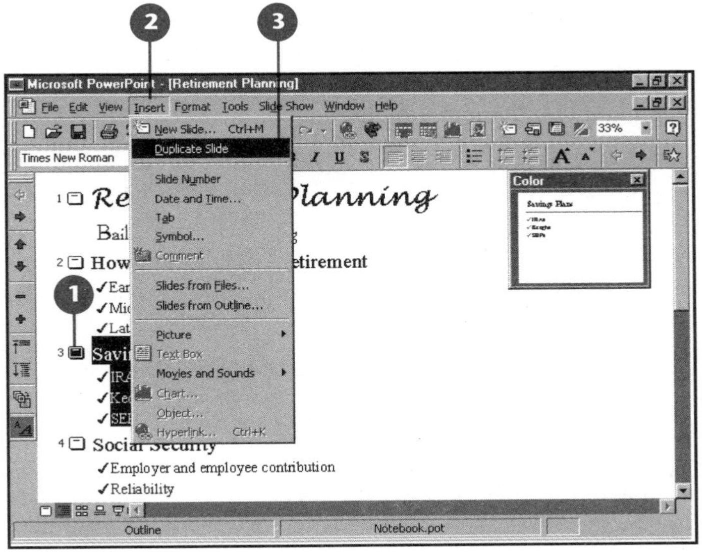

Insert an Outline from Another Application

1. Click the Insert menu.
2. Click Slides From Outline.
3. Locate and then click the file containing the outline you want to insert.
4. Click Insert.

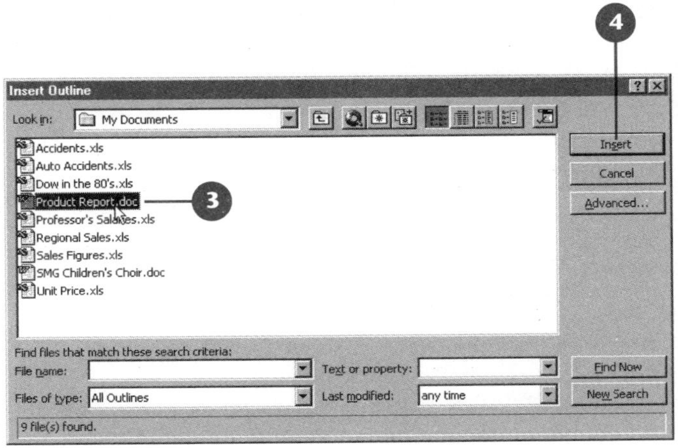

Rearranging Slides

You can instantly rearrange slides in Outline view or Slide Sorter view. You can use either the Move Up and Move Down button to move selected slides up or down through the outline, or you can use the Cut and Paste buttons to first cut the slides you want to move and then paste them in the new location. Outline view also lets you collapse the outline down to its major points so you can more easily see its structure. A horizontal line appears below a collapsed slide in Outline view.

TIP

Use Slide Sorter view to rearrange your slides quickly. *A vertical bar appears next to the slide you are moving as you drag a slide in Slide Sorter view. It indicates where the slide will drop when you release the mouse button.*

Rearrange Slides in Outline View

1. Click the Outline View button.
2. Click the slide icon of the slide or slides you want to move.
3. Click the Move Up button to move the slide up or the Move Down button to move the slide down. Repeat until the slide is where you want it.

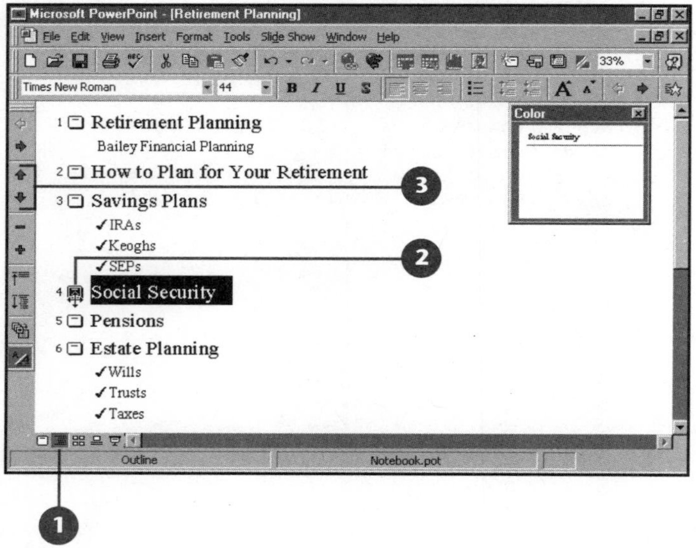

Rearrange Slides in Slide Sorter View

1. Click the Slide Sorter View button.
2. Click the slide you want to move and then drag it to a new location.

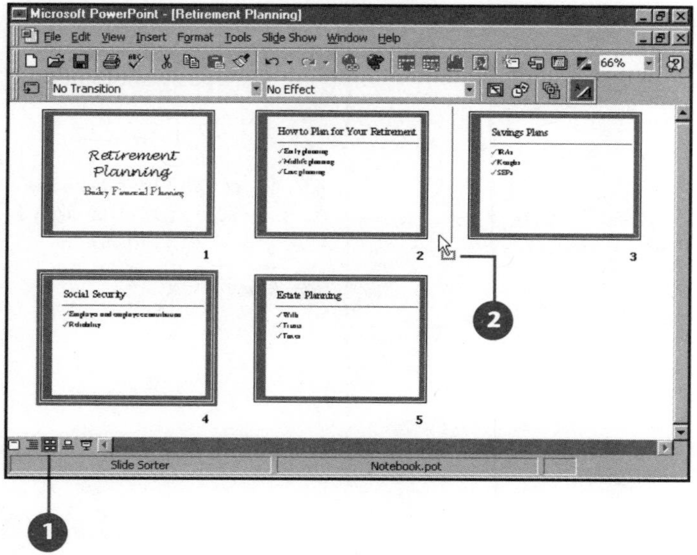

TIP

Select slide effectively in Outline view. *To select an entire slide in Outline view, click the slide icon. To select more than one slide, press and hold the Ctrl key while you click the slide icon.*

Expand All button

Collapse button

Collapse and Expand Slides in Outline View

- In Outline view, click the Collapse button to collapse the selected slide or slides.
- Click the Expand button to expand the selected slide or slides.
- Click the Collapse All button to collapse all slides.
- Click the Expand All button to expand all slides.

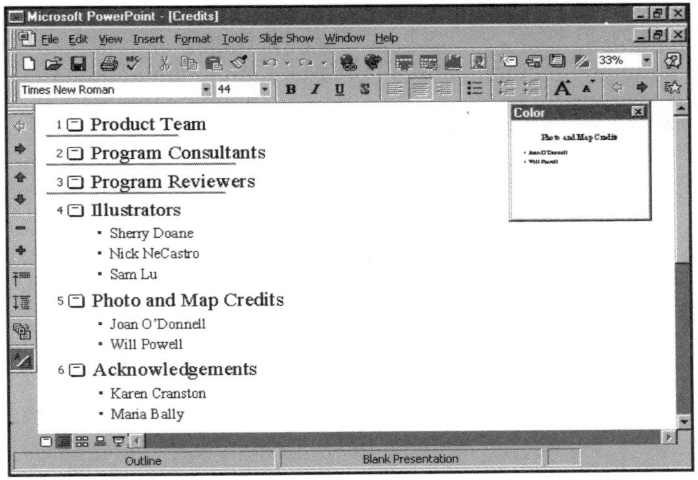

Move a Slide with Cut and Paste

1. In Outline or Slide Sorter view, select the slide or slides you want to move.
2. Click the Cut button on the Standard toolbar.
3. Click the new location.
4. Click the Paste button on the Standard toolbar.

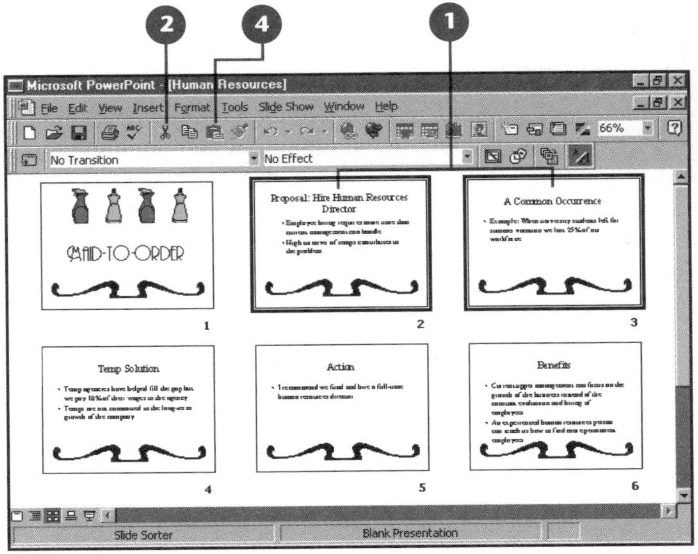

10

Controlling Slide Appearance with Masters

If you want an object, such as a company logo or clip art, to appear on every slide in your presentation, you can place it on the slide master. You can also hide the object from any slide you want. However, you can also create unique slides that don't follow the format of the masters. If you change your mind, you can easily restore a master format to a slide you altered. As you make changes to the master, you might find it helpful to view a miniature of the slide, complete with text and graphics, using the Slide Miniature window.

TIP

Objects on the slide master. *An object you place on the slide master will not appear on the title slide unless you also place it on the title master.*

Include an Object on Every Slide

1. Click the View menu, point to Master, and then click Slide Master.
2. Add the object you want and fine-tune its size and placement.
3. Click Close on the Master toolbar.

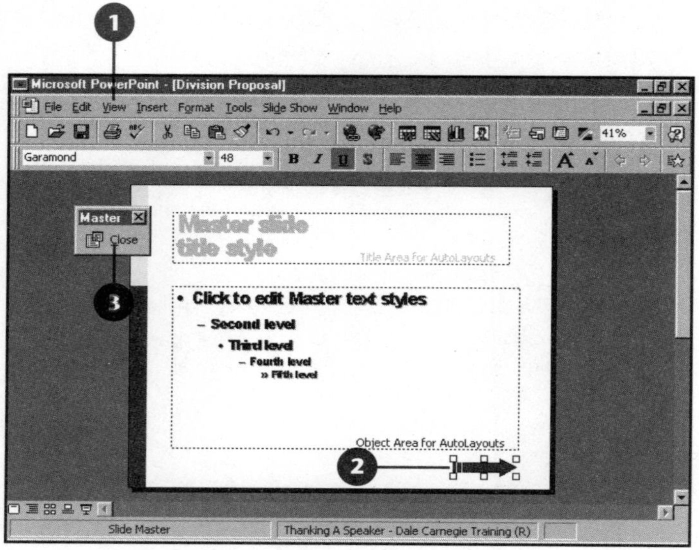

Hide Master Background Objects on a Slide

1. Display the slide whose background object you want to hide.
2. Click the Format menu.
3. Click Background.
4. Click the Omit Background Graphics From Master check box to select it.
5. Click Apply.

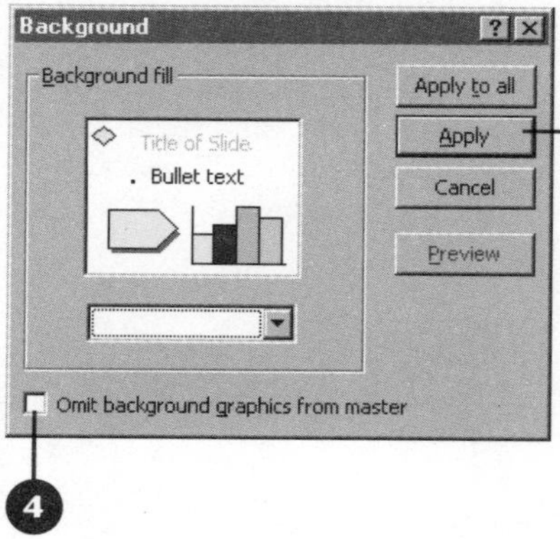

TIP

Apply a change to all slides. *To apply a change you make to all slides instead of an individual slide, click Apply To All instead of Apply.*

TRY THIS

Make a slide format different from the master. *Display the slide you want to change. Make the changes. Your changes now override master formatting, and even if you change the master, this slide will retain the features you changed.*

Reapply the Master to a Changed Slide

1. Right-click the changed slide in Slide view.
2. Click Slide Layout.
3. Click Reapply.

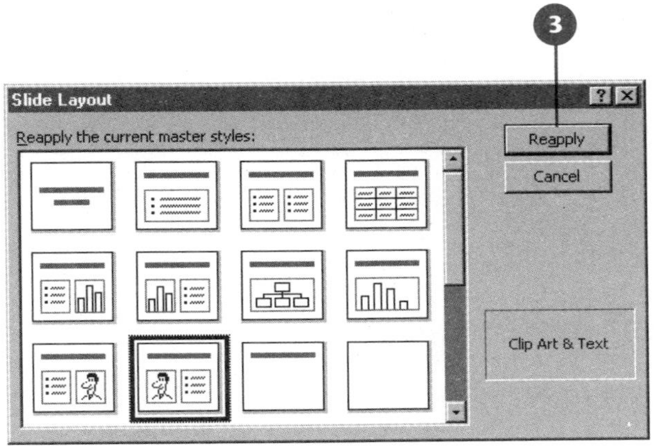

View a Miniature

1. Click the View menu.
2. Click Slide Miniature.

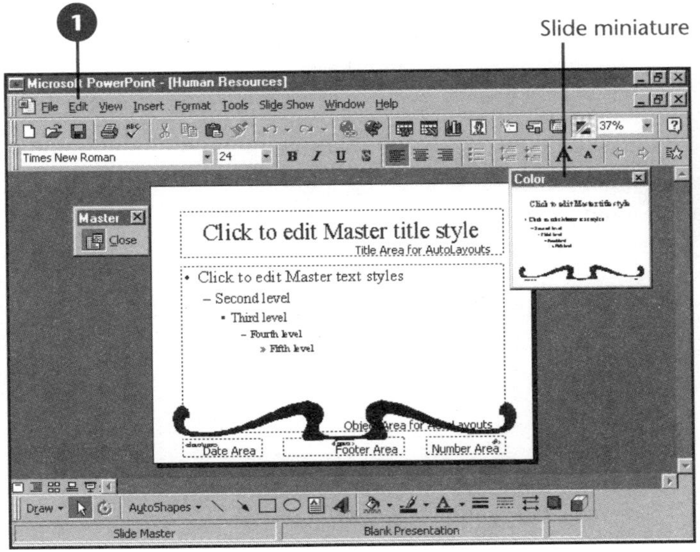

10

Applying a Color Scheme

You can apply a color scheme to an individual slide or to all the slides in a presentation. Each template offers one or more standard color schemes from which to choose, and you can also create your own color schemes, and then save them so you can apply them to other slides and even other presentations.

Choose a Color Scheme

1. Right-click a blank area of a slide.
2. Click Slide Color Scheme.
3. If necessary, click the Standard tab to view the available color schemes.
4. Click the color scheme you want.
5. Click Apply to apply the color scheme to the slide you are viewing, or click Apply To All to apply the color scheme to the entire presentation.

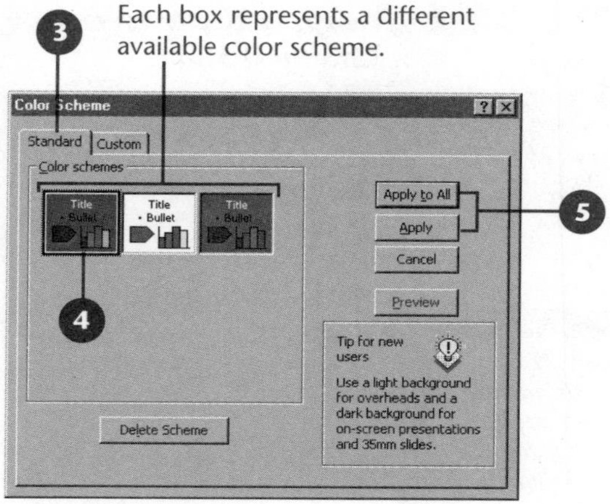

Delete a Color Scheme

1. Open the Color Scheme dialog box.
2. If necessary, click the Standard tab to view the available color schemes.
3. Locate and click the scheme you want to delete.
4. Click Delete Scheme.

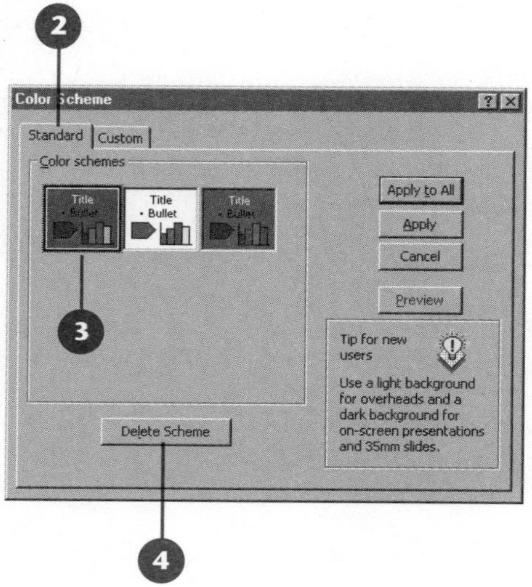

TIP

Apply a color scheme from one presentation to another. *Open both presentations, and then repeat the steps of the task "Apply the Color Scheme of One Slide to Another."*

"I really like this color scheme—I'd like to apply it to a different slide."

Apply the Color Scheme of One Slide to Another

1. Click the Slide Sorter View button.
2. Click the slide with the color scheme you want to apply.
3. Click the Format Painter button on the Formatting toolbar once to apply the color scheme to one slide, or double-click to apply the color scheme to multiple slides.
4. Select the slide or slides to which you want to apply the color scheme. This can be in the current presentation or in another open presentation.
5. If you are applying the scheme to more than one slide, press Esc to cancel Format Painter. If you are applying the scheme to only one slide, Format Painter cancels automatically.

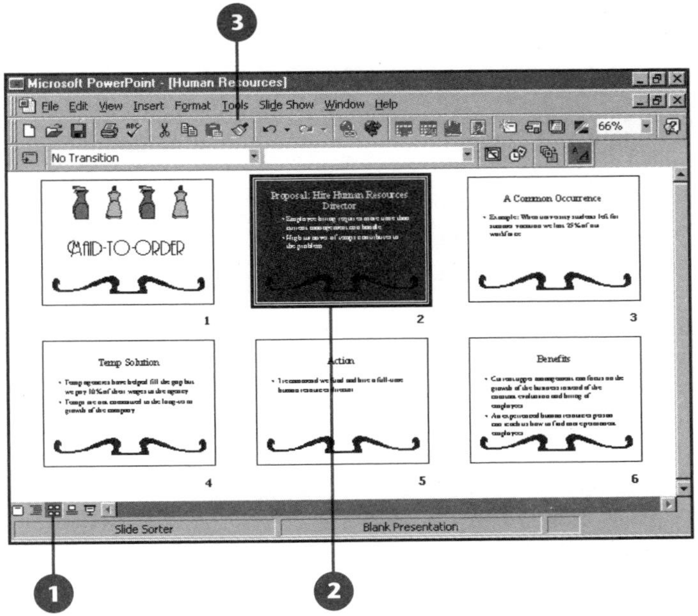

10

Changing the Color Scheme

You might like a certain color scheme, all except for one or two colors. You can change an existing color scheme and apply your changes to the entire presentation or just to a few slides. Once you change a color scheme, you can add it to your collection of color schemes so that you can make it available to any slide in the presentation.

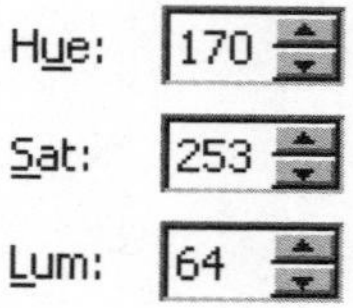

Change a Standard Color Scheme Color

1. In Slide view, right-click a blank area of the slide whose color scheme you want to change, and then click Slide Color Scheme.
2. Click the Custom tab.
3. Click the element you want to change in the Scheme Colors list.
4. Click Change Color.
5. Click a color on the Standard tab.
6. Click OK.
7. Click Apply to apply the changed color scheme to the current slide, or click Apply To All to apply the changed scheme to all slides.

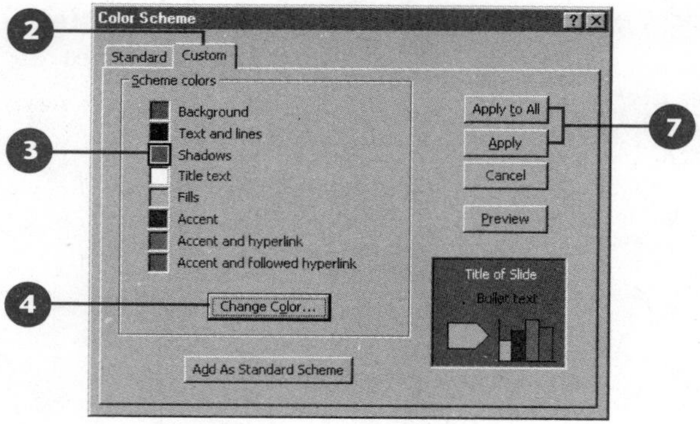

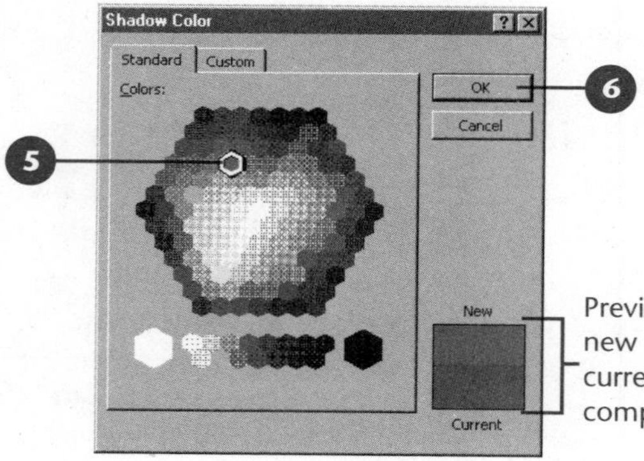

Preview box shows the new color and the current color so you can compare them.

Choose a Nonstandard Color

1. In the Color Scheme dialog box, click the Custom tab.
2. Click the element you want to color in the Scheme Colors list.
3. Click Change Color.

THE PROPERTIES OF COLORS	
Characteristic	**Description**
Hue	The color itself; every color is identified by a number, determined by the number of colors available on your monitor.
Saturation	The intensity of the color. The higher the number the more vivid the color.
Luminosity	The brightness of the color, or how close the color is to black or white. The larger the number, the lighter the color.

"How can I create a custom color scheme?"

4. In the Color dialog box that opens (the name depends on which element you chose), click the Custom tab.
5. Drag across the palette until the pointer is over the color you want, or set the Hue, Sat, Lum, Red, Green, and Blue values manually.
6. Click OK. The color appears in the Scheme Colors list.
7. Click Apply to make the new color part of the color scheme for the current slide, or click Apply To All to make it part of the entire presentation.

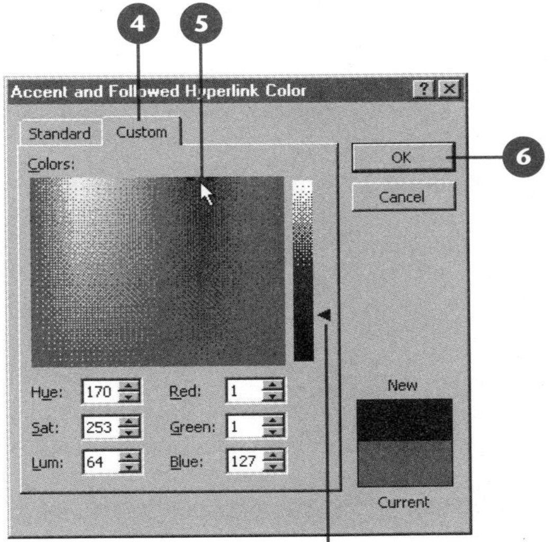

Moving the slider changes the luminosity for the current color.

Save a Changed Color Scheme

1. In the Color Scheme dialog box, click the Custom tab.
2. Change the color scheme until all eight colors are as you want them.
3. Click Add As Standard Scheme. Your new scheme now appears on the Standard tab.

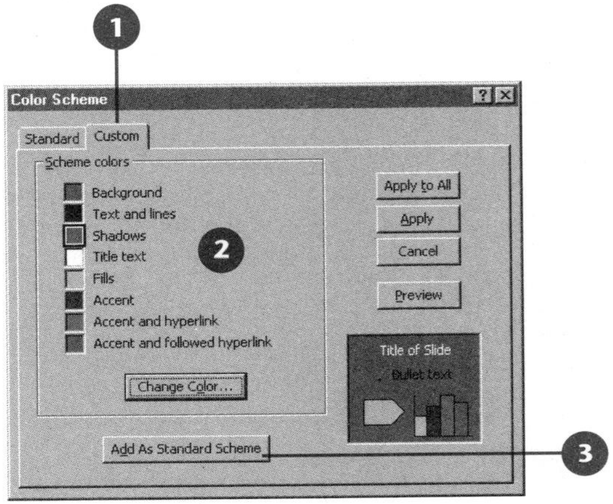

10

Printing a Presentation

You can print all elements of your presentation—the slides, an outline, the notes, and handouts—in either color or black and white. The Print dialog box offers standard Windows features, giving you the option to print multiple copies, to specify ranges, to access printer properties, and to print to a file.

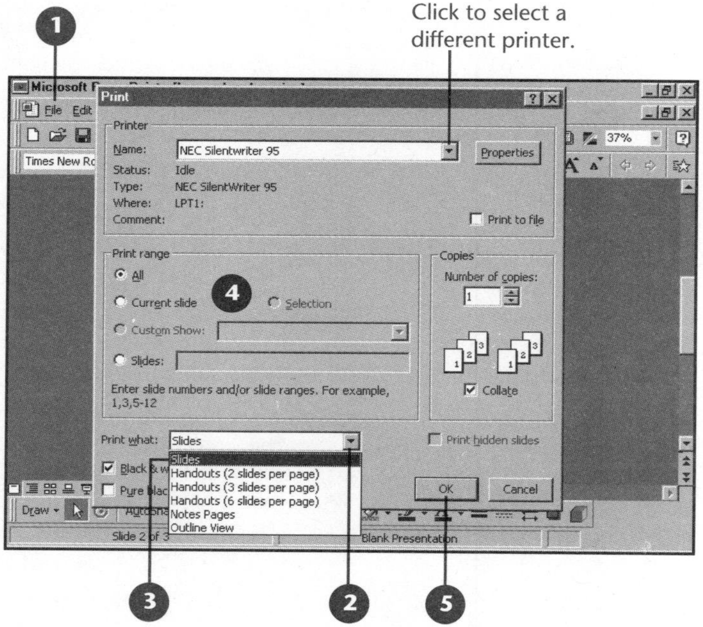

TIP

Print an outline. *Switch to Outline view, and then choose how you want your slides to look by clicking the Expand All, Collapse All, or Show Formatting button. Click the File menu, and then click Print. Click the Print What drop-down arrow, and then click Outline View. Click OK to print.*

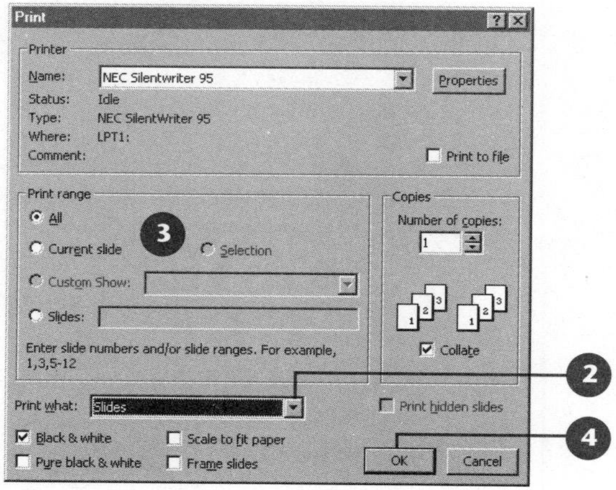

TRY THIS

Print a custom show. *Click the File menu and then click Print. Click the Custom Show drop-down arrow, click the custom show you want to print, and then click OK.*

Print a Presentation

1. Click the File menu, and then click Print.

2. Click the Print What drop-down arrow.

3. Click what you want to print.

4. Change settings in the Print dialog box as necessary.

5. Click OK.

Click to select a different printer.

Print a Single Slide or a Range of Slides

1. Click the File menu, and then click Print.

2. If necessary, click the Print What drop-down arrow, and then click Slides.

3. In the Print Range area, select the slides you want to print.

4. Click OK.

11

Designing a Presentation with PowerPoint 97

IN THIS SECTION

Although well-illustrated slides can't make up for a lack of content, you have a much better chance of capturing your audience's attention if your slides are vibrant and visually interesting. You can easily enhance a slide by adding a graph, a chart, or a picture—one of your own or one of the hundreds that come with Office 97. If you have the appropriate hardware, such as a sound card and speakers, you also might want to include sound files and video clips in your presentation.

PowerPoint also lets you create custom slide shows that can include special features, such as visual, sound, and animation effects. For example, you can program special *transitions* or actions between slides. You can also control how each element of the slide is introduced to the audience using *animations*. You can add *action buttons* to your presentation that the presenter can click to activate a hyperlink and jump instantly to another slide in the presentation. A PowerPoint presentation can really come alive with the proper use of narration and music. With PowerPoint you can record a narration and insert it directly into your slide show.

Inserting Slides from Other Presentations

To insert slides from other presentations in a slide show, you can open the presentation and copy and paste the slides you want, or you can use the *Slide Finder* feature. With Slide Finder, you don't have to open the presentation first; instead, you view "snapshots" of each slide in a presentation and then insert only the ones you select. With Slide Finder, you can also create a list of favorite presentations that you often use as source material.

Insert Slides from Slide Finder

1. Click the Insert menu.
2. Click Slides From Files, and then click the Find Presentation tab, if necessary.
3. Click Browse, locate and select the file you want, and then click Open.
4. Click Display to display a miniature of each slide.
5. Select the slides you want to insert.
   - To insert just one slide, click the slide, and then click Insert.
   - To insert multiple slides, click each slide you want to insert, and then click Insert.
   - To insert all the slides in the presentation, click Insert All.

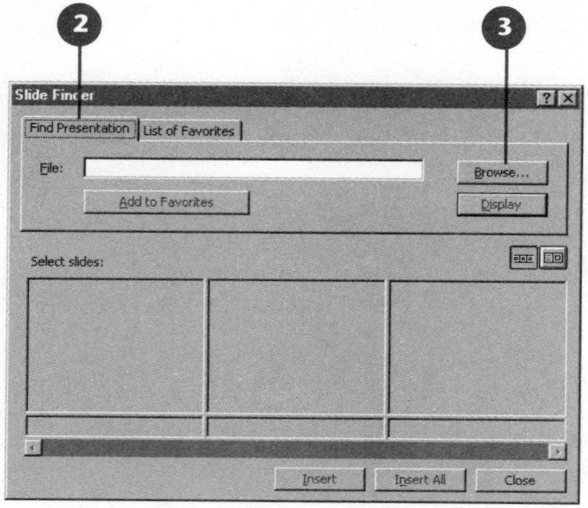

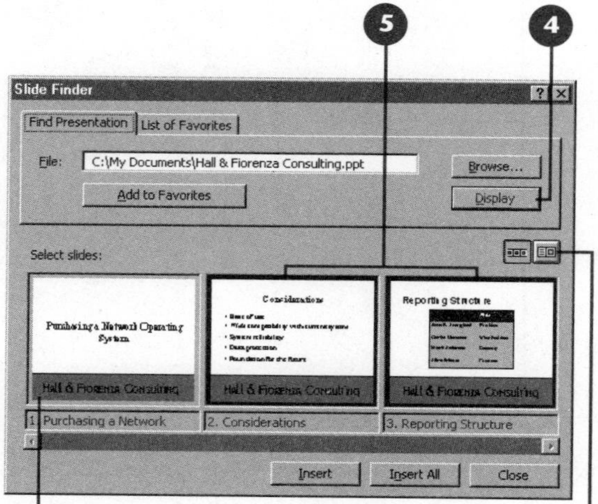

When you display miniatures, you see a miniature of each slide with its title underneath.

Click to display only the slide titles.

> **TIP**
>
> **Select slides in Slide Finder.** *To select a group of adjacent slides, click the first slide, press Shift, and then click the last slide. To select a group of nonadjacent slides, press and hold Ctrl and each slide you want to insert.*

> **TIP**
>
> **Remove a presentation from your list of favorites.** *To remove a presentation from your list of favorites, click the presentation on the List Of Favorites tab in Slide Finder, and then click Remove.*

> **TRY THIS**
>
> **Insert slides over a network.** *To insert slides from presentations stored on other computers in your company's network, click the Insert menu, click Slides From File, click the Browse button, click the Look In drop-down arrow, and then click the network drive that contains the presentation you want to use. Slide Finder gives you the same access to those slides as it would to slides on your local hard drive.*

Display Slide Titles in Slide Finder

1. In Slide Finder, click the Titles button.

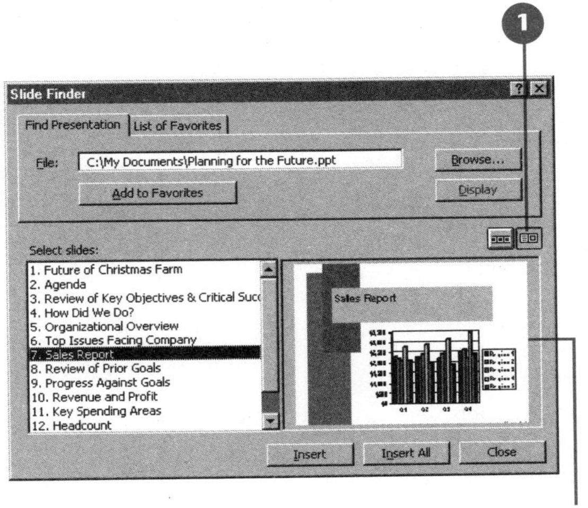

Preview of the top selected slide

Add a Presentation to List of Favorites

1. In Slide Finder, locate the file you want to add to the list of favorites.
2. Click Add To Favorites.
3. Click the List Of Favorites tab.
4. Click Close.

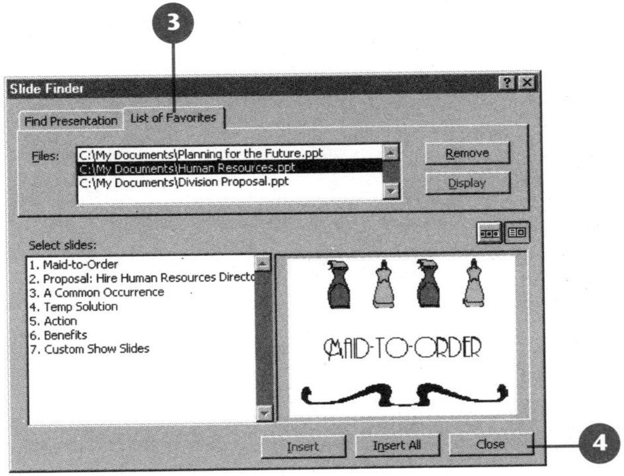

11

Inserting a Graph Chart in a Slide

You can insert an existing chart from a program such as Microsoft Excel, or you can create one from scratch using the graph program that comes with the Office 97 suite, *Microsoft Graph.* Graph uses two views to display the information that makes up a graph: the *datasheet*, a spreadsheet-like grid of rows and columns that contains your data, and the *chart*, the graphical representation of the data.

Create a Graph Chart

1. Start Microsoft Graph in one of the following ways:
   - To create a graph on an existing slide, display the slide on which you want the graph to appear, and then click the Insert Chart button on the Standard toolbar.
   - To create a graph on a new slide, click the Insert New Slide button on the Standard toolbar, click the Chart AutoLayout, click OK, and then double-click the chart placeholder to add the chart and datasheet.
2. Replace the sample data in the datasheet with your own data.
3. Edit and format the data in the datasheet as appropriate.
4. Click the Close button on the datasheet to close it and view the chart.
5. Click outside the chart to exit Microsoft Graph.

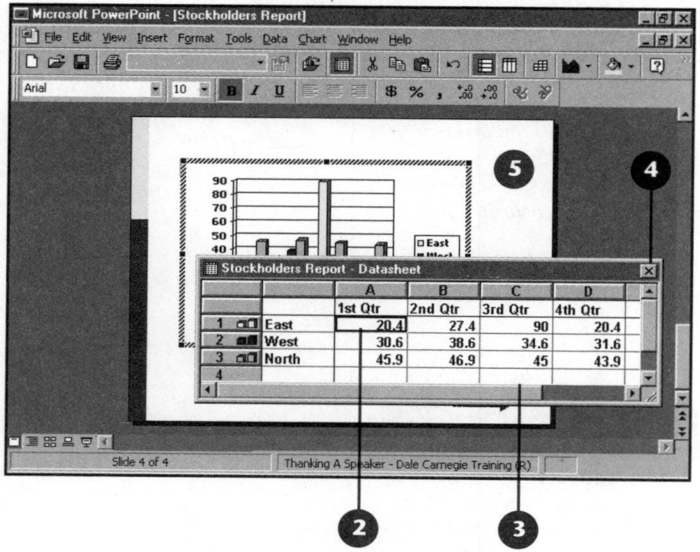

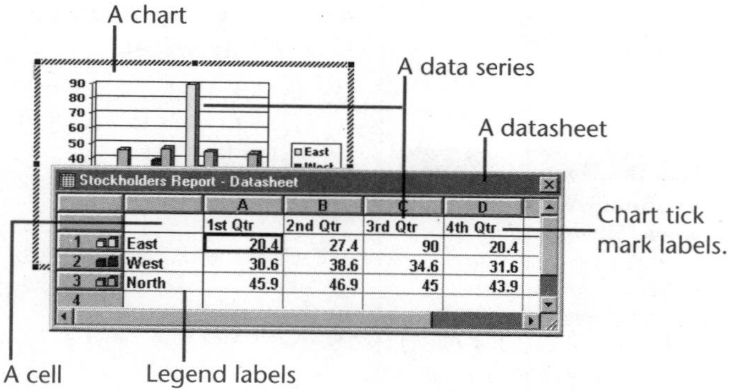

Entering Graph Data

You enter graph data in the datasheet either by typing it or by inserting it from a different source. The datasheet is designed to make data entry easy, but if your data resides elsewhere, it's better not to retype it—you might make mistakes, and you would have to update your data twice. When the data that form the bases of your graph are located elsewhere, it's usually best to link your data to the graph object.

If you type data into a cell already containing data, your entry replaces the cell contents. The cell you click is called the *active cell;* it has a thick border.

SEE ALSO

See "Viewing the Excel Window" on page 116 for more information on about active cells.

Enter Data in the Datasheet

1. If necessary, double-click Microsoft Graph, and then click the View Datasheet button on the Standard toolbar.
2. Delete the sample data by clicking the upper left heading button to select all the cells and then pressing Delete.
3. Click a cell to make it active.
4. Type the data you want entered in the cell.
5. Press Enter to move the insertion point down one row to the next cell, or press Tab to move the insertion point right to the next cell.

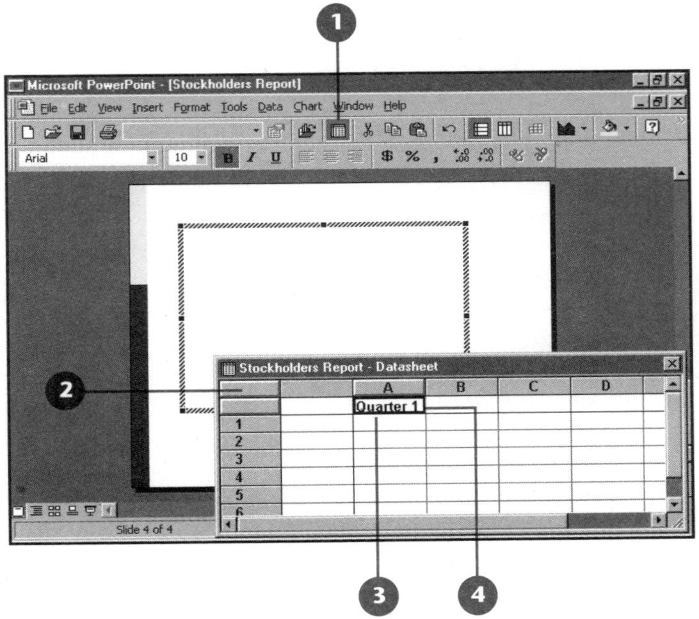

11

Selecting a Chart Type

Your chart is what your audience will see, so make sure to take advantage of PowerPoint's chart formatting options. You start by choosing the chart type you want. There are 18 chart types, available in 2-D and 3-D formats, and for each chart type you can choose from a variety of formats. If you want to format your chart beyond the provided formats, you can customize any chart object to your own specifications and can then save those settings so that you can apply that chart formatting to any chart you create.

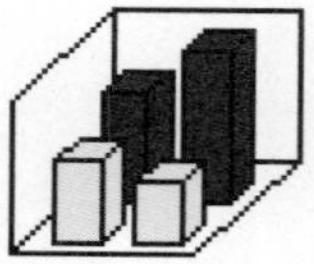

Select a Chart Type

1. If necessary, close the datasheet to view the chart.
2. Click the Chart Type drop-down arrow on the Standard toolbar.
3. Click the button corresponding to the chart type you want.

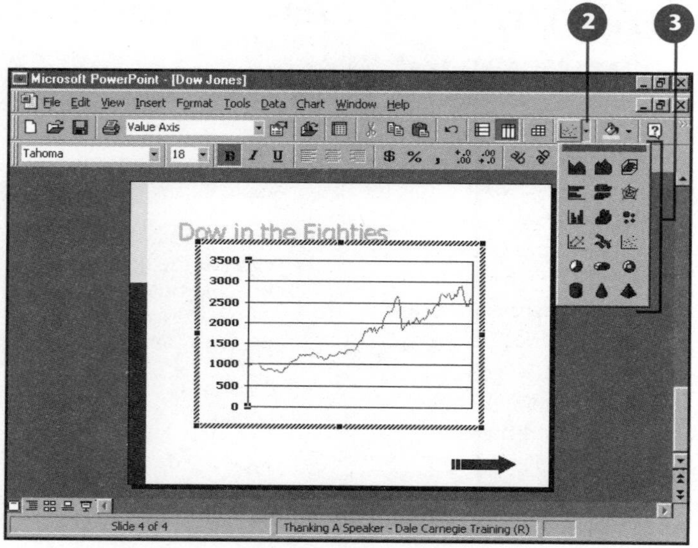

Apply a Standard Chart Type

1. Click the Chart menu, and then click Chart Type.
2. Click the Standard Types tab.
3. Click the chart type you want.
4. Click the chart sub-type you want. *Sub-types* are variations on the chart type.
5. Click OK.

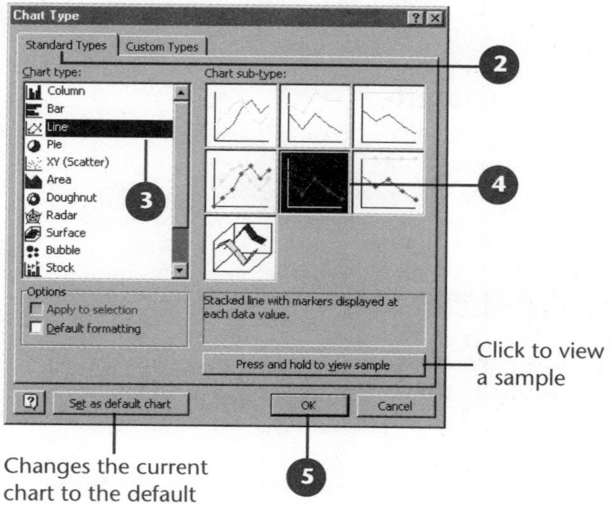

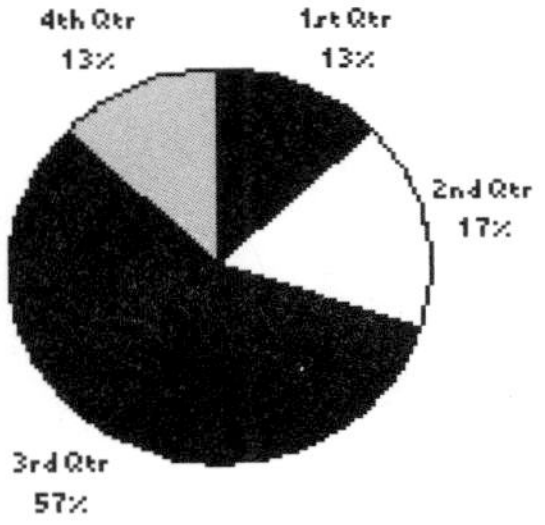

"I put a lot of work into creating this chart—how can I save the formatting to apply to other charts?"

Apply a Custom Chart Type

1. Click the Chart menu, and then click Chart Type.
2. Click the Custom Types tab.
3. Click the Built-In option button.
4. Click the chart type you want.
5. Click OK.

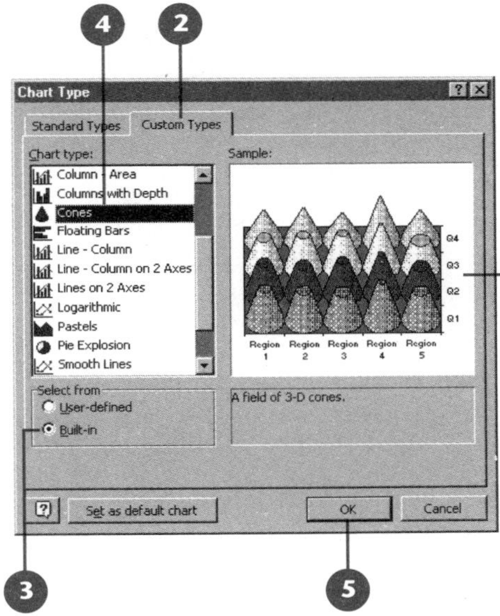

Create a Custom Chart Type

1. Click the Chart menu, and then click Chart Type.
2. Click the Custom Types tab.
3. Click the User-Defined option button.
4. Click Add.
5. Type a name and description for the chart.
6. Click OK twice.

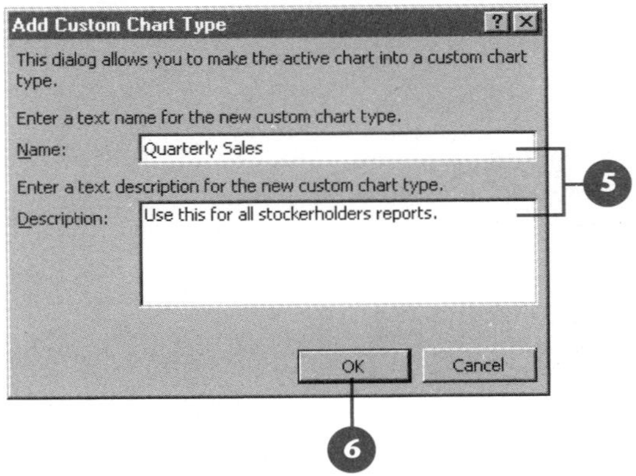

Formatting Chart Objects

Chart objects are the individual elements that make up a chart, such as an axis, the legend, or a data series. The *plot area* is the bordered area where the data are plotted. The *chart area* is the area between the plot area and the Microsoft Graph object selection box. As with any Microsoft utility, Graph treats all these elements as objects, which you can format and modify.

> **TIP**
>
> **Use the mouse button to select a chart quickly.** *You can simply click a chart object to select it, but this can by tricky if you aren't using a zoomed view since the chart objects are often quite small.*

Select a Chart Object

1. Click the Chart Objects drop-down arrow on the Standard toolbar.
2. Click the chart object you want to select.

   When a chart object is selected, selection handles appear.

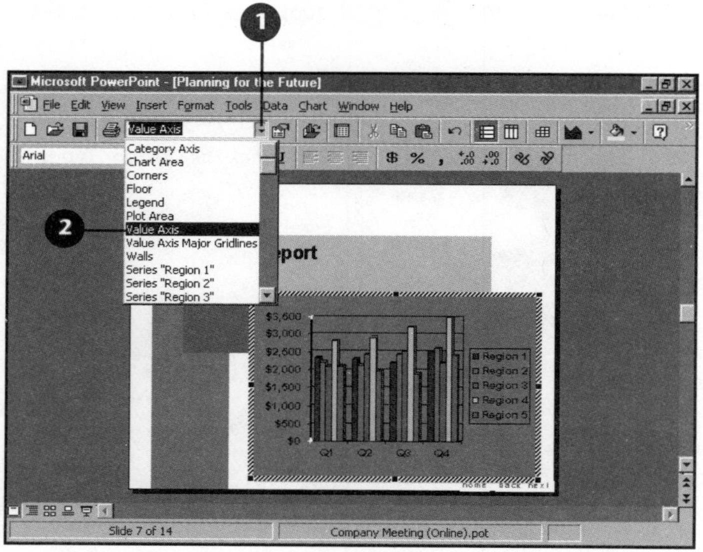

Format a Chart Object

1. Right-click the chart object you want to format, such as an axis or legend or data series.
2. Click the Format command that appears. For an axis, for example, the command is Format Axis.
3. Click the appropriate tab(s), and select the options you want to apply.
4. Click OK.

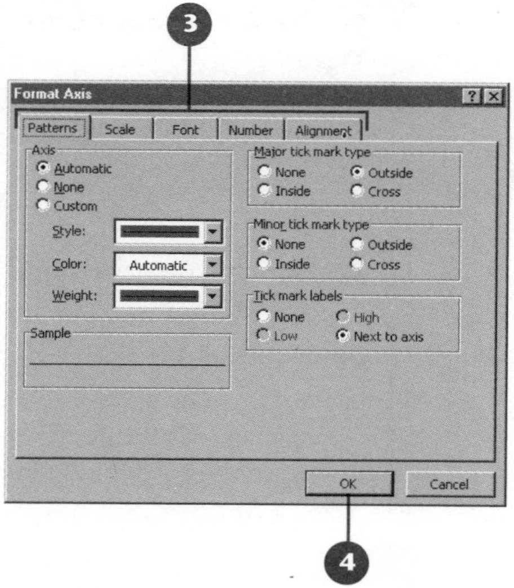

TRY THIS

Change the angle of an axis. *Right-click the axis, click Format Axis, click the Alignment tab, and then select a rotation.*

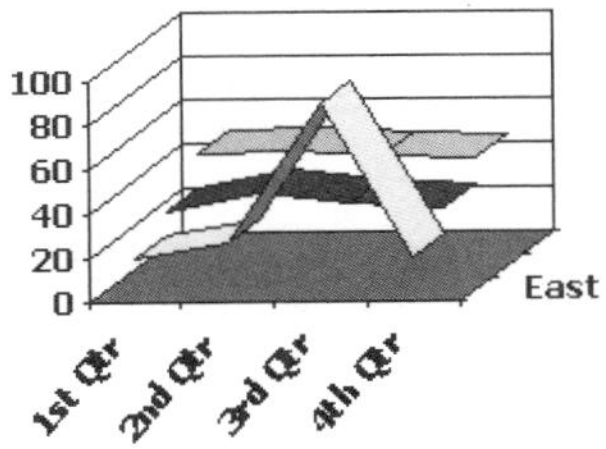

Customize a Chart

1. Click the Chart menu, and then click Chart Options.
2. Click the tab corresponding to the chart object you want to customize.
3. Make the necessary changes.
4. Click OK.

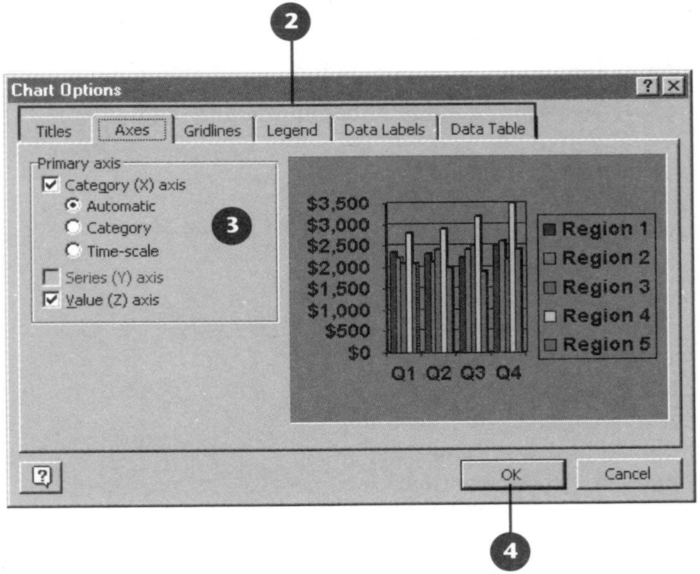

11

Creating Slide Transitions

In order to give your presentation more visual interest, you can add transitions between slides. For example, you can create a "fading out" effect so that the old slide fades out and is replaced by the new slide, or you can have one slide appear to "push" another slide out of the way. When you add a transition effect to a slide, the effect takes place between the previous slide and the selected slide. You can also add sound effects to your transitions, though you need a sound card and speakers to play these sounds.

Specify a Transition

1. View your presentation in Slide Sorter view.
2. Click the slide to which you want to add a transition effect.
3. Click the Slide Transition Effects drop-down arrow.
4. Click the transition effect you want.

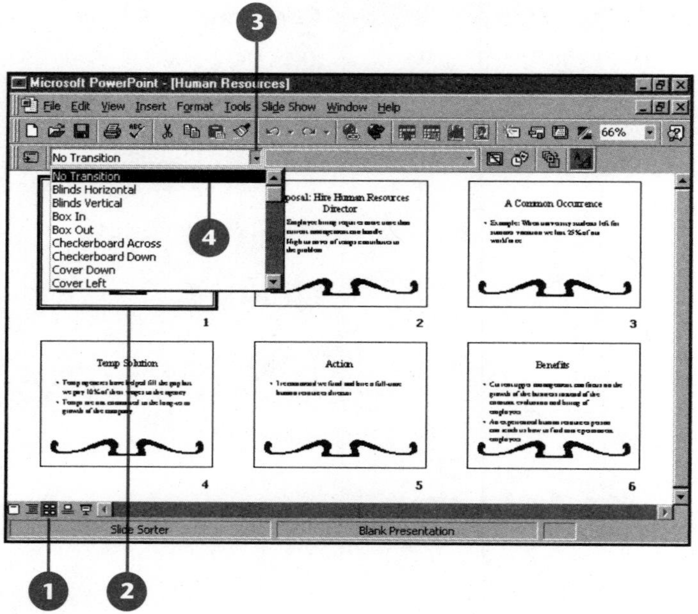

Apply a Transition to All Slides in a Presentation

1. Click the Slide Show menu, and then click Slide Transition.
2. Click the Effect drop-down arrow.
3. Click the transition you want.
4. Click Apply To All.

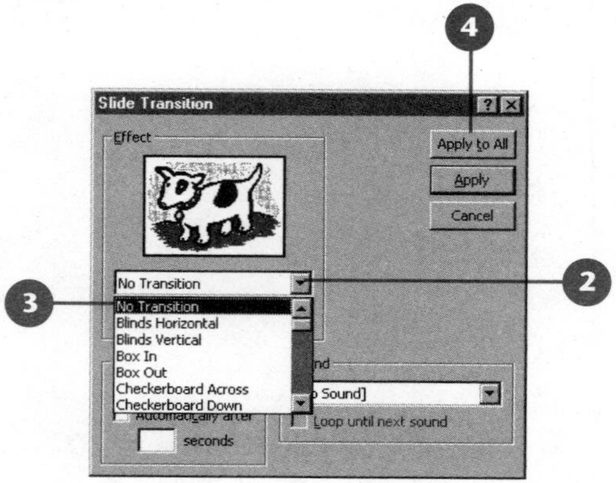

TIP

View a transition in Slide Sorter view. *In Slide Sorter view, click a slide's transition icon to view the transition's appearance.*

Set Transition Effect Speeds

1. In Slide or Slide Sorter view, click or display the slide whose transition effect you want to edit.
2. Click the Slide Show menu, and then click Slide Transition.
3. Click the Slow, Medium, or Fast option button in the Slide Transition dialog box.
4. Click Apply.

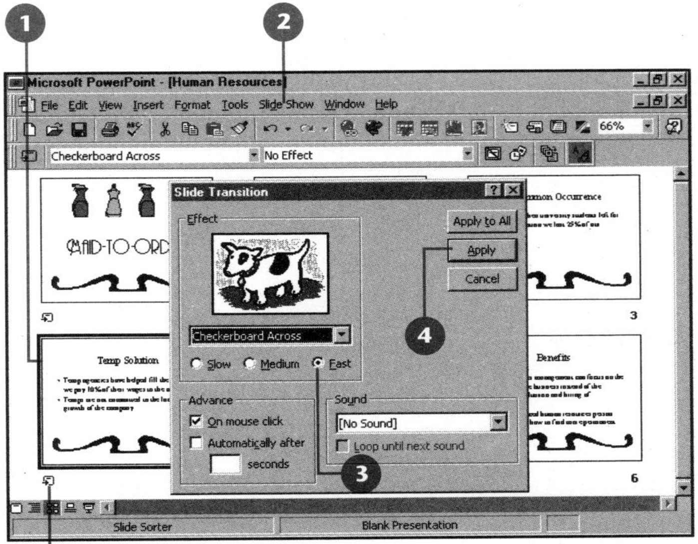

Icon indicates slide has a transition.

TRY THIS

Record your own sounds and use them as slide transitions. *If you have a microphone, use the Sound Recorder accessory that comes with Windows to record and save a sound. In the Slide Transition dialog box, click the Sound drop-down arrow, click Other Sound, locate and select the sound you created in the Add Sound dialog box, and then click OK.*

Add Sound to a Transition

1. In Slide or Slide Sorter view, click or display the slide for which you want to add a transition sound.
2. Click the Slide Show menu, and then click Slide Transition.
3. Click the Sound drop-down arrow, and then click the sound you want.
4. Click Apply.

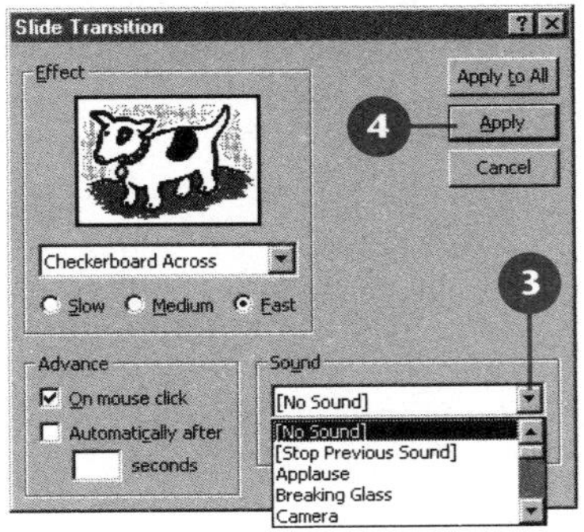

11

Adding Animation

You can use animation to introduce objects onto a slide one at a time or with special animation effects. For example, a bulleted list can appear one bulleted item at a time, or a picture or chart can fade gradually into the slide's foreground. PowerPoint supports many different kinds of animations. Some of these are called *preset animations* and are effects that PowerPoint has designed for you. Many of the preset animations contain sounds. You can also design your own *customized animations*, including your own special effects and sound elements.

Use Preset Animation

1. Select the object you want to animate.
2. Click the Slide Show menu, and then point to Preset Animation.
3. Click the animation you want.

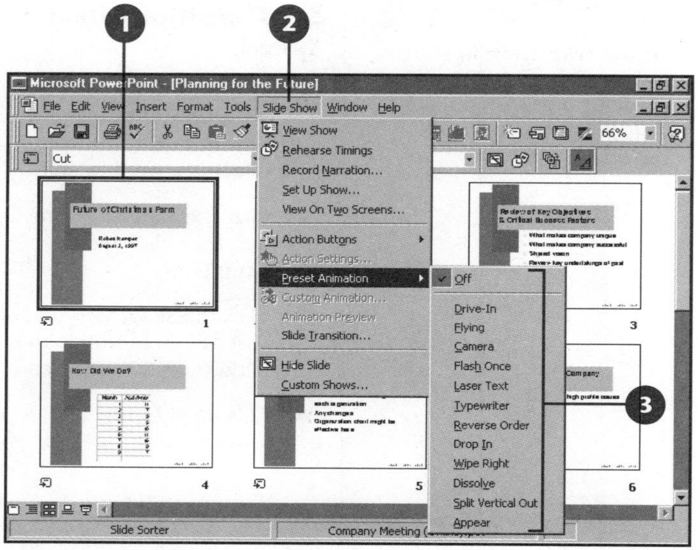

Preview an Animation

1. In Slide view, display the slide containing the animation you want to preview.
2. Click the Slide Show menu, and then click Animation Preview.

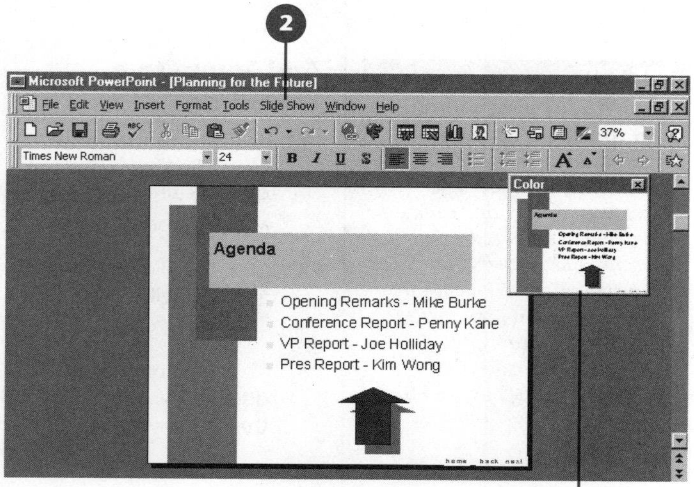

Click the window to play the animation

"How can I animate an object on my slide?"

Apply a Customized Animation

1. In Slide view, right-click the object to which you want to apply a customized animation.
2. Click Custom Animation.
3. On the Effects tab, click the Entry Animation And Sound drop-down arrow.
4. Click the effect you want.
5. Click Preview.
6. Click OK.

List of custom animations

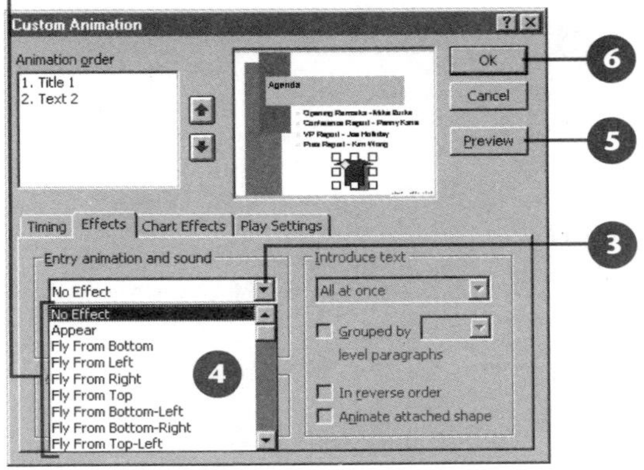

TIP

You can use a sound effect from one of your own sound files. *Click Other Sound at the bottom of the sound list, and then select the sound you want.*

Add Sound to an Animation

1. Right-click the object in the Slide View window, and then click Custom Animation.
2. Choose an effect from the list of animation effects.
3. Click the Entry Animation And Sound drop-down arrow.
4. Click the sound effect you want.
5. Click Preview to preview the animation and sound effect.
6. Click OK.

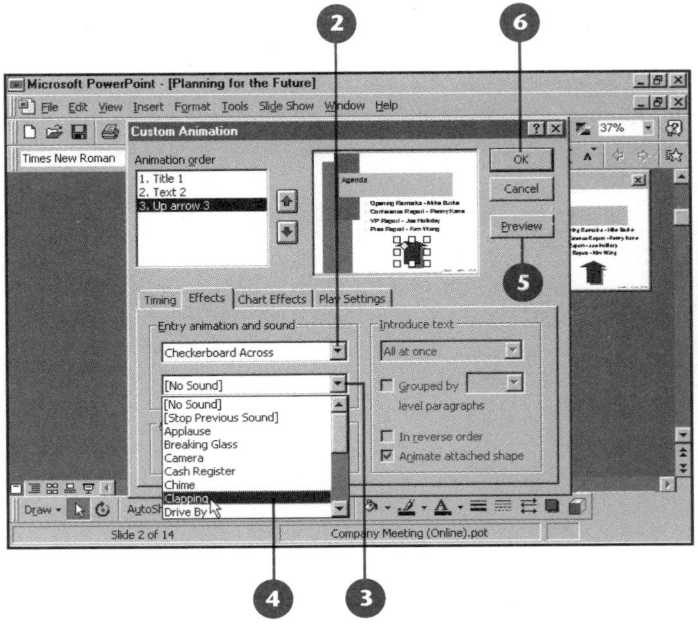

Using Specialized Animations

You can apply animations to your objects in different ways. For example, for a text object, you can introduce the text on your slide all at once or by word or letter. Similarly, you can introduce bulleted lists one bullet item at a time and apply different effects to older items, such as graying the items out, as they are replaced by new ones. You can animate charts by introducing chart series or chart categories one at a time.

Animate Text

1. Right-click the selected text object, and then click Custom Animation.
2. Choose an effect from the list of animation effects.
3. Click the Introduce Text drop-down arrow, and click All At Once, By Word, or By Letter.
4. Click Preview.
5. Click OK.

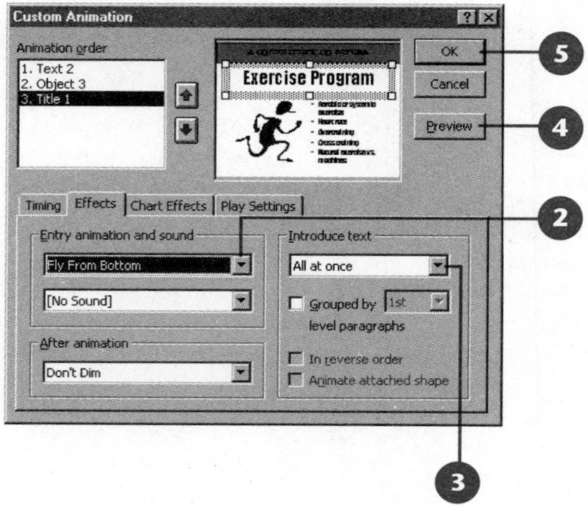

Animate Bulleted Lists

1. Right-click the bulleted text, and then click Custom Animation.
2. Choose an effect from the list of animation effects.
3. If necessary, check the Grouped By check box.
4. Select at what level (1st, 2nd, 3rd and so forth) bulleted text will be animated.
5. Click Preview.
6. Click OK.

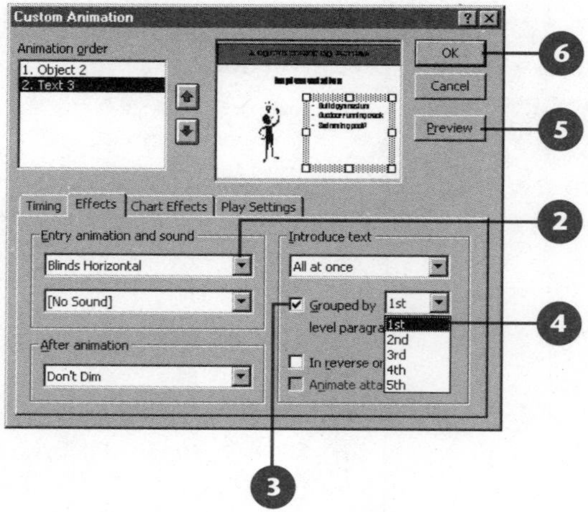

TIP

You can make text appear in reverse order. *To make the text appear in reverse order, such as from the last bulleted list item to the first, click the In Reverse Order check box to select it.*

Dim Text After It Is Animated

1. Right-click the text, and then click Custom Animation.
2. Choose an effect from the list of animation effects.
3. Click the After Animation drop-down arrow.
4. Click the option you want.
5. Click Preview.
6. Click OK.

Click to hide text as new objects enter the slide.

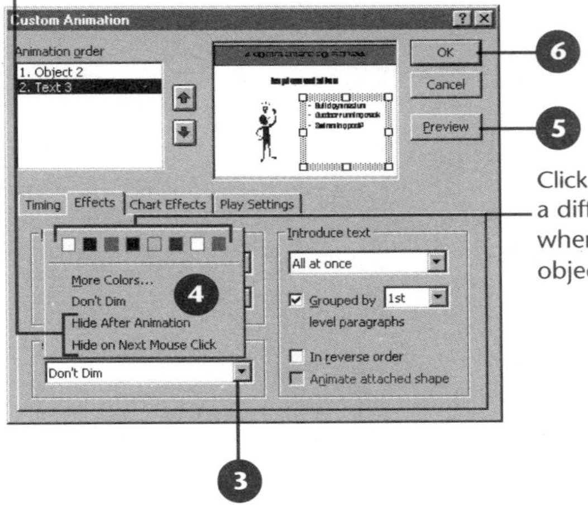

Click to give the text a different color when the next object is animated.

Chart Animation Options

1. In Slide view, right-click the chart, and then click Custom Animation.
2. On the Chart Effects tab, click the Introduce Chart Elements drop-down arrow.
3. Click the order in which chart elements should be introduced.
4. Click Preview.
5. Click OK.

"How can I make the bars on my bar chart appear one at a time with a neat animation effect?"

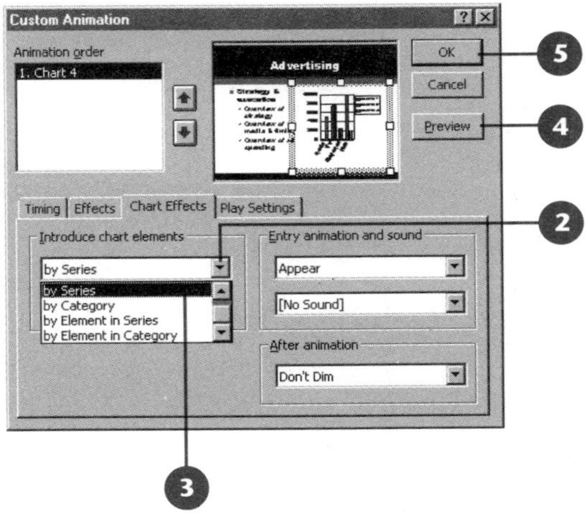

11

Adding Action Buttons

When you create a self-running presentation to be used at a kiosk, you might want a user to be able to move easily to specific slides or to a different presentation altogether. To give an audience this capability, you insert *action buttons*, which a user can click to jump to a different slide or different presentation. Clicking an action button activates a *hyperlink*, a connection between two locations in the same document or in different documents.

SEE ALSO

See "Using and Removing Hyperlinks" on page 48 for more information on about hyperlinks.

Insert a Forward or Backward Action Button

1. Click the Slide Show menu.
2. Point to Action Buttons, and then choose the action button you want.
3. Drag on the slide, and then release the mouse button when the action button is the size you want.
4. If necessary, fill out the Action Settings dialog box, and then click OK

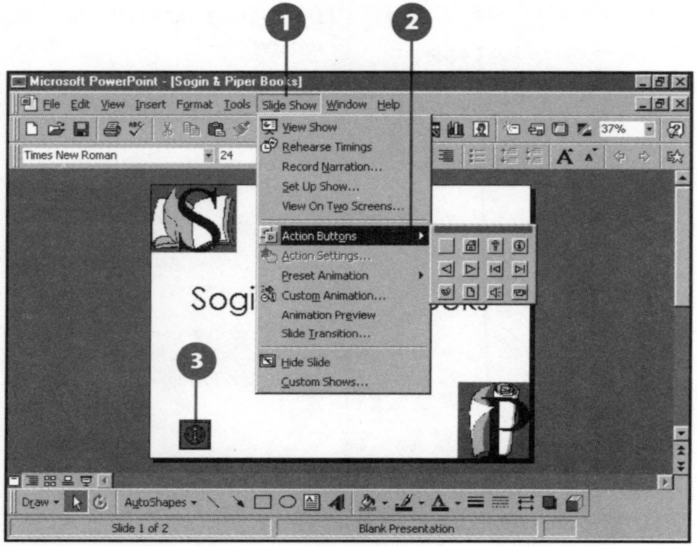

Test an Action Button

1. Click the Slide Show View button.
2. Display the slide containing your action button.
3. Click the action button.

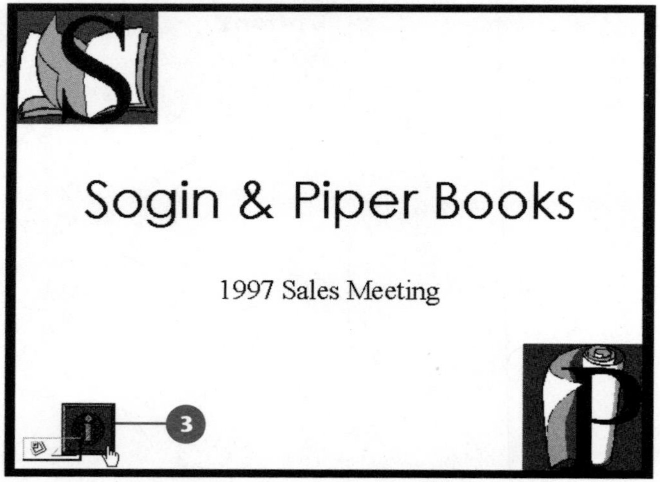

TIP

Use the Return action button to jump back to your last slide. *If you want your audience to be able to return to the slide they were previously viewing, regardless of its location in the presentation, insert the Return action button.*

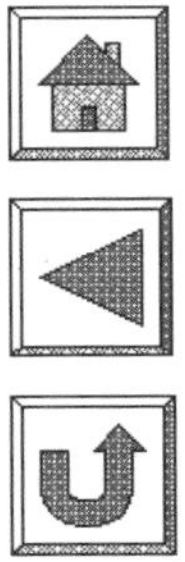

TIP

Create a square action button. *Press Shift as you drag to create a square action button.*

Create an Action Button to Go to a Specific Slide

1. Click the Slide Show menu, and then point to Action Buttons.
2. Click the Custom action button.
3. Drag to insert the action button on the slide.
4. Click the Hyperlink To option button, click the drop-down button, and then click Slide from the list of hyperlink destinations.
5. Select the slide you want the action button to jump you to, and then click OK twice.
6. Right-click the action button, and then click Add Text.
7. Type the name of the slide the action button points to.
8. Click outside the action button to deselect it.
9. Run the slide show and test the action button.

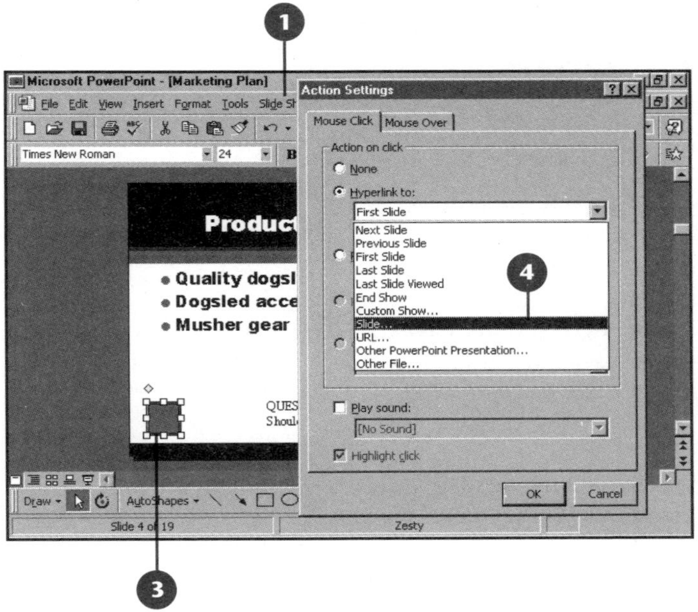

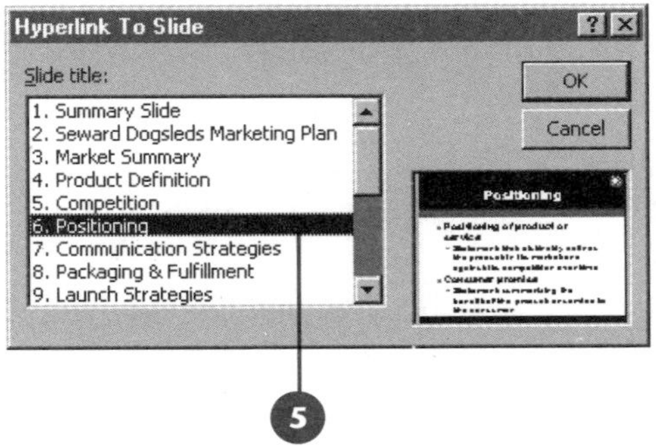

11

Creating a Custom Slide Show

If you plan to show a slide show to more than one audience, or you use a show regularly for different audiences, you don't have to create a separate slide show for each audience. Instead, you can create a *custom slide show* that allows you to specify which slides from the presentation you will use and the order in which they will appear.

Create a Custom Slide Show

1. Click the Slide Show menu, and then click Custom Shows.
2. Click the New button.
3. Type a name for the show in the Slide Show Name box.
4. Double-click the slides you want to include in the show in the order you want to present them.
5. Click OK.
6. Click Close.

List of custom slide shows for this presentation.

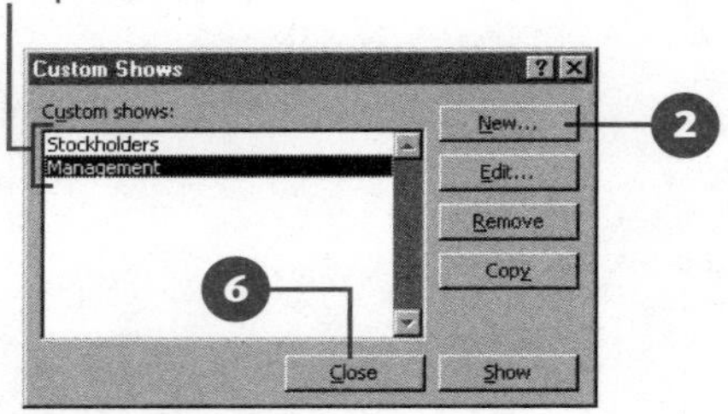

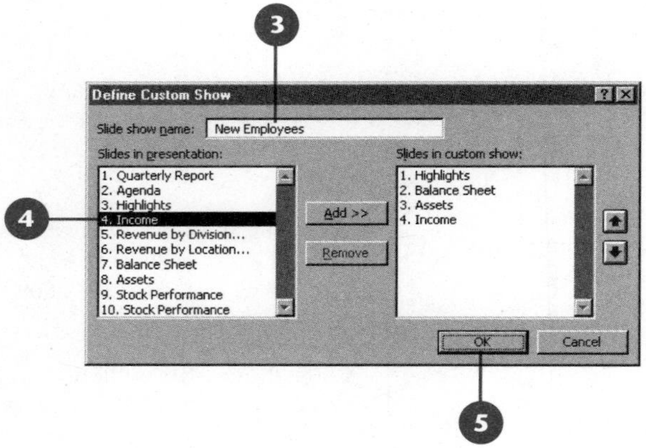

TIP

Use the Set Up Show command on the Slide Show menu to display a custom slide show. *In the Set Up Show dialog box, click the Custom option button and choose the slide show from the custom slide show list.*

Show a Custom Slide Show

1. Click the Slide Show menu, and then click Custom Shows.
2. Click the custom slide show you want to run.
3. Click Show.

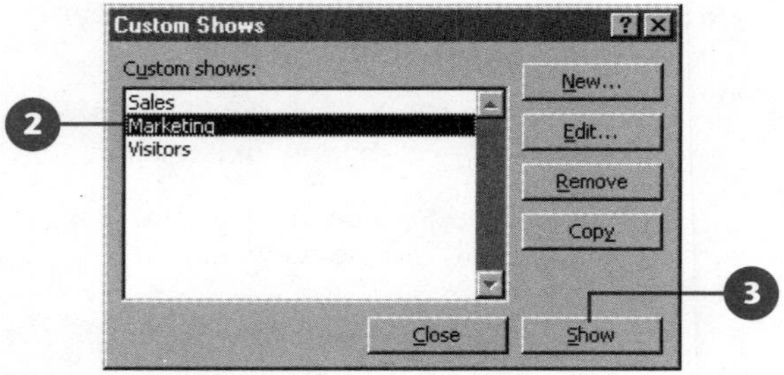

TIP

Remove a custom slide show. *To remove a custom show, click the custom slide show you want to remove in the Custom Shows dialog box, and then click the Remove button.*

TRY THIS

Create a custom slide show from an existing one. *To create a custom slide show that is similar to an existing custom show, click the existing custom show in the Custom Shows dialog box, and then click the Copy button. A new custom show is created named Copy Of <Existing Show>. Click the Edit button to edit the copy, and give the new custom slide show its own name.*

Edit a Custom Slide Show

1. Click the Slide Show menu, and then click Custom Shows.
2. Click the show you want to edit.
3. Click the Edit button.
4. In the Define Custom Show dialog box, edit the slides as necessary:
   - ◆ To remove a slide from the show, click the slide in the Slides In Custom Show list, and then click Remove.
   - ◆ To move a slide up or down in the show, click the slide in the Slides In Custom Show list, and then click the Up arrow or Down arrow button.
   - ◆ To add a slide, click the slide in the Slides In Presentation list and then click the Add button. The slide appears at the end of the Slides In Custom Show list.
5. Click OK.
6. Click Close.

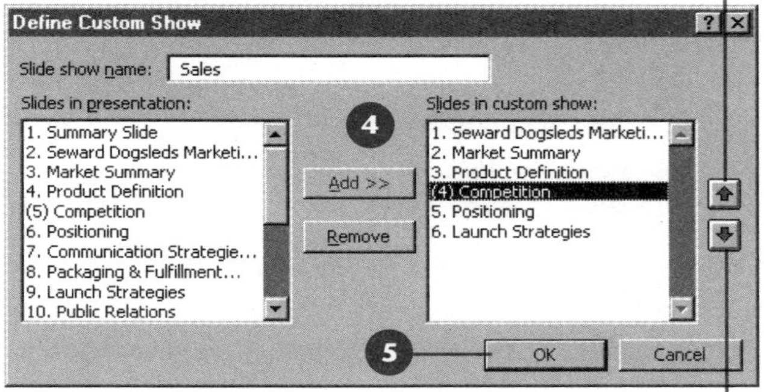

Enhancing Clip Art

Once you have inserted clip art into your presentation, you can adapt it to meet your needs. Perhaps the clip is too small to be effective, or you don't quite like the colors it uses. Like any object, you can resize or move the image. You can also control the image's colors, brightness, and contrast using the Picture toolbar. You can use these same methods with bitmapped pictures.

TIP

Show the Picture toolbar. *If the Picture toolbar does not appear when you select a piece of clip art or a picture, click View, point to Toolbars, and then click Picture.*

TIP

Restore original settings. *Click the object whose settings you want to restore, and then click the Reset Picture button on the Picture toolbar.*

Change Image Contrast

1. Click the object whose contrast you want to increase or decrease.
2. To choose the contrast you want:
   - Click the More Contrast button on the Picture toolbar to increase color intensity, resulting in less gray color.
   - Click the Less Contrast button on the Picture toolbar to decrease color intensity, resulting in more gray color.

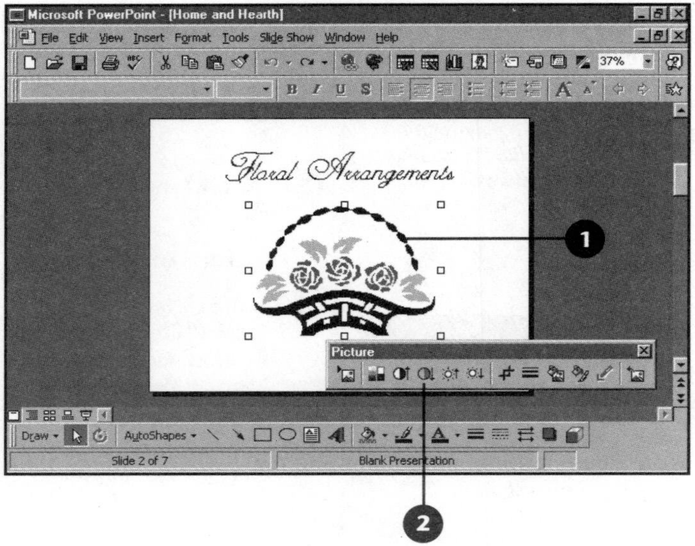

Change Image Brightness

1. Click the object whose brightness you want to increase or decrease.
2. To choose the image brightness you want:
   - Click the More Brightness button on the Picture toolbar to lighten the object colors by adding more white.
   - Click the Less Brightness button on the Picture toolbar to darken the object colors by adding more black.

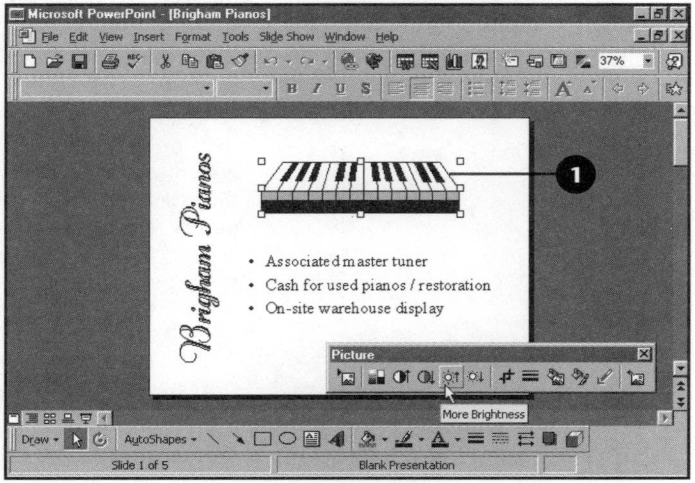

12

Working with Access 97

IN THIS SECTION

Microsoft Access 97 is a database program that allows you to:

- Store an almost limitless amount of information
- Organize information in a way that makes sense for how you work
- Retrieve information based on selection criteria you specify
- Create forms that make it easier to enter information
- Generate meaningful and insightful reports that can combine data, text, graphics, and even sound

What Is a Database?

Database is a rather technical word for a collection of information that is organized as a list. This definition might be oversimplified, but essentially, whenever you use or make a list of information—names, addresses, products, customers, or invoices—you are using a database. A database that you store on your computer, however, is much more flexible and powerful than a simple list you keep on paper, in your cardfile, or in your address book.

Understanding Access Databases

In Access, a database consists of tables, their relationship to one another (if any), reports, queries, filters, forms, and macros.

Parts of a database

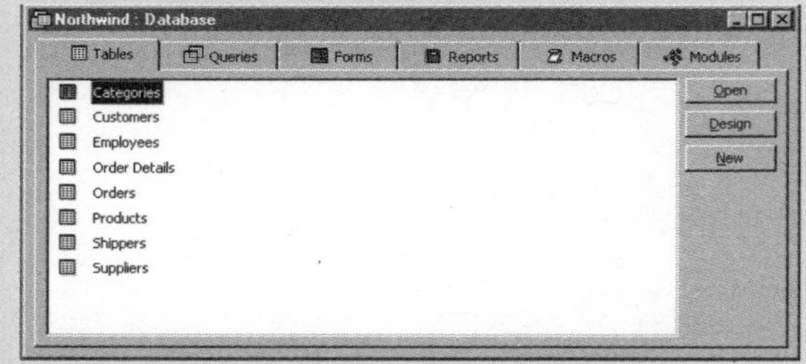

Tables are where you store information related to a specific part of your business or work. For example, the Northwind database contains a table of customer information. Another table stores purchasing information, and still another table contains product information. Tables are organized into rows and columns. Each row represents a set of information called a *record*. In the Customers table in the Northwind database, for example, each row represents a customer record, which is the information related to a specific customer. Columns represent a specific piece of information, called a *field*. For example, in the Customers table, the customer's company name is stored in the Company Name field.

In addition you can relate the tables to each other based on a field the tables have in common. By relating two tables to each other, you can work with data from both tables as if they were one larger table.

A table with rows and columns

Customers : Table

Customer ID	Company Name	Contact Name	Co
ALFKI	Alfreds Futterkiste	Maria Anders	Sales Repre
ANATR	Ana Trujillo Emparedados y helados	Ana Trujillo	Owner
ANTON	Antonio Moreno Taquería	Antonio Moreno	Owner
AROUT	Around the Horn	Thomas Hardy	Sales Repre
BERGS	Berglunds snabbköp	Christina Berglund	Order Admin
BLAUS	Blauer See Delikatessen	Hanna Moos	Sales Repre
BLONP	Blondel père et fils	Frédérique Citeaux	Marketing M
BOLID	Bólido Comidas preparadas	Martín Sommer	Owner
BONAP	Bon app'	Laurence Lebihan	Owner
BOTTM	Bottom-Dollar Markets	Elizabeth Lincoln	Accounting
BSBEV	B's Beverages	Victoria Ashworth	Sales Repre
CACTU	Cactus Comidas para llevar	Patricio Simpson	Sales Agent
CENTC	Centro comercial Moctezuma	Francisco Chang	Marketing M
CHOPS	Chop-suey Chinese	Yang Wang	Owner
COMMI	Comércio Mineiro	Pedro Afonso	Sales Assoc
CONSH	Consolidated Holdings	Elizabeth Brown	Sales Repre
DRACD	Drachenblut Delikatessen	Sven Ottlieb	Order Admin

Record: 1 of 91

To locate information in a table (or in multiple tables) you create a query. A *query* is simply a question you ask of a database to help you locate specific information. For example, if you want to know which customers placed orders in the last six months, you can create a query in which you ask Access to examine the contents of the Order Date field in the Orders table and to find all the records in which the purchase date is less than six months ago.

Queries in a database

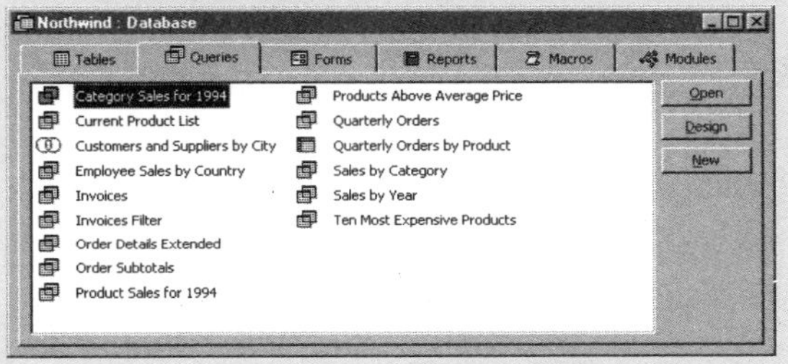

After Access has retrieved the records that match the specifications in your query, you can sort or filter the information with still more specific criteria, so that you can focus on exactly the information you need—no more or less.

To make it easier to enter information into your tables, you can create customized *forms* that direct you to enter the correct information, check it for errors, and then store the information in the proper table. A form usually displays all the fields for one record at a time, making it easier for you to focus on a particular record.

A form in Access

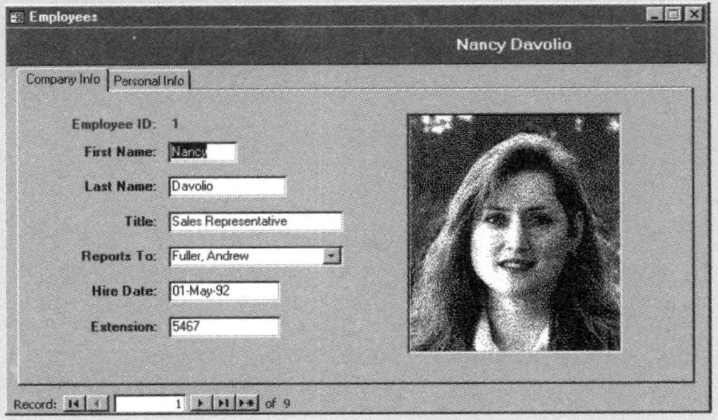

After you have retrieved and organized only the specific information you want, you can display and print this information as a *report*. In Access you can create a simple report that displays each record's information, or you can customize a report to include calculations, charts, graphics, and other features to go beyond the numbers and really emphasize the information in the report.

A report in Access

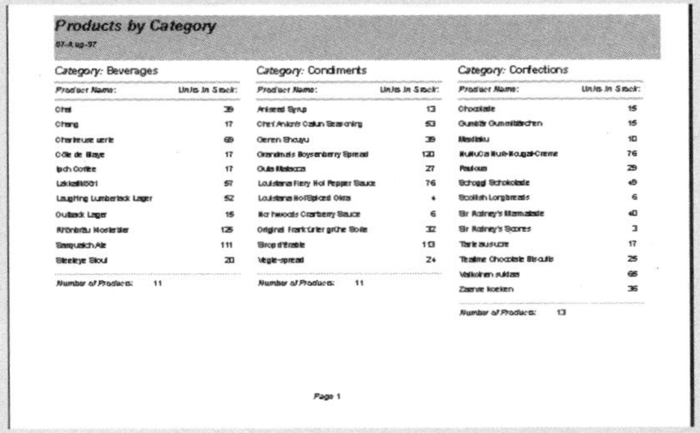

To automate a series of Access commands, you can create a *macro*. With macros, you can perform a series of commands with a click of a button.

In addition, you can automate many Access database procedures and combine them with Microsoft Visual Basic programs to create modules. *Modules* allow you to expand upon and integrate Access commands and macros with Microsoft Visual Basic, as well as other Microsoft Office 97 programs.

Viewing the Access Window

The *title bar* displays the name of the open program.

The *menu bar* contains menu items that represent groups of related commands.

The *toolbar* contains buttons that you click to carry out commands.

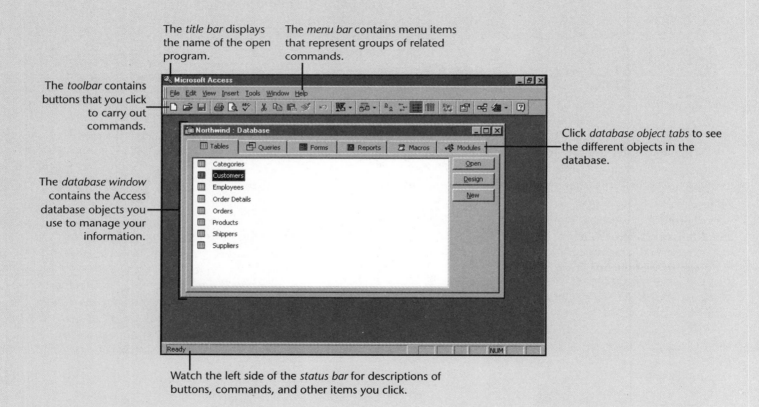

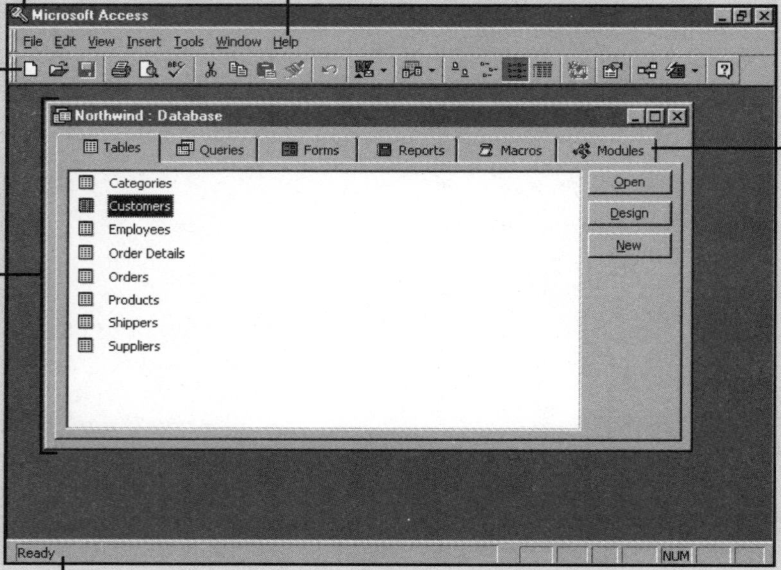

Click *database object tabs* to see the different objects in the database.

The *database window* contains the Access database objects you use to manage your information.

Watch the left side of the *status bar* for descriptions of buttons, commands, and other items you click.

Viewing Multiple Tables

When you open multiple tables at once, you can arrange the Table windows so that you can see all open tables at the same time. For example, you can use the Tile Horizontally command on the Window menu to display the Table windows one above the other or you can use the Tile Vertically command to display the windows side by side. Each Table window contains scroll bars so that you can move around in each table. When you want several tables open but prefer to see only one at a time, you can use the Cascade command. This command staggers the arrangement of Table windows, so that the active Table window remains on top of a stack of windows.

View Multiple Tables

1. Click the Window menu, and then click:
   - Tile Vertically to display Table windows side by side.
   - Tile Horizontally to display Table windows one above the other.
   - Cascade to display Table windows stacked and offset so that you can see the title bars of the other windows.
2. Click any part of a window to make it active.

Active title bar

1

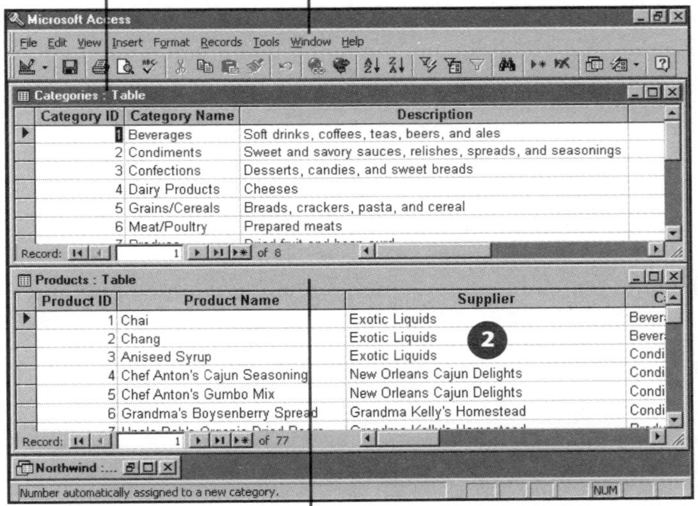

2

Inactive title bar

12

Moving to a Specific Record in a Table

When you scroll through a table in Datasheet view, you are simply viewing different parts of the table; the insertion point (cursor) stays in its original location in the first record. If you type any text, it would appear in the first record, regardless of which record is currently visible. To move the insertion point to a specific record, you must click the record (or a field in the record). If the record you want to select is not visible, you can use the navigation buttons to move to the next, previous, first, or last record. Or you can type the number of the record (if you know it) in the Specific Record box to move to that record. The Go To command also provides a fast way to move to a specific record.

Move to a Record Using the Mouse Button

- Current Record icon.

  Indicates the current record.
- Specific Record box.

  To move to a new record, select the current record number and then type the new record number.
- New Record button.

  Click to create a new, blank row at the end of the table.
- Selection bar.

  Click to the left of a record to select it.
- First Record button.

  Click to move to the first record in the table.
- Previous Record button.

  Click to move to the previous record in the table.
- Next Record button.

  Click to move to the next record in the table.
- Last Record button.

  Click to move to the last record in the table.

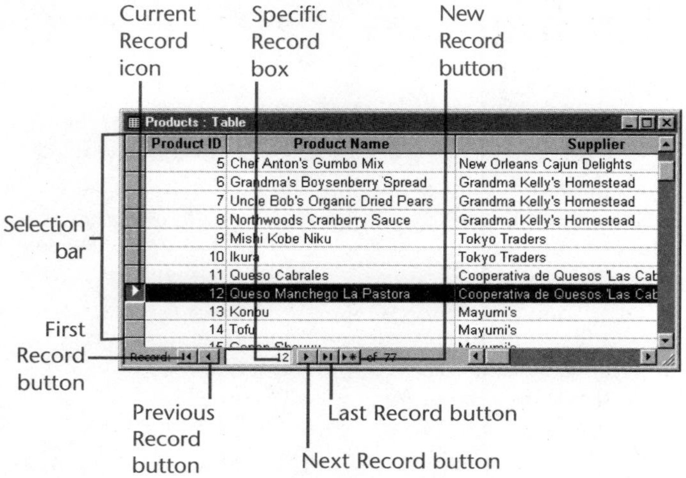

Viewing Specific Records Using a Filter

Instead of displaying all the records in a table, you can use a *filter* to display only those records that you want to see. You can display records based on a specific value in one field or on multiple values in multiple fields. You can filter by selecting the field value on which to base the filter in Datasheet view, or by using the Filter By Form feature to help you create more complex filters involving multiple field values. After you apply a filter, Access displays only those records that match your specifications. You can remove a filter to return the datasheet to its original display.

Filter a Table by Selection

1. Display the table in Datasheet view.
2. Position the insertion point anywhere in the specific field value on which you want to base the filter.
3. Click the Filter By Selection button on the Table Datasheet toolbar. Notice that the bottom of the Table window tells you the number of records matching your filter criteria. Also the notation "FLTR" in the status bar indicates that a filter is currently in effect.

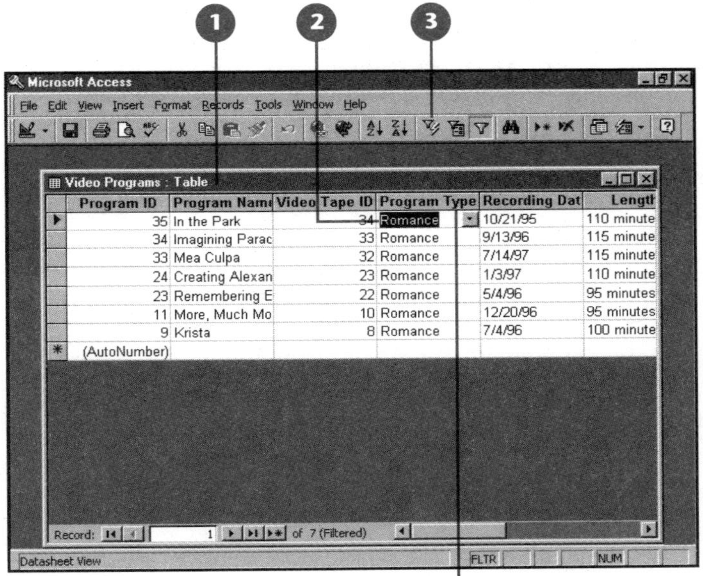

The records are filtered to show only the Romance program type.

Clear a Filter from a Table

1. Click the Apply/Remove Filter button on the Table Datasheet toolbar. Notice that the status bar removes the indication that the table is filtered.

12

Changing the Order of Records in a Table

You can change the order in which records appear in a table by *sorting* the records. You can select a field and then sort the records by the values in that field in either ascending or descending order. *Ascending* order means that records appear in alphabetical order (for text fields), from earliest to most recent (for date fields), or from smallest to largest (for numeric fields). *Descending* order means that records appear in reverse alphabetical order (for text fields), from most recent to earliest (for date fields), and from largest to smallest (for numeric fields). You can also change the order of records based on multiple fields.

Arrange Records in Ascending Order Based on One Field

1. Display the table in Datasheet view.
2. Position the insertion point anywhere in the field that contains the values by which you want to sort the records.
3. Click the Sort Ascending button on the Table Datasheet toolbar.

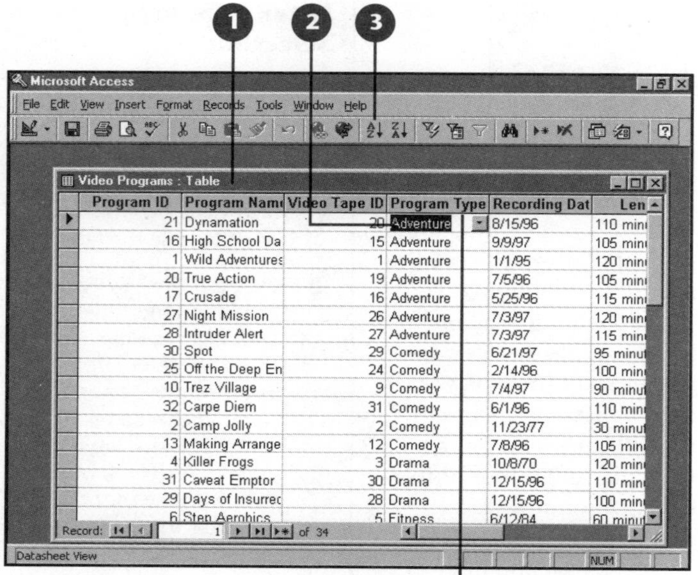

Records sorted by the Program Type field in ascending (alphabetical) order

TIP

You can specify a sort order when designing a table. *Changing the order of records displayed in a table is not the same as specifying the sort order when you first design the table. Use the Sort feature when designing a table to display records in the order that you are likely to use most often, and then use the Sort Ascending and Sort Descending buttons to handle the exceptions when you display the table in Datasheet view.*

Arrange Records in Descending Order Based on One Field

1. Display the table in Datasheet view.
2. Position the insertion point anywhere in the field that contains the values by which you want to sort the records.
3. Click the Sort Descending button on the Table Datasheet toolbar.

Records sorted by the Program Type field in descending (reverse alphabetical) order

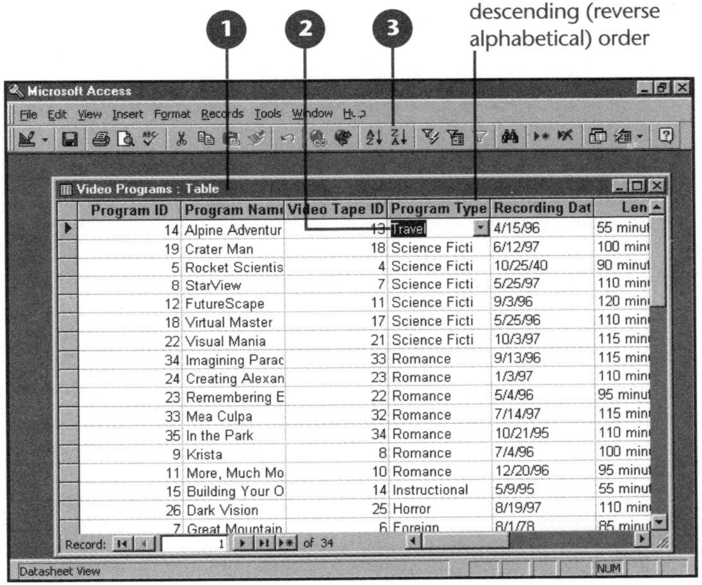

12

Understanding Different Types of Queries

There are several different types of queries you can use: select queries, crosstab queries, action queries, and parameter queries.

- A *select query* retrieves and displays records in the Table window in Datasheet view.
- A *crosstab query* displays summarized values (sums, counts, and averages) from one field in a table and groups them by one set of fields listed down the left side of the datasheet and another set of fields listed across the top of the datasheet.
- An *action query* performs operations on the records that match your criteria. There are four kinds of action queries: *delete queries* delete matching records from a table; *update queries* make changes to matching records in a table; *append queries* add new records to the end of a table (records not matching your criteria are added to the table); and *make-table* queries create new tables based on matching records.
- A *parameter query* allows you to prompt for a single piece of information to use as selection criteria in the query. For example, instead of creating separate queries to retrieve customer information for each state in which you do business, you could create a parameter query that prompts you to enter the name of a state and then continues to retrieve those specific records from that state.

Creating Queries in Access

As with most objects you create in a database, you have several ways to create a query. You can create a query from scratch or use a wizard to guide you through the process of creating a query. With the Query Wizard, Access helps you create a simple query to retrieve the records you want. All queries you create and save are listed on the Queries tab in the Database window. You can then double-click a query to run it and display the results. When you run a select query, the query results will show only the selected fields for each record in the table that matches your selection criteria. Of course, once you have completed a query, you can further customize it in Design view. As always, you can begin creating your query in Design view without using the wizard at all.

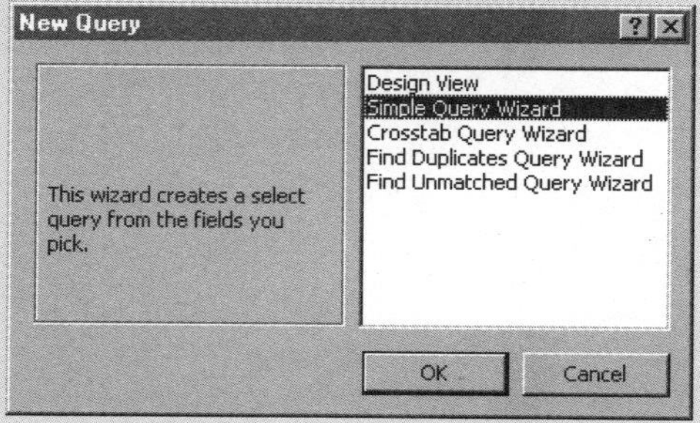

Creating a Query from Scratch

Although a wizard can be a big help when you are first learning to create a query, you do not need to use the wizard. If you prefer, you can create a query without the help of a wizard. Instead of answering questions in a series of dialog boxes, you can start working in Design view right away.

SEE ALSO

See "Creating a Query Using the Query Wizard" on page 210 for another way to create a query.

Create a Query from Scratch

1. In the Database window, click the Queries tab, and then click New.
2. In the New Query dialog box, click Design View.
3. Select the table or query containing the records you want to retrieve.
4. Click Add.
5. Repeat steps 3 and 4 for each table or query you want to use.
6. Click Close to display the query in Design view.
7. In the field list at the top part of the Design view window, double-click each field you want to include in the query.
8. In the Design grid, enter the contents of the field you want to search for in the Criteria box.
9. Click the Sort drop-down arrow to specify a sort order for records when they appear in the query results.

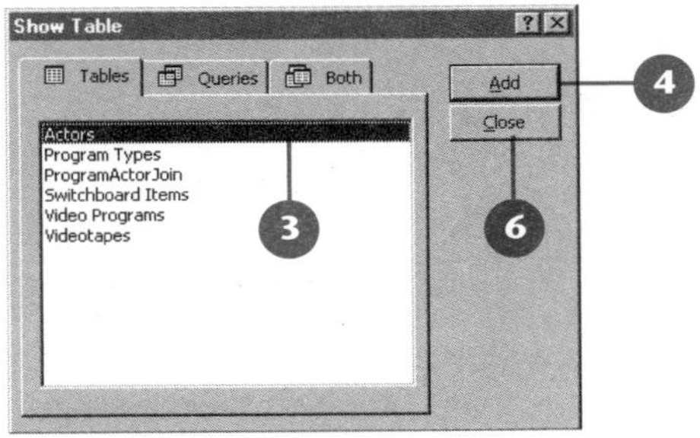

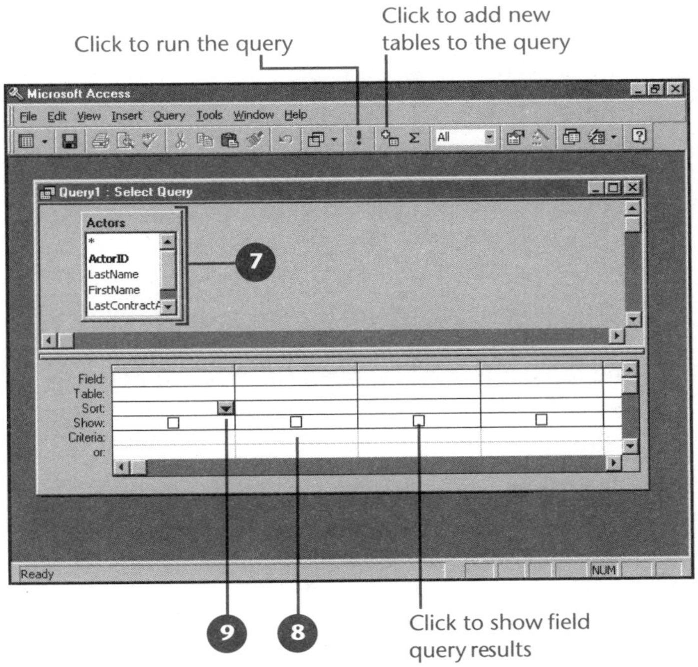

Creating a Query Using the Query Wizard

When you create a query, you can choose from several different kinds of queries. By choosing the Query Wizard, you can specify the records you want to retrieve and specify other kinds of queries you want to create. The Query Wizard guides you through each step. All you do is answer a series of questions about your query, and Access creates a query with your data.

"How do I create a query quickly and easily?"

Create a Query Using the Query Wizard

1. On the Queries tab in the Database window, click the New button, and then click the wizard that corresponds to the kind of query you want to create.
2. Click the Tables/Queries drop-down arrow, and select a table with fields to include in the query.
3. Specify the fields that you want included in the query.
4. Click Next to continue.
5. If you have selected numeric or date fields in step 3, you can indicate whether you want to see detail or summary information. If you choose Summary, click Summary Options to specify the calculation for each field. Select averages, counts, and minimum and maximum values, and then click OK.
6. Click Next to continue.

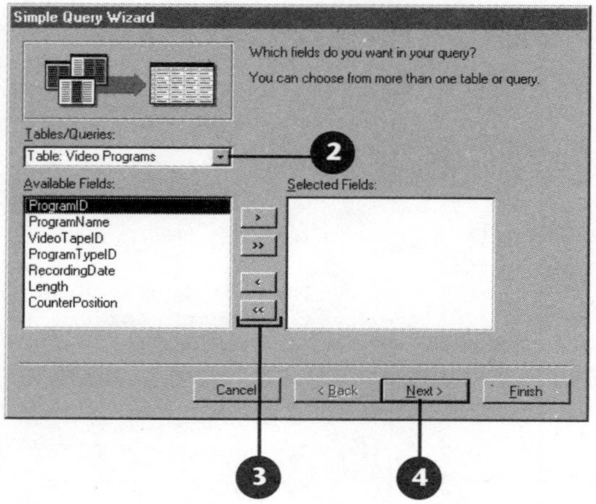

Click to specify the summary calculations.

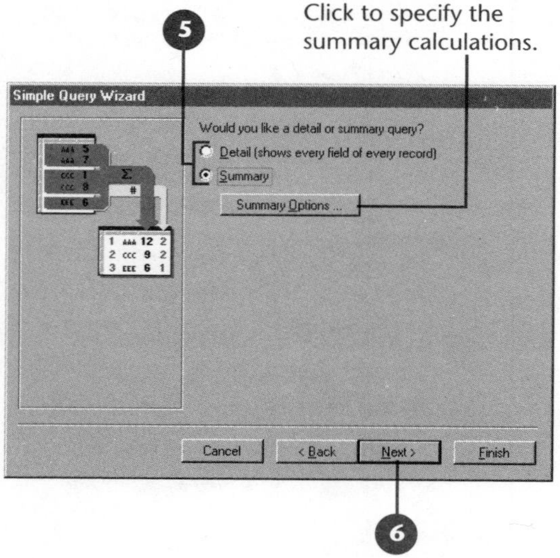

TIP

Use Query options to create a query. *You can also begin creating a query by clicking the Query option on the New Object drop-down list and clicking a query wizard you want to use.*

TIP

Include a field from another source. *To do this, click the Tables/Queries drop-down arrow if you want to include a field from another source.*

SEE ALSO

See "Understanding Different Types of Queries" on page 208 for more information on queries you can create.

7. In the final wizard dialog box, type the name of the query.
8. Click an option to preview the query or display it in Design view.
9. Click Finish.

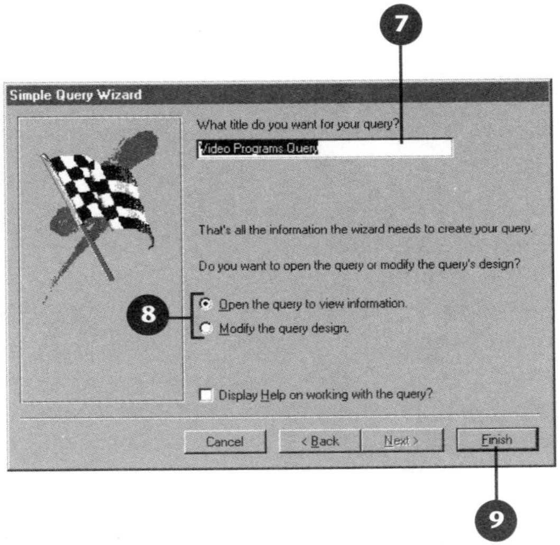

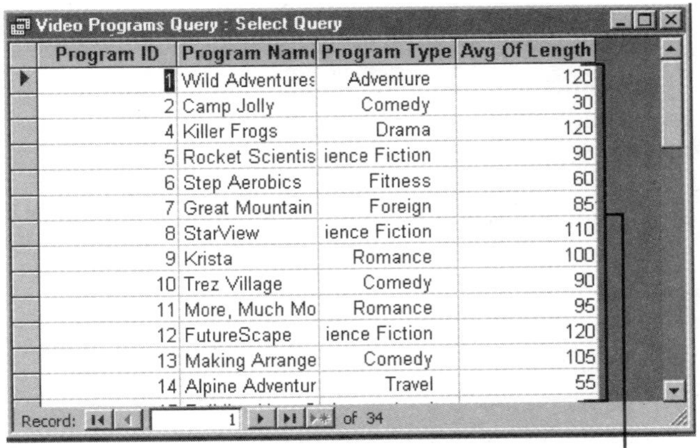

Records retrieved in a query.

12

Retrieving Only the Records You Want

For each field you include in a query, you can specify criteria that a record must match to be selected when you run the query. For example, you can create a query to retrieve only those records for customers located in a particular city. To view records for customers located in either New York City *or* Boston, you can expand your search with an *OR condition*. You can also narrow your search with an *AND condition*. For example, you could view the records for customers with offices in both New York City *and* Boston; a customer must have offices in both cities to be included in the query results. You can also create a *parameter query* so that the query prompts you to provide specific criteria each time you run the query.

Specify Criteria in a Query

1. Display the query in Design view.
2. Click the Criteria box for the field for which you want to define a selection criterion.
3. Type the first criterion you want for the query.
4. Click the Run button on the Query Design toolbar.

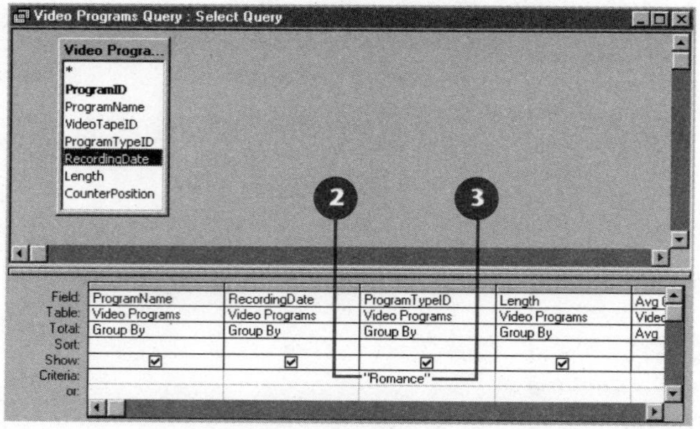

Expand Criteria with an OR Condition

1. Display the query in Design view.
2. In the Criteria row, type the first criteria you want for the query.
3. For each additional OR criteria, enter the criteria in a separate "or" row for the field.
4. Click the Run button on the Query Design toolbar.

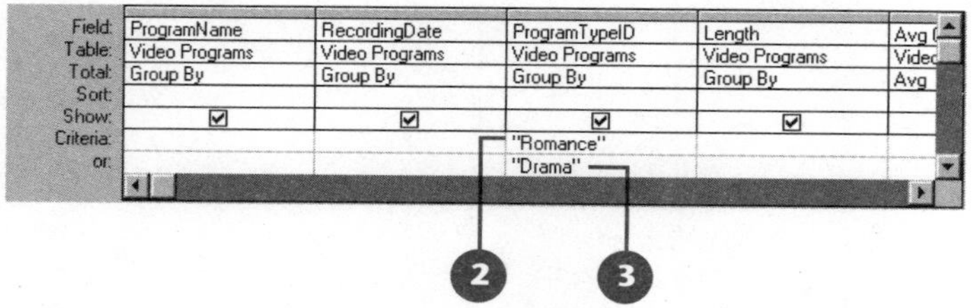

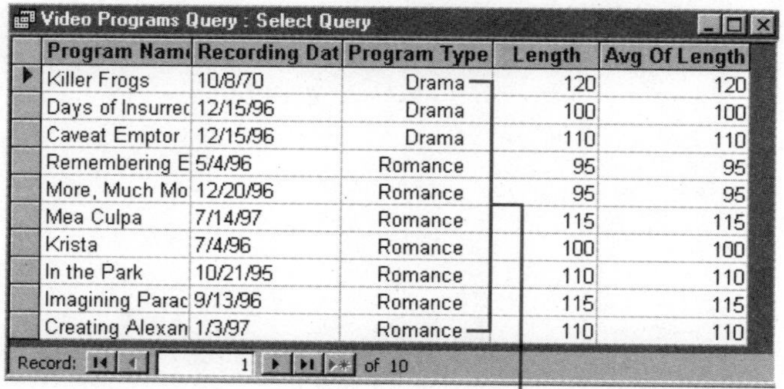

The program type field can contain *either* Drama or Romance to be included in the query results.

TIP

Specify text to search for in your selection criteria. *When the criterion is a text value, it must be enclosed in quotation marks. Access will insert the quotation marks for you after you type the value and press Tab or Enter.*

Restrict Criteria with an AND Condition

1. Display the query in Design view.
2. In the Criteria row, enter the first criteria you want for the query.
3. In the same Criteria row, enter the additional AND criterion for another field in the query.
4. Click the Run button on the Query Design toolbar.

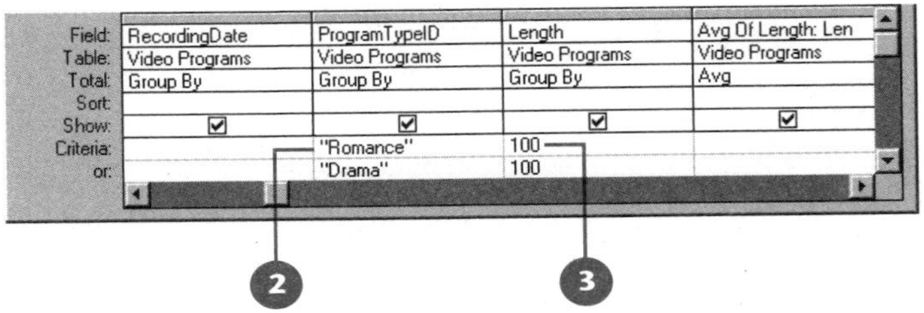

The record must contain both values to be included in the query results.

TIP

You can sort the retrieved records. *In Datasheet view, you can select a field and then click the Sort Ascending or Sort Descending button on the Table Datasheet toolbar to sort the query results in either ascending or descending order by the values in the selected field.*

Create a Parameter Query to Prompt You for Criteria

1. Display the query in Design view.
2. Click the Criteria box for the field for which you want to be prompted to enter a value.
3. Type the text of your prompt surrounded by square brackets.
4. Run the query.
5. Enter criteria information.
6. Click OK.

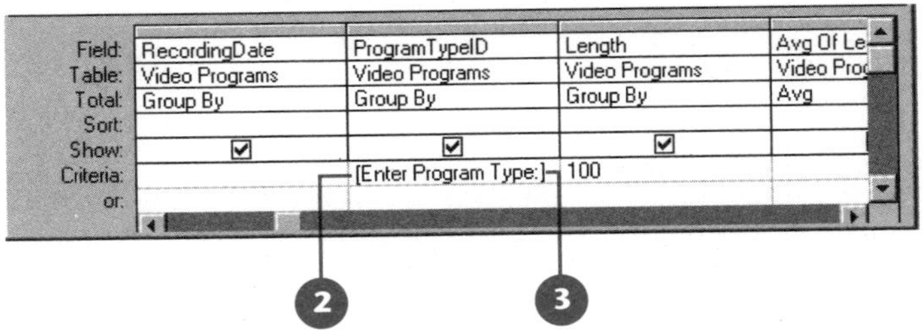

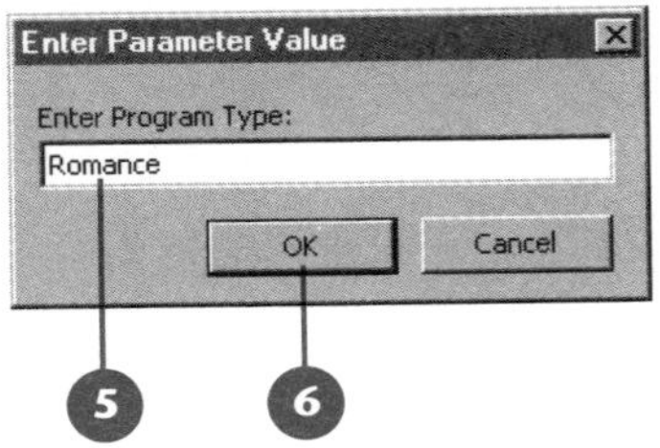

12

Saving a Customized Filter

If you enter a series of criteria in a filter that you expect you might need again, or if you create a rather complex filter, consider saving the criteria as a query. In many ways, a query is simply a filter you have decided to save. However, queries also have other unique capabilities that extend beyond what you can accomplish in a filter. For now, however, you can create a simple query by saving a filter you have already created.

TIP

You can run a filter that you saved as a query. *Click the Queries tab on the Database window, and then double-click the name of the filter that you saved as a query.*

Save a Filter as a Query

1. Display the filtered table in Datasheet view.
2. Click the Records menu, point to Filter, and then click Advanced Filter/Sort. The details of the filter appear in Design view.
3. Click the File menu, and then click Save As Query.
4. In the Query Name box, type the name you want to assign to the query. If you enter the name of an existing query, Access will ask if you want to over-write the existing query. Be sure to answer "No" if you want to retain the original query, so you can give the new query a different name.
5. Click OK to save the filter as a query. The query you have just saved appears on the Queries tab in the Database window.

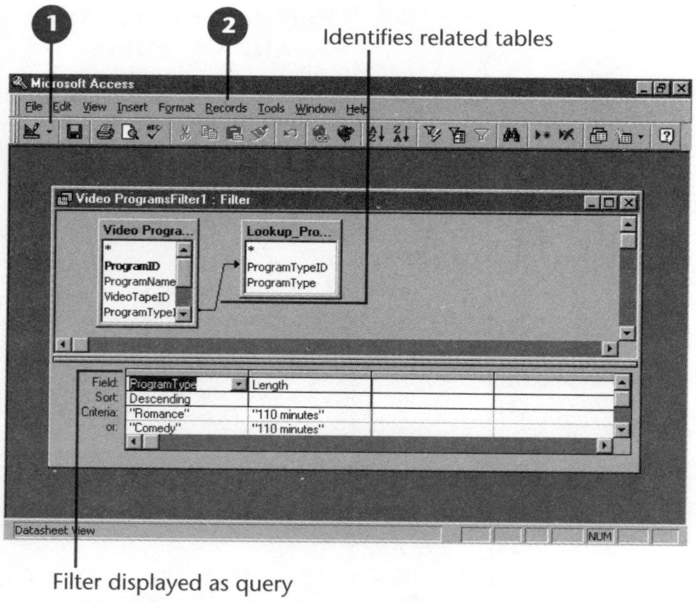

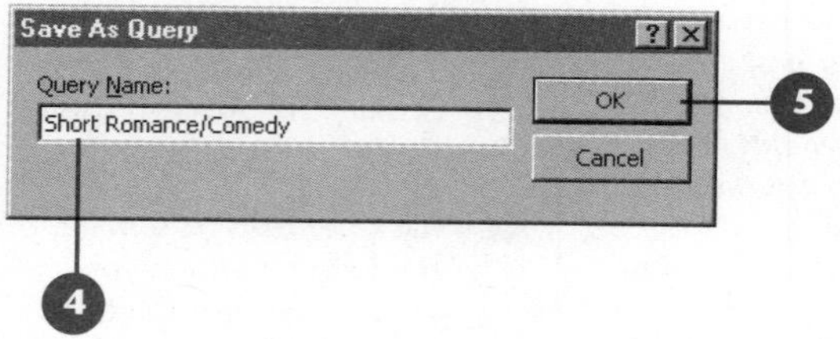

13

Creating a Database with Access 97

IN THIS SECTION

When you need to manage information not already in an existing Microsoft Access 97 database, you can create a new database. Creating a database involves:

- Planning the database to determine the kind of information it will contain
- Creating the tables
- Establishing the necessary relationships between tables
- Entering or importing information into the tables

After you have created a database and worked with it for a while, your information needs might change. If so, you can always modify the design of the tables to meet any new information requirements.

Planning a Database

Planning a database is an important first step in creating your own database. Although you can always make changes to your database when necessary, a little planning before you begin can save you a lot of time later on. For example, when you create a table in a database, you specify the type of data that will be stored in each field. Although you can change the field type (for example, from text to a number), you would need to reenter all the information for that field for all the records in the table if you change the data type after you have entered data in this field. It's better to plan ahead and anticipate possible uses of your information. Think about the information you need to keep track of, when you need it, and the questions you need to answer using this information. Think about how you currently keep a record of this information and what you would like to do differently. In many respects, creating a new database in Access gives you the opportunity to rethink your information requirements.

Planning Tables

Because a database can contain multiple tables, consider organizing your database information into several tables—each one containing only the fields related to a specific topic—rather than one large table that contains all the fields you need for the entire database. For example, you could create a Customers table that contains only customer information and an Orders table that contains only customer order information.

Establishing Table Relationships

Sometimes you'll want to retrieve data from multiple tables at the same time. For example, you might want to view information from both a Customers table and an Orders table so that you could see which orders were placed by specific customers. In order to retrieve data from multiple tables, you need to establish the necessary relationships between tables through the use of a common field. A *common field* is a field that exists in more than one table so that you can connect the tables. For example, a Customers table might contain a CustomerID field. You could include this same field in an Orders table so that you could connect the two tables. The CustomerID field would be the common field in this relationship.

Other than the common field, take care to avoid creating the same fields in multiple tables. This saves space and reduces errors caused by incorrectly updating the same information in multiple tables.

Specifying a Primary Key

When planning a table, you should also identify the primary key. The *primary key* is one or more fields whose values uniquely identify each record in a table. For example, a Social Security number field in a personnel table would be the primary key, because each employee has a unique Social Security number. Although designating a primary key is not mandatory, doing so is a good idea because the primary key facilitates sorting and locating the data you want to see.

Assigning a primary key to a table also facilitates establishing relationships between tables

When you use the primary key as the common field to establish a relationship between two tables, it's called the *foreign key* in the second table. In the previous example, the CustomerID field would be the primary key in the Customers table and a foreign key in the Orders table.

Choosing How to Create a Database File

As with most other objects you create in Access, you can create a new database file using one of the Database Wizards or you can use the Blank Database option to create and name a database file. A Database Wizard guides you through the process of naming a new database file and specifying the tables for your database. For each table, you can indicate the fields it should contain. Using a wizard you can choose from several types of tables and fields, including customer and contact information tables. If you create a blank database, you must name the database file and then start creating new tables from the Database window.

New Database button
If Access is already open, click to create a new database using a wizard (or a blank database).

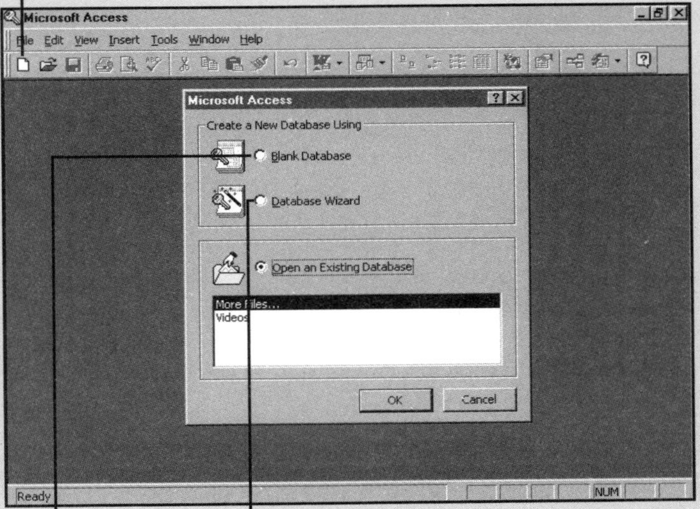

Click to create a new blank database.

Click to create a new database using a wizard.

Creating a Database with a Wizard

Access provides a variety of Database Wizards you can use to create databases that are suitable for different business or personal information needs. Each wizard guides you through the process of creating all the tables you need to create a database that you can begin using right away. These wizards also create useful queries, reports, and forms that will make it easier to use the database. You can even have Access supply data in the tables so you can see the database in action.

Create a Database with a Wizard

1. Start Access, click the Database Wizard option button, and then click OK. Or, if Access is already open, click the New Database button on the Database toolbar.
2. Click the Databases tab and double-click the wizard for the kind of database you want to create.
3. Click the Save In drop-down arrow, and then select the drive and the folder in which you want to store your database file.
4. In the File Name text box, type a filename for the database, or use the default filename. A database filename can contain up to 255 characters, including spaces, numbers, and symbols. When you type a filename, you can use both uppercase and lowercase letters.
5. Click Create.

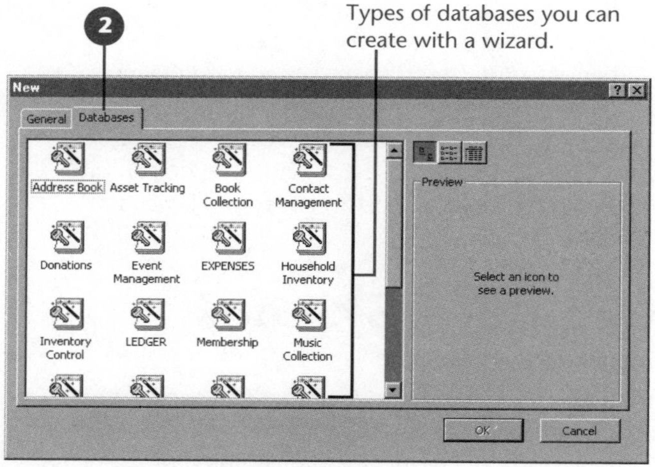

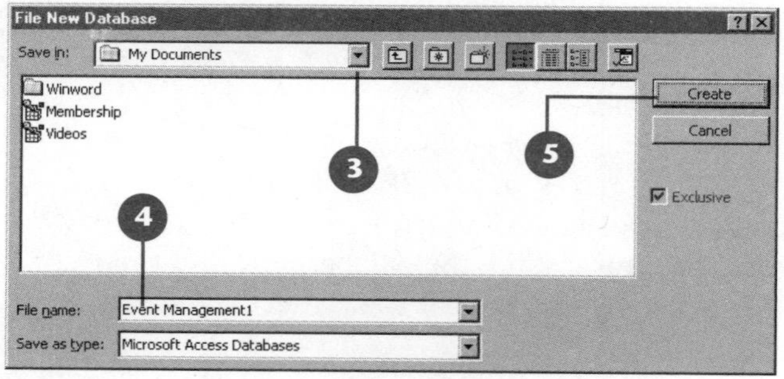

TIP

Working with a switchboard. *When you create a database using a wizard, Access automatically displays the Main Switchboard for the database. The* Main Switchboard *is a custom dialog box that allows you to use the features in your database. If you want to modify any of the other objects in the database, click the Restore button on the minimized Database window. If you click the Exit This Database button in the Main Switchboard, you will close the entire database.*

TRY THIS

Use the Address Book Wizard to create a database of your business or personal addresses. *If you are already in Access, click the New Database button on the Database toolbar. On the Databases tab, double-click Address Book and make your selections in the wizard dialog boxes.*

6. The first Database Wizard dialog box identifies the kind of information that you will be able to store in your new database. Each item corresponds to a table that you will create with the wizard. Click Next to continue.
7. On the left side of the dialog box, select a table.
8. Click the check box for each optional (unchecked) field you also want to include. If you change your mind, you can clear the check box for any optional field you want to exclude. Click Next to continue.
9. Click a style for the forms in the database, and then click Next to continue.
10. Click a style for the reports in the database, and then click Next to continue.
11. Type a name for your database (this name can be different from the database filename). Click Next to continue.
12. Indicate whether or not you want to start the new database right away. Click Finish to have Access build the database according to your selections.

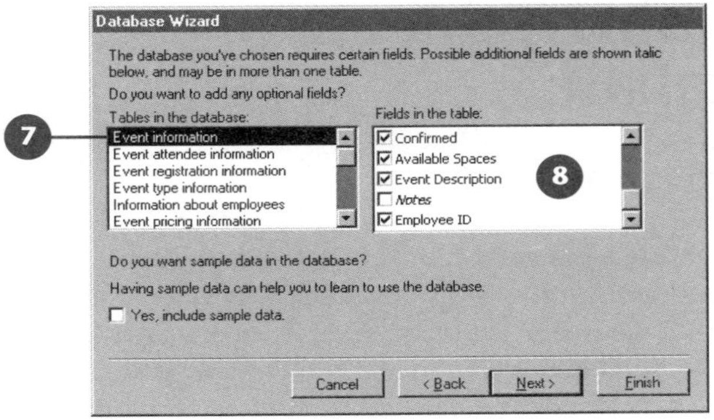

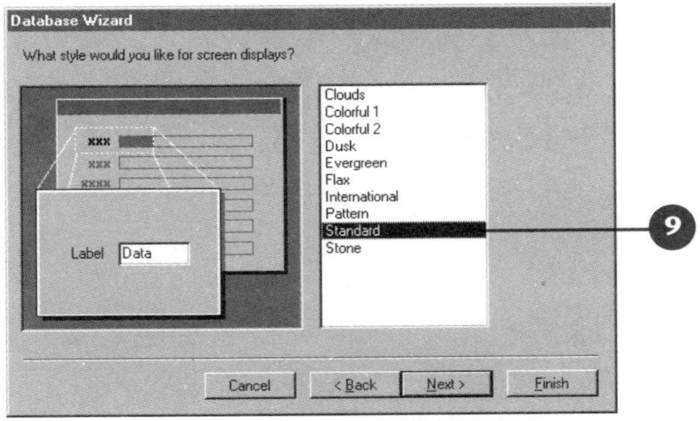

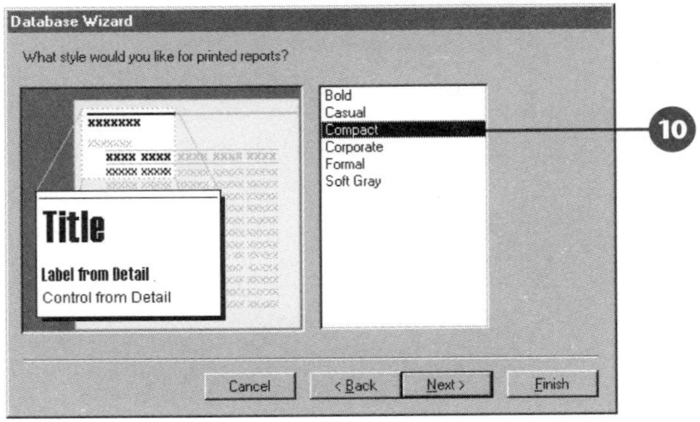

Creating Tables in a Database

After creating a database file, you need to create the tables in the database. You can also create additional tables in an existing database. There are several ways to create a new table: in Design view, in Datasheet view, with a Table Wizard, or by importing data from another program, such as Microsoft Excel. Depending on the method you choose, creating a table can involve one or more of the following:

- Specifying the fields for the table
- Determining the data type for each field
- Determining the field size (for text and number fields only)
- Assigning the primary key
- Saving and naming the table

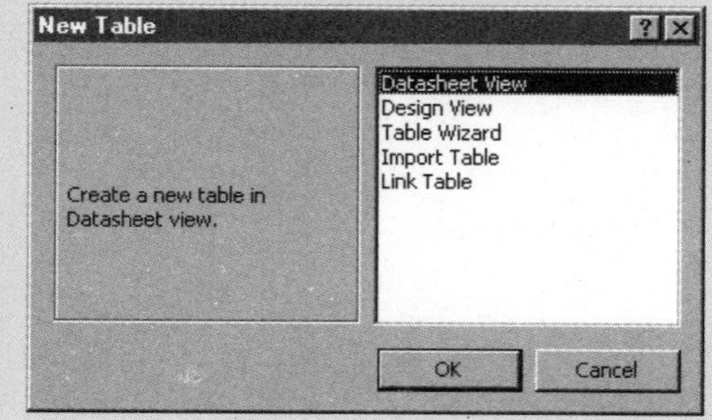

METHODS FOR CREATING A TABLE

Method	Description
Design	In Design view, you must specify the fields, specify the data type for each field, assign the size (for text view and number fields), assign the primary key, and save the table yourself.
Datasheet	When you create a table in Datasheet view, you can start viewing and entering data right away. Access automatically assigns the field type based on the kind of information you entered in the field, and it assigns a default field size for text and number fields. After you close and save the table, Access prompts you to identify a primary key or to have Access designate one for you.
Table	Using a Table Wizard, you select fields from sample wizard tables that are appropriate for the type of database you are creating. The data type and other field properties are already defined for each field.
Importing a table	When you import a table, all the field names and data types are retained with the imported data. However, you must name the new table and identify the primary key or have Access create a primary key for you. Also, you might need to change the field size and other properties after importing.
Linking a table	When you link a table, the table data is retrieved from a table in another database. Linking a table saves disk space because there is only one table rather than multiple tables with the same data. Linking a table saves time because there is no need to update the same information in more than one table.

Working in Design View

Click the *Primary Key button* to assign or remove the primary key designation for a field.

Click the *Insert Rows button* to add new fields to the table.

Click to switch to Datasheet view.

Click the *Delete Rows button* to remove selected fields from the table.

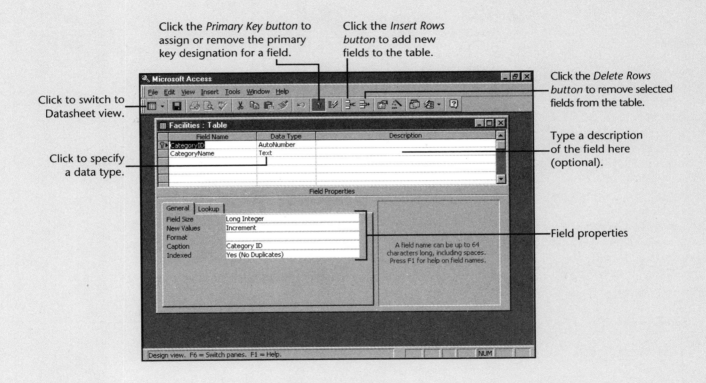

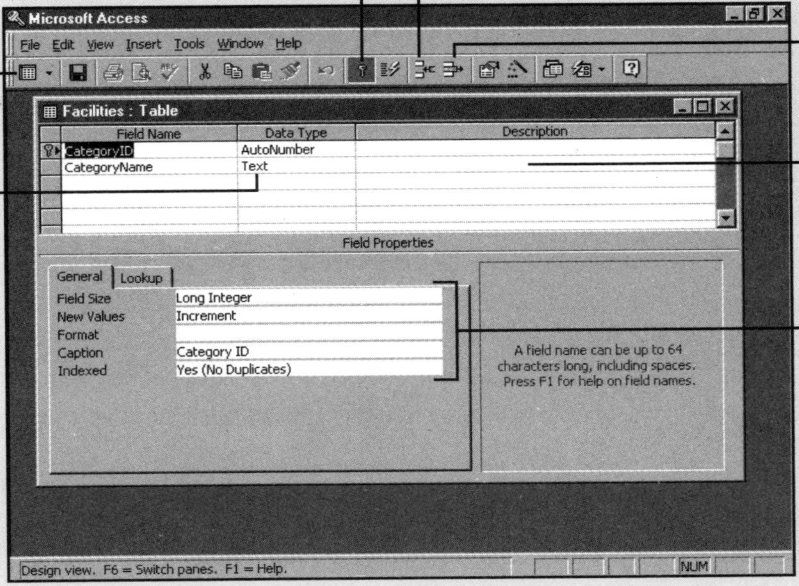

Type a description of the field here (optional).

Click to specify a data type.

Field properties

Creating Tables the Easy Way

One of the easiest ways to create a table is to use the Table Wizard. The *Table Wizard* displays a series of dialog boxes in which you can enter selections for your table. You choose from a number of tables suitable for a variety of databases and select the fields that you want to use. You can also rename the fields to what makes sense for you. With the wizard you also indicate any relationship between the new table and other tables in the database (if any), and you identify the primary key or have Access assign one for you.

Start the Table Wizard

1. On the Tables tab of the Database window, click New and then double-click Table Wizard.
2. Click the Business or Personal option button.
3. Choose the table that best matches your needs.
4. In the Sample Fields list, double-click each field you want to include in the table to copy the selected field to the Fields In My New Table list.
5. Click Next to continue.
6. Type a new name for the table or accept the suggested name.
7. Click the first option button to have the Table Wizard assign the primary key, or click the second option button to assign your own primary key. Click Next to continue. If you choose to assign your own primary key, you will see another dialog box describing primary key options. After you specify your primary key preferences, click OK to return to the Table Wizard.

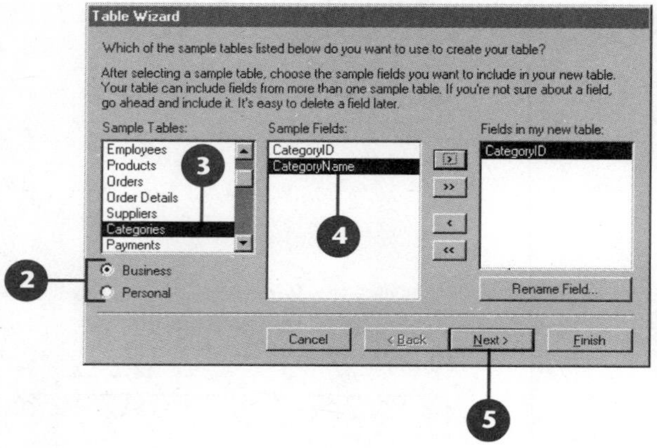

Table Wizard
Which of the sample tables listed below do you want to use to create your table?
After selecting a sample table, choose the sample fields you want to include in your new table. Your table can include fields from more than one sample table. If you're not sure about a field, go ahead and include it. It's easy to delete a field later.
Sample Tables:
Sample Fields:
Fields in my new table:
Employees
Products
Orders
Order Details
Suppliers
Categories
Payments
CategoryID
CategoryName
CategoryID
Business
Personal
Rename Field...
Cancel
< Back
Next >
Finish
2
3
4
5

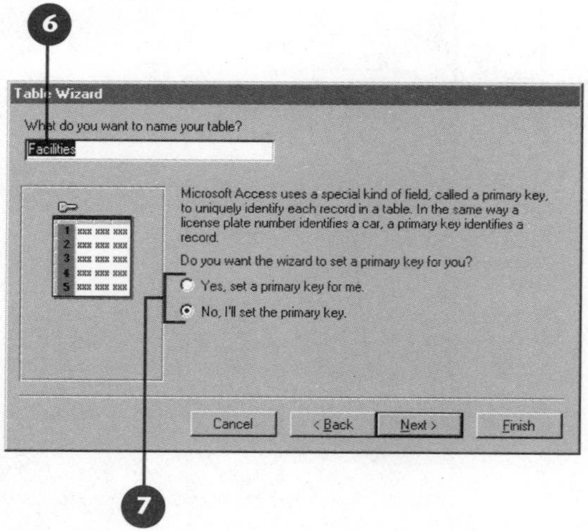

Table Wizard
What do you want to name your table?
Facilities
Microsoft Access uses a special kind of field, called a primary key, to uniquely identify each record in a table. In the same way a license plate number identifies a car, a primary key identifies a record.
Do you want the wizard to set a primary key for you?
Yes, set a primary key for me.
No, I'll set the primary key.
Cancel
< Back
Next >
Finish
6
7

SEE ALSO

See "Creating Tables in a Database" on page 220 for information on the different ways to create database tables.

"What's the easiest way to create tables for my database?"

8. Review the relationships of this new table with the other tables in the database. If you want to make any changes to the relationships, select the relationship you want to change, click the Relationships button, specify the new table relationships, and click OK. Then click Next to continue.

9. Indicate whether you want to start entering data right away (either in Datasheet view or in a form that Access creates for you) or whether you want to see the table's design in Design view.

10. Click Finish to complete the wizard and create the table.

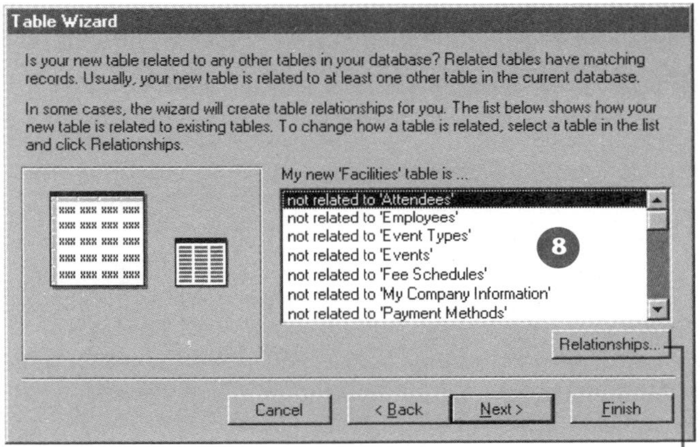
Table Wizard
Is your new table related to any other tables in your database? Related tables have matching records. Usually, your new table is related to at least one other table in the current database.
In some cases, the wizard will create table relationships for you. The list below shows how your new table is related to existing tables. To change how a table is related, select a table in the list and click Relationships.
My new 'Facilities' table is ...
not related to 'Attendees'
not related to 'Employees'
not related to 'Event Types'
not related to 'Events'
not related to 'Fee Schedules'
not related to 'My Company Information'
not related to 'Payment Methods'
8
Relationships...
Cancel
< Back
Next >
Finish

Click to specify table relationships

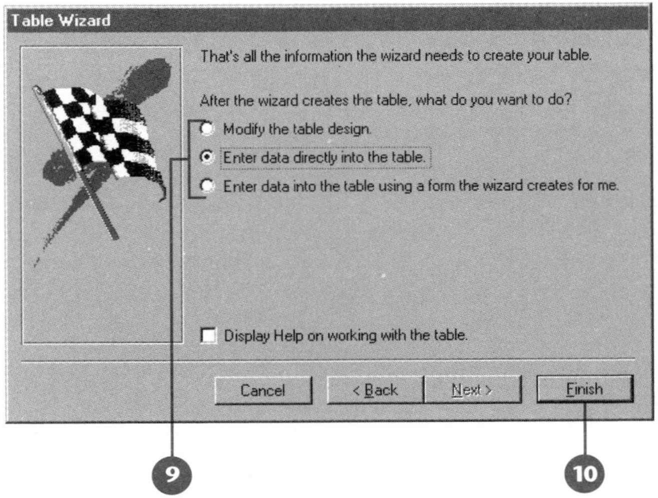
Table Wizard
That's all the information the wizard needs to create your table.
After the wizard creates the table, what do you want to do?
Modify the table design.
Enter data directly into the table.
Enter data into the table using a form the wizard creates for me.
Display Help on working with the table.
Cancel
< Back
Next >
Finish
9
10

Working with Fields

In Design view, you can add new fields to your table. You add a field by inserting a row, entering the field name, and specifying its data type and other properties. If your table includes a field you no longer need, you can delete the field—and any data you might have already entered in the table for this field. You can also change the order of the fields in Design view.

SEE ALSO

See "Understanding Access Databases" on page 200 for more information about working with fields.

Add a New Field

1. Display the table in Design view.
2. Click the row selector for the field that will be below the new field you want to insert.
3. Click the Insert Rows button on the Table Design toolbar.
   A new blank row appears above the row you selected.
4. In the Field Name column, type the name of the new field. A field name can contain up to 255 characters (including letters and numbers).
5. Press Tab to move to the Data Type column.
6. Click the drop-down arrow and specify the data type you want to assign to the field, or press Tab to accept the default Text data type.
7. Press Tab to move to the Description column.
8. Type a brief description (optional) of the kind of information this field can contain or include data entry instructions.
9. Set any additional properties for the field.

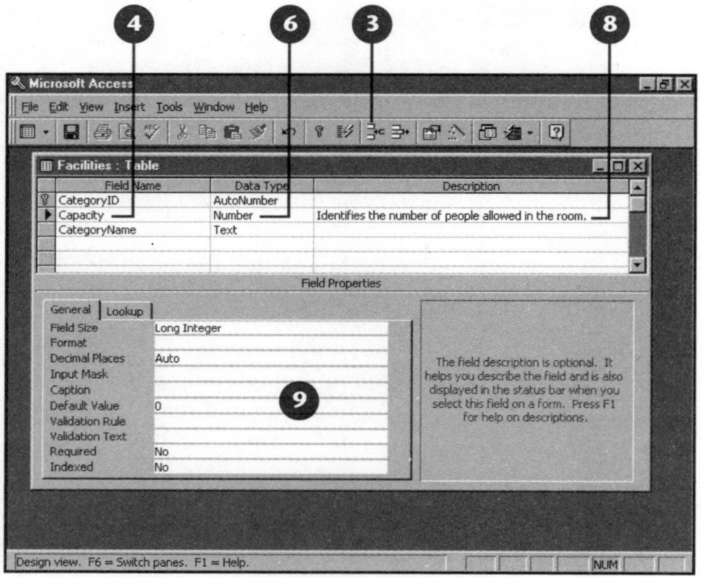

Exploring Different Ways to Create Reports

As with most objects you create in a database, you have several ways to create a report. With the AutoReport Wizard, Access creates a simple report (either columnar or tabular) based on the data in the currently selected table or query. With the Report Wizard you can specify the kind of report you want to create, and the Report Wizard guides you through each step of the process. All you do is answer a series of questions about your report, and Access builds a report with your data, using your formatting preferences.

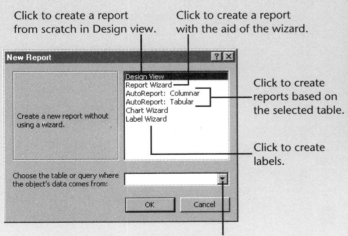

Once you have completed a report, you can further customize it in Design view. As always, you can begin creating your report in Design view without using a wizard at all.

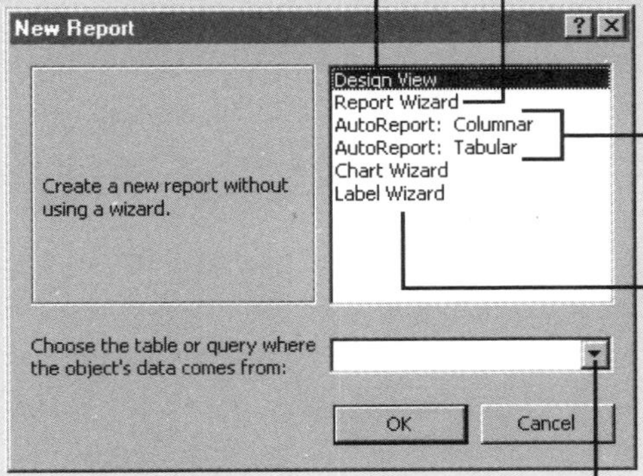
Click to create a report from scratch in Design view.
Click to create a report with the aid of the wizard.
New Report
Design View
Report Wizard
AutoReport: Columnar
AutoReport: Tabular
Chart Wizard
Label Wizard
Create a new report without using a wizard.
Choose the table or query where the object's data comes from:
OK
Cancel
Click to create reports based on the selected table.
Click to create labels.
Click to specify the table or query that contains the data you want to report.

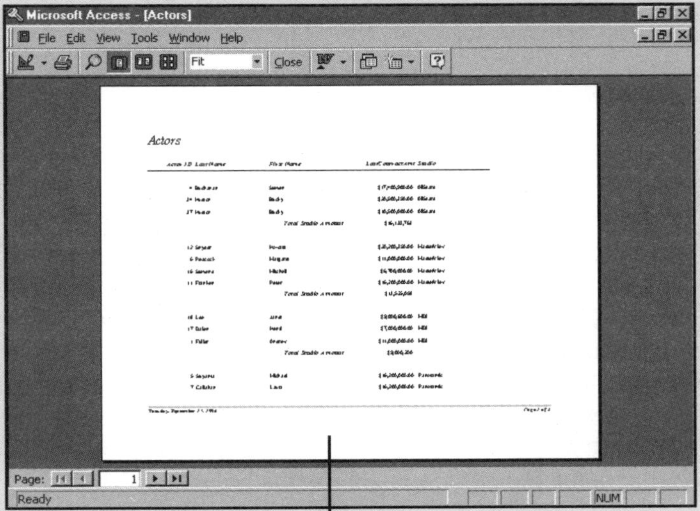
Microsoft Access - [Actors]
File Edit View Tools Window Help
Fit
Close
Actors
Page:
Ready
NUM

Preview of a report created with the Report Wizard

Creating a Report the Easy Way

To create a simple report in Access, you can use the AutoReport Wizard. This wizard quickly arranges the data in the selected table or query as an attractively formatted report. In a report created with the AutoReport: Columnar Wizard, each record's data is displayed vertically—that is, each field of data for each record appears on a line by itself. With the AutoReport: Tabular Wizard, the data for each record is arranged horizontally with each field appearing in a column, as in Datasheet view. After creating a report, you can save and name it.

TRY THIS

View multiple pages. *If your report contains more than one page, click the Multiple Pages button on the Print Preview toolbar, and then move the mouse to select the number and arrangement of pages you want to see.*

Create a Report with the AutoReport Wizard

1. In the Database window, click the Reports tab, and then click New.
2. Click AutoReport: Columnar (to display records in a column) or click AutoReport: Tabular (to display records in rows).
3. Click the drop-down arrow for choosing a table or query on which to base the report, and then click the table or query you want.
4. Click OK.

   After a moment, Access creates a report and displays it in the Print Preview window. From Print Preview, you can save, print, or close the report, or you can switch to Design view to modify it.

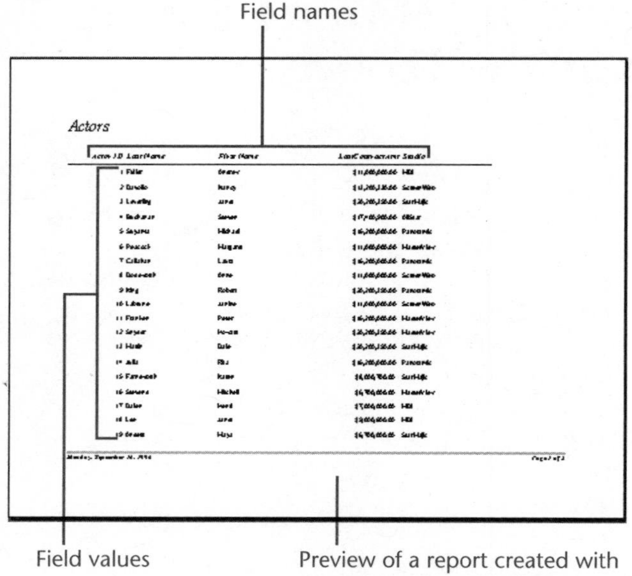

Preview of a report created with the AutoReport: Tabular Wizard.

Save a Report

1. Click the File menu, and then click Save.
2. Type a name for your report.
3. Click OK.

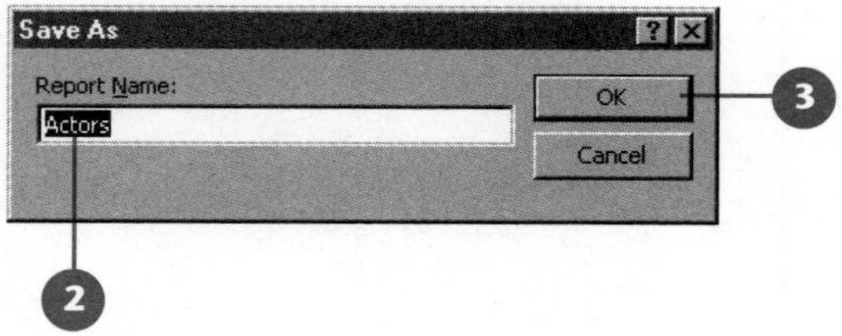

Modifying a Report in Design View

Formatting toolbar

Click the *Sorting And Grouping button* to specify ways to group and sort records, and to hide or display grouping headers and footers.

Click the *AutoFormat button* to choose from a variety of formatting and layout options.

This *page header* appears at the top of each page of the report.

The *grouping header* appears before each grouping of records.

The *detail section* displays fields for each detail record.

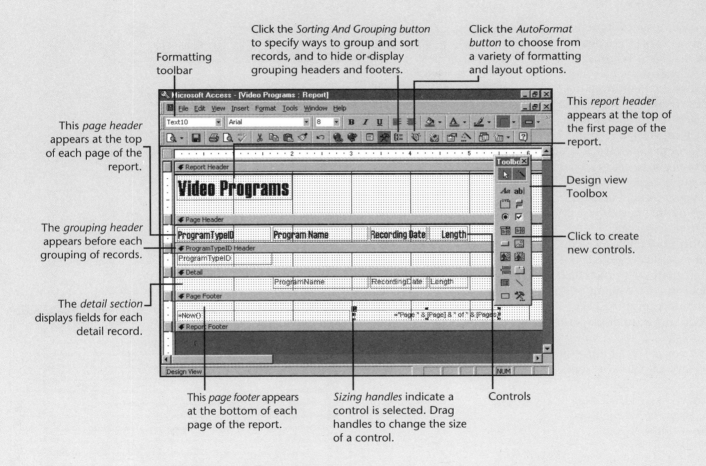

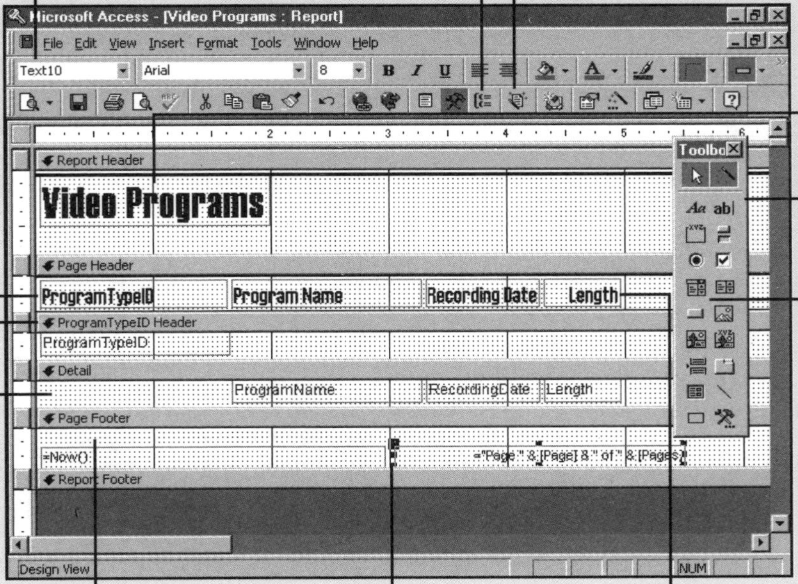

This *report header* appears at the top of the first page of the report.

Design view Toolbox

Click to create new controls.

This *page footer* appears at the bottom of each page of the report.

Sizing handles indicate a control is selected. Drag handles to change the size of a control.

Controls

Creating a Form the Easy Way

To create a simple form in Access, you can use one of the AutoForm Wizards. These wizards quickly arrange the fields from the selected table or query as an attractively formatted form. In a form created with the AutoForm: Columnar Wizard, you see each record's data displayed vertically—that is, each field of data for each record appears on a line by itself. With the AutoForm: Tabular Wizard, you see each record's data horizontally, with each field appearing in a column. With the AutoForm: Datasheet Wizard the form displays the records in Datasheet view. After you create a form, you can save and name it so that you can use it again. Any form you save is listed on the Forms tab of the Database window.

Create a Simple Form with the AutoForm Wizard

1. In the Database window, click the Forms tab, and then click New.
2. Click AutoForm: Columnar (to display records in a column), or click AutoForm: Tabular (to display records in rows), or click AutoForm: Datasheet (to display records in Datasheet view).
3. Click the drop-down arrow for choosing a table or query on which to base the form, and then click the name of the table or query you want.
4. Click OK.

After a moment, Access creates a form and displays it in Form view.

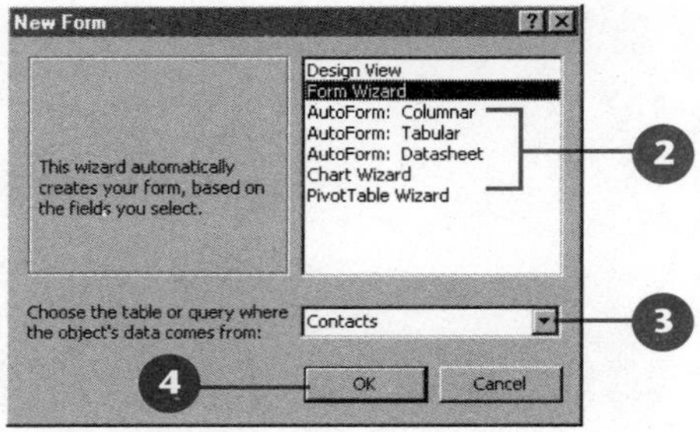

Preview of form created with AutoForm: Column Wizard

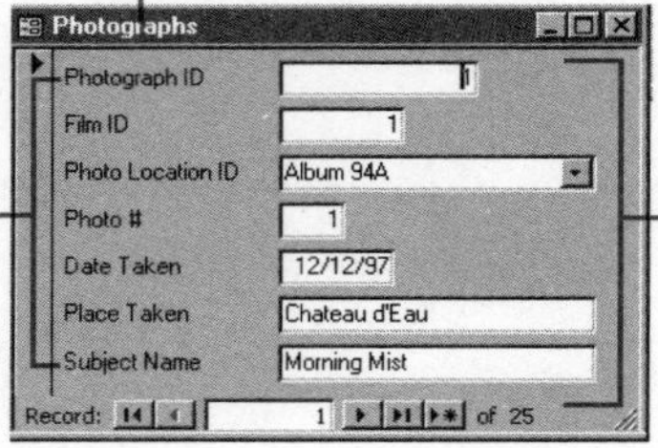

Field values

Field names

Preview of form created with AutoForm: Tabular Wizard

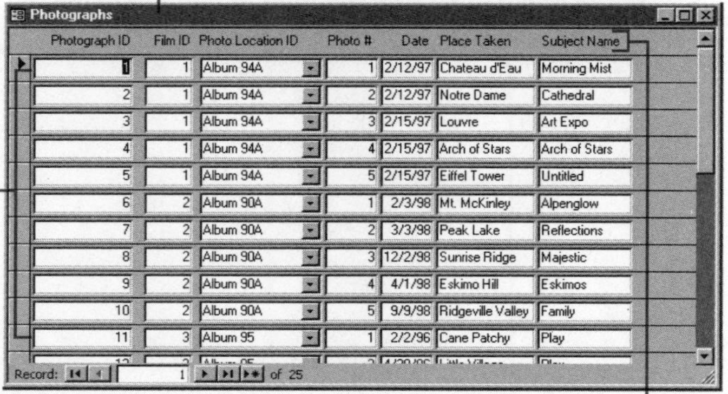

Field values

Field names

TRY THIS

Create a form instantly with the AutoForm command. *In the Database window, open the table or query that contains the data you want to display in a form. Click the New Object drop-down arrow on the Database toolbar, and then click AutoForm. After a moment, Access generates a simple (but unformatted) columnar form.*

SEE ALSO

See "Displaying a Form in Design View" on page 230 for more information about views.

Form created with AutoForm: Datasheet Wizard

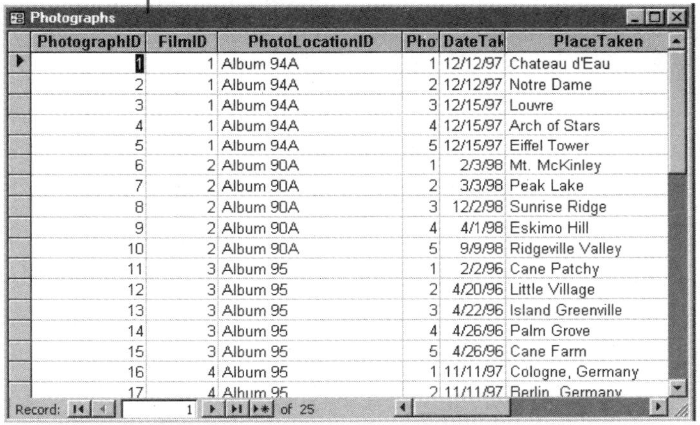

PhotographID	FilmID	PhotoLocationID	Pho	DateTak	PlaceTaken
1	1	Album 94A	1	12/12/97	Chateau d'Eau
2	1	Album 94A	2	12/12/97	Notre Dame
3	1	Album 94A	3	12/15/97	Louvre
4	1	Album 94A	4	12/15/97	Arch of Stars
5	1	Album 94A	5	12/15/97	Eiffel Tower
6	2	Album 90A	1	2/3/98	Mt. McKinley
7	2	Album 90A	2	3/3/98	Peak Lake
8	2	Album 90A	3	12/2/98	Sunrise Ridge
9	2	Album 90A	4	4/1/98	Eskimo Hill
10	2	Album 90A	5	9/9/98	Ridgeville Valley
11	3	Album 95	1	2/2/96	Cane Patchy
12	3	Album 95	2	4/20/96	Little Village
13	3	Album 95	3	4/22/96	Island Greenville
14	3	Album 95	4	4/26/96	Palm Grove
15	3	Album 95	5	4/26/96	Cane Farm
16	4	Album 95	1	11/11/97	Cologne, Germany
17	4	Album 95	2	11/11/97	Berlin, Germany

Save a Form

1. With the form displayed, click the Save button on the Form View toolbar.
2. In the Save As dialog box, type the name for your form.
3. Click OK.

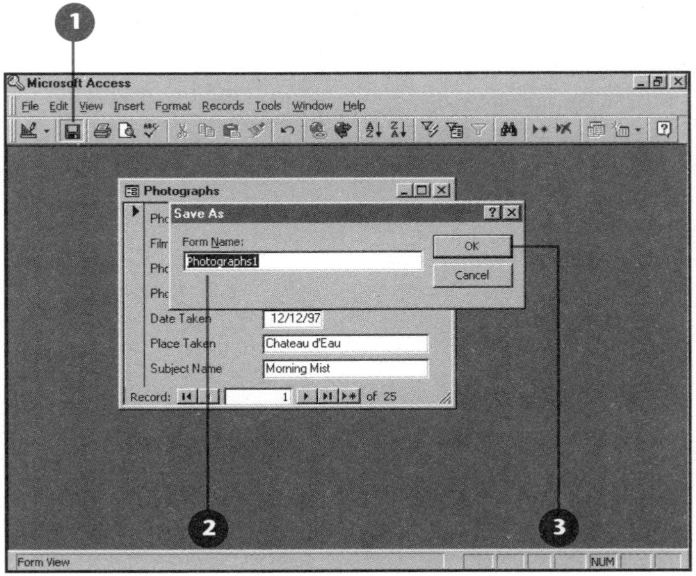

Displaying a Form in Design View

After you create a form, you might decide to modify certain features (called controls) in the form to make it easier to use. For example, you might want more descriptive labels to identify each field. Or you might create a box around a group of fields to help the user identify and complete related fields. To modify a form, you must display the form in Design view, which you can do from the Forms tab in the Database window or from Form view. The View button lets you switch between Form view and Design view so that you can easily modify a form and view the results.

Display a Form in Design View

1. In the Database window, click the Forms tab.
2. Click the form you want to use.
3. Click Design.

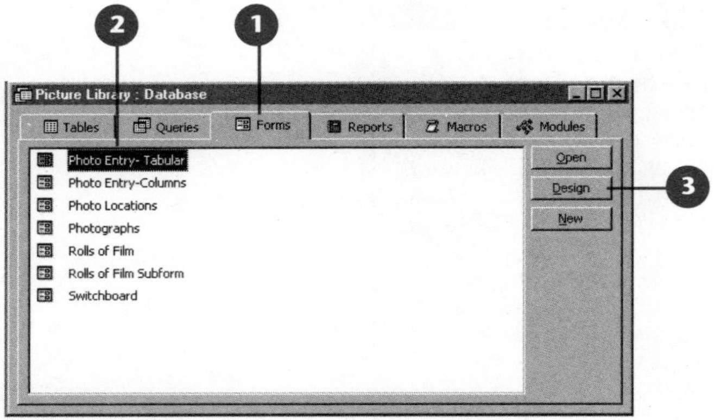

Switch Between Views

1. In Design view, click the View drop-down arrow to display the form in Form view so you can enter information.
2. In Form view, click the View drop-down arrow to display the form in Design view so you can modify the form.

View button
Click to switch between views.

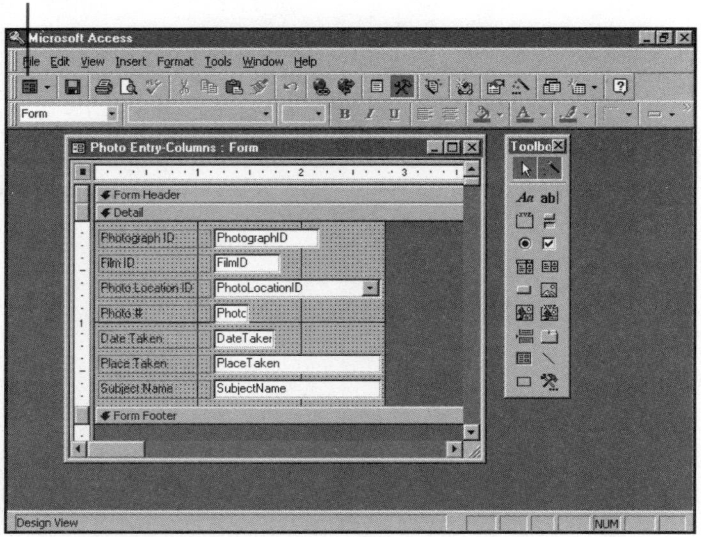

14

Communicating and Scheduling with Outlook 97

IN THIS SECTION

If, like many people, you're juggling a scheduler, an address book, and an e-mail address list, and you're cluttering your desk and computer with reminder notes and to-do lists, help is here—Microsoft Outlook 97.

Outlook 97 integrates all the common planning, scheduling, organization, and management tools into one simple and flexible system.

- *Inbox* receives and stores your incoming messages.
- *Contacts* clears your desk of the standard card file and compiles multiple addresses, phone numbers, e-mail and Web addresses, and any personal information you need or want about each contact.
- *Calendar* replaces your daily or weekly planner and helps you schedule meetings and block time for activities.
- *Tasks* organizes and tracks your to-do list.
- *Notes* provides a place to jot random notes that you can group, sort, and categorize.
- *Journal* automatically records your activities and is more convenient than keeping a diary by hand.

Outlook 97 provides a single place to plan, organize, and manage every aspect of your work and personal life.

Viewing the Outlook Window

Title bar
The title bar shows the program name, Microsoft Outlook, preceeded by the Outlook folder you have open, in this case, Inbox.

Standard toolbar
Outlook opens with the Standard toolbar on screen; other toolbars are available in some folders.

Menu bar
The Compose menu changes to Calander, Contacts, Tasks, Journal, or Notes depending on which folder you are using.

Folder bar
The name of the folder in which you are working appears here.

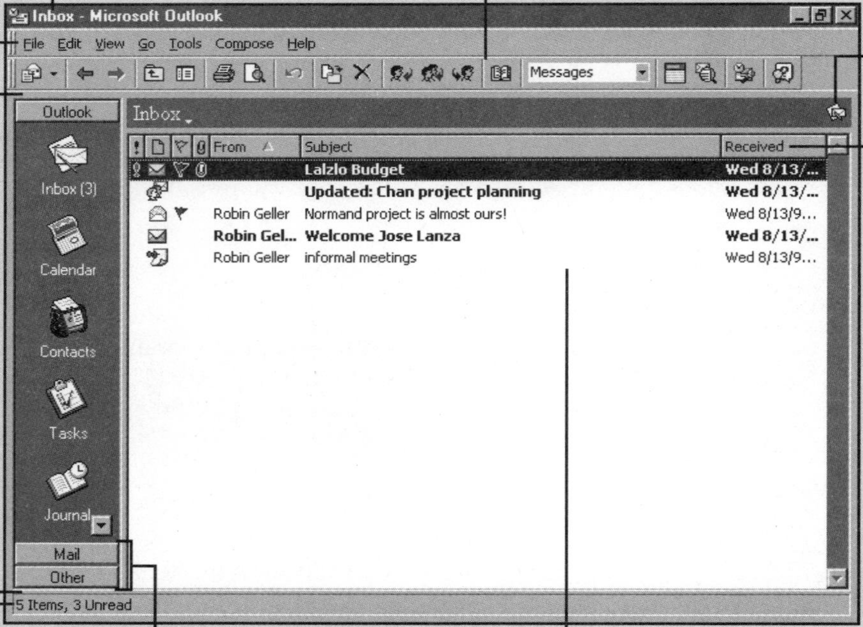

Column buttons
Each folder has different column buttons that you can use to change the way the contents are organized. Click a column button to switch between *ascending* (low to high, A to Z, or early to late) and *descending* (high to low, Z to A, or late to early) order.

Outlook bar
The Outlook bar, also called the Navigation bar, is always visible and contains shortcut icons you can click to move among all the groups and folders. You can add additional shortcut icons here to quickly open other folders on your system or network.

Status bar
The status bar indicates the number of items you have stored or saved in a folder, for example, two notes, five appointments, seven messages, and so on.

Group buttons
The various components of Outlook (such as Calendar, Contacts, etc.) are split into three groups by default. Click a Group button to display shortcuts for that group's components.

Information viewer
This part of the screen changes to different views, depending on the folder you are using. In this figure, you see a list of e-mail messages in the Inbox.

Moving Around Outlook

As you work, you'll need to switch between the Outlook folders frequently and create new *items* such as tasks, contacts, e-mail messages, and appointments. Imagine you are revising your list of tasks. Then you call a business associate who recommends you contact her colleague. You add him to your Address Book and then send him an e-mail message. He then calls to arrange a meeting. To accomplish all this, you need to move smoothly from Tasks to Contacts to Inbox to Calendar in a short amount of time.

TIP

Create a new item quickly. *To create an item that's appropriate for the open folder, click the New Item button on the Standard toolbar. For example, if Calendar is open, the Appointment dialog box opens.*

Display Folder Icons and Open a Folder

1. Click a group button on the Outlook bar.
2. If necessary, click the Scroll button to display the icon you want.
3. Click any icon on the Outlook bar for the folder you want to open.

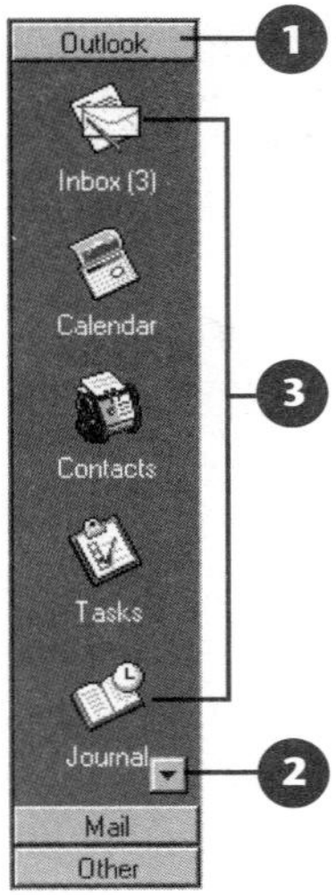

Create a New Item for Any Folder

1. Click the New Item drop-down arrow on the Standard toolbar.
2. Click the type of item you want to create.

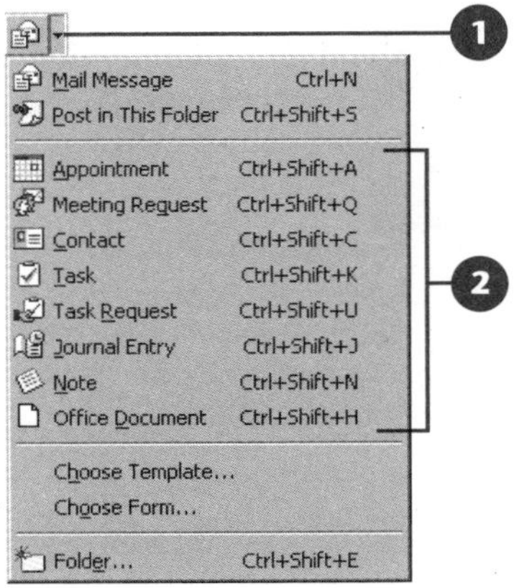

14

Creating a Contact

A *contact* is a person or company that you communicate with. One contact often has several mailing addresses; various phone and fax numbers; and e-mail addresses and Web sites. You can store all this data in the Contacts folder along with more detailed information, such as job title, birthdays and anniversaries. When you double-click a contact, you open a dialog box in which you can edit the contact information. You can also edit most contact information from within the information viewer.

TIP

Create multiple new contacts. *Once you are finished creating a contact you can click File, and then click Save And New to close the completed contact and open a new untitled contact.*

Create a New Contact

1. Click the New Item drop-down arrow on the Standard toolbar, and then click Contact.
2. Fill in information on the General tab. You can enter address (postal and e-mail) and phone numbers or select categories to help you organize your contacts.
3. Click Save and Close.

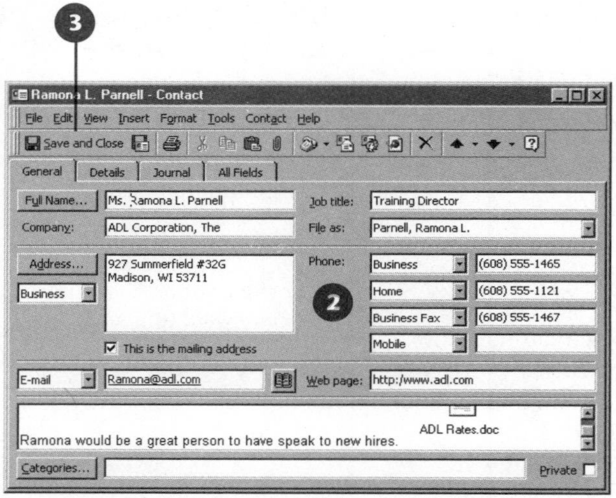

Move Around the Contact Information Viewer

1. Click Contacts on the Outlook bar.
2. Click the View drop-down arrow on the Standard toolbar, and then click Detailed Address Cards or Address Cards.
3. Click the button for the first letter of the name under which the contact is filed.

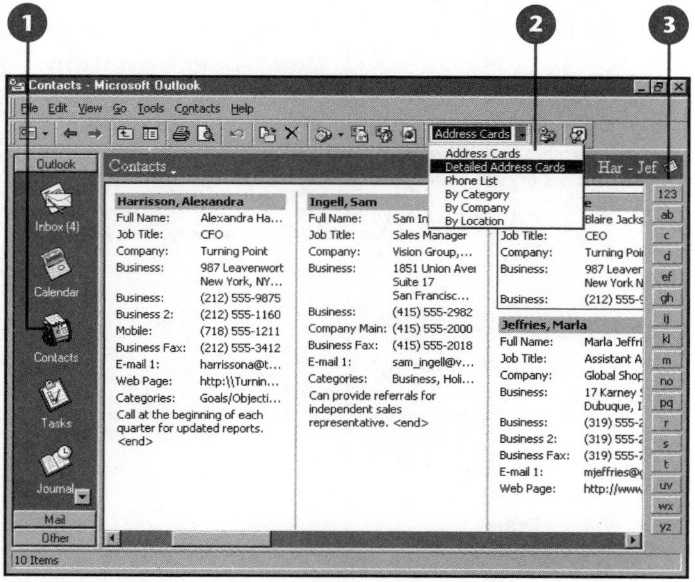

TIP

Delete a contact. *You can remove any contact from your list by clicking the contact you want to delete, and then clicking the Delete button on the Standard toolbar. Any journal entries that refer to that contact remain intact.*

Open and Close an Existing Contact Card

1. Click Contacts on the Outlook bar.
2. Find the contact you want.
3. Double-click the contact you want to open.
4. Click the Close button.

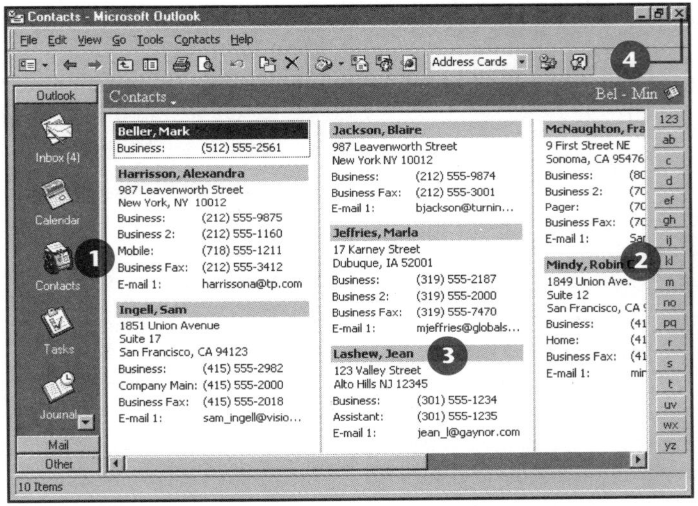

TIP

Trouble editing contact information? *If you try but can't edit a contact's information from a particular view, you need to turn on in-cell editing. Click the View menu, click Format View, click the Allow In-Cell Editing check box to select it, and then click OK.*

Update Existing Contact Information

1. Click Contacts on the Outlook bar.
2. Click the View drop-down arrow on the Standard toolbar.
3. Click Detailed Address Cards.
4. Click in the contact you want to change.
5. Use the usual editing commands to edit the information.

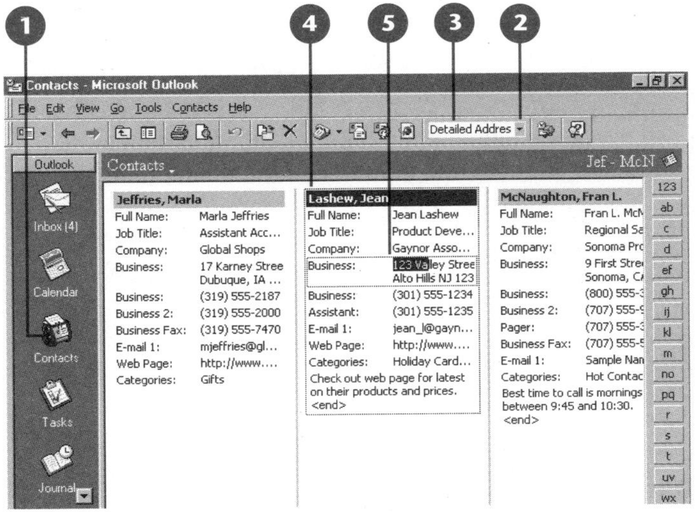

14

Creating and Sending an E-Mail Message

E-mail messages are a quick and effective way to communicate with others. They follow a standard memo format, with lines for the sender, recipient, date, and subject. To send an e-mail, you need to enter the recipient's complete e-mail address. You can also send the same e-mail to more than one person. Using the Address book makes entering e-mail addresses quick and easy.

> **TIP**
>
> **An important note about e-mail addresses.** *An e-mail address is not case sensitive (that is, capitalization doesn't matter) and cannot contain spaces.*

New Mail Message button

Create and Send an E-Mail Message

1. Click the New Mail Message drop-down arrow on the Standard toolbar.
2. Click Mail Message.
3. Click the To button.
4. Select an Address Book.
5. Click a name, and if necessary, press Ctrl while you click other names.
6. Click the To, Cc, or Bcc button. (To sends the message to the selected names; Cc sends a courtesy copy; Bcc sends a blind courtesy copy)
7. When you have finished selecting names, click OK.
8. Click in the Subject box, and type a brief description of your message.
9. Click in the message box, and type the text of your message and attach files as necessary.
10. Click the Options tab and then select the options you want.
11. Click the Send button on the Standard toolbar.

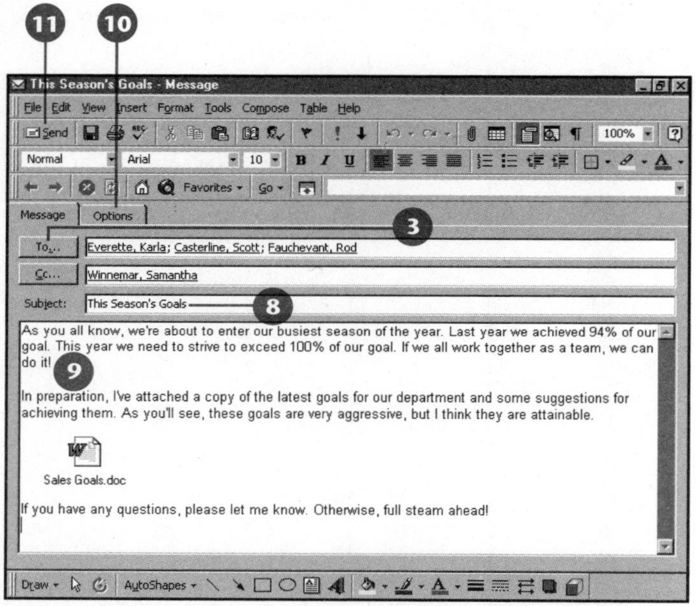

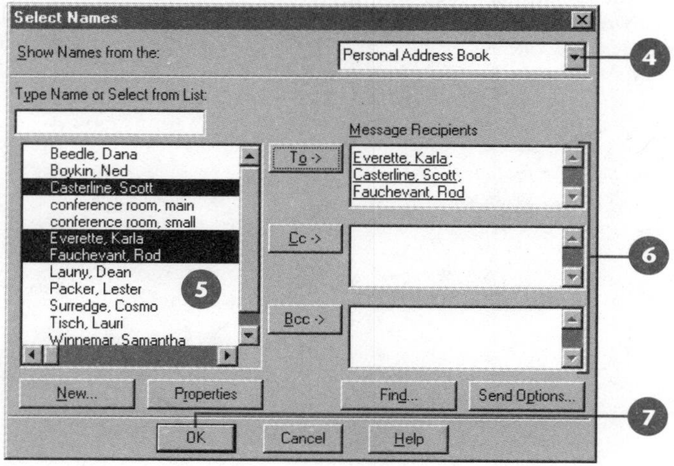

TIP

Compose a message now, but send it later. *To save a partially written message in the Inbox without sending it, click the Save button on the Standard toolbar, and then click the Close button in the upperright corner of the dialog box to close it. When you're ready to send the message, double-click it in the Inbox and then click the Send button on the Standard toolbar.*

TIP

A note about the e-mail editor used in this section. *The e-mail editor used in this section is Microsoft Word. To set Word as your e-mail editor, click the Tools menu, click Options, click the E-Mail tab, click the Use Microsoft Word As The E-mail Editor check box, and then Click OK.*

TIP

What if an e-mail address isn't in the Address Book? *If the e-mail address you need isn't in the Address Book, but you know the person's exact and complete address, you can type it directly in the To box in the Message dialog box. (Use a semicolon to separate two or more addresses.)*

Find a Name in the Address Book

1. Click the To button in the Message tab of the Message dialog box.
2. Select the Address Book you want to search.
3. Click Find.
4. Type the first several letters of the name you want to find.
5. Click OK.
6. Click the To, Cc, or Bcc button.
7. Click OK.

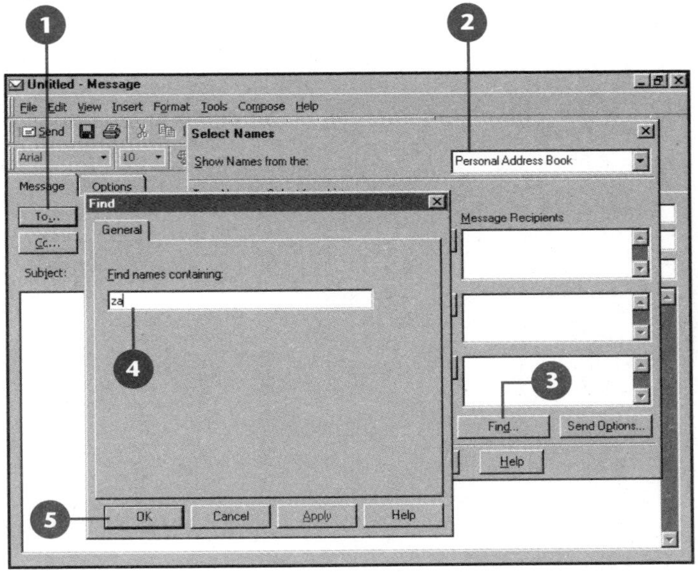

Add a Name to an Address Book

1. Click the Address Book button on the Standard toolbar.
2. Select the Address Book to which you want to add an entry.
3. Click the New Entry button on the toolbar.
4. Select an Entry Type, and then click OK.
5. Enter address information, and then click OK.
6. Click the Close button.

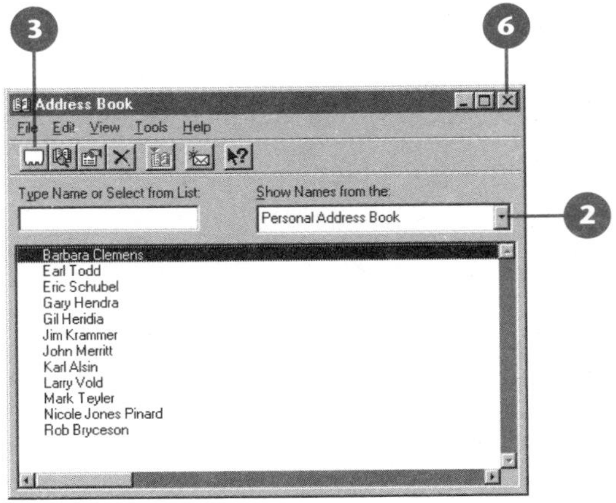

Attaching a File to an E-Mail Message

In addition to exchanging messages, sharing files is a powerful aspect of e-mail. You can attach one or more files to a message. The recipient then opens the file from the program in which it was created. You can also add text (called an AutoSignature) that appears at the bottom of every message you send. A signature commonly includes your name, mailing address, phone number, and e-mail address. Some people add a general greeting to their AutoSignature.

TIP

Use drag-and-drop to attack a file quickly. *You can quickly attach a file to an e-mail message by dragging it from the desktop or Windows Explorer to the message box.*

Attach a File to a Message

1. Click in the message box in the Message tab of the Message dialog box.
2. Click the Insert File button on the Standard toolbar.
3. Click the As Attachment check box.
4. Click the Look In drop-down arrow, and select the drive and folder in which the file is stored.
5. Double-click the file you want to attach to the message.

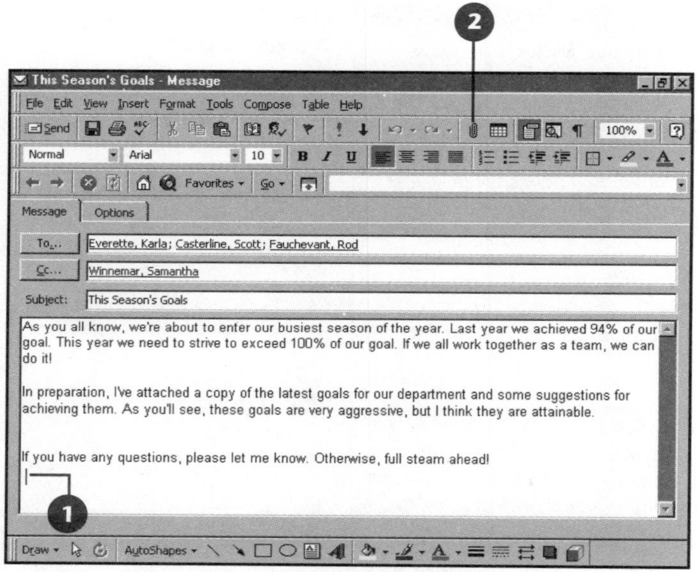

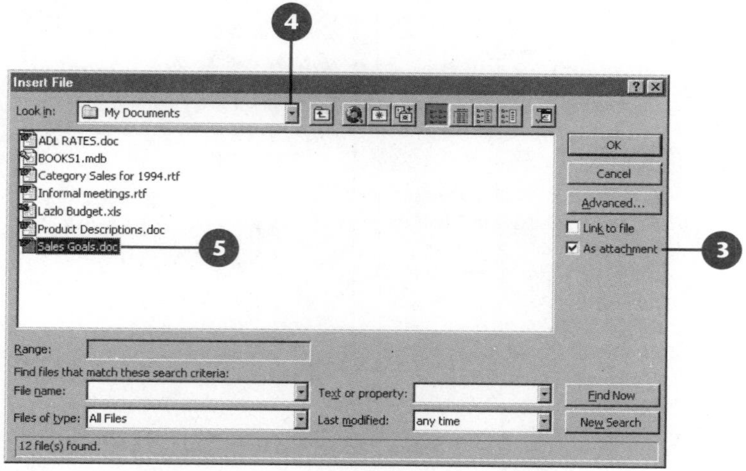

TRY THIS

Create a signature. *Add a signature to all your out going e-mail messages. Include your name, mailing address, phone and fax numbers, e-mail address, and Web site, if you have one. Add a special message at the end, such as a holiday greeting, or your personal motto.*

Create an AutoSignature

1. Click the New Message drop-down arrow, and then click New Message.
2. Type the information you want include in the AutoSignature, and then select and format the text.
3. Click the Tools menu, and then click AutoSignature.
4. Click Yes to confirm the autosignature.
5. Click the Close button, and then click No to save changes.

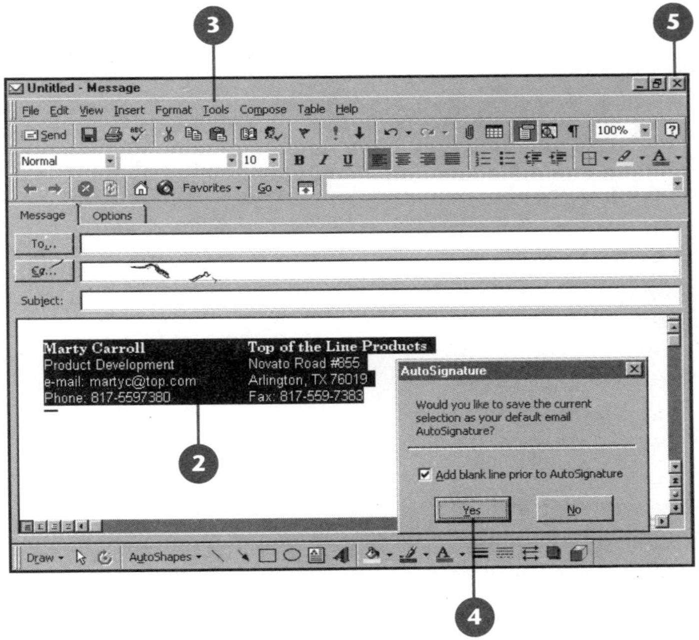

Reading and Replying to an E-Mail Message

You can receive e-mail messages anytime day or night, even when your computer is turned off. New messages appear in the Inbox along with any messages you haven't yet stored or deleted. A message flag appears next to any message that has a set importance or sensitivity level. The message flags, along with the sender's name and subject line, help you determine the content of a message and which one you want to open, read, and respond to first.

Preview and Open a Message

1. Click Inbox on the Outlook bar.
2. Click the AutoPreview button on the Standard toolbar.
3. Double-click the message you want to open.

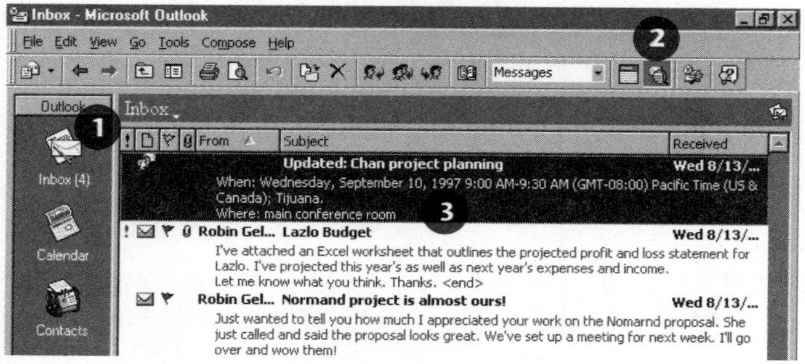

Inbox - Microsoft Outlook
File Edit View Go Tools Compose Help
Messages
Outlook
Inbox
Inbox (4)
Calendar
Contacts
From
Subject
Received
Updated: Chan project planning
Wed 8/13/...
When: Wednesday, September 10, 1997 9:00 AM-9:30 AM (GMT-08:00) Pacific Time (US & Canada); Tijuana.
Where: main conference room
Robin Gel... Lazlo Budget
Wed 8/13/...
I've attached an Excel worksheet that outlines the projected profit and loss statement for Lazlo. I've projected this year's as well as next year's expenses and income.
Let me know what you think. Thanks. <end>
Robin Gel... Normand project is almost ours!
Wed 8/13/...
Just wanted to tell you how much I appreciated your work on the Nomarnd proposal. She just called and said the proposal looks great. We've set up a meeting for next week. I'll go over and wow them!
1
2
3

Reply to a Message

1. Click Inbox on the Outlook bar.
2. Click the message to which you want to respond.
3. Click the Reply button or click the Reply To All button on the Standard toolbar.
   - Reply responds to only the message's sender.
   - Reply To All responds to the sender and all other recipients of the message.
4. Type your message at the top of the message box.
5. Click the Send button on the Standard toolbar.

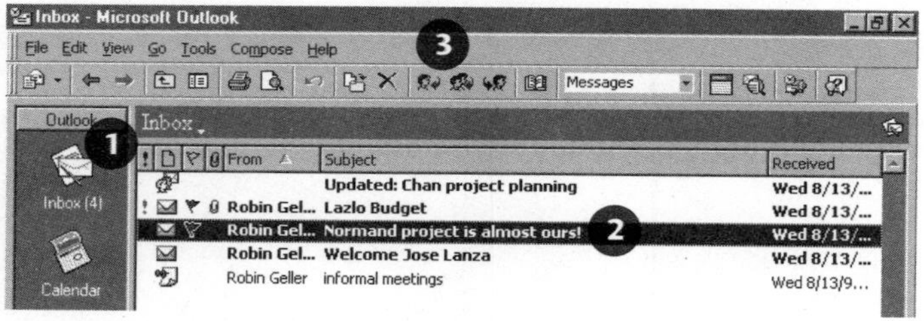

Inbox - Microsoft Outlook
File Edit View Go Tools Compose Help
Messages
Outlook
Inbox
Inbox (4)
Calendar
From
Subject
Received
Updated: Chan project planning
Wed 8/13/...
Robin Gel... Lazlo Budget
Wed 8/13/...
Robin Gel... Normand project is almost ours!
Wed 8/13/...
Robin Gel... Welcome Jose Lanza
Wed 8/13/...
Robin Geller informal meetings
Wed 8/13/9...
1
2
3

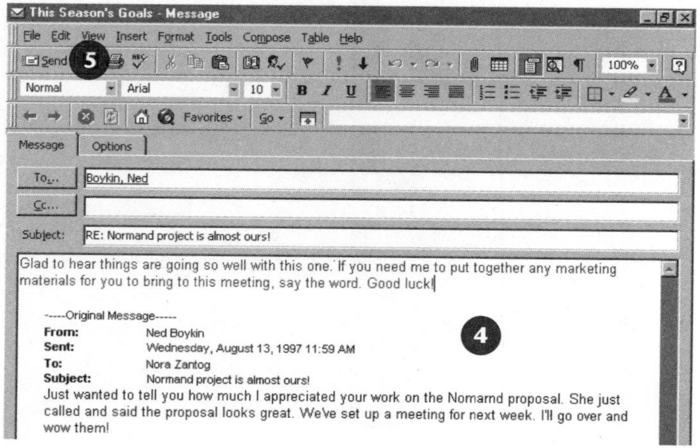

This Season's Goals - Message
File Edit View Insert Format Tools Compose Table Help
Send
100%
Normal
Arial
10
Favorites
Go
Message
Options
To...
Boykin, Ned
Cc...
Subject:
RE: Normand project is almost ours!
Glad to hear things are going so well with this one. If you need me to put together any marketing materials for you to bring to this meeting, say the word. Good luck!
-----Original Message-----
From: Ned Boykin
Sent: Wednesday, August 13, 1997 11:59 AM
To: Nora Zantog
Subject: Normand project is almost ours!
Just wanted to tell you how much I appreciated your work on the Nomarnd proposal. She just called and said the proposal looks great. We've set up a meeting for next week. I'll go over and wow them!
4
5

SEE ALSO

See "Creating and Sending an E-Mail Message" on page 236 for more information about addressing e-mail messages and entering text.

TIP

Get new mail quickly. *The moment you receive new mail, the New Mail icon appears next to the clock on the taskbar. You can double-click the icon to switch to your Inbox. Depending on your e-mail service, you might have to log onto a network or dial into a service provider to receive new mail.*

TRY THIS

Reply from within an open a message. *Just click the Reply, Reply To All, or Forward buttons on the Standard toolbar from within the open message, and then reply or forward the message as usual.*

TIP

Outlook adds a note when you reply to a message. *Whenever you reply to or forward an e-mail message, Outlook adds a note indicating when you replied or forwarded the message to that message's mail icon in your Inbox.*

Forward a Message

1. Click Inbox on the Outlook bar.
2. Click the message you want to forward.
3. Click the Forward button on the Standard toolbar.
4. Click the To button or the Cc button, and then select recipients for this message.
5. Type new text and attach files, if any, at the top of the message box.
6. Click the Send button on the Standard toolbar.

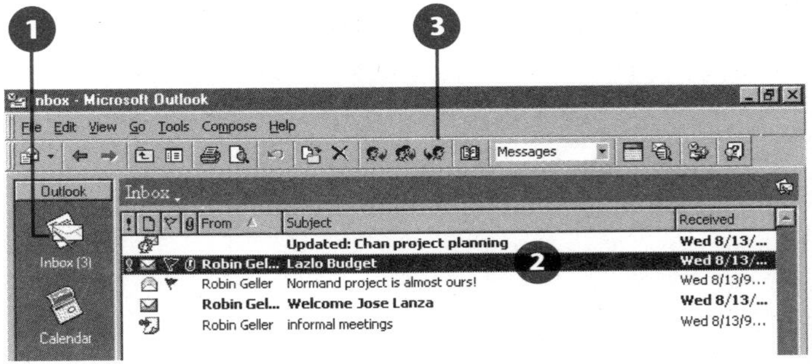

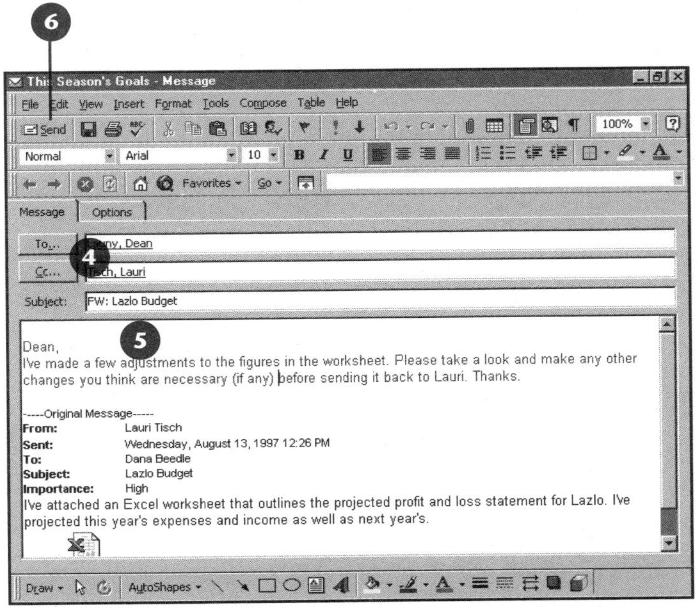

14

Managing E-Mail Messages

To avoid an overly cluttered Inbox, remember to routinely clear the Inbox of messages that you have read and responded to. You can save messages as files, move messages to other folders or subfolders, and delete messages you no longer need. Storing messages in other folders and deleting unwanted messages make it easier to see new messages and clear your computer's resources for new activities.

TIP

Select multiple messages or other items at one time. *To select two or more adjacent messages, click the first message, press and hold the Shift key while you click the last message. To select two or more nonadjacent messages, click the first message, press and hold the Ctrl key while you click each additional message.*

Save Messages as Files

1. Click Inbox on the Outlook bar.
2. Click the message you want to save as a file.
3. Click the File menu, and then click Save As.
4. Click the Save In drop-down arrow, and then select the drive and folder in which you want to store the message.
5. Click the Save As Type drop-down arrow, and then click the file type you want.
6. Type a new name in the File Name box.
7. Click Save.

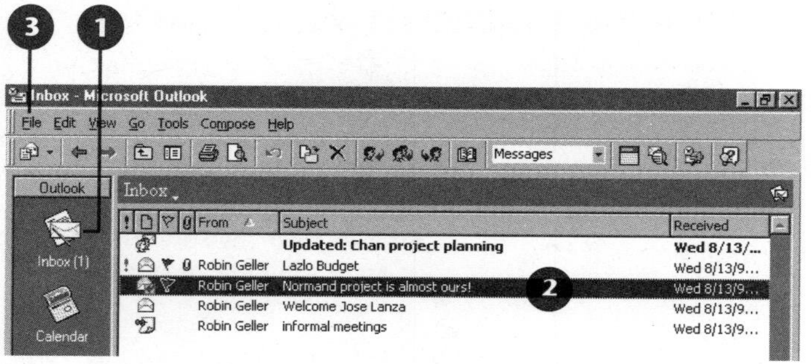

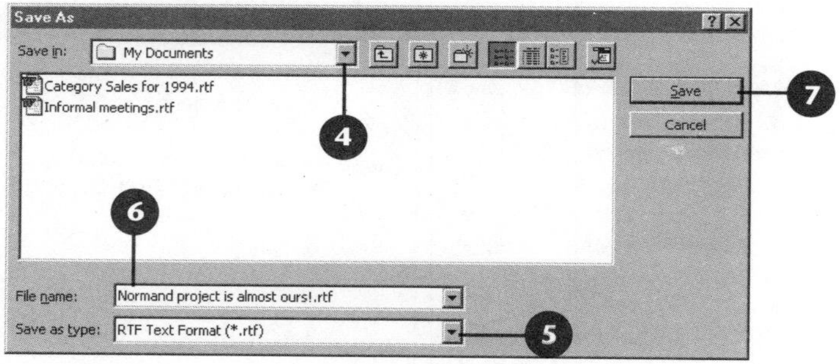

Delete Unwanted Messages

1. On the Outlook bar, click Inbox, Outbox, Sent Items, or the folder in which you store messages.
2. Select the message or messages you want to move to the Deleted Items folder.
3. Click the Delete button on the Standard toolbar.

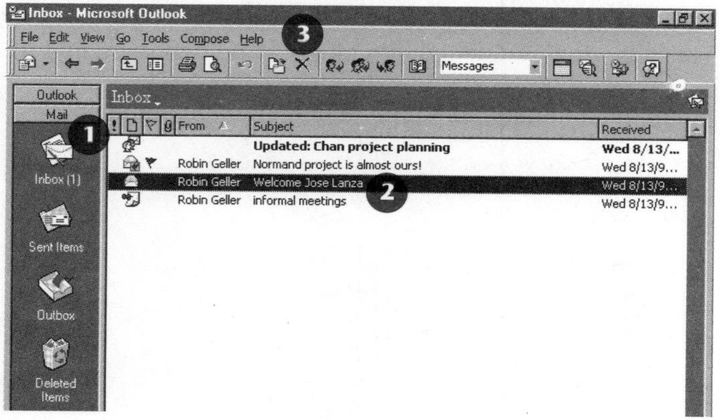

TIP

Retrieve messages from the Deleted Items folder. *Items remain in the Deleted Items folder until you empty it. To retrieve messages from the Deleted Items folder, click Deleted Items on the Outlook bar, and then drag an item to the Inbox or to any other shortcut icon on the Outlook bar. To empty the Deleted Items folder and permanently delete its contents, right-click Deleted Items on the Outlook bar, click Empty "Deleted Items" Folder, and then click Yes to confirm the deletion.*

14

Create a New Folder in Outlook

1. Click the File menu, point to Folder, and then click Create Subfolder.
2. Type a name for the new folder, such as Quarterly Reports.
3. Click the Folder Contains drop-down arrow, and then click the type of item you want to store here.
4. Click the folder in which you want to file this subfolder.
5. If necessary, type a description of the folder.
6. Click OK.

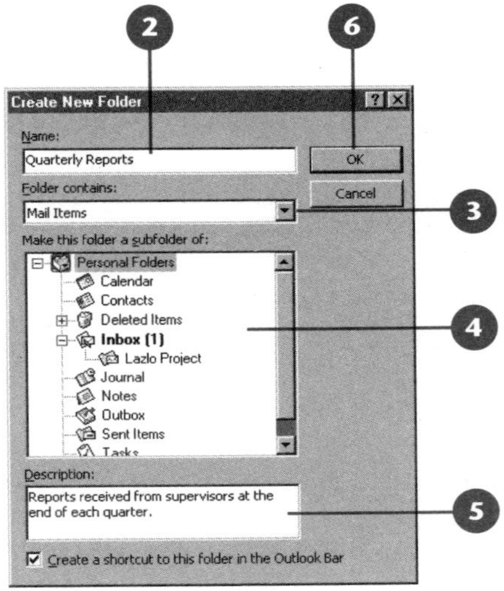

Organize Your Messages in Folders

1. Click Inbox on the Outlook bar.
2. Select the message or messages you want to move.
3. Click the Move To Folder button on the Standard toolbar.
4. Click Move To Folder.
5. Click the folder where you want to move the message.
6. Click OK.

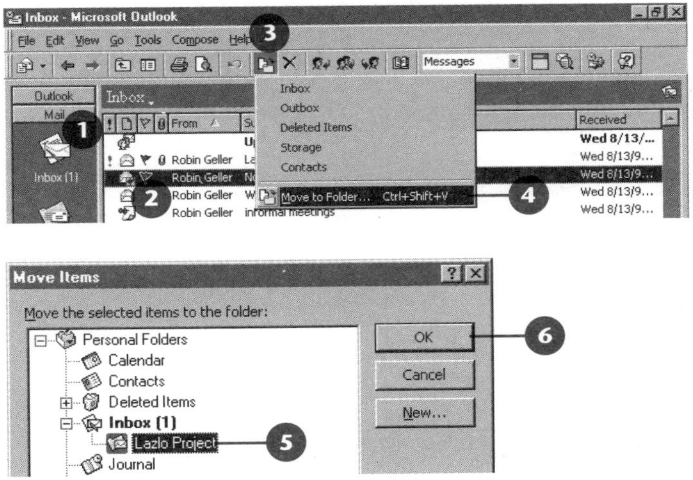

Viewing Your Schedule

The *Calendar* is an electronic version of the familiar paper daily planner. You can schedule time for completing specific tasks, meetings, vacations and holidays, or for any other activity with the Calendar. People using Outlook and Schedule+ can exchange messages, meeting requests, and appointments, however, neither can read the other's calendar. To view Schedule+ calendar information, you'll need to import it into Outlook.

SEE ALSO

See "Managing Tasks" on page 254 for more information about task lists.

Switch Views

The Calendar displays your schedule in a typical daily planner format or in list format. You can select:

- Day/Week/Month: Displays your schedule in a planner format; you can change between a daily, weekly, or monthly planner.
- Active Appointments: Lists all the appointments and meetings scheduled from the current day forward.
- Events: Lists all the current and future scheduled events.
- Annual Events: Lists all the current and future events that occur only once a year.
- Recurring Appointments: Lists all appointments that take place regularly.

Banner
Shows the date for open day; displays bar indicating a scheduled event.

Click to the left of any week to view that week's schedule.

Click any date to view that day's schedule.

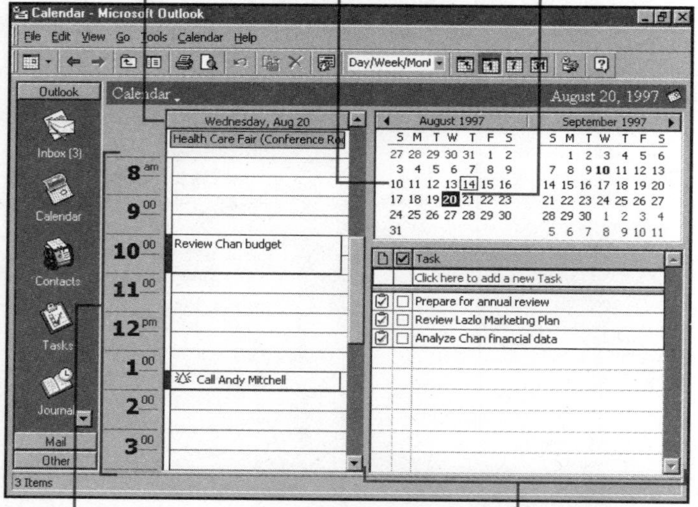

Time Bar
Shows the hours in day view (as in this figure), or days in weekly and monthly views; displays scheduled appointments and meetings.

Task Pad
Lists tasks you need to complete and shows completed tasks crossed out.

> **TIP**
>
> **Exchange information with Schedule+.** *People using Outlook and Schedule+ can exchange messages, meeting requests, and appointments. However, neither can read the other's calendar. Once you open an item from the Outlook Inbox, you will no longer be able to read it in Schedule+. If you want to use Schedule+ 7.0 rather than the Outlook Calendar, click the Tools menu, click Options, click the Calendar tab, click the Use Microsoft Schedule+ 7.0 As My Primary Calendar check box, and then click OK.*

> **SEE ALSO**
>
> *See "Viewing Items in Groups," "Sorting Items," and "Viewing Specific Files Using Filters" on pages 261, 262, and 263 for more information about how to display specific types of tasks in the Task Pad.*

Open a Calendar from Schedule+

1. Click the File menu, and then click Import And Export.
2. Double-click Import From Schedule+ Or Another Application Or File.
3. Double-click Schedule+ 7.0 or Schedule+ 1.0.
4. Click Browse, and then double-click the file you want to open.
5. Click the button for the option you want to use.
6. Click Next, and then make sure the files you want converted to Outlook are selected.
7. Click Finish.

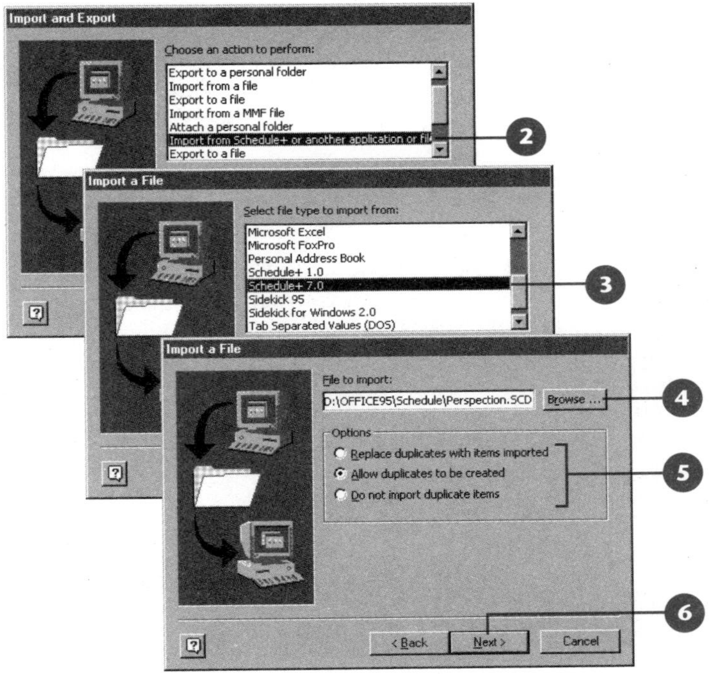

Fields and entries from Schedule+ are converted into their appropriate Outlook folders.

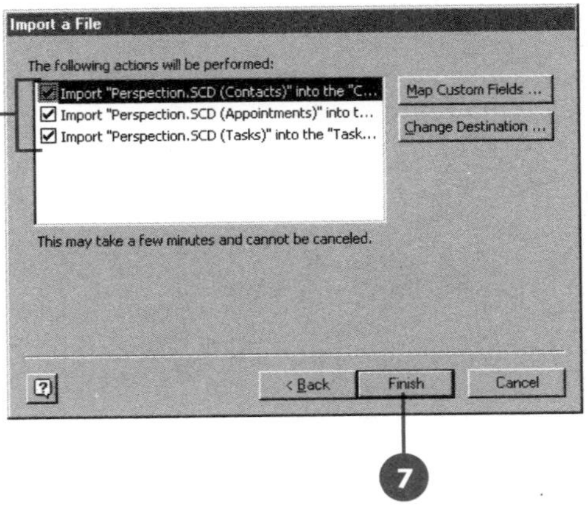

Scheduling an Appointment or Event

An *appointment* is any activity you schedule that doesn't include other people or resources. An *event* is any appointment that lasts one or more full days (24 hours increments), such as a seminar, conference, or vacation. You can mark yourself available (free or tentative) or unavailable (busy or out of the office) to others during a scheduled appointment or event. You use the same dialog box to schedule an appointment or event, the only difference is whether the All Day Event check box is selected or cleared.

SEE ALSO

See "Viewing Your Schedule" on page 244 for more information about moving around the Calendar.

Schedule an Appointment

1. Click Calendar on the Outlook bar.
2. Switch to Day/Week/Month view.
3. Drag to select a block of time in the Time Bar.
4. Right-click the selected block, and then click New Appointment.
5. Fill in the text boxes and set other options on the Appointment tab as needed.
   - Type where the meeting will take place, or select a location from the drop-down list.
   - Type details or notes for the appointment, or insert a file.
   - Select Categories to help your sort, group, or filter your appointments.
   - Check the Private check box if you do not want others to see this appointment.
6. Click the Save And Close button on the Standard toolbar.

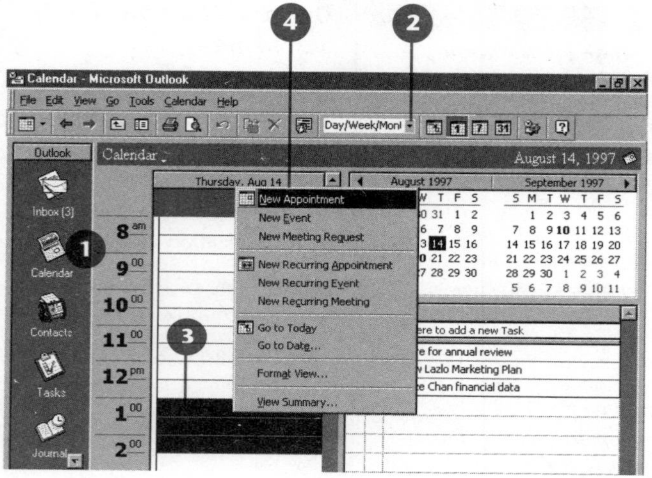

Mark your availability to others as Free, Tentative, Busy, or Out Of Office.

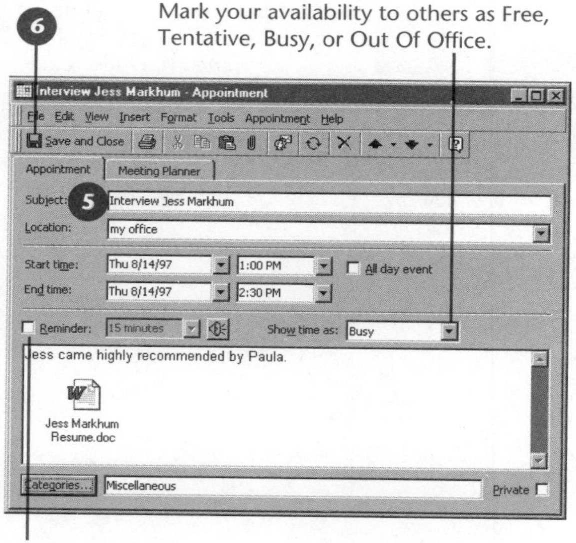

Click to set an alarm to notify you a certain amount of time before the appointment.

TIP

Switch between an appointment or event. *To change an appointment to an event or vice versa, click the All Day Event check box.*

TRY THIS

Schedule an appointment or event without starting Outlook. *Click the New Appointment button on the Office Shortcut Bar to open the Appointment dialog box. Complete the Appointment tab of the dialog box as usual.*

Block Time for an Event

1. Click Calendar on the Outlook bar.
2. Switch to Day/Week/Month view.
3. Double-click the date heading.
4. Fill in the text boxes, and set other options on the Appointment tab as needed.
   - Type where the meeting will take place, or select a location from the drop-down list.
   - Set an alarm to notify you a certain amount of time before the event.
   - Mark your availability to others as Free, Tentative, Busy, or Out Of Office.
   - Type notes and details of the event, or attach a file.
   - Select Categories to help you sort, group, and filter your events.
5. Click the Save And Close button on the Standard toolbar.

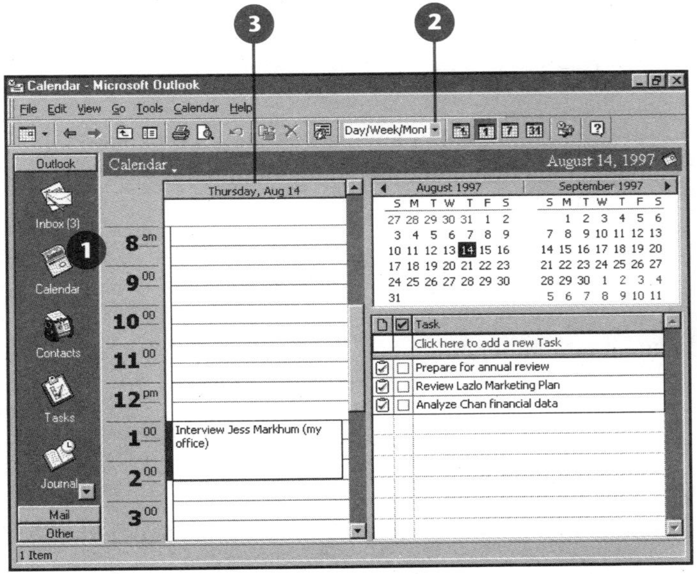

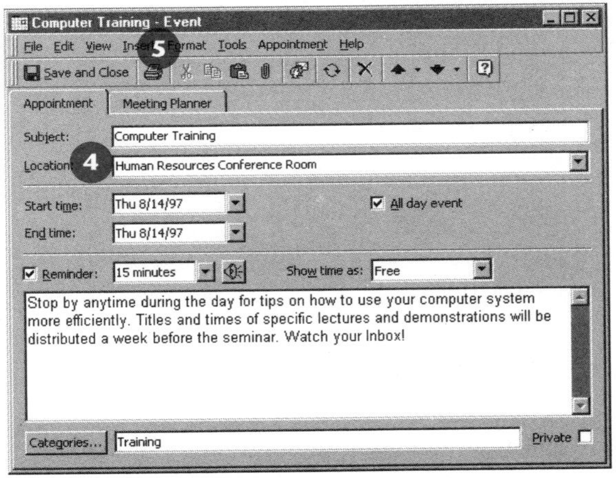

Rescheduling an Appointment or Event

A basic fact of life is that things change—appointments and events might be moved to another day or time, or event relocated. Outlook provides you the flexibility to easily reuse your Calendar as your schedule changes.

TIP

Drag an appointment to reschedule it quickly. *Reschedule an appointment or event quickly by dragging it to a new time on the Time Bar or to a new day in the Date Navigator in Day/Week/Month view. Press and hold the Ctrl key as you drag the appointment or event to copy it to another date or time.*

Reschedule an Appointment or Event

1. Click Calendar on the Outlook bar.
2. Switch to a view that shows the appointment or event you want to change on the time Bar.
3. Double-click the appointment or event.
4. Make whatever changes you want.
5. Click the Save And Close button on the Standard toolbar.

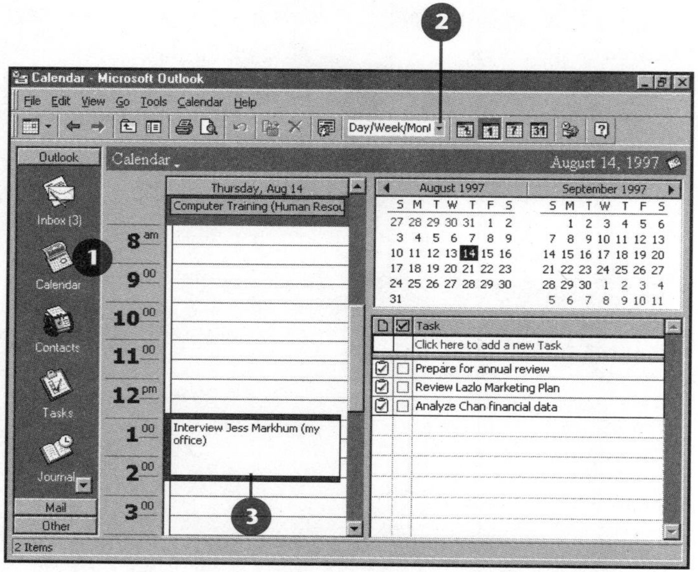

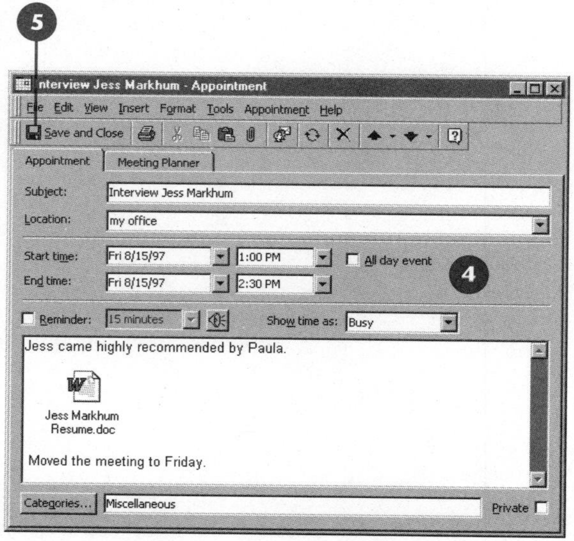

Planning a Meeting

The Calendar's *Meeting Planner* helps you organize meetings quickly, sends e-mail messages to all recipients announcing the meeting, and tracks their responses. As long as everyone is connected to the same network, you can use their Calendars to determine when other people and resources are available so you can select the best time to schedule a meeting. If you invite people who live in other time zones, Calendar converts their schedule times to your time zone.

TRY THIS

Send an agenda, meeting minutes, or other necessary documents to meeting invitees. *Attach the file to the meeting request just as you would attach a file to any other e-mail message.*

Create and Send a Meeting Request

1. Click Calendar on the Outlook bar.
2. Click the Plan A Meeting button on the Standard toolbar.
3. Click Invite Others.
4. Type a name or click one or more names in the list.
5. Click the Required, Optional, or Resources button.
6. When you have selected all the people and resources you want, click OK.
7. Click AutoPick to find the first common available time for all participants.
8. Click Make Meeting.
9. Type a brief description of the meeting in the Subject box.
10. Type any notes or attach files as needed.
11. Click Categories and assign keywords as needed.
12. Click the Send button on the Standard toolbar to send meeting requests.

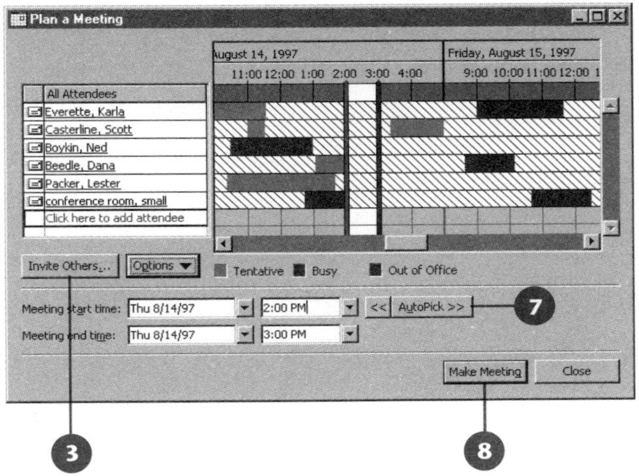

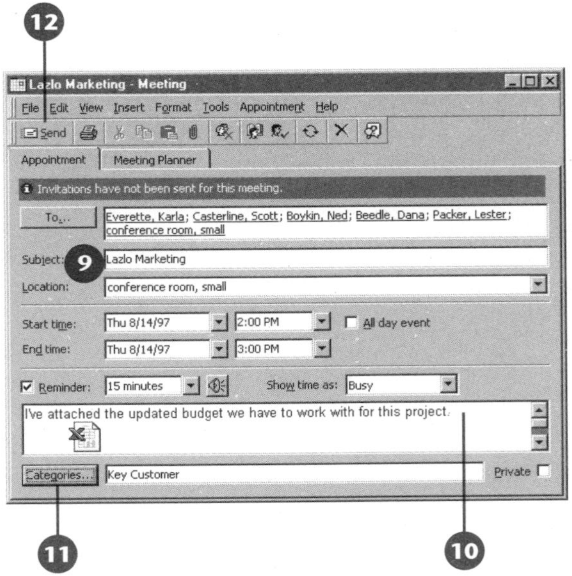

14

Rescheduling or Canceling a Meeting

Even the best laid plans sometimes change. This is especially true when you gather together a group of people to schedule a meeting. You might need to change the date of a meeting, switch the time, move the location, or even cancel the meeting. When you do this from Outlook's Calendar, you can be assured that everyone who have been invited to the meeting receives an update.

TIP

Turn an appointment into a meeting. *Open the appointment, click the Invite Attendees button on the Standard toolbar, add people and resources, enter a location if necessary, and then click the Send button on the Standard toolbar.*

Reschedule a Meeting

1. Click Calendar on the Outlook bar.
2. Switch to the view that shows the meeting you want to change.
3. Double-click the meeting you want to change.
4. Make any necessary changes on the Appointment tab.
5. Click the Send And Close button on the Standard toolbar.

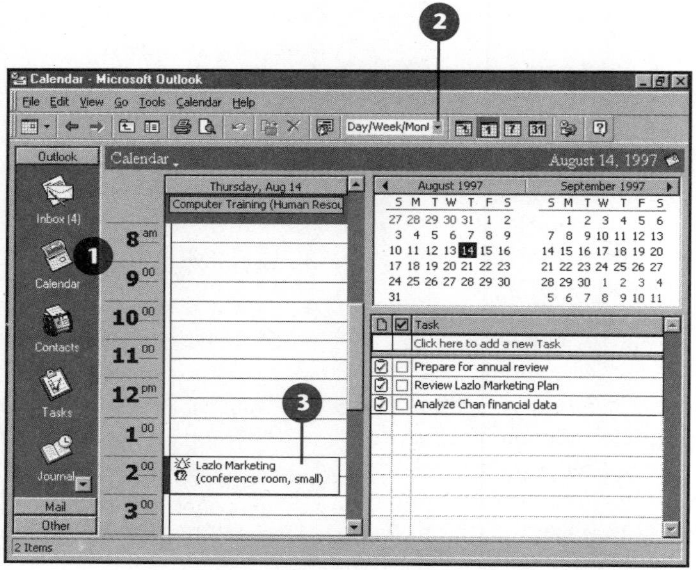

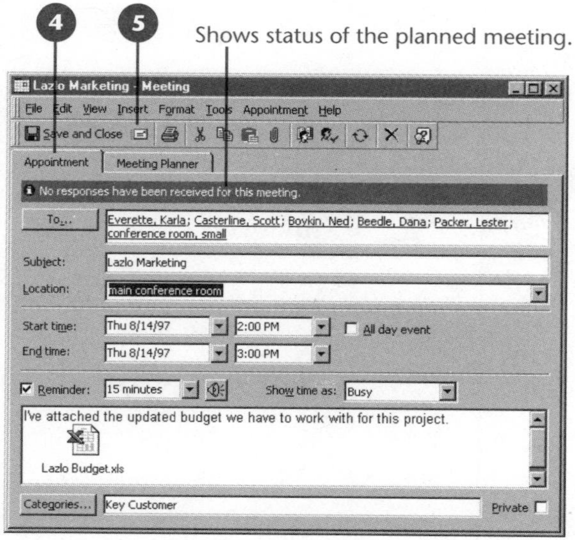

TIP

What happens when you delete a meeting? *When you cancel a meeting you must decide whether to send a cancelation notice as you delete the meeting. The cancellation notice sends an e-mail message to all invited people, notifying them that the meeting is canceled, and frees any reserved resources.*

SEE ALSO

See "Planning a Meeting" on page 249 for more information about scheduling a meeting.

Cancel a Meeting

1. Click Calendar on the Outlook bar.
2. If necessary, switch to Day/Week/Month view.
3. Click a scheduled meeting on the Time Bar.
4. Click the Delete button on the Standard toolbar.
5. Click the Send Cancellation And Delete Meeting option button.
6. Click OK.

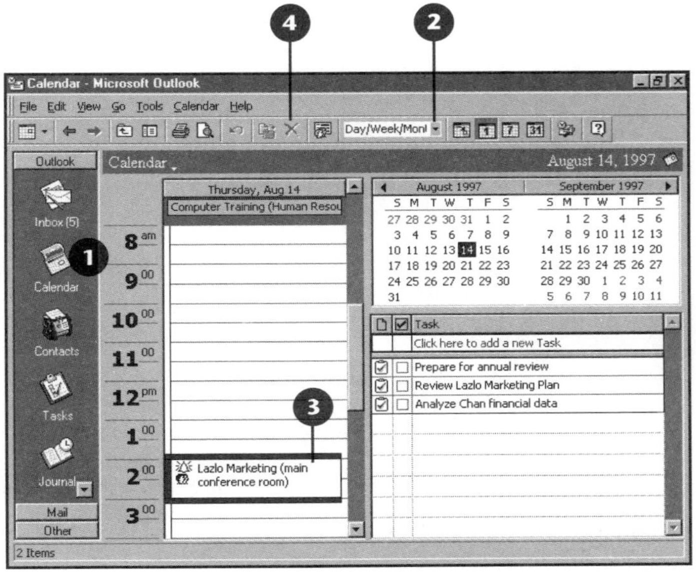

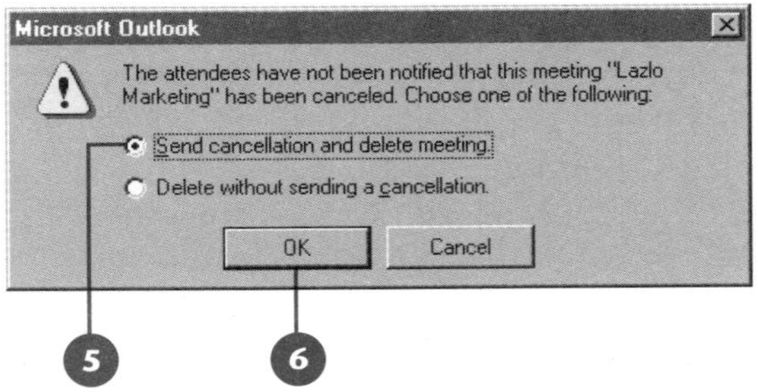

Changing a Meeting's Attendees List

As a meeting gets closer, you might want to revise the attendee list or reserve a certain resource. For example, you might want to have a supervisor attend a later meeting rather than the upcoming planning meeting. Or someone new was just assigned to the project and you want to invite them. Or you decide to reserve a white board to take notes on during the meeting. You can make these changes and send out an update message to everyone quickly from Outlook's Calendar.

SEE ALSO

See "Planning a Meeting" on page 249 for more information about scheduling a meeting.

Change Invited People or Resources

1. Click Calendar on the Outlook bar.
2. Switch to the view that shows the meeting you want to change.
3. Double-click the meeting on the Time Bar.
4. Click the Meeting Planner tab.
5. Select the names of those you no longer want at the meeting, or select the resources you longer want reserved, and then press Delete.
6. Click Invite Others.
7. Click the name of the person you want to invite or the resource you need at the meeting.
8. Click the Required, Optional, or Resources button.
9. Click OK.
10. Click the Send Update To Attendees And Close button on the Standard toolbar.

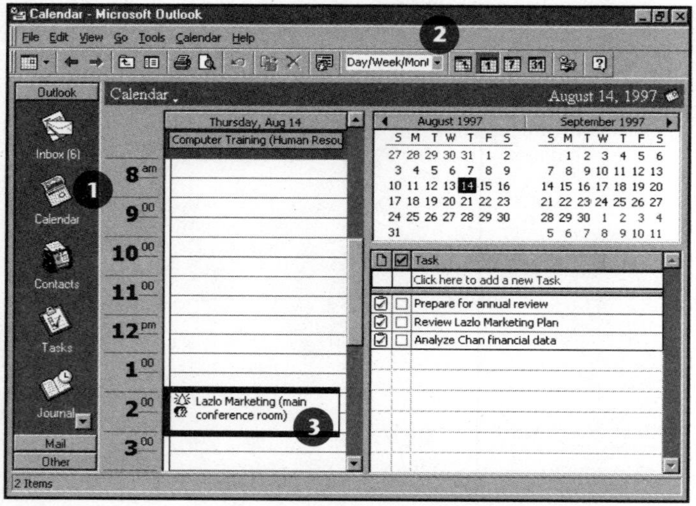

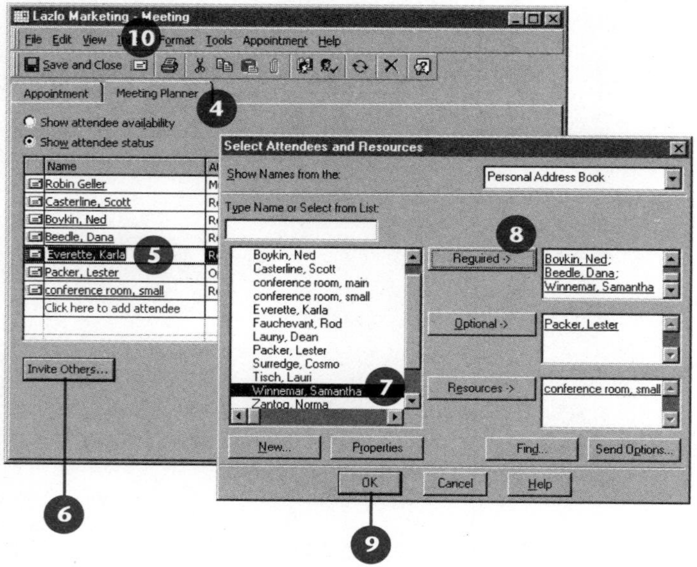

15

Managing Information with Outlook 97

IN THIS SECTION

Microsoft Outlook 97 provides an easy and efficient way to track and organize all the information that lands on your desk. Create a to-do list and assign the items on the list to others as needed from *Tasks*. Rather than cluttering your desk or obscuring your computer with sticky pad notes, use *Notes* to jot down your immediate thoughts, ideas, and other observations. With everything related to your work in one place, you can always locate what you need—whether it be a file, a note related to a specific project, or even the time of a phone call with a certain contact. Just check the *Journal* timeline to find it. As you create or work with any Outlook item—that is a task, note, journal entry, contact, appointment, and so on—you can assign *categories*—common words or phrases—so you can locate any tagged item related to a particular person, project, or other category.

Outlook 97 also provides three related, but distinct, tools with which to organize and locate information. *Group* organizes items based on a particular *field* (an element that stores a particular type of information). *Sort* arranges items in ascending or descending order according to a specified field. *Filter* shows items that match a specific criteria, such as "High Priority." You can group, sort, and filter by more than one field.

Managing Tasks

A common Monday chore is to create a list of activities that you should accomplish that week. Outlook *Tasks* is better than that traditional to-do list. You can create a to-do list with deadlines and cross off items as you complete them. Overdue tasks remain on your list until you finish them or delete them. You can also delegate a particular task to someone else by sending them a *Task Request*, complete with deadlines and related attachments. Either way, you can track a task's status and progress, estimated and actual hours, mileage, and other associated billing costs. A task remains in the Calendar Task Pad and in Tasks until you check it off or delete it.

SEE ALSO

See "Viewing Your Schedule" on page 244 for information about the Calendar Task Pad.

Create a New Task

1. Click the New Item drop-down arrow on the Standard toolbar, and then click Task.
2. Type a description of the task.
3. Set a timeframe, status, priority, alarm, categories, or any other option.
4. Type any relevant notes, or attach related files.
5. Click the Save And Close button on the Standard toolbar.

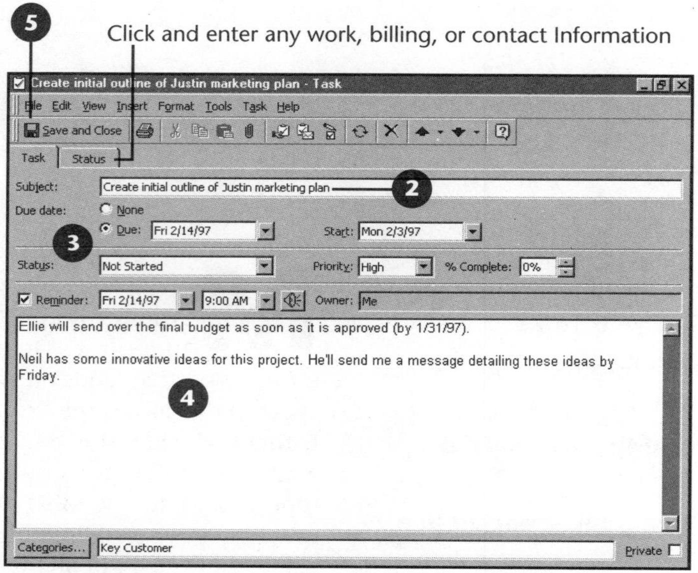

Assign a New Task to Someone Else

1. Click the New Item drop-down arrow on the Standard toolbar, and then click Task Request.
2. Type a name or e-mail address of the person who you are assigning the task.
3. Fill in the subject, timeframe, status, notes, categories, and other options.
4. Click the Send button on the Standard toolbar.

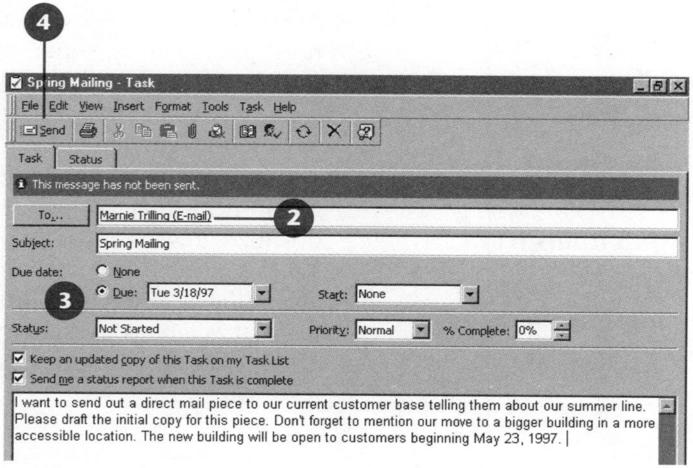

TIP

Make a task recurring. *Double-click an existing task on the Task List or Calendar Task Pad to edit it, or create a new task, click the Recurrence button on the Standard toolbar. Set a recurrence pattern, and then click OK. When the task is set up as you'd like, click the Save And Close button on the Standard toolbar.*

TIP

Insert a file into a task. *Double-click an existing task to open it, or create a new task. Click the Insert File button on the Standard toolbar. Click the Insert As Text Only, Attachment, or Shortcut option button, and then double-click the file you want to insert.*

TRY THIS

Enter a new task quickly. *To add a task quickly in either the Calendar Task Pad or the Task List, click the Click Here To Add A New Task box, type a name or brief description of the task, enter a deadline, enter any information necessary, and then press the Enter key.*

Track Tasks Assigned to Others

1. Click the Tools menu, and then click Options.
2. Click the Tasks/Notes tab.
3. Click the Keep Updated Copies Of Assigned Tasks On My Task List check box to select it.
4. Click the Send Status Reports When Assigned Tasks Are Completed check box to select it.
5. Click OK.

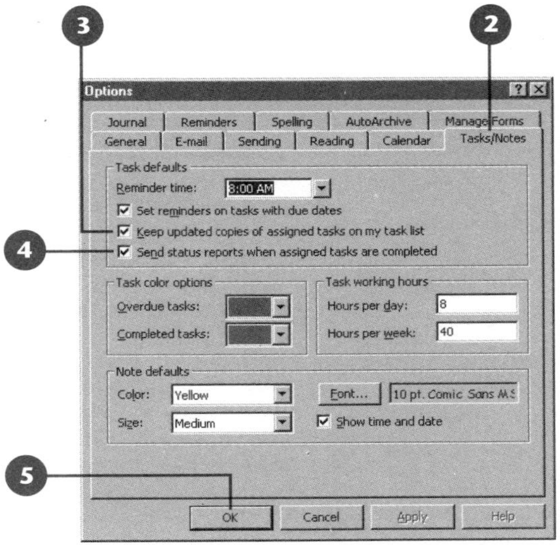

Delete Tasks from the Task List

1. Click Tasks on the Outlook bar.
2. Click the task you want to delete.
3. Click the Delete button on the Standard toolbar.

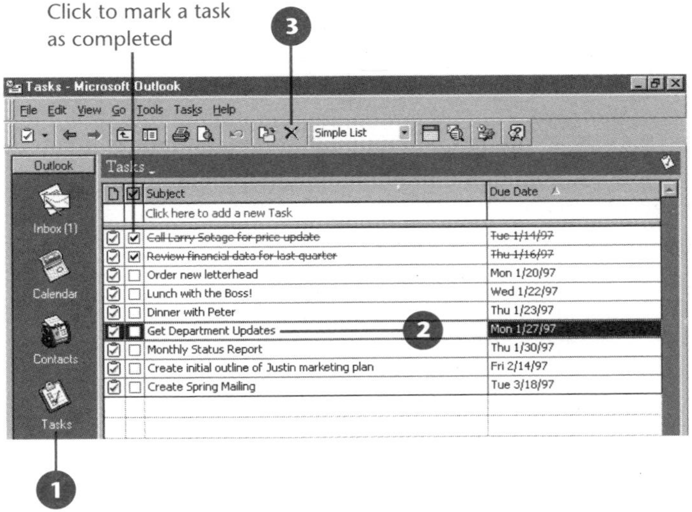

15

Recording Items in the Journal

The *Journal* is a diary of all the activities and interactions from your day. With everything organized on a timeline, you can see an overview of what you accomplished when and how long certain activities took. It also provides an alternate way to locate a particular item or file. The Journal can automatically record entries for your phone calls, e-mail messages, tasks or meeting requests and responses, faxes, and documents on which you've worked. You must record tasks, appointments, personal conversations, and existing documents manually.

SEE ALSO

See "Creating a Contact" on page 234 for information about the Contact window.

Automatically Record New Items and Documents

1. Click the Tools menu, and then click Options.
2. Click the Journal tab.
3. Click the check boxes for the items you want to record in the Journal automatically.
4. Click the check boxes of the contacts for whom you want to record the selected items.
5. Click the check boxes of the Office 97 programs that you want to record files from.
6. Click OK.

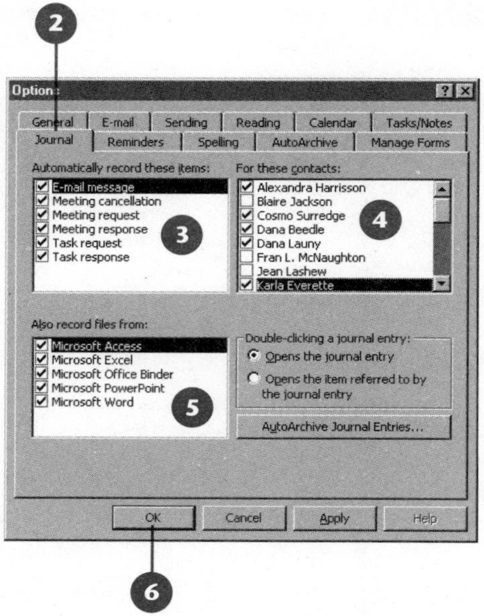

Manually Record Existing Files and Outlook Items

1. Click the items or files you want to record.
2. Click the Tools menu, and then click Record In Journal.

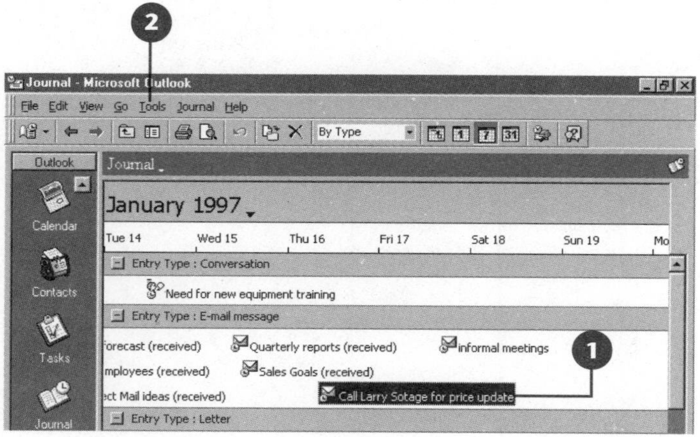

TIP

Automatically create journal entries for a contact. *When creating a new contact or editing an existing one, click the Journal tab in the Contact window, and then click the Automatically Record Journal Entries For This Contact check box.*

TIP

Manually record an existing activity for a contact. *Double-click an existing contact for whom you want to record an activity to open it. Click the Journal tab in the Contact window, and then click the New Journal Entry button. Enter the necessary information and click the Save And Close button on the Standard toolbar.*

TRY THIS

Manually record an existing document in the Journal. *Display the My Documents folder or the folder that contains your files. Drag the file from its folder in the information viewer onto the Journal icon on the Outlook bar. Make any changes necessary in the Journal Entry window, and then click the Save And Close button on the Standard toolbar.*

3. Set the entry type, contact, company, start time, duration, notes, and categories.
4. Click the Save And Close button on the Standard toolbar.

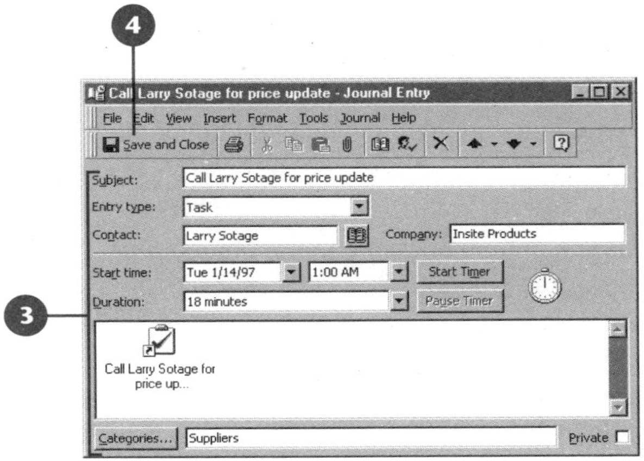

15

Manually Record a Personal Interaction

1. Click the New Item drop-down arrow on the Standard toolbar, and then click Journal Entry.
2. Type a description.
3. Click the Entry Type drop-down arrow, and then click the type of interaction you want to record.
4. If necessary, enter a contact, company, start time, duration, notes, and categories.
5. Click the Save And Close button on the Standard toolbar.

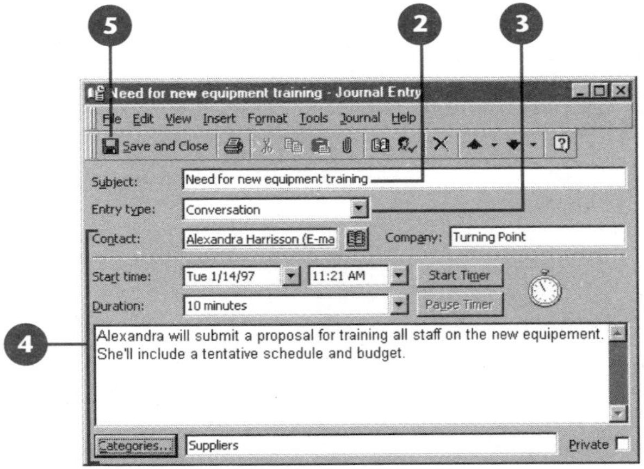

Working with Journal Entries

Journal entries and their related items, documents, and contacts are easy to open, move, and even delete. When you modify a journal entry, its associated item, document, or contact is not affected. Likewise, when you modify an item, document, or contact, any existing related journal entries remain unchanged. If you no longer need a journal entry, you can select the entry and press Delete or click the Delete button to remove it.

TIP

Expanding and collapsing entry types. *When you switch to the Journal to view the recorded items, some entries' types might be expanded to show all items and other might be collapsed to hide all items. You can easily switch between expanded and collapsed views by double-clicking an Entry Type bar.*

Open a Journal Entry and Its Recorded Item

1. Click Journal on the Outlook bar.
2. If necessary, double-click the entry type to display its items.
3. Double-click the item, document, contact name, or so on.

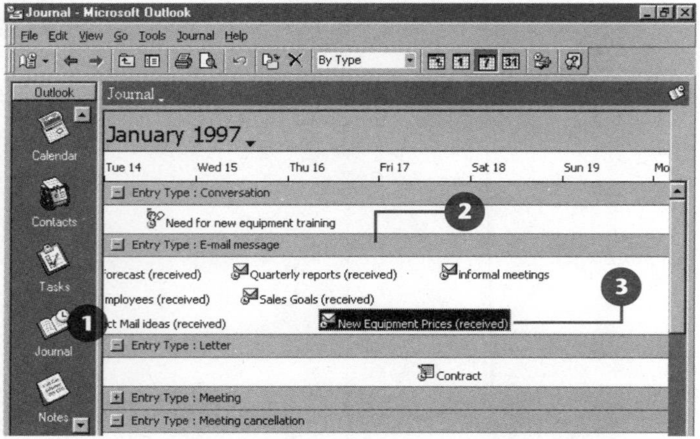

View Journal Entries for a Contact

1. Click Contacts on the Outlook bar.
2. Double-click a contact name.
3. Click the Journal tab.
4. Click the Show drop-down arrow, and then click the type of entries you want to view.
5. Click the Save And Close button on the Standard toolbar.

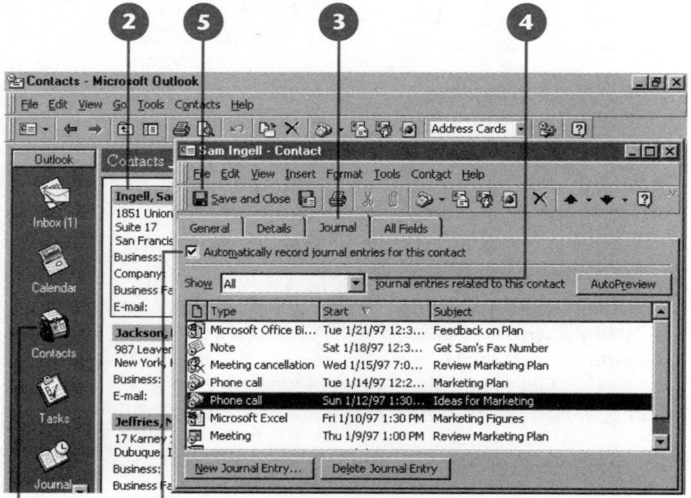

Click to record every item or activity related to this person in the Journal.

Viewing Information in a Timeline

A *timeline* is an easy way to view the chronological order of recorded items, documents, and activities in the Journal. Each item appears at the date and time it originated. A solid bar indicates the duration of any activity that takes place over a period of time.

TIP

Create a new journal entry quickly. *Double-click in the white area below the Entry Type bar to open a new journal entry. Fill in the Journal Entry window as usual.*

TRY THIS

Move to a specific Journal date. *Click the month and year listed at the top of the information viewer to display a calendar. Click the month and year at the top of the calendar to display a list of months. Click the month you want to switch to, and then click the exact date you want to view.*

Change the Location of Items and Documents in a Timeline

1. Click Journal on the Outlook bar.
2. Double-click the journal entry you want to move.
3. Click the Start Date drop-down, and then click a new day.
4. Click the Start Time drop-down arrow, and then click a new time.
5. Click the Save And Close button on the Standard toolbar.

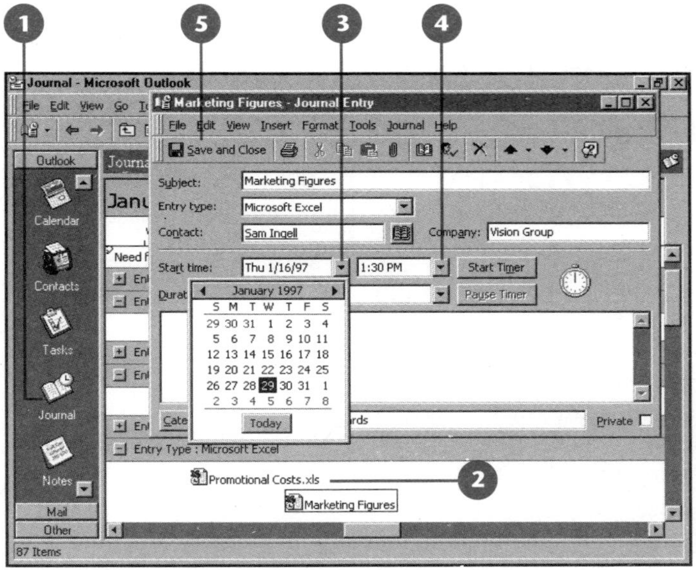

15

Display Time Scales

- Click the Day button on the Standard toolbar to see one day at a time.
- Click the Week button on the Standard toolbar to view a week at a time.
- Click the Month button on the Standard toolbar to look at 30 days.
- Click the Go To Today button on the Standard toolbar to move to the current day.

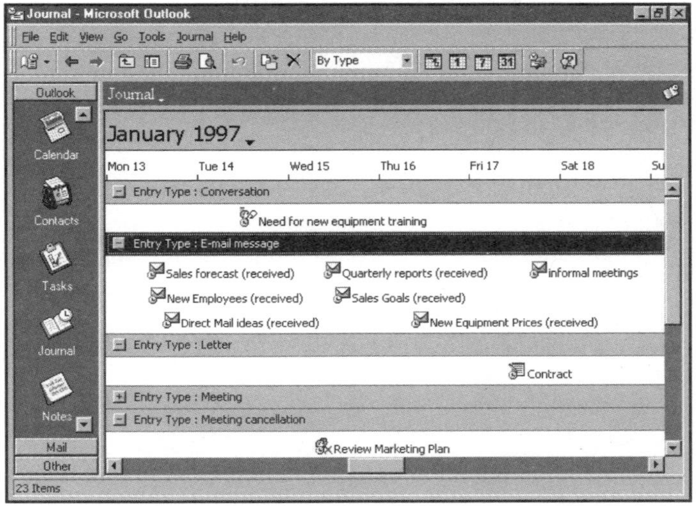

Organizing Information by Categories

A *category* is one or more keywords or phrases you assign to items so you can later find, group, sort, or filter them. Categories provide additional flexibility in how you organize and store items and files. With categories you can store related items in different folders or unrelated items in the same folder and still compile a complete list of items related to a specific category. Outlook starts you off with a *Master Category List* of some common categories, but you can add or remove them to fit your purposes.

TIP

Create a mailing list. *You can export a specific category of contacts using Microsoft's Word Mail Merge to create a mailing list.*

Assign and Remove Categories to and from an Outlook Item

1. Click any Outlook item to select it.
2. Click the Edit menu, and then click Categories.
3. Click check boxes to assign and remove categories.
4. Click OK.

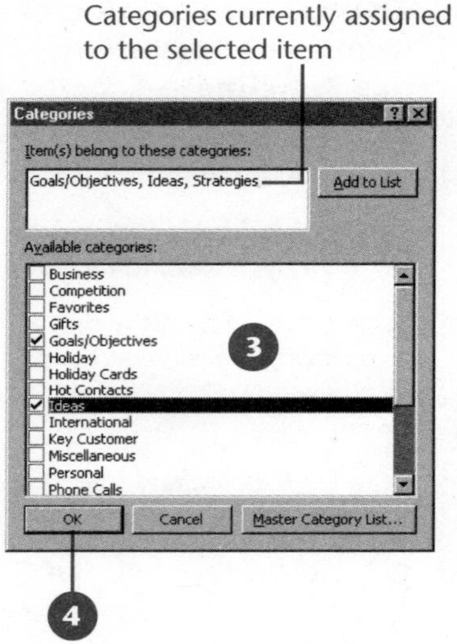

Add or Remove a Category

1. Click any Outlook item to select it.
2. Click the Edit menu, and then click Categories.
3. Click Master Category List.
4. Type a new category name, or click the category you want to remove.
5. Click Add or Delete.
6. Click OK.
7. Click OK.

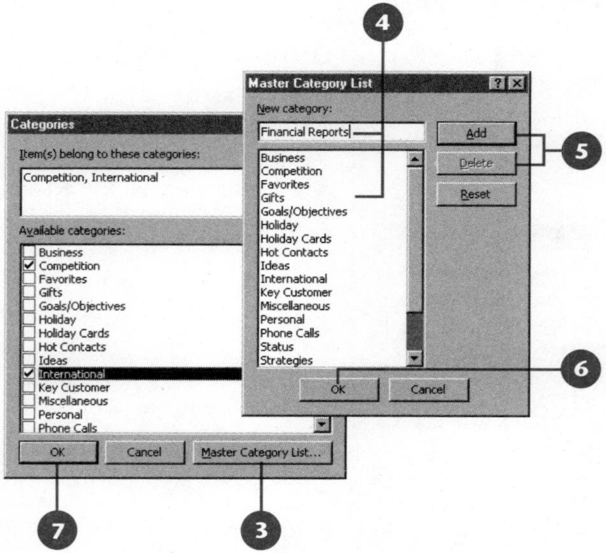

Viewing Items in Groups

As the number of items in Outlook grows, you'll want to be able to view related items. A *group* is any set of items with a common element, such as an assigned category, priority level, or associated contact name. You can group items only in a table or timeline view. If an item has more than one entry listed in the field by which you are grouping (for example, three categories), that item appears in every relevant group, and changes you make to the item in one group will appear in all copies of that item.

TIP

Ungroup items. *Click the View menu, click Group By, and then click Clear All.*

Group By Box button

Group Items

1. Click the View drop-down arrow on the Standard toolbar, and then click a table view.
2. Click the Group By Box button on the Standard toolbar.
3. Drag the first column heading to the Group By box.
4. Drag any subsequent headings to the Group By box in the order by which you want to group them.

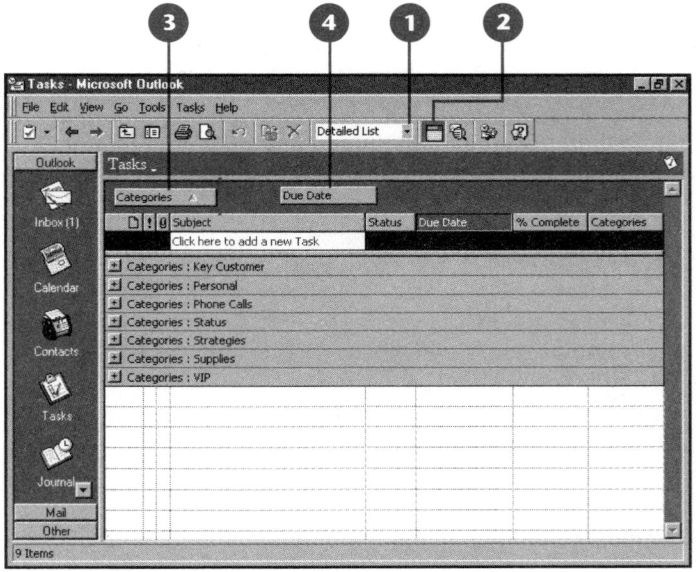

View Grouped Items or Headings

Refer to the table for commands to show or hide grouped items and headings.

VIEWING GROUPED ITEMS AND HEADINGS

To	Click
Show items in a group	Expand button
Hide items in a group	Collapse button
Show all items in all groups	View, point to Expand/Collapse Groups, click Expand All
Show only all group headings	View, point to Expand/Collapse Groups, click Collapse All
Save new view settings	View, click Group By, click the Expand Collapse Defaults drop-down arrow, click As Last Viewed, click OK

Sorting Items

Sometimes you'll want to organize items in a specific order. For example, tasks from high to low priority or in alphabetical order by category. A *sort* arranges items in ascending (A to Z, low to high, recent to distant) or descending (Z to A, high to low, distant to recent), alphabetical, numerical, or chronological order. You can sort items by one or more fields; you can also sort grouped items. Items must be in a table view to sort.

Sort a List of Items in a Table

1. Click the View drop-down arrow on the Standard toolbar, and then click a table view.
2. Click the View menu, and then click Sort.
3. Click the Sort Items By drop-down arrow, and then click a field.
4. Click the Ascending or Descending option button.
5. Click the Then By drop-down arrow, and then click a second sort element and sort order, if necessary.
6. Click OK.

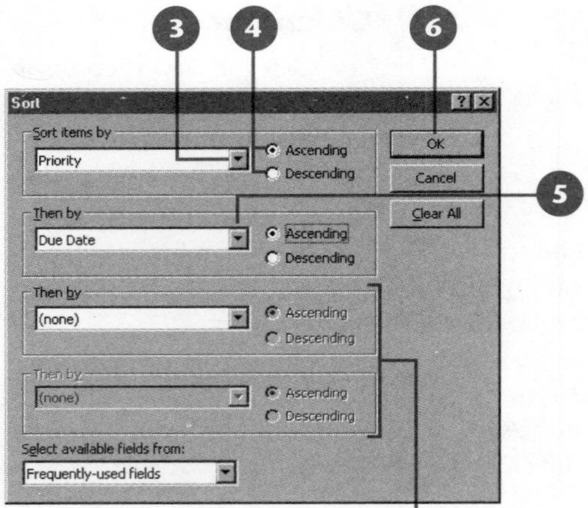

Click these drop-down arrows for additional sort elements, if necessary.

TRY THIS

Sort grouped items. *Try grouping items and then sorting them. If you choose the same element to sort and group by, the groups are sorted instead of the individual items.*

Remove a Sort

1. Click the View menu, and then click Sort.
2. Click Clear All.
3. Click OK.

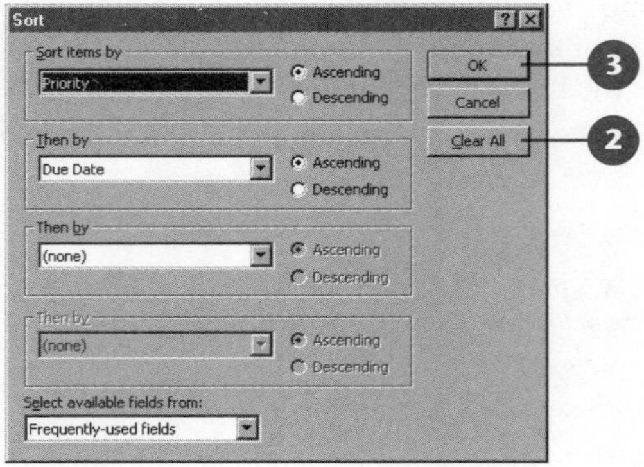

SEE ALSO

See "Viewing Items in Groups" on page 261 for more information about grouping items.

Viewing Specific Files Using Filters

A *filter* isolates the items or files that match certain specifications, such as all appointments with a certain a contact or any documents you created last week. If you select two or more filter criteria, only those items and files that meet all the criteria are listed. "Filter Applied" appears in the lower left corner of the status bar as a reminder that you filtered the items and files you are viewing.

> **TIP**
>
> **Create a filter that fits your needs.** *You can filter for any or all of the options available in the Filter dialog box. For example, you might want to filter for a specific word in a certain field, for all items with a particular status, or for all items received from or sent to someone on a specific day.*

Set a Filter to Show Certain Items and Files

1. Click the View menu, and then click Filter.
2. Type a word to search for.
3. Click the In drop-down arrow, and then click a field.
4. Enter in the status, sender, recipient, or timeframe as necessary.
5. Click OK.

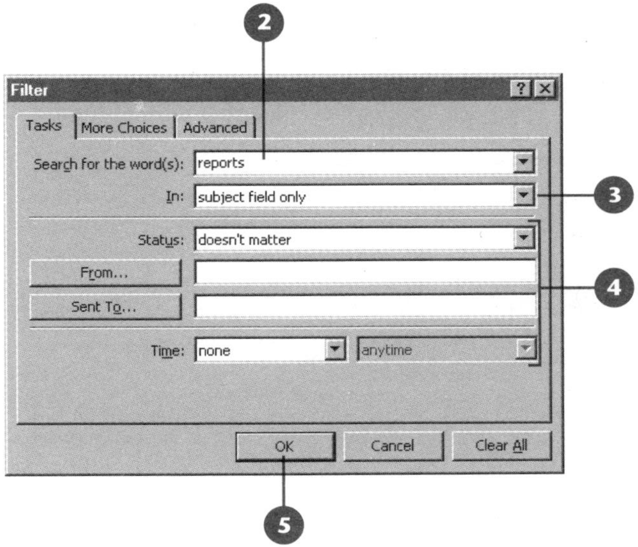

Remove a Filter

1. Click the View menu, and then click Filter.
2. Click Clear All.
3. Click OK.

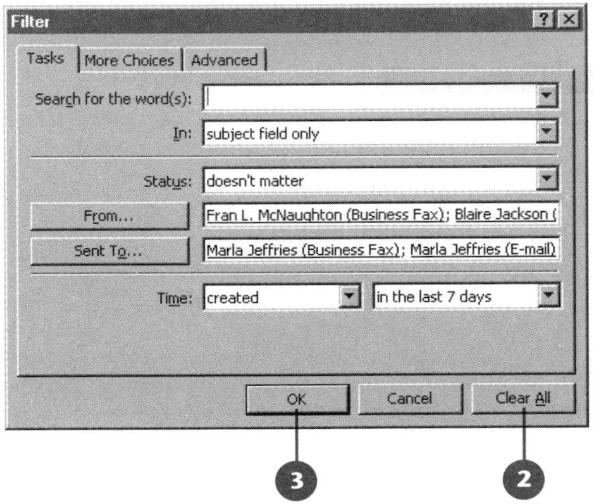

Printing Items from Outlook

You can print any item in Outlook 97. The default or preset printing option is Memo style, which adds a footer (text at the bottom of a page) with the print date, your name, and a page number. Other printing options are available in table, calendar, and card views. You cannot print from a timeline or icon view. You should try to preview your documents before you print to make sure the pages look like you expect.

TRY THIS

Print using the default settings. *Select a view and the item or items you want to print, and then click the Print button on the Standard toolbar.*

Print Preview button

Preview an Item Before Printing

1. If necessary, click an Outlook item to select it.
2. Click the Print Preview button on the Standard toolbar.
3. Click the Page Up or Page Down button on the Print Preview toolbar to move between pages.
4. Click the pointer on a page to zoom in and out.
5. Click the Close button on the Print Preview toolbar.

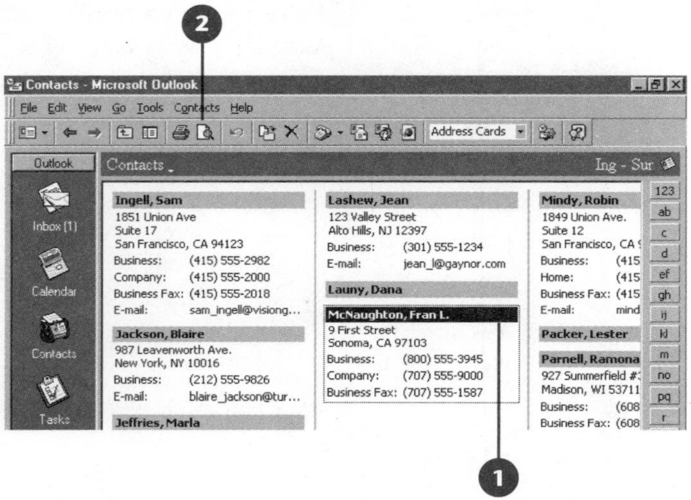

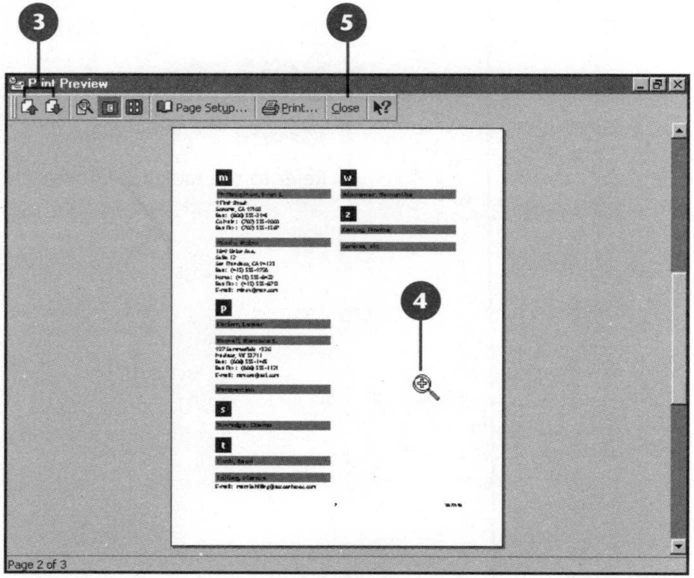

TIP

Print categorized items. *Sort items by categories or find a particular category, select one or more items, and then print.*

Print button

Print an Item or View

1. Click the File menu, and then click Print, or click the Print button on the Print Preview toolbar.
2. Type the number of copies you want.
3. Choose a style from the Print Style list.
4. Specify a print range, if necessary.
5. Click OK.

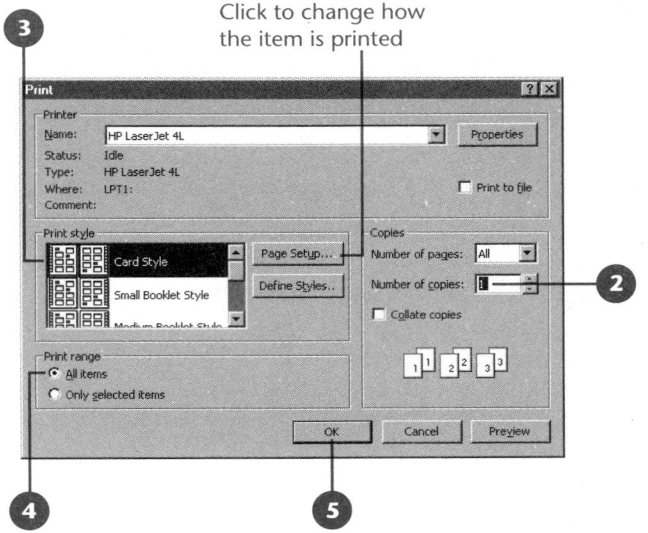

Printing Options Available in Different Views

Refer to the table for information on the printing options available in the different views.

PRINTING OPTIONS

View	Default	Prints
Table	Table	All items in a list in the visible columns
Calendar	Daily	Each day from 7 A.M. to 7 P.M. on a separate page with tasks and notes
	Weekly	Each week from midnight to midnight on a separate page
	Monthly	Each month on a separate page
	Tri-Fold	Three equal columns with one day, one month, and tasks each in its own column
Card	Card	All contact cards with letter tabs and headings and six blank cards at the end
	Phone List	Names and phone numbers for all contacts with letter tabs and headings

Writing Miscellaneous Notes

Notes replace the random scraps of paper on which you might jot down reminders, questions, thoughts, ideas, or directions. Like the popular sticky notes, you can move a note anywhere on your screen and leave it displayed as you work. Any edits you make to a note are saved automatically. The ability to color-code, size, categorize, sort, or filter notes makes these notes even more handy than their paper counterparts.

TIP

Change the look of Notes. *To change the note color, size, font, and display, click the Tools menu, click Options, and then click the Tasks/Notes tab. Select the Note Default options you want to change.*

TIP

Delete a note. *Select the note or notes you want to delete, and then click the Delete button on the Standard toolbar.*

Write a New Note

1. Click the New Item drop-down arrow on the Standard toolbar.
2. Click Note.
3. Type the text of the note.
4. Drag the note to any location on your screen or close it.

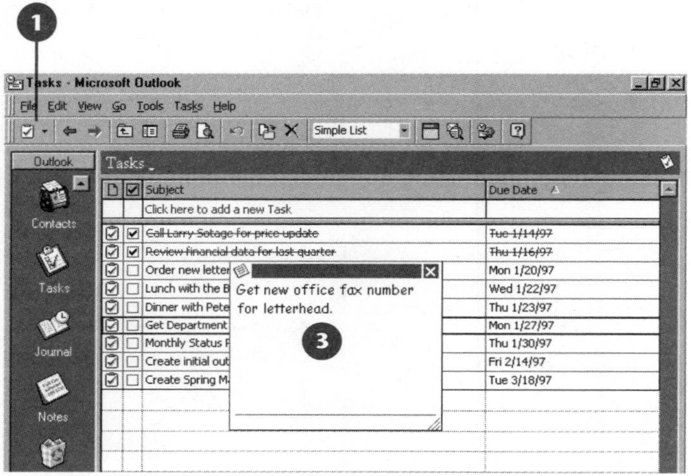

Open and Close a Note

1. Click Notes on the Outlook bar.
2. Double-click the note you want to open.
3. Click the Close button to close the note.

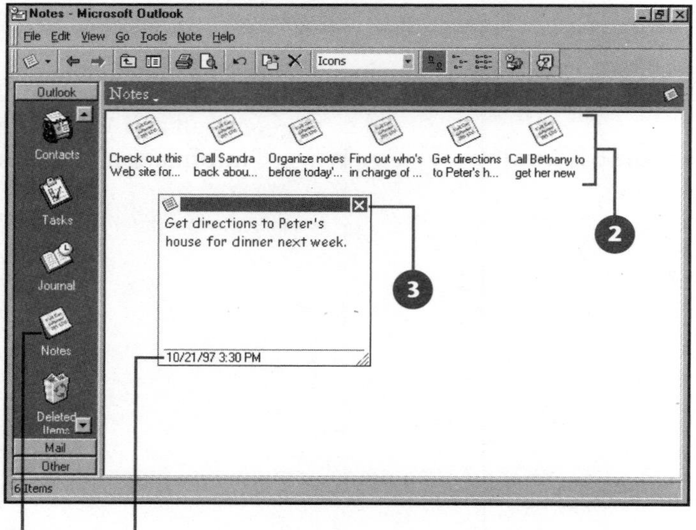

Indicates the date and time you wrote the note

16

Communicating and Scheduling with Outlook 98

IN THIS SECTION

Installing Outlook 98

Moving Around Outlook

Attaching a File to E-Mail

Creating a Contact

Creating and Sending an E-Mail Message

Using Stationery

Reading and Replying to an E-Mail Message

Managing E-Mail Messages

Viewing Your Schedule

Scheduling an Event

Rescheduling an Event

Planning a Meeting

Rescheduling or Canceling a Meeting

Changing a Meeting's Attendees List

If, like many people, you're juggling a scheduler, an address book, and an e-mail address list, and you're cluttering your desk and computer with reminder notes and to-do lists, help is here—Microsoft Outlook 98.

Outlook 98 integrates all the common planning, scheduling, organization, and management tools into one simple and flexible system.

- *Inbox* receives and stores your incoming messages.
- *Contacts* clears your desk of the standard card file and compiles multiple addresses, phone numbers, e-mail and Web addresses, and any personal information you need about each contact.
- *Calendar* replaces your daily or weekly planner and helps you schedule meetings and block time for activities.
- *Tasks* organizes and tracks your to-do list.
- *Notes* provides a place to jot random notes that you can group, sort, and categorize.
- *Journal* automatically records your activities.

Outlook 98 provides a single place to plan, organize, and manage every aspect of your work and personal life.

Installing Outlook 98

Since there are many ways to send and receive e-mail, Microsoft Outlook 98 allows you to customize your installation to best fit how you work everyday. Outlook 98 can be used with the most common e-mail servers including SMTP/POP3 or IMAP4 and Microsoft Exchange Server. Outlook 98 also works well with other messaging services such as Microsoft Mail, Compu-Serve, and LotusNotes. So, whether you are sending e-mail messages, scheduling meetings with others, or just in need of a personal management system, Outlook 98 provides the necessary tools for your information management needs.

Optimizing the Outlook Setup

1. Start the Outlook 98 Setup Wizard to begin installing Outlook 98.
2. Read the information in each setup dialog box, and then enter the required information. Click Next to continue.
3. In the Installation Option dialog box, click the drop-down arrow, and then select the option that best fits your needs:
   - Minimal Installation
   - Standard Installation
   - Enhanced Installation
   - Full Installation
4. Read the information in each setup dialog box, and then enter the required information. Click Next to continue.
5. Click Finish in the last setup dialog box.

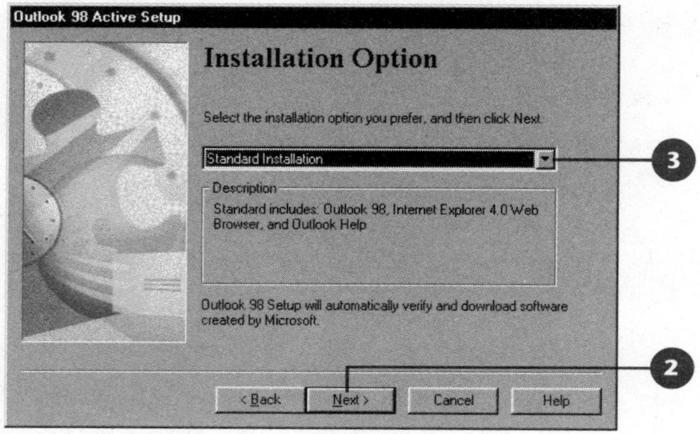
Outlook 98 Active Setup
Installation Option
Select the installation option you prefer, and then click Next.
Standard Installation
Description
Standard includes: Outlook 98, Internet Explorer 4.0 Web Browser, and Outlook Help
Outlook 98 Setup will automatically verify and download software created by Microsoft.
< Back
Next >
Cancel
Help
3
2

E-MAIL SERVICE OPTIONS

Service	Feature Summary
Internet Only	E-mail access; send and receive meeting requests; use with Microsoft Exchange Server; manage personal tasks, contacts, appointments, and calendar
Corporate Or Workgroup	Use with Microsoft Exchange Server, message recall and voting buttons, complete group scheduling interpretable with Schedule+, share contact information; use with MS Mail and third party mail programs; manage personal tasks, contacts, appointments, and calendar
No E-Mail	Manage personal tasks, contacts, appointments, and calendar; no e-mail or Internet access

Viewing the Outlook Window

Title bar
The title bar shows the program name, Microsoft Outlook, preceded by the Outlook folder you have open, in this case, Inbox.

Standard toolbar
Outlook opens with the Standard toolbar on screen; other toolbars are available in some folders.

Menu bar
The menu bar gives you access to all the menu options. Simply click a menu name to display a list of related commands, and then click the command you want to issue.

Folder Banner
The name of the folder in which you are working appears here.

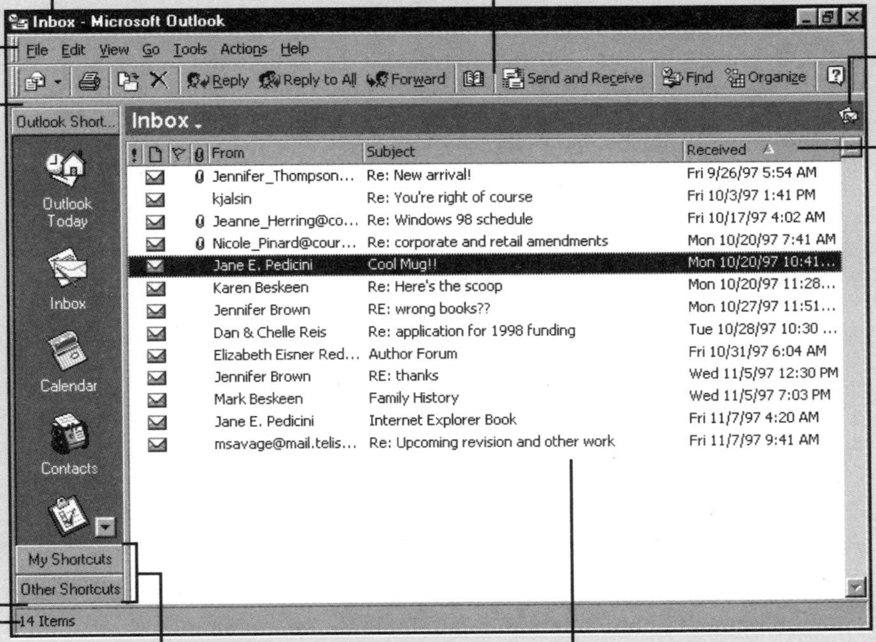

Column buttons
Each folder has different column buttons that you can use to change the way the contents are organized. Click a column button to switch between *ascending* (low to high, A to Z, or early to late) and *descending* (high to low, Z to A, or late to early) order.

Outlook Bar
The Outlook Bar is always visible and contains shortcut icons you can click to move among all the groups and folders. You can add additional shortcut icons here to quickly open other folders on your system or network.

Status bar
The status bar indicates the number of items you have stored or saved in a folder, for example, two notes, five appointments, seven messages, and so on.

Group buttons
The various components of Outlook (such as Calendar, Contacts, etc.) are split into three groups by default. Click a group button to display shortcuts for that group's components.

Information viewer
This part of the screen changes to different views, depending on the folder you are using. In this figure, you see a list of e-mail messages in the Inbox.

Moving Around Outlook

As you work, you'll need to switch between the Outlook folders frequently and create new *items* such as tasks, contacts, e-mail messages, and appointments. Imagine you are revising your list of tasks. Then you call a business associate who recommends you contact her colleague. You add him to your Address Book and then send him an e-mail message. He then calls to arrange a meeting. To accomplish all this, you need to move smoothly from Tasks to Contacts to Inbox to Calendar with a single click.

TIP

Create a new item quickly. *To create an item that's appropriate for the open folder, click the New Item button on the Standard toolbar. For example, if Calendar is open, the Appointment dialog box opens.*

Display Folder Icons and Open a Folder

1. Click a group button on the Outlook Bar.

   Note that the New Item button name changes depending on the folder in which you are currently working.

2. If necessary, click the Scroll button to display the icon you want.
3. Click any folder icon on the Outlook bar that you want to open.

Create a New Item for Any Folder

1. Click the New Item drop-down arrow on the Standard toolbar.
2. Click the type of item you want to create.

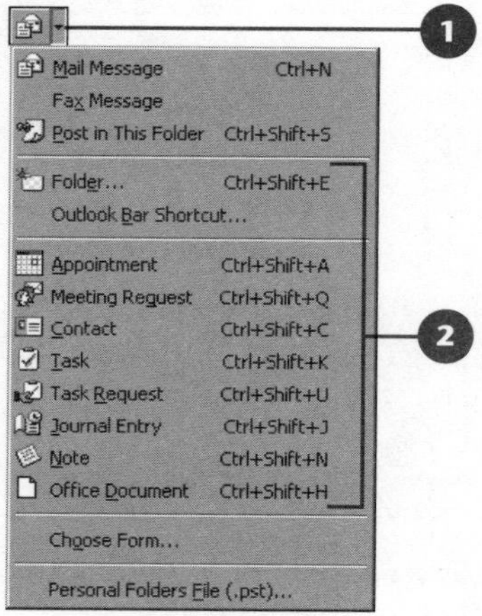

Attaching a File to E-Mail

In addition to exchanging messages, sharing files is a powerful aspect of e-mail. You can attach one or more files, such as a picture or a document, to a mail message. The recipient of the e-mail then opens the file from the program in which it was created. For example, suppose you are working on a report that needs to be presented today by a colleague in another part of the country. After you finish the report, you can attach the report file to a mail message and send the message with the attached report directly to your colleague. Attaching a file to a message becomes very handy when you want to deliver a file promptly.

TIP

Use drag-and-drop to attach a file quickly. *You can quickly attach a file to an e-mail message by dragging it from the desktop or Windows Explorer to the message box.*

Attach a File to a Message

1. Compose a new message, or open an existing message.
2. Click the Insert File button on the Standard toolbar.
3. Click the Look In drop-down arrow, and then select the drive and folder that contains the file you want to attach.
4. Click the file you want to attach to the message.
5. Click OK.

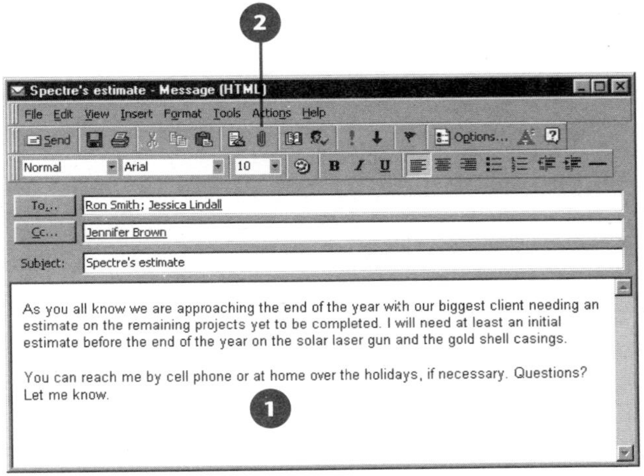

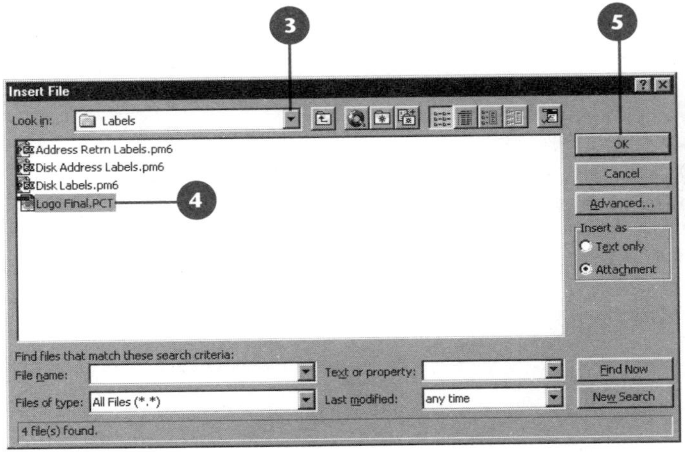

16

Creating a Contact

A *contact* is a person or company that you communicate with. One contact often has several mailing addresses, various phone and fax numbers, e-mail addresses, and Web sites. You can store all this data in the Contacts folder along with more detailed information, such as job title, birthdays and anniversaries. When you double-click a contact, you open a dialog box in which you can edit the contact information. You can also edit most contact information from within the information viewer.

> **TIP**
>
> **Create multiple new contacts.** *Once you are finished creating a contact you can click File, and then click Save And New to close the completed contact and open a new untitled contact.*

Create a New Contact

1. Click the New Item drop-down arrow on the Standard toolbar, and then click Contact.
2. Fill in information on the General tab. You can enter addresses (postal and e-mail) and phone numbers. Select Categories to help you organize your contacts.
3. Click the Save and Close button on the Standard toolbar.

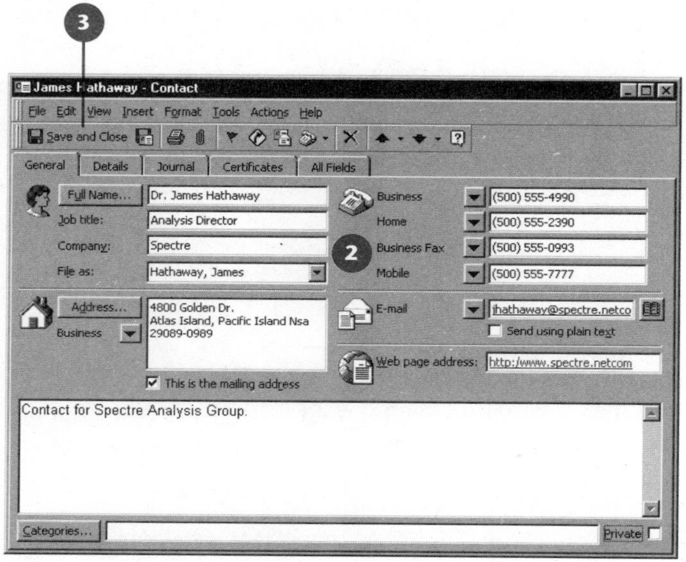

Move Around the Contact Information Viewer

1. Click Contacts on the Outlook Bar.
2. Click the View menu, point to Current View, and then click Detailed Address Cards.
3. Click the button for the first letter of the name under which the contact is filed.

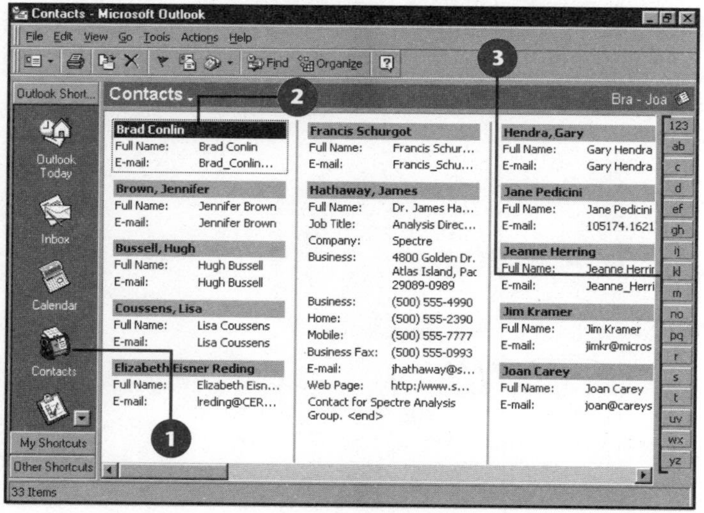

TIP

Delete a contact. *You can remove any contact from your list by clicking the contact you want to delete, and then clicking the Delete button on the Standard toolbar. Any journal entries that refer to that contact remain intact.*

Open and Close an Existing Contact Card

1. Click Contacts on the Outlook Bar.
2. Find the contact you want, and then double-click it.
3. Click the Close button.

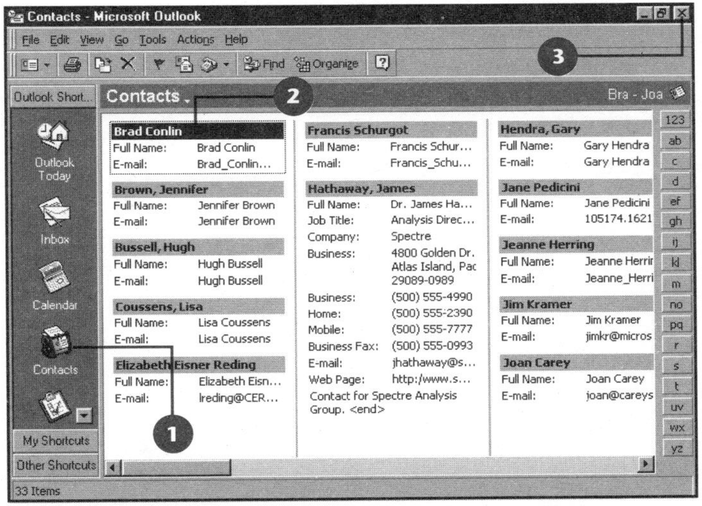

Update Existing Contact Information

1. Click Contacts on the Outlook Bar.
2. Click the View menu, point to Current View, and then click Detailed Address Cards.
3. Click in the contact card you want to change.
4. Use the usual editing commands to update the information.

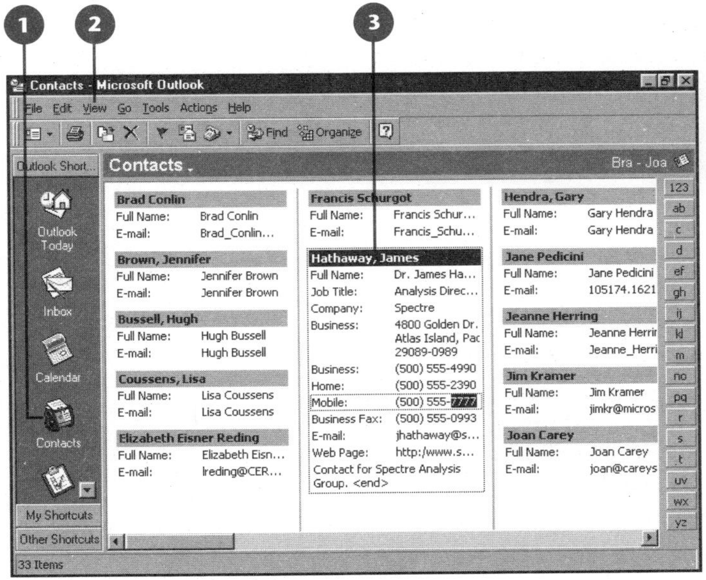

TIP

Trouble editing contact information? *If you try but can't edit a contact's information from a particular view, you need to turn on in-cell editing. Click the View menu, point to Current View, click Edit Current View, click Format, and then click the Allow In-Cell Editing check box, and then click OK twice.*

Creating and Sending an E-Mail Message

E-mail messages are a quick and effective way to communicate with others. They follow a standard memo format. To send a message, you need to enter the recipient's complete e-mail address. You can send the same message to more than one person. Using the Address Book makes entering e-mail addresses quick and easy.

TIP

An important note about e-mail addresses. *An e-mail address is not case sensitive (that is, capitalization doesn't matter) and cannot contain spaces.*

New Mail Message button

Create and Send an E-Mail Message

1. Click the New Mail Message drop-down arrow on the Standard toolbar.
2. Click Mail Message.
3. Click the To button.
4. Select an Address Book.
5. Click a name, and if necessary, press Ctrl while you click other names.
6. Click the To, Cc, or Bcc button. (To sends the message to the selected names; Cc sends a courtesy copy; Bcc sends a blind courtesy copy.)
7. When you have finished selecting names, click OK.
8. Click in the Subject box, and type a brief description of your message.
9. Click in the message box, and type the text of your message. Attach files as necessary.
10. Click the Options button on the Standard toolbar, select the options you want, and then click Close.
11. Click the Send button on the Standard toolbar.

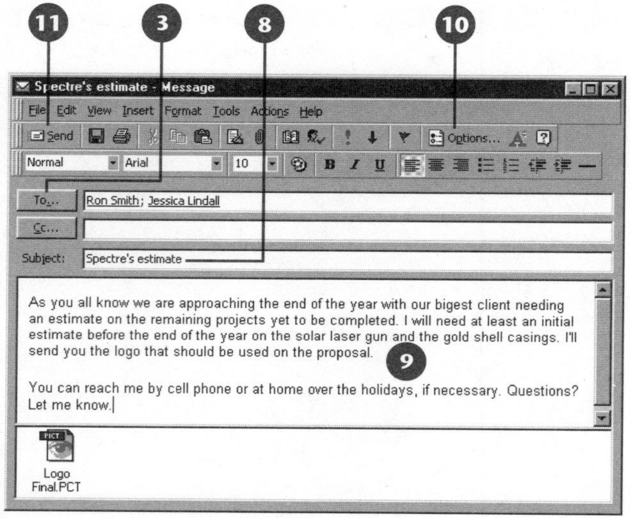

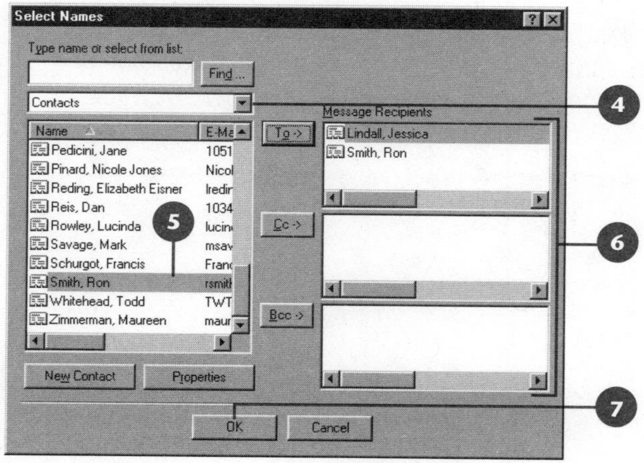

TIP

Compose a message now, but send it later. *To save a partially written message without sending it, click the Save button on the Standard toolbar, and then click the Close button in the upper right corner of the dialog box to close it. When you're ready to send the message, open the Drafts folder, double-click the message, and then click the Send button on the Standard toolbar.*

Find a Name in the Address Book

1. Click the To button in the Message dialog box.
2. Select the Address Book you want to search.
3. Click Find.
4. Type the first several letters of the name you want to find.
5. Click Find Now.

   The Find People dialog box expands to display the people found.
6. Click the To, Cc, or Bcc button.
7. Click OK.

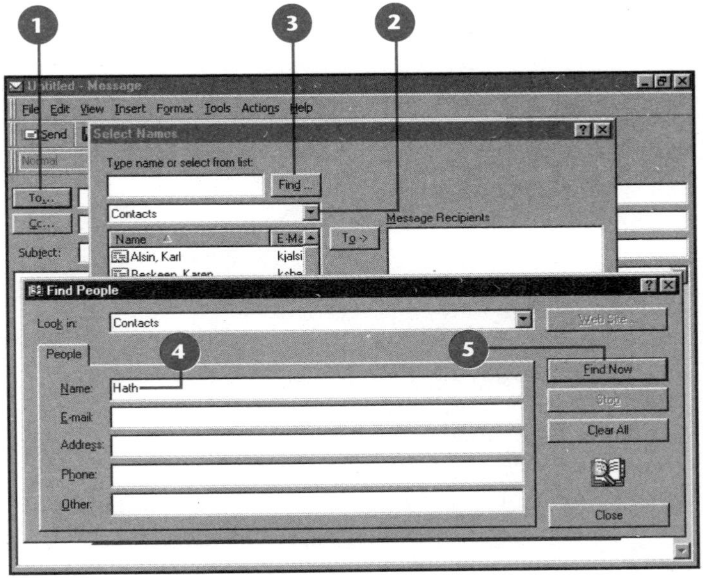

16

TIP

What if an e-mail address isn't in the Address Book? *If the e-mail address you need isn't in the Address Book, but you know the person's exact and complete address, you can type it directly in the To box in the Message dialog box. (Use a semicolon to separate two or more addresses.)*

Add a Name to an Address Book

1. Click the Tools menu, and then click Address Book.
2. Click the New Contact button on the toolbar.
3. Enter all the necessary personal and business information, and then click OK.
4. Click the Close button.

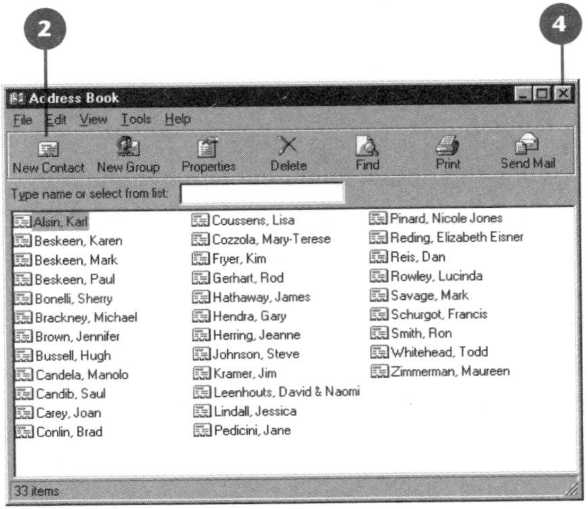

Using Stationery

Tired of the typical bland, unexciting look of e-mail? Outlook 98 now gives you the ability to create and add custom stationery and a personalized signature to your e-mail. Stationery can include background images, different text fonts, a signature, and even a personal Business Card. A *signature* is any file, either text file or graphic file, you choose to use as your signature. A *Business Card* is your, or someone else's, contact information from the Address Book. Any type of computer or digital device can read the Business Card.

Create Stationery

1. Click the Tools menu, click Options, and then click the Mail Format tab.
2. Click Stationery Picker.
3. Click a stationery from the list, or click New to create your own stationery.
4. Click OK, and then click OK again.

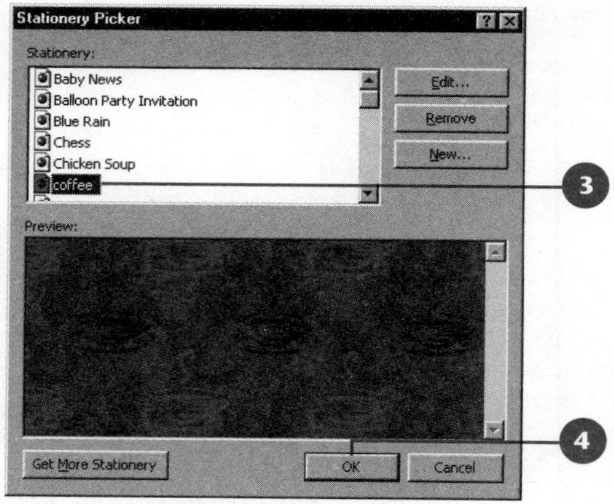

Create a Signature

1. Click the Tools menu, click Options, and then click the Mail Format tab.
2. Click Signature Picker and then click New.
3. Enter a name for your signature in the top text box, and then click Next.
4. Type your signature text.
5. Select the signature, and then use the Font and Paragraph buttons to customize the text.
6. Click Finish, click OK, and then click OK again.

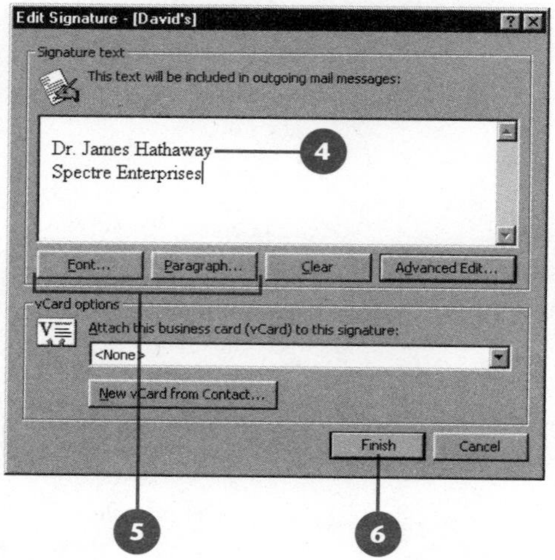

TIP

Create a message using other stationery. *Click Inbox on the Outlook Bar, click the Actions menu, point to New Mail Message Using, and then click a stationery.*

SEE ALSO

See "Creating a Contact" on page 272 for information on contact cards.

Create a Business Card

1. Click the Tools menu, click Options, and then click the Mail Format tab.
2. Click Signature Picker.
3. Click an existing signature in the Signature box, and then click Edit. Or create a new signature.
4. Click New vCard From Contact.
5. Click a contact in the Name box.
6. Click Add, and then click OK.
7. Click OK three times to close the dialog boxes.

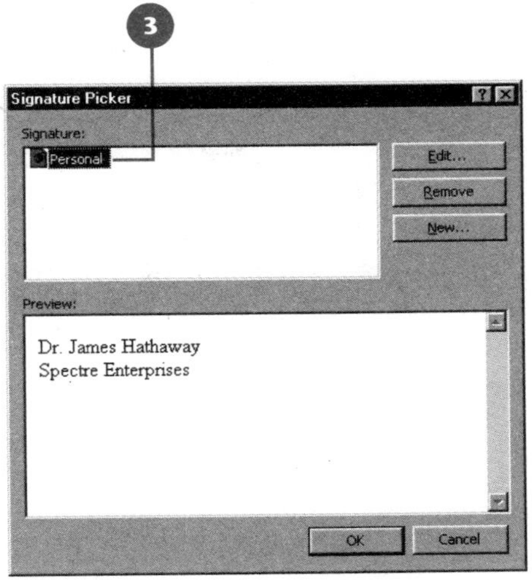

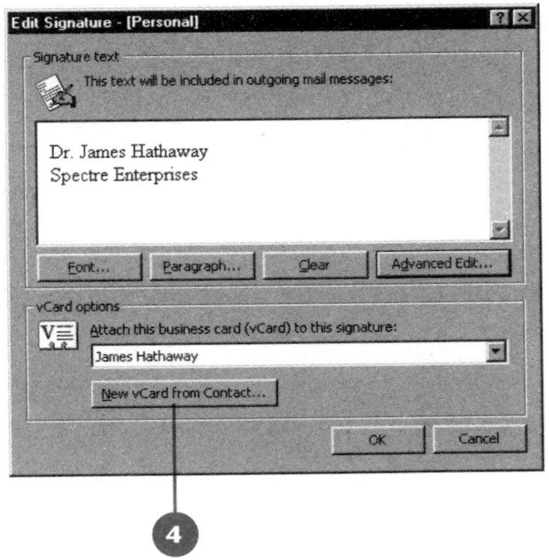

16

Reading and Replying to an E-Mail Message

You can receive e-mail messages anytime day or night, even when your computer is turned off. New messages appear in the Inbox along with any messages you haven't yet stored or deleted. A message flag appears next to any message that has a set importance or sensitivity level. The message flags, along with the sender's name and subject line, help you determine the content of a message and which one you want to open, read, and respond to first.

SEE ALSO

See "Creating and Sending an E-Mail Message" on page 274 for more information about addressing e-mail messages and entering text.

Preview and Open a Message

1. Click Inbox on the Outlook Bar.
2. Click the View menu, and then click AutoPreview.
3. Double-click the message you want to open.

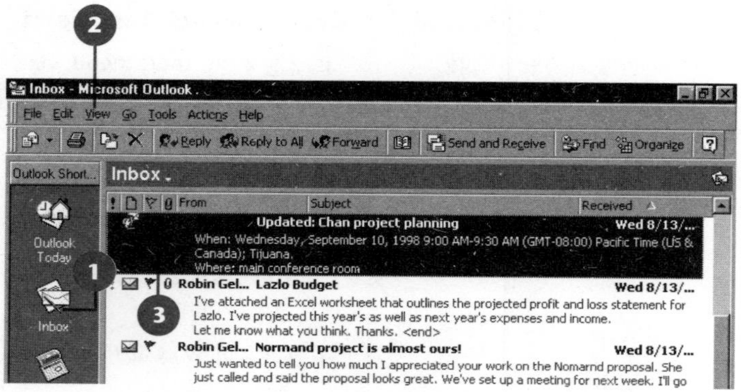

Reply to a Message

1. Click Inbox on the Outlook Bar.
2. Click the message to which you want to respond.
3. Click the Reply button or click the Reply To All button on the Standard toolbar.
   - Reply responds to only the message's sender.
   - Reply To All responds to the sender and all other recipients of the message.
4. Type your message at the top of the message box.
5. Click the Send button on the Standard toolbar.

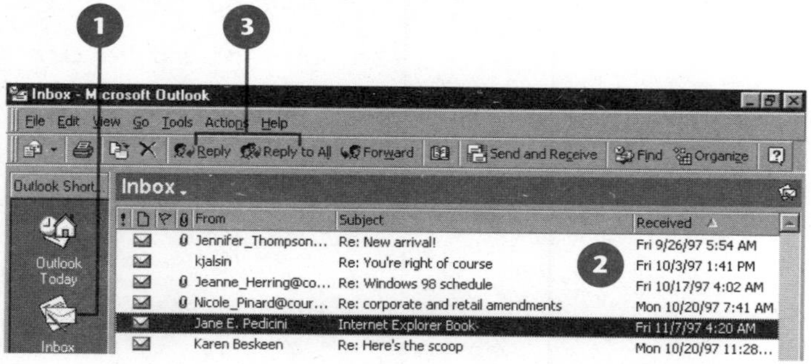

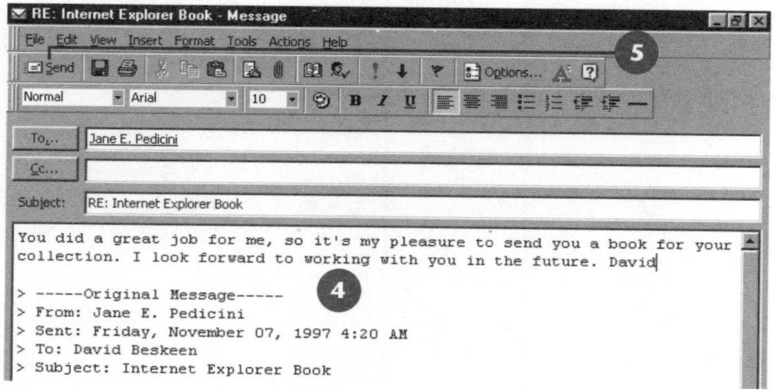

TIP

Get new mail quickly. *The moment you receive new mail, the New Mail icon appears next to the clock on the taskbar. You can double-click the icon to switch to your Inbox. Depending on your e-mail service, you might have to log onto a network or dial into a service provider to receive new mail.*

TRY THIS

Reply from within an open message. *Just click the Reply, the Reply To All, or the Forward button on the Standard toolbar from within the open message, and then reply or forward the message as usual.*

TIP

Outlook adds a note to a message when you reply. *Whenever you reply to or forward an e-mail message, Outlook adds a note indicating when you replied or forwarded the message. Outlook also adds a flag to the message icon in the Inbox indicating that you replied to the message.*

Forward a Message

1. Click Inbox on the Outlook Bar.
2. Click the message you want to forward.
3. Click the Forward button on the Standard toolbar.
4. Click the To button or Cc button, and then select recipients for this message.
5. Type new text at the top of the message box, and attach any files if appropriate.
6. Click the Send button on the Standard toolbar.

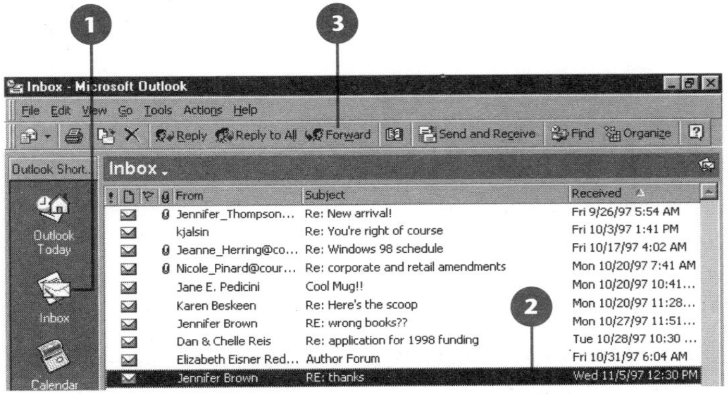

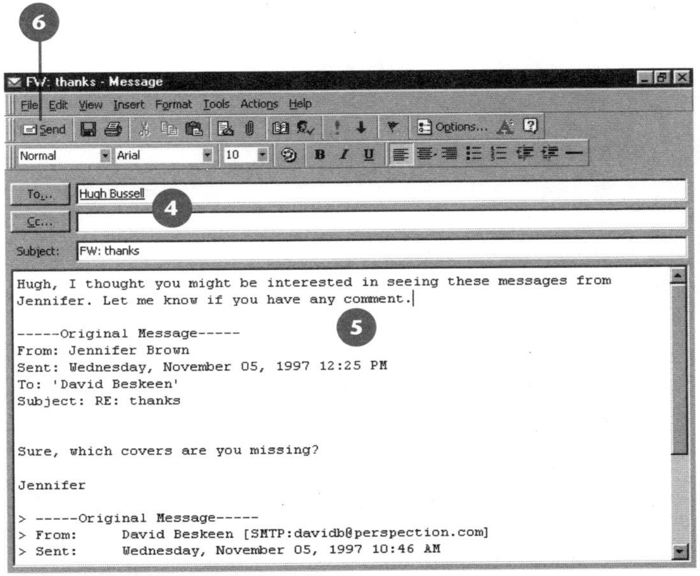

16

Managing E-Mail Messages

To avoid an overly cluttered Inbox, remember to routinely clear the Inbox of messages that you have read and responded to. You can save messages as files, move messages to other folders or subfolders, and delete messages you no longer need. Storing messages in other folders and deleting unwanted messages make it easier to see new messages and clear your computer's resources for new activities.

Save Messages as Files

1. Click Inbox on the Outlook Bar.
2. Click the message you want to save as a file.
3. Click the File menu, and then click Save As.
4. Click the Save In drop-down arrow, and then select the drive and folder in which you want to store the message.
5. Click the Save As Type drop-down arrow, and then click the file type you want.
6. Type a new name in the File Name box.
7. Click Save.

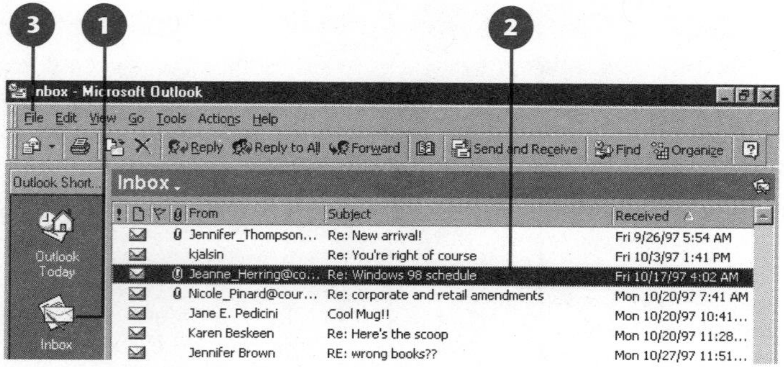

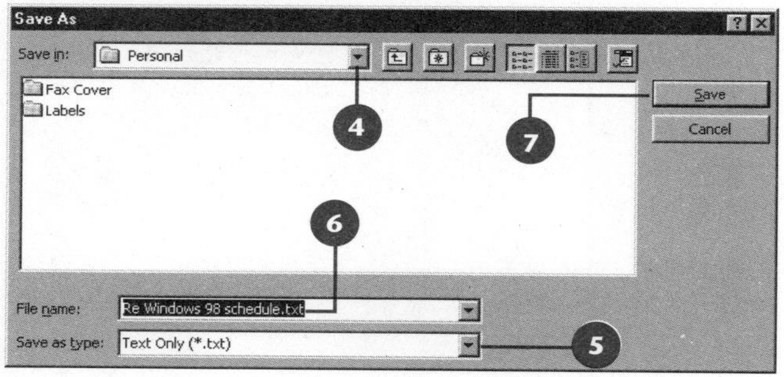

Delete Unwanted Messages

1. Click Inbox, Outbox, Sent Items, or the folder in which you store messages on the Outlook Bar.
2. Select the message or messages you want to move to the Deleted Items folder.
3. Click the Delete button on the Standard toolbar.

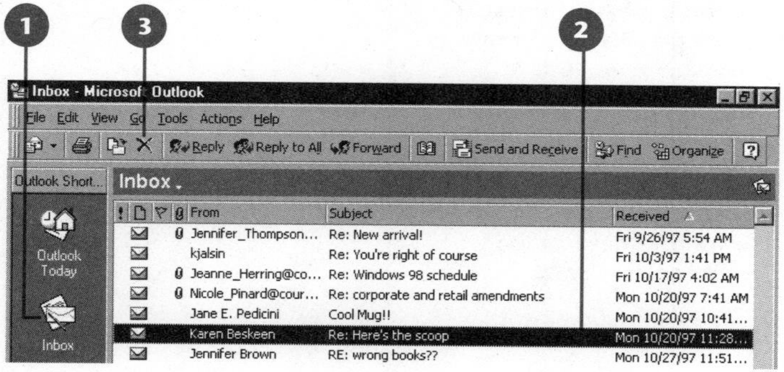

TIP

Select multiple messages at one time. *To select two or more adjacent messages, click the first message, press and hold the Shift key while you click the last message. To select two or more nonadjacent messages, click the first message, press and hold the Ctrl key while you click each additional message.*

TIP

Retrieve messages from the Deleted Items folder. *Items remain in the Deleted Items folder until you empty it. To retrieve messages from the Deleted Items folder, click Deleted Items on the Outlook Bar, and then drag an item to the Inbox or to any other shortcut icon on the Outlook Bar. To empty the Deleted Items folder and permanently delete its contents, right-click Deleted Items on the Outlook Bar, click Empty "Deleted Items" Folder, and then click Yes to confirm the deletion.*

Create a New Folder in Outlook

1. Click the File menu, point to Folder, and then click New Folder.
2. Type a name for the new folder.
3. Click the Folder Contains drop-down arrow, and then click the type of item you want to store here.
4. Click the folder in which you want to file this subfolder.
5. Click OK.

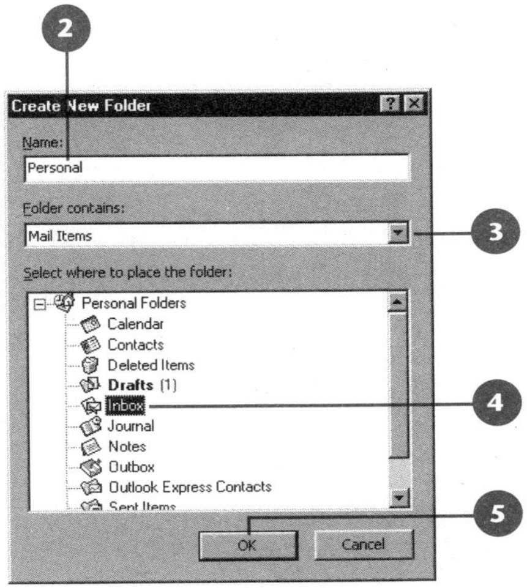

TIP

Organize items within a folder. *Click one of the column buttons until the items in the folder are organized the way you want them.*

16

Move Messages to a Different Folder

1. Click Inbox on the Outlook Bar.
2. Select the message or messages you want to move.
3. Click the Move To Folder button on the Standard toolbar, and then click Move To Folder.
4. Click the folder where you want to move the messages.
5. Click OK.

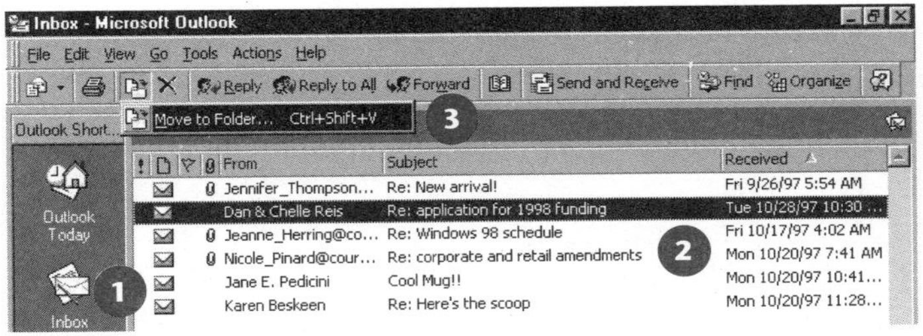

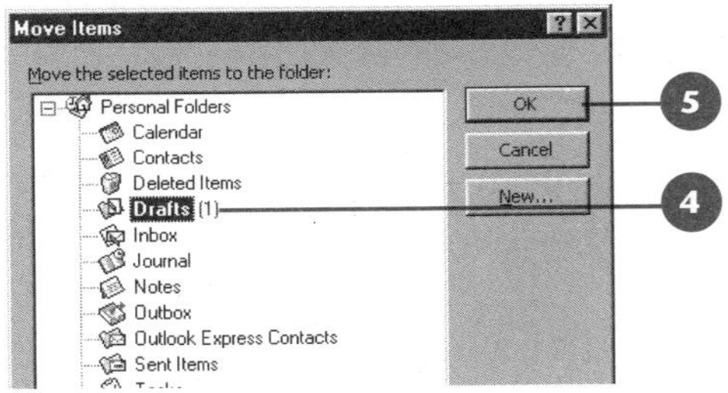

Viewing Your Schedule

The *Calendar* is an electronic version of the familiar paper daily planner. You can schedule time for completing specific tasks, meetings, vacations and holidays, or for any other activity with the Calendar. People using Outlook and Schedule+ can exchange messages, meeting requests, and appointments; however, neither can read the other's calendar. To view Schedule+ calendar information, you'll need to import it into Outlook.

SEE ALSO

See "Managing Tasks" on page 292 for more information about task lists.

Calendar Views

The Calendar displays your schedule in a typical daily planner format or in list format. Click the View menu, and then point to Current View to display the available options. You can select:

- Day/Week/Month: Displays your schedule in a planner format; you can change between a daily, a weekly, or a monthly planner.
- Day/Week/Month With AutoPreview: Displays your schedule in a planner format showing the first three lines of the appointment; you can change between a daily, a weekly, or a monthly planner.
- Active Appointments: Lists all the appointments and meetings scheduled from the current day forward.
- Events: Lists all the current and future scheduled events.
- Annual Events: Lists all the current and future events that occur only once a year.
- Recurring Appointments: Lists all appointments that take place regularly.
- By Category: Lists all appointments by category.

Banner
Shows the date for selected day; displays bar indicating a scheduled event.

Date Navigator
Click to the left of any week to view that week's schedule.

Click any date to view that day's schedule.

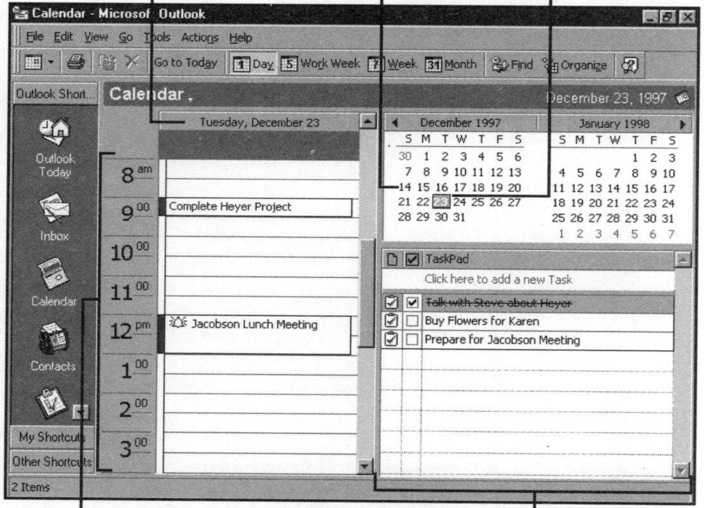

Time Bar
Shows the hours in day view (as in this figure) or days in weekly and monthly views; displays scheduled appointments and meetings.

Task Pad
Lists tasks you need to complete and shows completed tasks crossed out.

TIP

Exchange information with Schedule+. *If you want to use Schedule+ 7.0 rather than the Outlook Calendar, click the Tools menu, click Calendar Options, click the Use Microsoft Schedule+ As My Primary Calendar check box, and then click OK.*

SEE ALSO

See "Viewing Items in Groups," "Sorting Items," and "Viewing Specific Files Using Filters" on pages 300, 301, and 302 for more information about how to display specific types of tasks in the TaskPad.

Open a Calendar from Schedule+

1. Click the File menu, and then click Import And Export.
2. Double-click Import From Another Program Or File.
3. Double-click Schedule+ 7.0 or Schedule+ 1.0.
4. Click Browse, and then double-click the file you want to open.
5. Click the button for the option you want to use.
6. Click Next, and then make sure the files you want converted to Outlook are selected.
7. Click Finish.

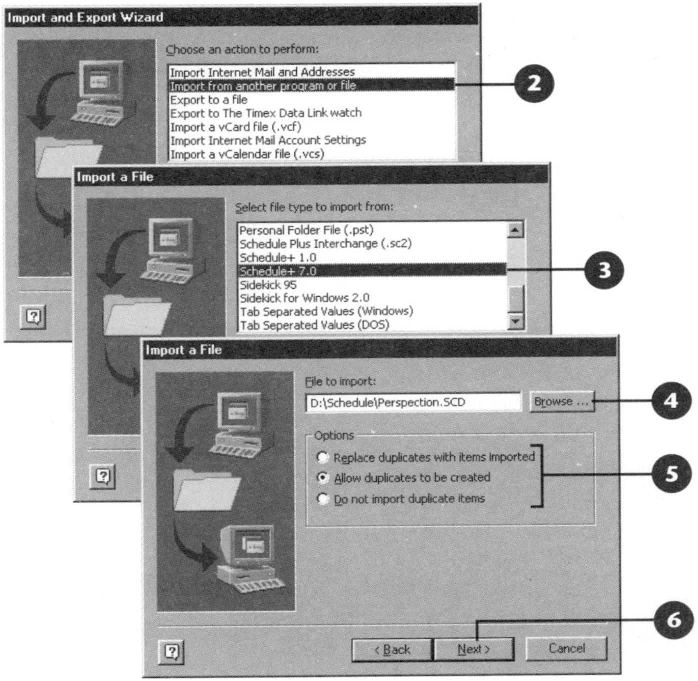

Fields and entries from Schedule+ are converted into their appropriate Outlook folders.

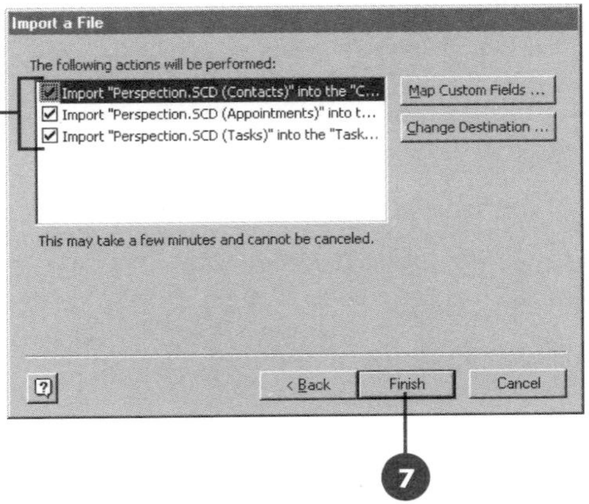

Scheduling an Event

An *appointment* is any activity you schedule that doesn't include other people or resources. An *event* is any appointment that lasts one or more full days (24 hours increments), such as a seminar, a conference, or a vacation. You can mark yourself available (free or tentative) or unavailable (busy or out of the office) to others during a scheduled appointment or an event. You use the same dialog box to schedule an appointment or an event; the only difference is whether the All Day Event check box is selected or cleared.

SEE ALSO

See "Viewing Your Schedule" on page 282 for more information about moving around the Calendar.

Schedule an Appointment

1. Click Calendar on the Outlook Bar.
2. Drag to select a block of time in the Time Bar.
3. Right-click the selected block, and then click New Appointment.
4. Fill in the text boxes, and set other options on the Appointment tab as needed.
   - Type where the meeting will take place, or select a location from the drop-down list.
   - Type details or notes for the appointment, or insert a file.
   - Click Categories to help you sort, group, or filter your appointments.
   - Click the Private check box if you do not want others to see this appointment.
5. Click the Save And Close button on the Standard toolbar.

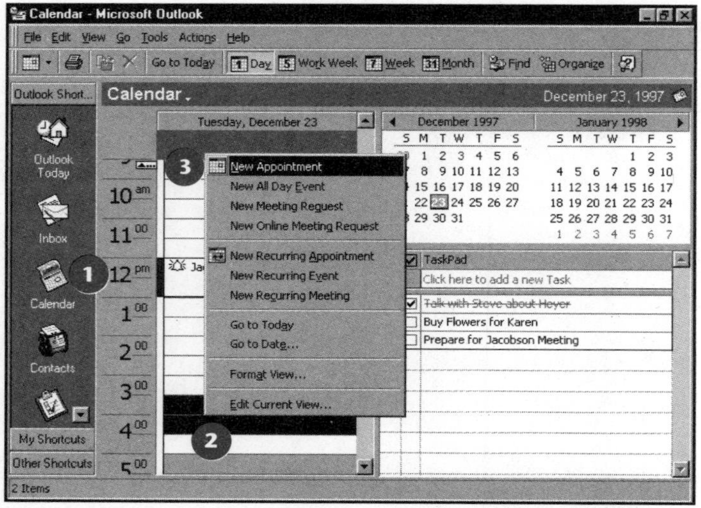

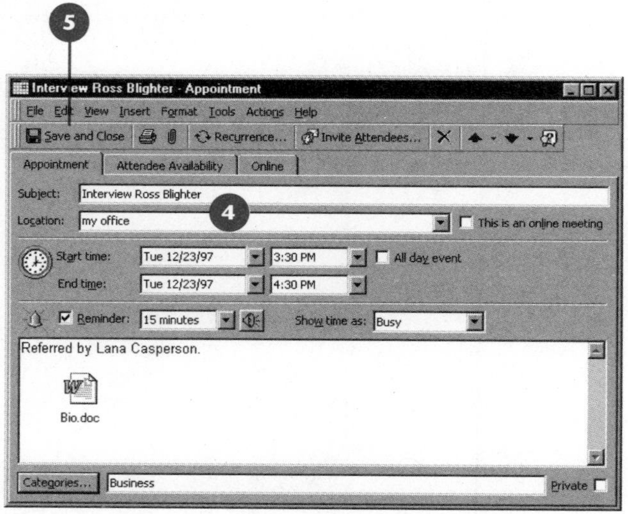

TIP

Switch between an appointment or an event. *To change an appointment to an event or vice versa, click the All Day Event check box.*

TRY THIS

Schedule an appointment or event without starting Outlook. *Click the New Appointment button on the Office Shortcut Bar to open the Appointment dialog box. Complete the Appointment tab of the dialog box as usual.*

Block Time for an Event

1. Click Calendar on the Outlook Bar.
2. Double-click the date heading.
3. Fill in the text boxes, and set other options on the Appointment tab as needed.
   - Type where the meeting will take place, or select a location from the drop-down list.
   - Set an alarm to notify you a certain amount of time before the event.
   - Mark your availability to others as Free, Tentative, Busy, or Out Of Office.
   - Type notes and details of the event, or attach a file.
   - Click Categories to help you sort, group, and filter your events.
4. Click the Save And Close button on the Standard toolbar.

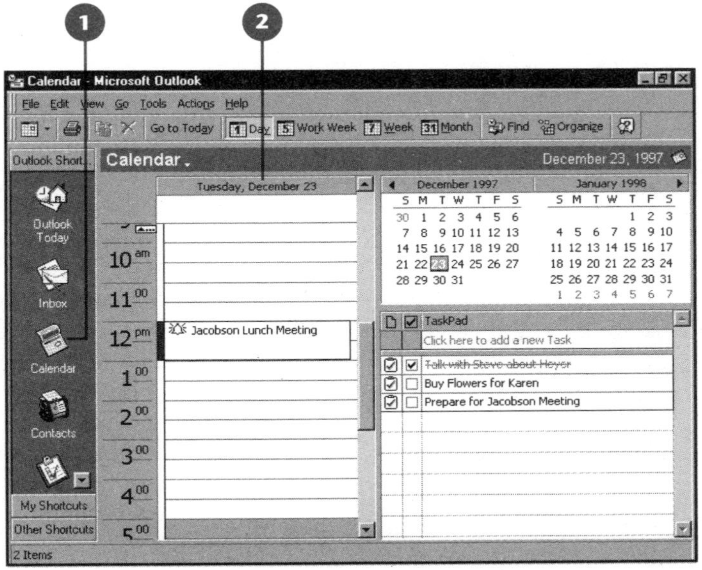

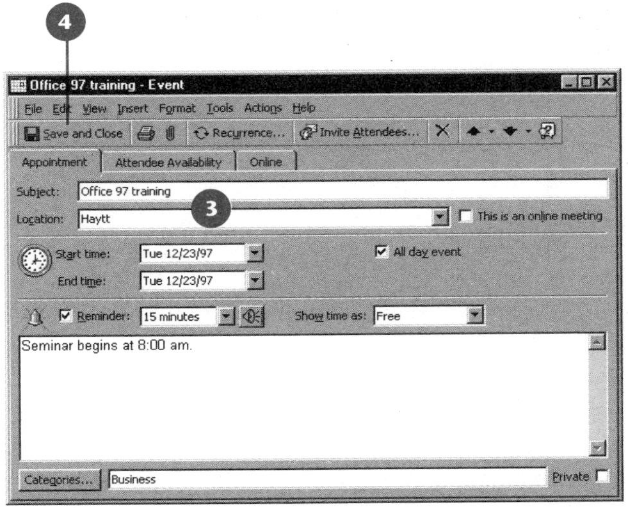

16

Rescheduling an Event

A basic fact of life is that things change—appointments and events might be moved to another day or time or even relocated. Outlook provides you the flexibility to easily revise your Calendar as your schedule changes.

TIP

Drag an appointment to reschedule it quickly. *Reschedule an appointment or event quickly by dragging it to a new time on the Time Bar or to a new day in the Date Navigator in Day/Week/Month view. Press and hold the Ctrl key as you drag the appointment or event to copy it to another date or time.*

Reschedule an Appointment or an Event

1. Click Calendar on the Outlook Bar.
2. Switch to a view that shows the appointment or the event you want to change.
3. Double-click the appointment or the event on the Time Bar.
4. Make whatever changes you want.
5. Click the Save And Close button on the Standard toolbar.

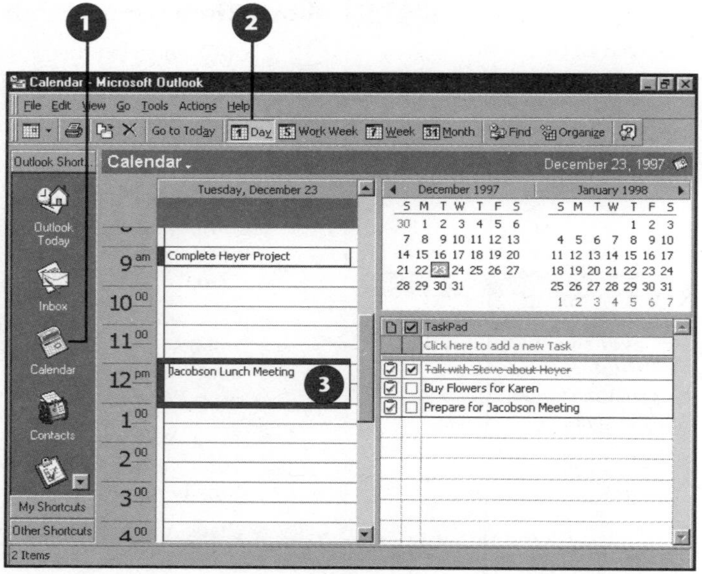

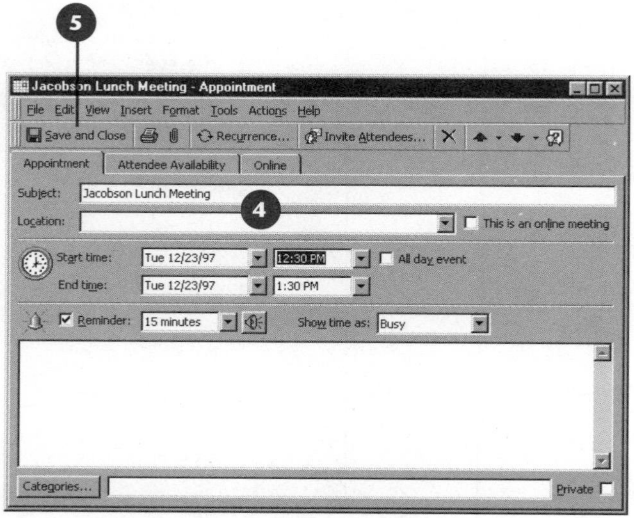

Planning a Meeting

The Calendar's *Meeting Planner* helps you to organize meetings quickly, sends e-mail messages to all recipients announcing the meeting, and tracks their responses. As long as everyone is connected to the same network, you can use their Calendars to determine when other people and resources are available so that you can select the best time to schedule a meeting. If you invite people who live in other time zones, Calendar converts their schedule times to your time zone.

TRY THIS

Send an agenda, meeting minutes, or other necessary documents to meeting invitees. *Attach the file to the meeting request just as you would attach a file to any other e-mail message.*

Create and Send a Meeting Request

1. Click Calendar on the Outlook Bar.
2. Click the Actions menu, and then click Plan A Meeting.
3. Click Invite Others.
4. Type a name, or click one or more names in the list.
5. Click the Required, Optional, or Resources button.
6. Click the people and resources you want, and then click OK.
7. Click AutoPick to find the first common available time for all participants.
8. Click Make Meeting.
9. Type a brief description of the meeting in the Subject box.
10. Type any notes or attach files as needed.
11. Click Categories, and assign keywords as needed.
12. Click the Online tab for an online meeting over the Internet (optional).
13. Click the Send button on the Standard toolbar.

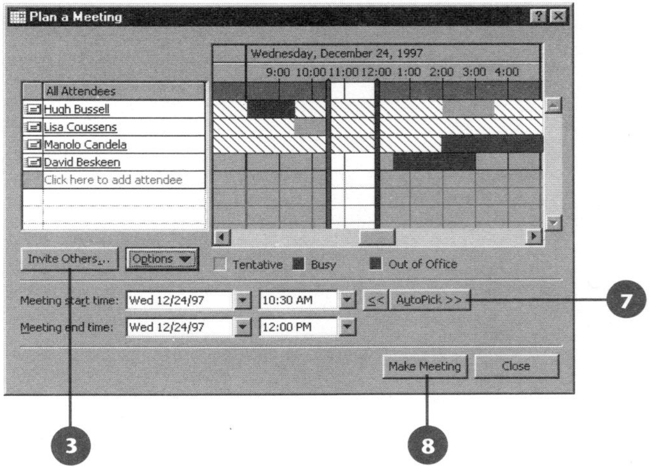

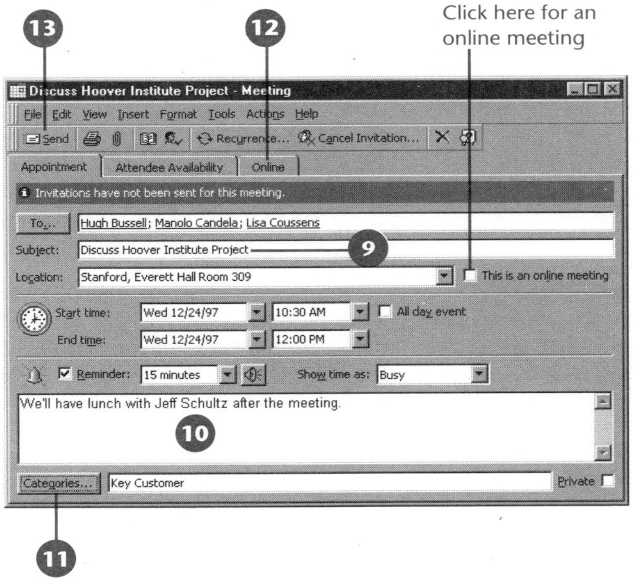

16

Rescheduling or Canceling a Meeting

Even the best laid plans sometimes change. This is especially true when you gather a group of people to schedule a meeting. You might need to change the date of a meeting, switch the time, move the location, or even cancel the meeting. When you do this from Outlook's Calendar, you can be assured that everyone who has been invited to the meeting receives an update.

> **TIP**
>
> **Turn an appointment into a meeting.** *Open the appointment, click the Invite Attendees button on the Standard toolbar, add people and resources, enter a location if necessary, and then click the Send button on the Standard toolbar.*

Reschedule a Meeting

1. Click Calendar on the Outlook Bar.
2. Switch to the view that shows the meeting you want to change.
3. Double-click the meeting on the Time Bar.
4. Make any necessary changes on the Appointment tab.
5. Click the Send button on the Standard toolbar.

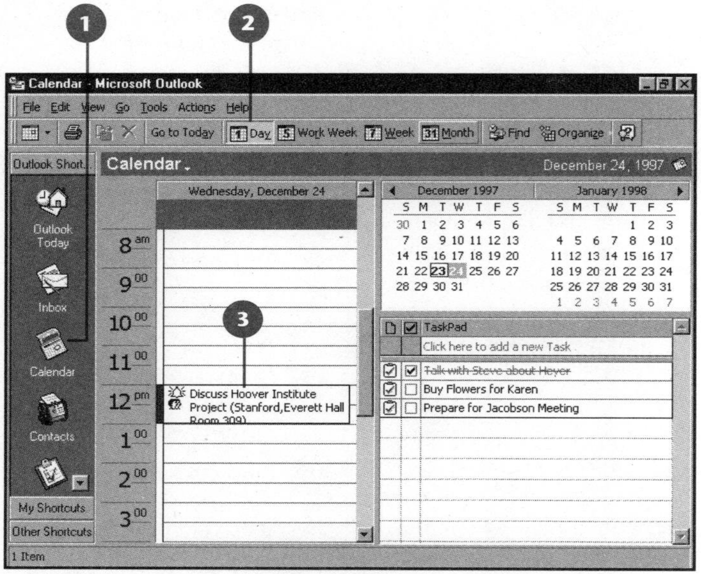

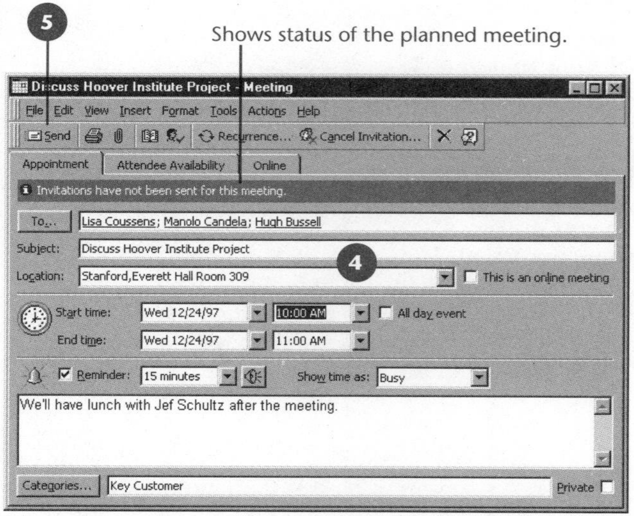

TIP

What happens when you delete a meeting? *When you cancel a meeting, you must decide whether to send a cancellation notice as you delete the meeting. The cancellation notice sends an e-mail message to all invited people, notifying them that the meeting is canceled, and frees any reserved resources.*

SEE ALSO

See "Planning a Meeting" on page 287 for more information about scheduling a meeting.

Cancel a Meeting

1. Click Calendar on the Outlook bar.
2. Switch to the view that shows the meeting you want to cancel.
3. Click the scheduled meeting on the Time Bar.
4. Click the Delete button on the Standard toolbar.
5. Click the Send Cancellation And Delete Meeting option button.
6. Click OK.

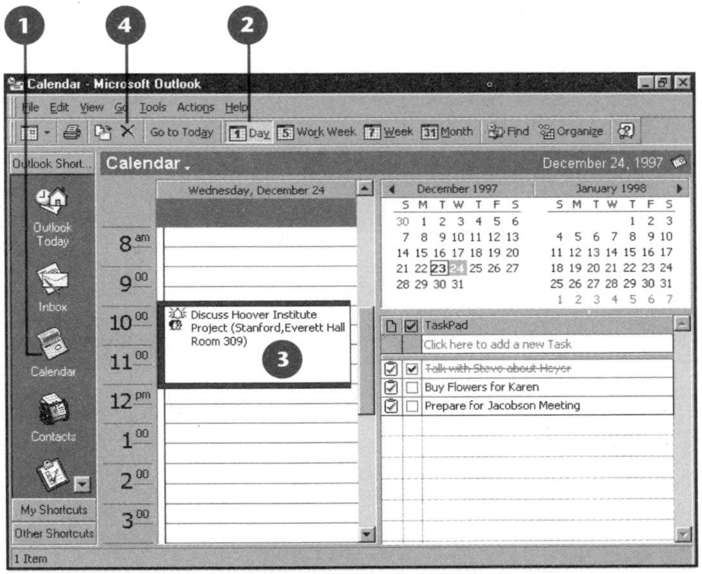

16

Changing a Meeting's Attendees List

As a meeting gets closer, you might want to revise the attendees list or reserve a certain resource. For example, you might want to have a supervisor attend a later meeting rather than the upcoming planning meeting. Or someone new was just assigned to the project, and you want to invite them. Or you decide to reserve a white board to take notes on during the meeting. You can easily make these changes and send out an update message to everyone from Outlook's Calendar.

SEE ALSO

See "Rescheduling or Canceling a Meeting" on page 288 for more information about changing a meeting.

Change Attendees List or Resources

1. Click Calendar on the Outlook Bar.
2. Switch to the view that shows the meeting you want to change.
3. Double-click the meeting on the Time Bar.
4. Click the Attendee Availability tab.
5. Select the names of those you no longer want at the meeting, or select the resources you no longer want reserved, and then press Delete.
6. Click Invite Others.
7. Click the name of the person you want to invite or the resource you need at the meeting.
8. Click the Required, Optional, or Resources button.
9. Click OK.
10. Click the Send Update button on the Standard toolbar.

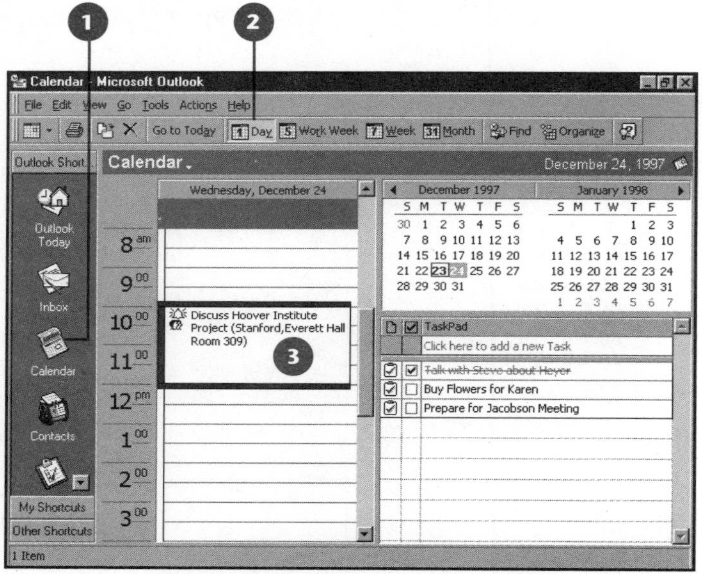

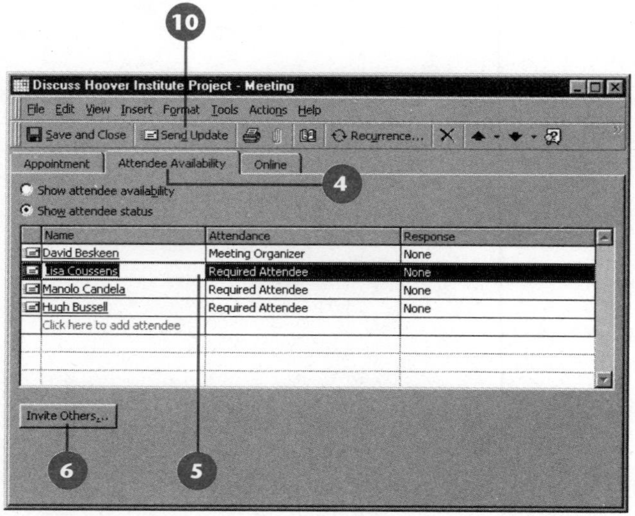

17

Managing Information with Outlook 98

IN THIS SECTION

Microsoft Outlook 98 provides an easy and efficient way to track and organize all the information that lands on your desk. Create a to-do list and assign the items on the list to others as needed from *Tasks*. Rather than cluttering your desk or obscuring your computer with sticky pad notes, use *Notes* to jot down your immediate thoughts, ideas, and other observations. With everything related to your work in one place, you can always locate what you need—whether it be a file, a note related to a specific project, or even the time of a phone call with a certain contact. Just check the *Journal* timeline to find it.

To help organize and locate information, Outlook allows you to group, sort, and filter items. *Group* organizes items based on a particular *field* (an element that stores a particular type of information). *Sort* arranges items in ascending or descending order according to a specified field. *Filter* shows items that match a specific criteria, such as "High Priority." You can group, sort, and filter by more than one field.

If you are interested in communicating with people around the world about things that interest you, then you will have fun with newsgroups. A *newsgroup* is a forum where people can share common interests, share ideas, ask and answer questions, and comment on a variety of subjects. You can find a newsgroup on almost any topic, from the serious to the lighthearted, from educational to controversial, and from business to social.

Managing Tasks

A common Monday chore is creating a list of activities that you should accomplish that week. Outlook *Tasks* is better than that traditional to-do list. You can create a to-do list with deadlines and cross off items as you complete them. Overdue tasks remain on your list until you finish them or delete them. You can also delegate a particular task to someone else by sending them a *Task Request*, complete with deadlines and related attachments. Either way, you can track a task's status and progress, estimated and actual hours, mileage, and other associated billing costs. A task remains in the Calendar TaskPad and in Tasks until you check it off or delete it.

SEE ALSO

See "Viewing Your Schedule" on page 282 for information about the Calendar TaskPad.

Create a New Task

1. Click the New Item drop-down arrow on the Standard toolbar, and then click Task.
2. Type a description of the task.
3. Set a timeframe, status, priority, alarm, categories, or any other option.
4. Type any relevant notes, or attach related files.
5. Click the Save And Close button on the Standard toolbar.

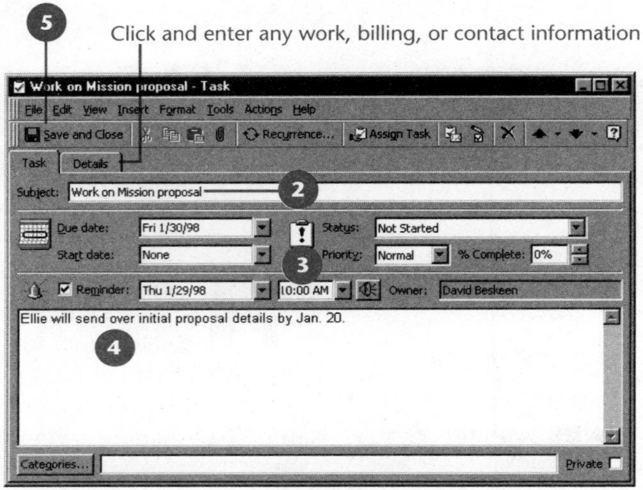

Assign a New Task to Someone Else

1. Click the New Item drop-down arrow on the Standard toolbar, and then click Task Request.
2. Type the name or e-mail address of the person you are assigning the task to, or click the To button and select a recipient from the list.
3. Fill in the subject, timeframe, status, notes, categories, and other options.
4. Click the Send button on the Standard toolbar.

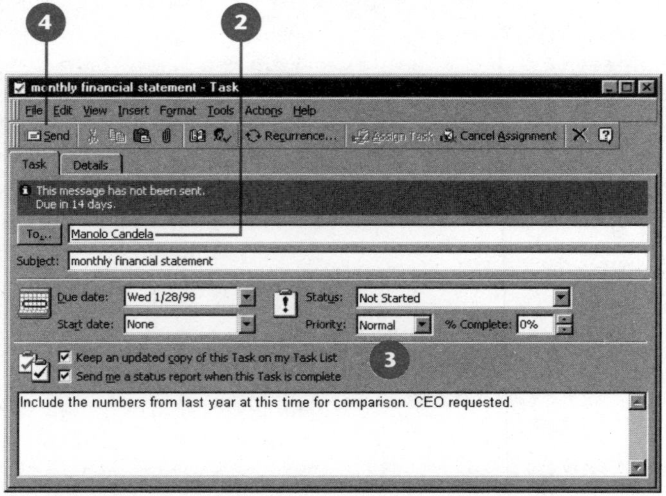

Delete Tasks from the Task List

1. Click Tasks on the Outlook Bar.
2. Click the task you want to delete.
3. Click the Delete button on the Standard toolbar.

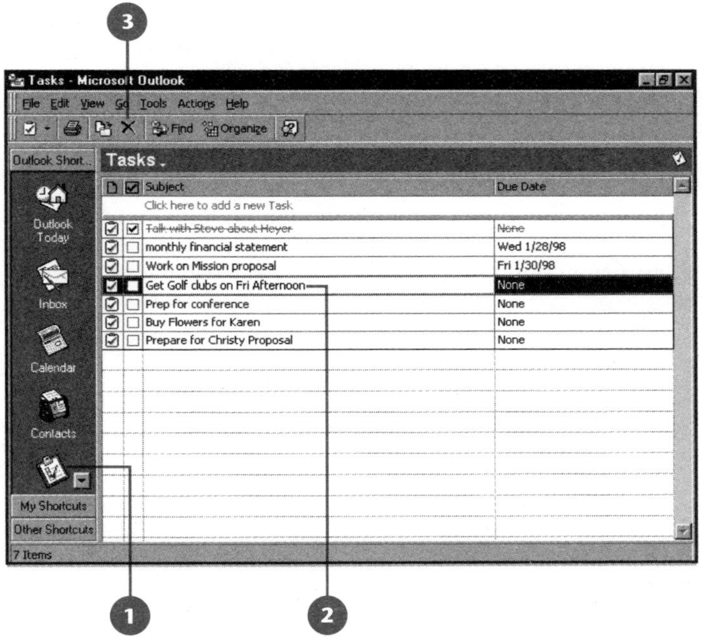

TIP

Make a task recurring. *Double-click an existing task on the Task List or Calendar TaskPad to edit it, or create a new task. Click the Recurrence button on the Standard toolbar, set a recurrence pattern, and then click OK. When the task is set up as you'd like, click the Save And Close button on the Standard toolbar.*

TIP

Insert a file into a task. *Double-click an existing task to open it, or create a new task. Click the Insert File button on the Standard toolbar. Click the Insert As Text Only, Attachment, or Shortcut option button, and then double-click the file you want to insert.*

TRY THIS

Enter a new task quickly. *To add a task quickly in either the Calendar TaskPad or the Tasks List, click the Click Here To Add A New Task box, type a name or a brief description of the task, enter a deadline, enter any information necessary, and then press the Enter key.*

Recording Items in the Journal

The *Journal* is a diary of all the activities and interactions from your day. With everything organized on a timeline, you can see an overview of what you accomplished when and how long certain activities took. It also provides an alternate way to locate a particular item or a file. The Journal can automatically record entries for your phone calls, e-mail messages, tasks, meeting requests and responses, faxes, and documents on which you've worked. You must record tasks, appointments, personal conversations, and existing documents manually.

SEE ALSO

See "Creating a Contact" on page 272 for information about the Contact window.

Automatically Record New Items and Documents

1. Click the Tools menu, and then click Options.
2. Click Journal Options, and then click the check boxes for the items you want to record in the Journal automatically.
3. Click the check boxes of the contacts for whom you want to record the selected items.
4. Click the check boxes of the Office 97 programs that you want to record files from.
5. Click OK, and then click OK again.

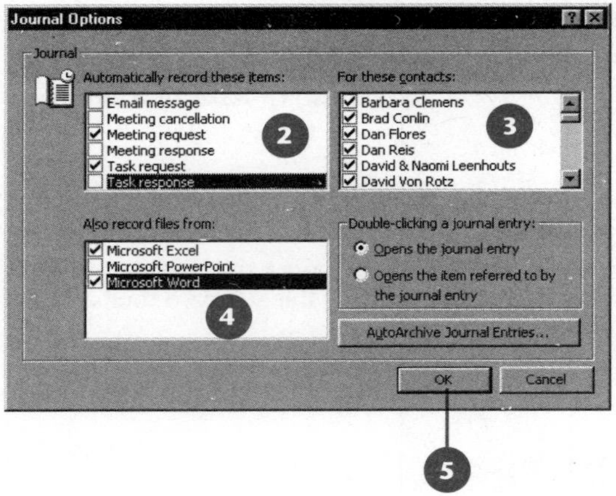

Manually Record a Personal Transaction

1. Click the items or the files you want to record.
2. Click the File menu, point to New, and then click Journal Entry.

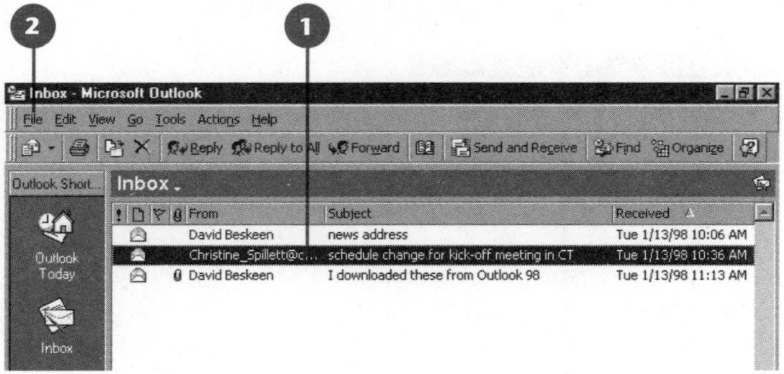

SEE ALSO

See "Working with Journal Entries" on page 296 for more information on journal entries.

3. Type a description of the journal entry.
4. Set the entry type, contact, company, start time, duration, notes, and categories.
5. Click the Save And Close button on the Standard toolbar.

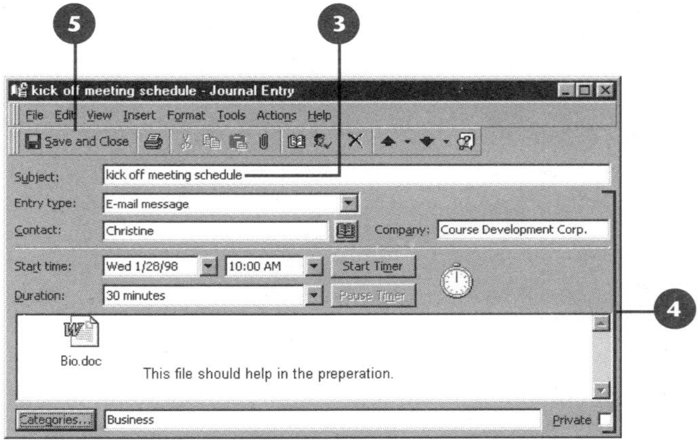

TRY THIS

Manually record an existing document in the Journal. *Display the My Documents folder or the folder that contains your file. Drag the file from its folder in the information viewer onto the Journal icon on the Outlook Bar. Make any changes necessary in the Journal Entry window, and then click the Save And Close button on the Standard toolbar.*

Manually Record an Activity for a Contact

1. Double-click an existing contact.
2. Click the Journal tab, and then click New Journal Entry
3. Type a description.
4. Click the Entry Type drop-down arrow, and then click the type of interaction you want to record.
5. If necessary, enter a contact, company, start time, duration, notes, and categories.
6. Click the Save And Close button on the Standard toolbar.

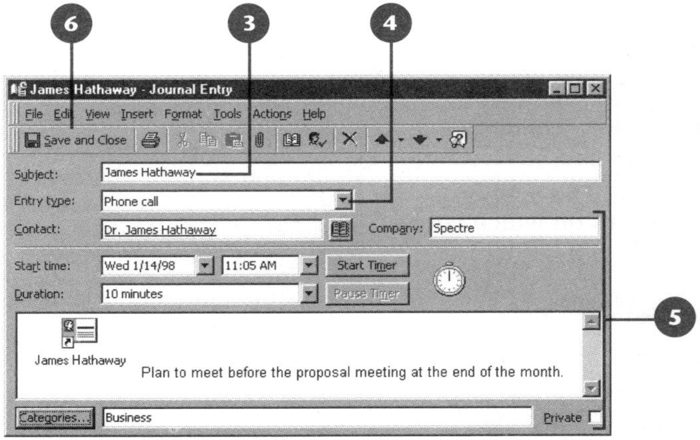

17

Working with Journal Entries

Journal entries and their related items, documents, and contacts are easy to open, move, and even delete. When you modify a journal entry, its associated item, document, or contact is not affected. Likewise, when you modify an item, document, or contact, any existing related journal entries remain unchanged. If you no longer need a journal entry, you can select the entry and press Delete or click the Delete button to remove it.

> **TIP**
>
> **Expanding and collapsing entry types.** *When you switch to the Journal to view the recorded items, some entries' types might be expanded to show all items and others might be collapsed to hide all items. You can easily switch between expanded and collapsed views by double-clicking on the Entry Type bar.*

Open a Journal Entry and Its Recorded Item

1. Click Journal on the Outlook Bar.
2. If necessary, double-click the Entry Type bar to display its items.
3. Double-click the item, document, contact name, or so on, to open it.

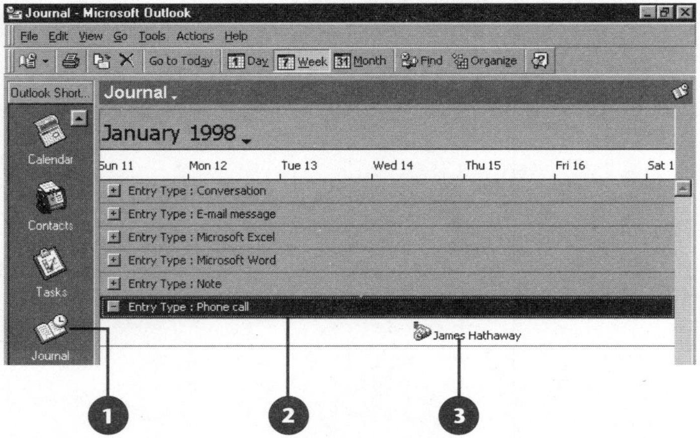

View Journal Entries for a Contact

1. Click Contacts on the Outlook Bar.
2. Double-click a contact name.
3. Click the Journal tab.
4. Click the Show drop-down arrow, and then click the type of entries you want to view.
5. Click the Save And Close button on the Standard toolbar.

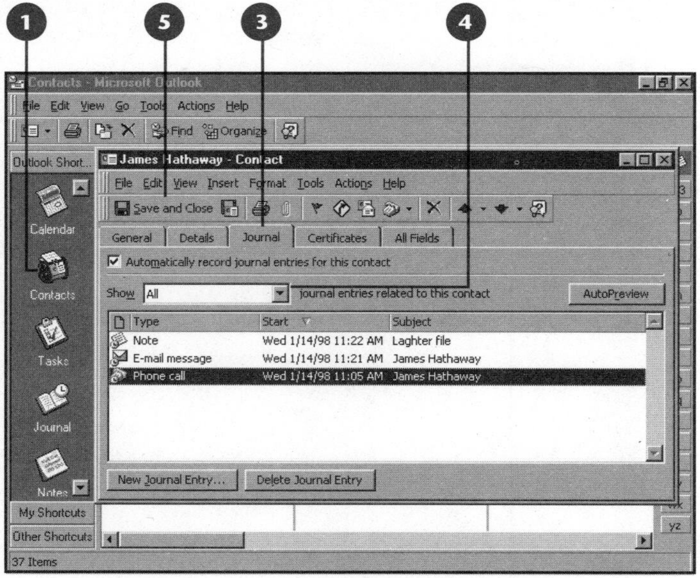

Viewing Information in a Timeline

A *timeline* is an easy way to view the chronological order of recorded items, documents, and activities in the Journal. Each item appears at the date and time it originated. A solid bar indicates the duration of any activity that takes place over a period of time.

TIP

Create a new journal entry quickly. *Double-click in the white area below the Entry Type bar to open a new journal entry. Fill in the Journal Entry window as usual.*

TRY THIS

Move to a specific Journal date. *Click the month and year listed at the top of the information viewer to display a calendar. Click and hold the month and year at the top of the calendar to display a list of months. Point to the month you want to switch to, and then click the exact date you want to view.*

Change the Location of Items and Documents in a Timeline

1. Click Journal on the Outlook Bar.
2. Double-click the journal entry you want to move.
3. Click the Start Date drop-down, and then click a new day.
4. Click the Start Time drop-down arrow, and then click a new time.
5. Click the Save And Close button on the Standard toolbar.

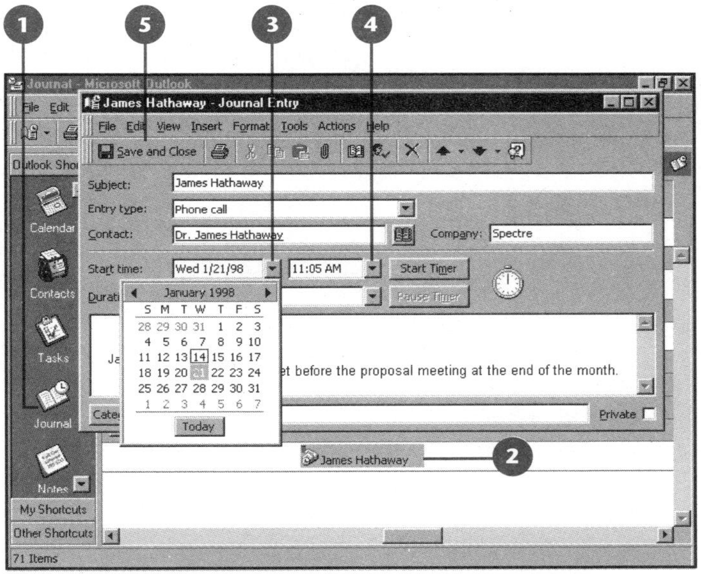

Display Time Scales

- Click the Day button on the Standard toolbar to see one day at a time.
- Click the Week button on the Standard toolbar to view a week at a time.
- Click the Month button on the Standard toolbar to look at 30 days.
- Click the Go To Today button on the Standard toolbar to move to the current day.

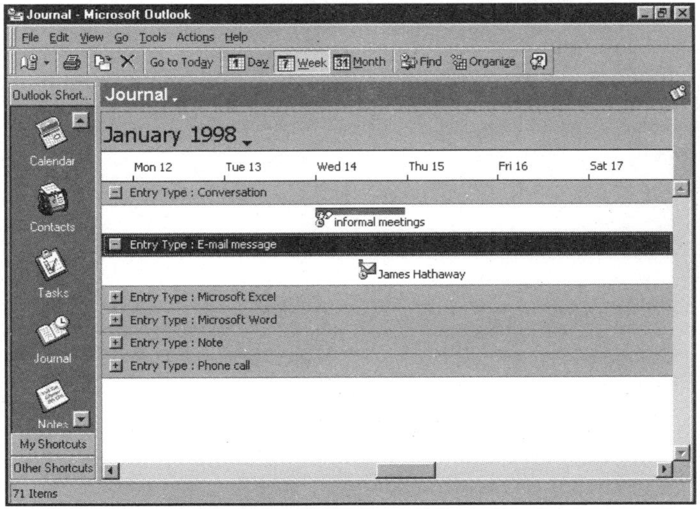

17

Organizing Information by Categories

A *category* is one or more keywords or phrases you assign to items so you can later find, group, sort, or filter them. Categories provide additional flexibility in how you organize and store items and files. With categories you can store related items in different folders or unrelated items in the same folder and still compile a complete list of items related to a specific category. Outlook starts you off with a *Master Category List* of some common categories, but you can add or remove them to fit your purposes.

TIP

Create a mailing list. *You can export a specific category of contacts using Microsoft Word's Mail Merge to create a mailing list.*

Assign and Remove Categories to and from an Outlook Item

1. Click any Outlook item to select it.
2. Click the Edit menu, and then click Categories.
3. Click check boxes to assign and remove categories.
4. Click OK.

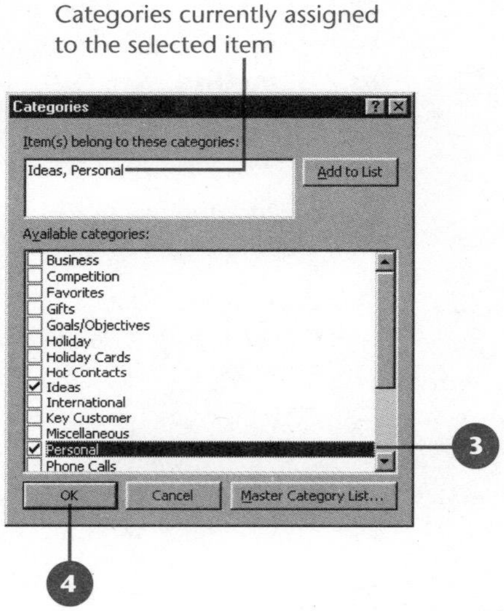

Add or Remove a Category

1. Click any item to select it.
2. Click the Edit menu, and then click Categories.
3. Click Master Category List.
4. Type a new category name, or click the category you want to remove.
5. Click Add or Delete.
6. Click OK.
7. Click OK again.

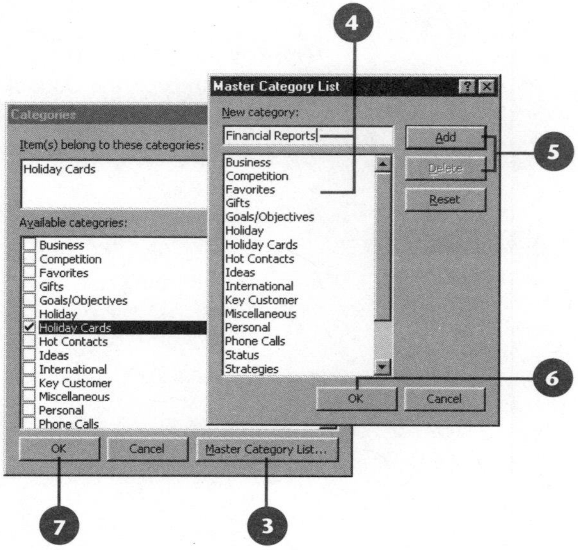

Organizing Folders

Because of the ever increasing use of e-mail as the primary means of communication between friends and business associates, there is a need to logically organize the volumes of e-mail that you receive. Outlook provides a way to organize each of your folders using certain criteria that you set. For example, you can set your Inbox to file incoming messages from a particular friend into an existing folder or a special folder that you create.

TIP

Use the Rules Wizard to set criteria for incoming messages. *Click the Tools menu, and then click Rules Wizard, or click Wizard Rules when the Organize feature is on.*

Organize Your Inbox Folder

1. Click Inbox on the Outlook Bar.
2. Click the Organize button on the Standard toolbar.
3. Click an e-mail item in the information viewer
4. Click Using Folders.
5. Click the Folder drop-down arrow, and then click a folder in the folder list, or click New Folder to create a new folder.
6. Click Move.

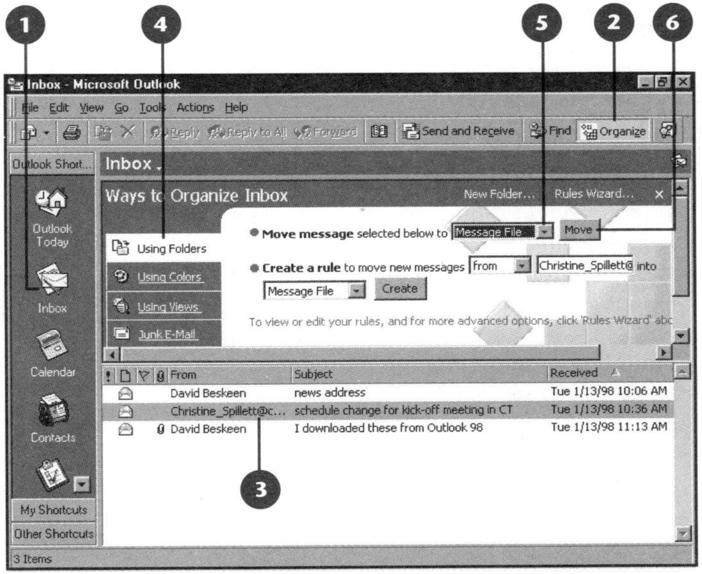

File Junk E-Mail

1. Click Inbox on the Outlook Bar.
2. Click the Organize button on the Standard toolbar.
3. Click Junk E-Mail.
4. Click the Color drop-down arrow, and then click Move.
5. Click Turn ON and then click Yes to create a Junk E-Mail folder.
6. Right-click a message, point to Junk E-Mail, and then click Add To Junk Senders List.

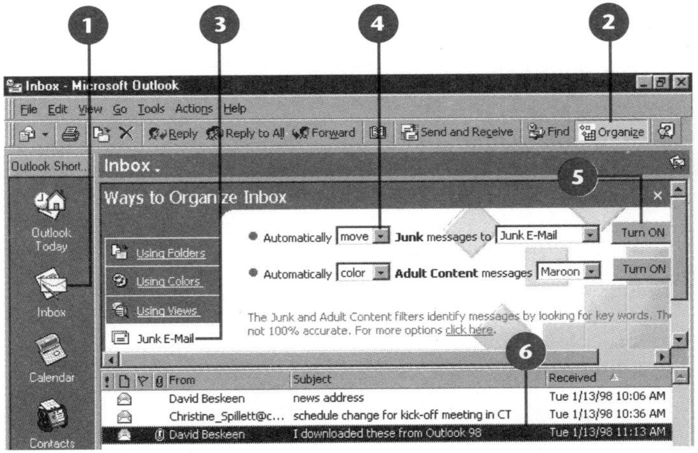

Viewing Items in Groups

As the number of items in Outlook grows, you'll want to be able to view related items. A *group* is any set of items with a common element, such as an assigned category, priority level, or associated contact name. You can group items only in a table or timeline view. If an item has more than one entry listed in the field by which you are grouping (for example, three categories), that item appears in every relevant group, and changes you make to the item in one group will appear in all copies of that item.

TIP

Ungroup items. *Right-click the Group By Box, and then click Don't Group By This Field.*

Group Items

1. Right-click a column button, and then click Group By Box.
2. Drag the column button to the Group By Box.
3. Drag any subsequent headings to the Group By Box in the order by which you want to group them.

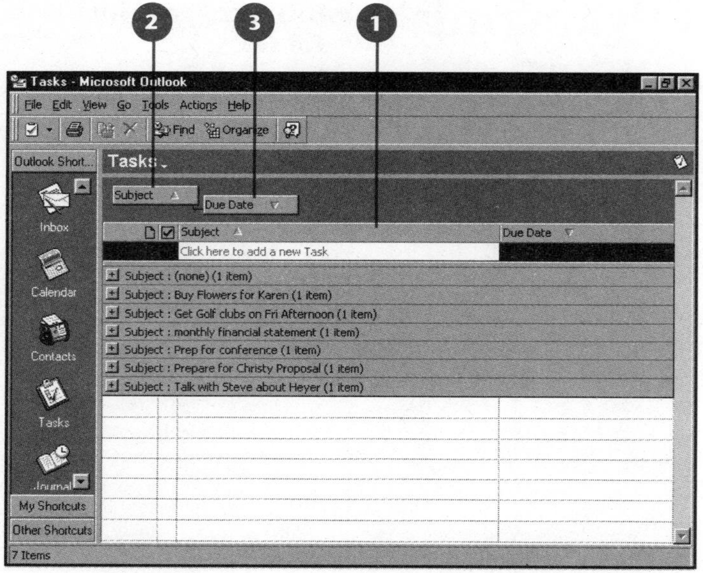

View Grouped Items or Headings

Refer to the table for commands to show or hide grouped items and headings.

VIEWING GROUPED ITEMS AND HEADINGS

To	Click
Show items in a group	Expand button
Hide items in a group	Collapse button
Show all items in all groups	View, point to Expand/Collapse Groups, click Expand All
Show only group headings	View, point to Expand/Collapse Groups, click Collapse All
Save new view settings	View, point to Current View, click Edit Current View, click Group By, click the Expand/Collapse Defaults drop-down arrow, click As Last Viewed, click OK twice

Sorting Items

Sometimes you'll want to organize items in a specific order. For example, tasks from high to low priority or in alphabetical order by category. A *sort* arranges items in ascending (A to Z, low to high, recent to distant) or descending (Z to A, high to low, distant to recent), alphabetical, numerical, or chronological order. You can sort items by one or more fields; you can also sort grouped items. Items must be in a table view to sort.

TRY THIS

Sort grouped items. *Try grouping items and then sorting them. If you choose the same element to sort and group by, the groups are sorted instead of the individual items.*

SEE ALSO

See "Viewing Items in Groups" on page 300 for more information about grouping items.

Sort a List of Items in a Table

1. Click the View menu, point to Current View, and then click Customize Current View.
2. Click Sort.
3. Click the Sort Items By drop-down arrow, and then click a field.
4. Click the Ascending or Descending option button.
5. Click the Then By drop-down arrow, and then click a second sort element and order, if necessary.
6. Click OK.
7. Click OK again.

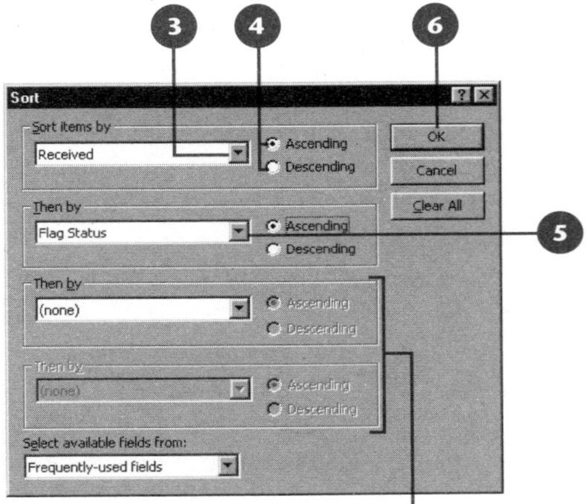

Click these drop-down arrows for additional sort elements, if necessary.

Remove a Sort

1. Click the View menu, point to Current View, and then click Customize Current View.
2. Click Sort.
3. Click Clear All.
4. Click OK.
5. Click OK again.

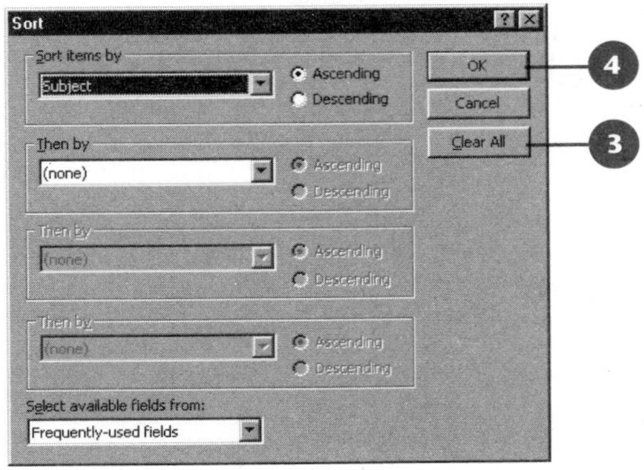

17

Viewing Specific Files Using Filters

A *filter* isolates the items or files that match certain specifications, such as all appointments with a certain contact or any documents you created last week. If you select two or more filter criteria, only those items and files that meet all the criteria are listed. "Filter Applied" appears in the lower left corner of the status bar as a reminder that you filtered the items and files you are viewing.

TIP

Create a filter that fits your needs. *You can filter for any or all of the options available in the Filter dialog box. For example, you might want to filter for a specific word in a certain field, for all items with a particular status, or for all items received from or sent to someone on a specific day.*

Set a Filter to Show Certain Items and Files

1. Click the View menu, point to Current View, and then click Customize Current View.
2. Click Filter.
3. Type a word to search for.
4. Click the In drop-down arrow, and then click a field.
5. Enter in the status, sender, recipient, or timeframe as necessary.
6. Click OK.
7. Click OK again.

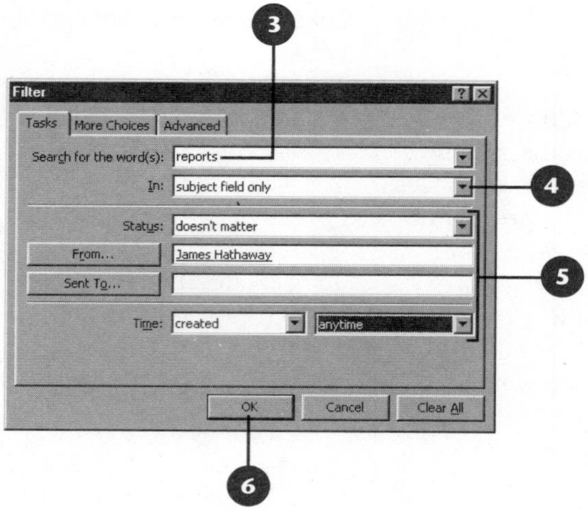

Remove a Filter

1. Click the View menu, point to Current View, and then click Customize Current View.
2. Click Filter.
3. Click Clear All.
4. Click OK.
5. Click OK again.

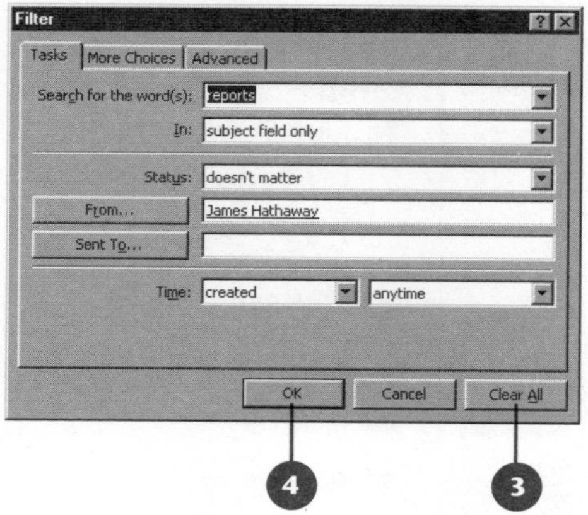

Using Outlook Today

If you like seeing all your appointments, tasks, and upcoming events in one summary view without having to switch between different views, then you'll like Outlook Today. Outlook Today displays information using the style of a Web page that makes it easy to open any piece of information by simply clicking it. You can easily customize Outlook Today, including options for how e-mail, calendar, tasks, and Web page links are displayed.

TIP

Create your own Outlook Today view. *Outlook Today is defined using HTML, which allows you to create your own Outlook Today view that could include specific company or workgroup information.*

Viewing Outlook Today

1. Click Outlook Today on the Outlook Bar.
2. Click any item to view it in more detail or to change it.

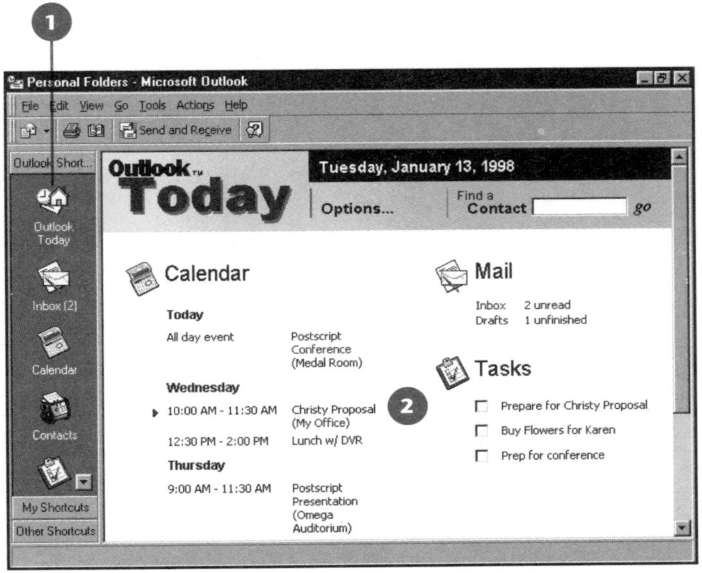

Customize Outlook Today

1. Click Options.
2. Set the options for displaying the Outlook Today page when the program starts, the number of days that appears under Calendar, the type of Task list, and the style of the page itself.
3. Click Back To Outlook Today.

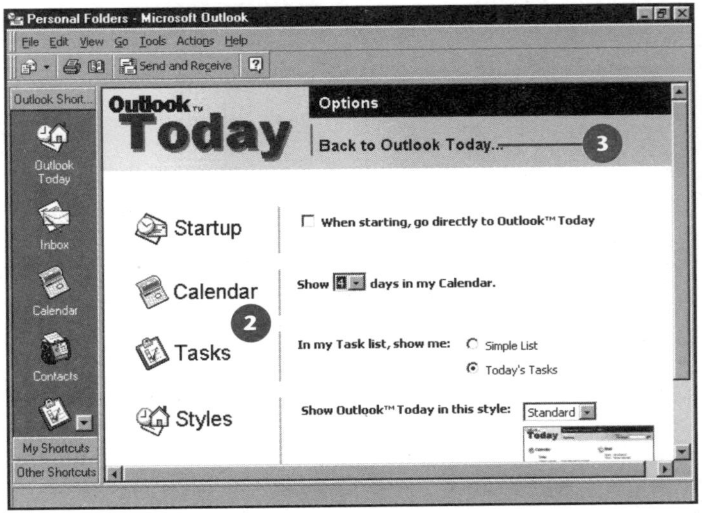

Printing Items from Outlook

You can print any item in Outlook. The default or preset printing style is different for each view depending on what type of information you are printing. There are other printing options available in table, calendar, and card views. You cannot print from a timeline or an icon view. You should try to preview your documents before you print to make sure the pages look like you expect them to.

TIP

Print categorized items. *Sort items by categories or find a particular category, select one or more items, and then print.*

Print button

Print an Item or View

1. Click the File menu, and then click Print, or click the Print button on the Print Preview toolbar.
2. Type the number of copies you want.
3. Choose a style from the Print Style list.
4. Specify a print range, if necessary.
5. Click OK.

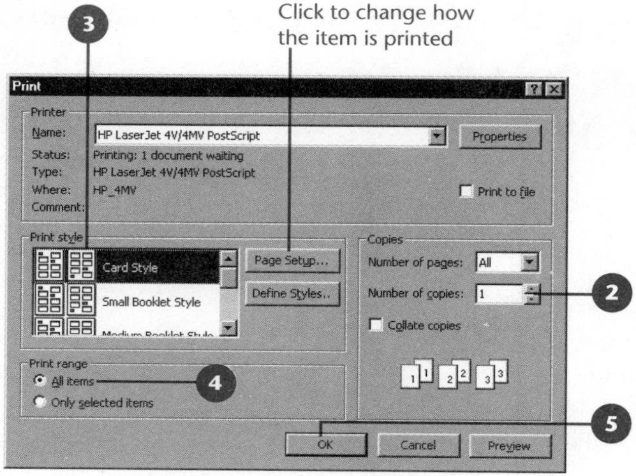

Printing Options Available in Different Views

Refer to the table for information on the printing options available in the different views.

PRINTING OPTIONS

View	Style	Prints
Table	Table	All items in a list in the visible columns
Calendar	Daily	Each day from 7 A.M. to 7 P.M. on a separate page with tasks and notes
	Weekly	Each week from midnight to midnight on a separate page
	Monthly	Each month on a separate page
	Tri-Fold	Three equal columns with one day, one month, and tasks each in its own column
Card	Card	All contact cards with letter tabs and headings and six blank cards at the end
	Phone Directory	Names and phone numbers for all contacts with letter tabs and headings

Viewing the News Window

Menu bar
The menu bar gives you access to all the menu options. Simply click a menu name to display a list of related menu commands, and then click the command you want to issue.

Toolbar
The toolbar contains buttons for commands you use in Outlook Express. The buttons change depending on which folder you are using in Outlook Express.

Folder List
The Folder List contains all the folders in Outlook Express. You can customize the folders to meet your needs.

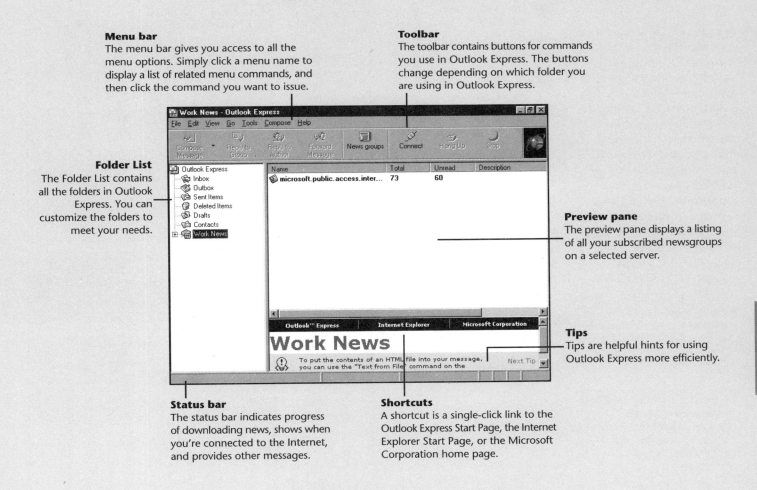

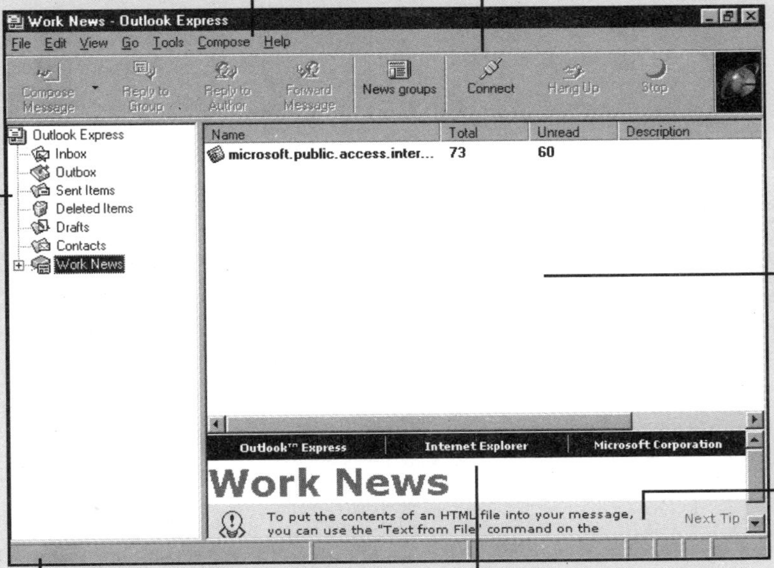

Preview pane
The preview pane displays a listing of all your subscribed newsgroups on a selected server.

Tips
Tips are helpful hints for using Outlook Express more efficiently.

Status bar
The status bar indicates progress of downloading news, shows when you're connected to the Internet, and provides other messages.

Shortcuts
A shortcut is a single-click link to the Outlook Express Start Page, the Internet Explorer Start Page, or the Microsoft Corporation home page.

17

Subscribing to a Newsgroup

Before you can participate in a newsgroup, you need a *newsreader program*, such as Outlook Express News, that allows you subscribe to newsgroups. *Subscribing* to a newsgroup places a link to a particular group in the server folder, providing easy access to the newsgroup. You can subscribe to as many newsgroups as you'd like. Before you subscribe to a newsgroup, it's a good idea to read some messages (called *articles*) and get a feel for the people and content. If you like what you see and want to regularly read or participate in the conversation threads, you can subscribe to that newsgroup.

TIP

Unsubscribe from a Newsgroup. *Right-click the newsgroup, and then click Unsubscribe From This Newsgroup.*

View a Newsgroup Without Subscribing

1. Click the Go menu, and then click News.
2. Click a news server in the Folder List.
3. Click the News Groups button on the toolbar.
4. Click a newsgroup you want to view.
5. Click Go To.

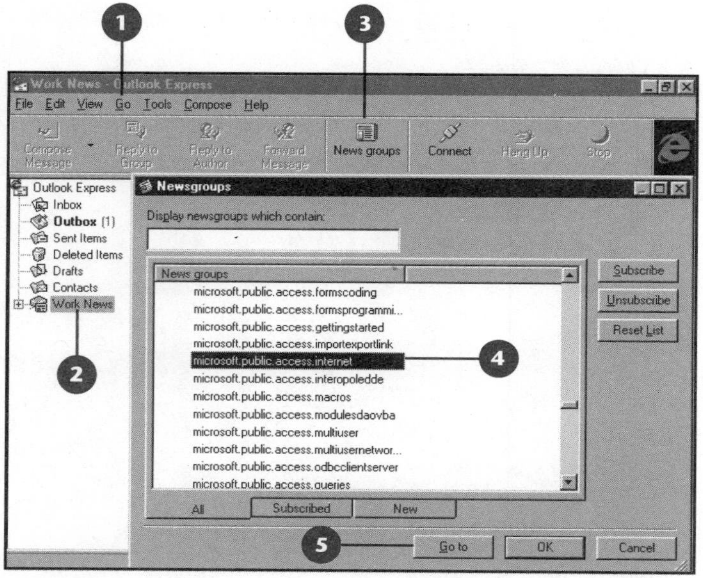

Subscribe to a Newsgroup

1. Right-click the newsgroup you want to subscribe to, and then click Subscribe To This Newsgroup on the shortcut menu.

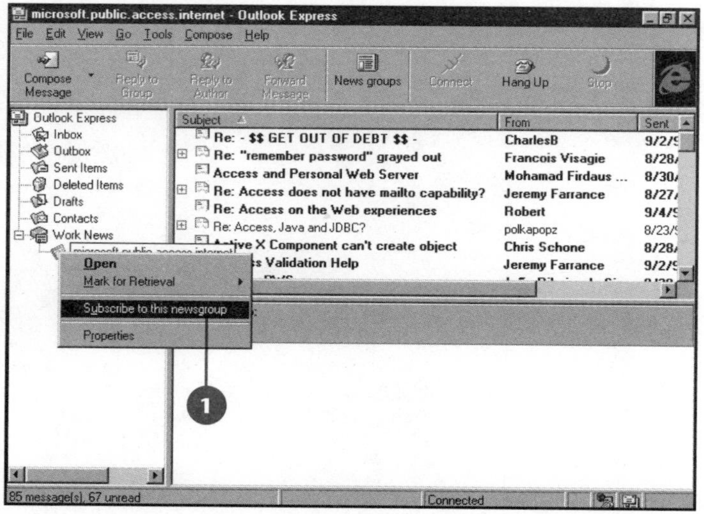

Reading and Posting News

After retrieving new newsgroup messages or message headers, you need to open the messages and read them. You can save any message to your hard drive for future reference. Periodically, you should clear your hard drive of old messages to free up space. Part of the fun of newsgroups is that you can participate in an ongoing discussion, respond privately to a message's author, or start a new conversation thread yourself by posting your own message on a topic. A *conversation thread* consists of the original message on a topic along with the responses that include the original message title preceded by "RE:".

Open and Read News Messages

1. Click the news server icon in the Folder List.
2. Double-click the newsgroup you want to read.
3. If necessary, click + (the plus sign) to the left of a message header to display all the reply headers for that message.
4. When you see a message or reply you want to read, click its header in the message list.
5. Read the message in the preview pane.

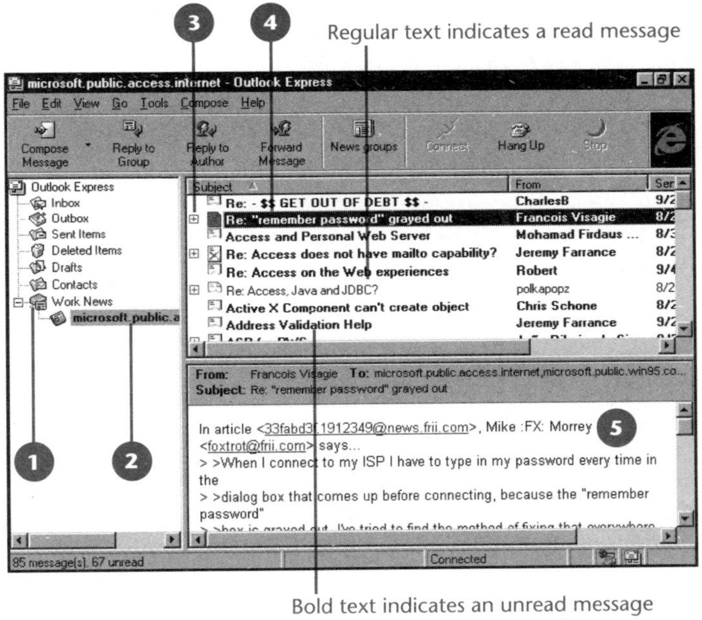

Post a New Message

1. Select the newsgroup to which you want to post a message.
2. Click the Compose Message button on the toolbar.
3. Type a subject for your message.
4. Type your message.
5. Click the Post button on the toolbar.

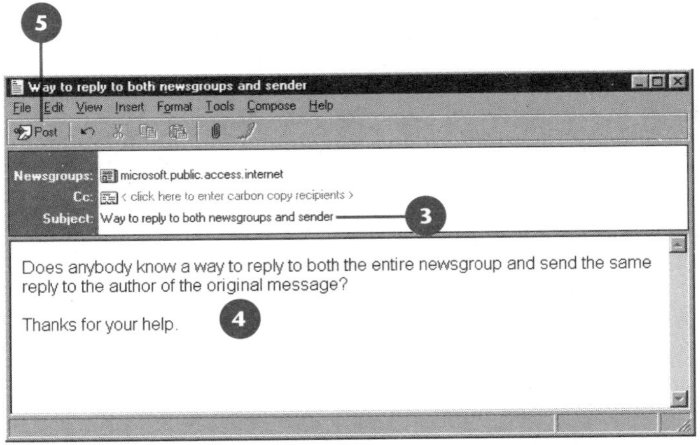

17

Writing Miscellaneous Notes

Notes replace the random scraps of paper on which you might jot down reminders, questions, thoughts, ideas, or directions. Like the popular sticky notes, you can move an Outlook note anywhere on your screen and leave it displayed as you work. Any edits you make to a note are saved automatically. The ability to color-code, size, categorize, sort, or filter notes makes these notes even more handy than their paper counterparts.

TIP

Change the look of Notes. *To change the note color, size, font, and display, click the Tools menu, click Options, and then click Notes Options. Select the options you want to change.*

TIP

Delete a note. *Select the note or notes you want to delete, and then click the Delete button on the Standard toolbar.*

Write a New Note

1. Click the New Item drop-down arrow on the Standard toolbar, and then click Note.
2. Type the text of the note.
3. Click the Close button.

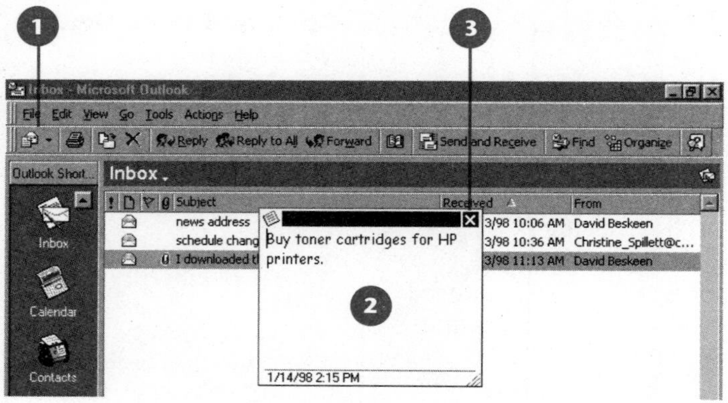

Open and Close a Note

1. Click Notes on the Outlook Bar.
2. Double-click the note you want to open and read.
3. Drag the note to any location on your screen or close it.
4. Click the Close button.

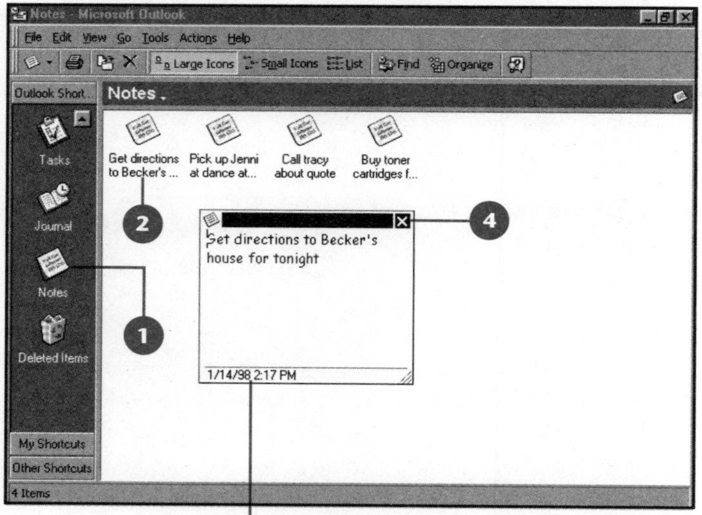

Indicates the date and time you wrote the note

18

Sharing Information Between Office 97 Programs

IN THIS SECTION

One of the most helpful aspects of Microsoft Office 97 is its ability to share information between programs. This means you can create and store information in the program that works best for that type of information, yet move that same information to another program for a specific purpose or presentation.

Consider an example. Sarah coordinates her local school district's soccer teams. She needs to send out monthly newsletters that show the scheduled dates and times for practices and games. In Access, she creates a database of team members and all their relevant information. She tracks the year-to-date expenses and plans the tentative schedules between teams in Excel. Every month, Sarah writes a form letter to the players in Word, imports the upcoming schedule from Excel, and then merges the form letter with Access to create the mailing.

This is just one scenario. As you work with Office 97 programs, you'll find many ways you'll want to share information between them.

Sharing Information Between Programs

Office 97 can convert data or text from one format to another using a technology known as *Object Linking and Embedding* (OLE). OLE allows you to move text or data between programs in much the same way as you move them within a program. The familiar cut and paste or drag and drop methods work between programs and documents just as they do within a document. In addition, all Office programs have special ways to move information from one program to another, including importing, exporting, embedding, linking, and hyperlinking.

Importing and Exporting

Importing and exporting information are two sides of the same coin. *Importing* copies a file created with the same or another program into your open file. The information becomes part of your open file, just as if you created it in that format, although formatting and program-specific information such as formulas can be lost. *Exporting* converts a copy of your open file into the file type of another program. In other words, importing brings information into your open document, while exporting moves information from your open document into another program file.

Embedding

Embedding inserts a copy of a file created in one program into a file created in another program. Unlike imported files, you can edit the information in embedded files with the same commands and toolbar buttons used to create the original file. The original file is called the *source file*, while the file in which it is embedded is called the *destination file*. Any changes you make to an embedded object appear only in the destination file; the source file remains unchanged.

Linking

Linking displays information from one file (the source file) in a file created in another program (the destination file). You can view and edit the linked object from either the source file or the destination file. The changes are stored in the source file but also appear in the destination file as well. As you work, Office 97 updates the linked object to ensure you always work with the most current information available.

Office 97 keeps track of all the drive, folder, and filename information for a source file. But, if you move or rename the source file, the link between files will break.

Once the link is broken, the information in the destination file becomes embedded rather than linked. In other words, changes to one copy of the file will no longer affect the other.

TERM	DEFINITION
source program	The program that created the original object
source file	The file that contains the original object
destination program	The program that created the document into which you are inserting the object
destination file	The file into which you are inserting the object

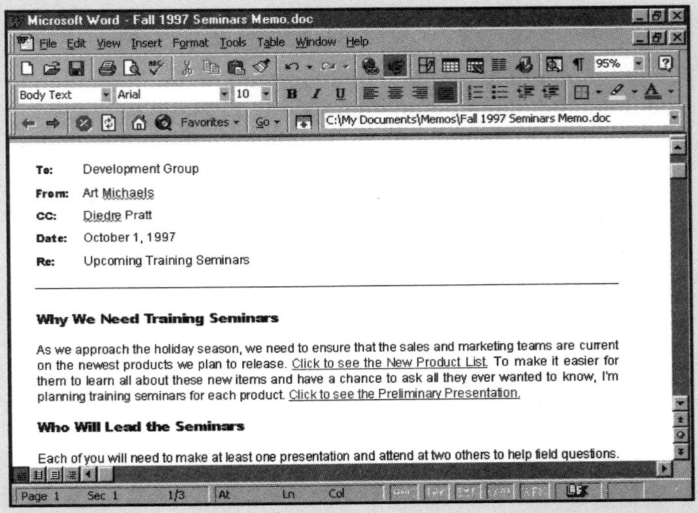

Microsoft Word - Fall 1997 Seminars Memo.doc
File Edit View Insert Format Tools Table Window Help
Body Text
Arial
10
95%
Favorites
Go
C:\My Documents\Memos\Fall 1997 Seminars Memo.doc
To: Development Group
From: Art Michaels
CC: Diedre Pratt
Date: October 1, 1997
Re: Upcoming Training Seminars
Why We Need Training Seminars
As we approach the holiday season, we need to ensure that the sales and marketing teams are current on the newest products we plan to release. Click to see the New Product List. To make it easier for them to learn all about these new items and have a chance to ask all they ever wanted to know, I'm planning training seminars for each product. Click to see the Preliminary Presentation.
Who Will Lead the Seminars
Each of you will need to make at least one presentation and attend at two others to help field questions.
Page 1 Sec 1 1/3 At Ln Col

Hyperlinking

The newest way to share information between programs—hyperlinks—comes from World Wide Web technology. A *hyperlink* is an object (either colored, underlined text or a graphic) you click to jump to a different location in the same document or a different document. (See "Creating Internet Documents With Office 97" on page 51 for more information about creating and navigating hyperlinks in Office 97 documents.) The following illustration is an example of hyperlinks in a Word document.

Importing and Exporting Files

When you *import* data, you insert a copy of a file (from the same or another program) into an open document. When you *export* data, you save an open document in a new format so that it can be opened in an entirely different program. For example, you might import an Excel worksheet into a Word document to create a one page report with text and a table. Or you might want to save the Excel worksheet as an earlier version of Excel so someone else can edit, format, and print it.

Import a File from the Same or Another Program

1. Click where you want to insert the imported file.
2. Click the Insert menu and then click File (in Word) or Slide From File (in PowerPoint), or click the File menu, point to Get External Data, and then click Import (in Access).
3. Click the Files Of Type drop-down arrow, and then click All Files.
4. If necessary, click the Look In drop-down arrow, and then select the drive and folder that contains the file you want to import.
5. Double-click the name of the file you want to import.
6. Edit the imported information with the open program's available commands.

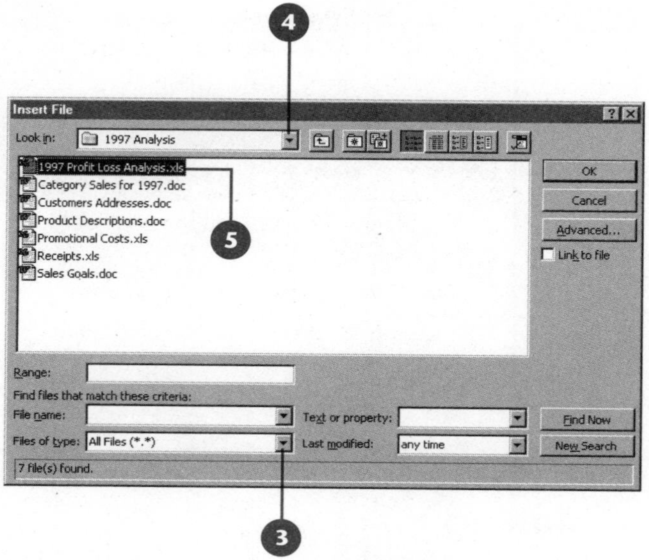

TIP

Use copy and paste to export information. *If you want to move only part of a file into your document, just copy the information you want to insert, and then paste the information in the file where you want it to appear.*

SEE ALSO

See "Saving a File" on page 10 for more information about saving a file as another file type.

Export a File to Another Program

1. Click the File menu, and then click Save As.
2. If necessary, click the Save In drop-down arrow, and then select the drive and folder in which you want to save the file.
3. Click the Save As Type drop-down arrow, and then click the type of file you want to save the document as.
4. If necessary, type a new name for the file.
5. Click Save.
6. Edit the file from within the new program.

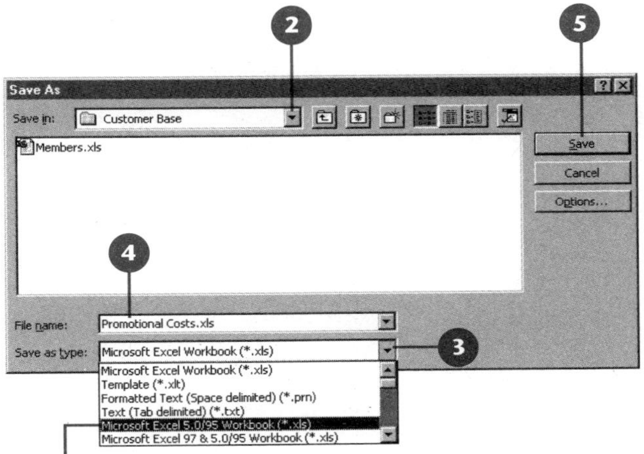

You might want to save a workbook in a different version of Excel or as another spreadsheet type so another person can edit, format, and print the file.

18

Embedding and Linking Information

Embedding inserts a copy of one document into another. Once data is embedded, you can edit it using the menus and toolbars of the program in which it was created (that is, the *source program*). *Linking* displays information stored in one document (the *source file*) into another (the *destination file*). You can edit the linked object from either file, although changes are stored in the source file.

TIP

Change an object from linked to embedded. *If you break the link between an linked object and its source file, it becomes merely embedded. To break a link, open the linked file, click the Edit menu, click Links, and then click the link you want to break. Finally, click Break Link, and then click Yes.*

Embed a Previously Created Object

1. Click where you want to embed the object.
2. Click the Insert menu, and then click Object.
3. Click the Create From File tab or option button.
4. Click Browse and then double-click the object you want to embed.
5. Click OK.

Places the object over your existing text rather than placing it between existing lines.

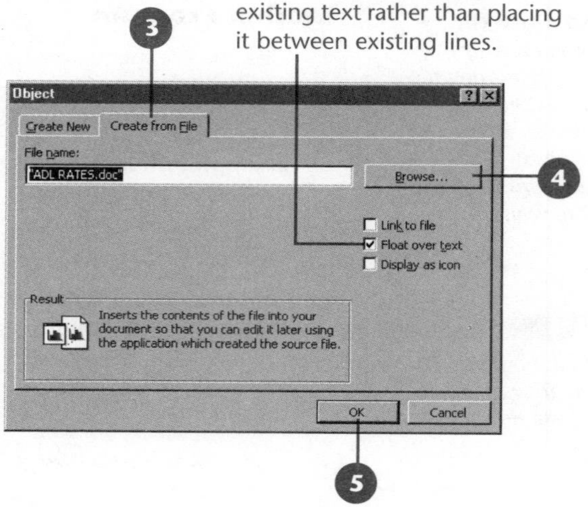

Embed a New Object

1. Click where you want to embed the object.
2. Click the Insert menu, and then click Object.
3. Click the Create New tab or option button.
4. Double-click the type of object you want to create.
5. Enter information in the new object using its commands.

Inserts the object as an icon rather than text.

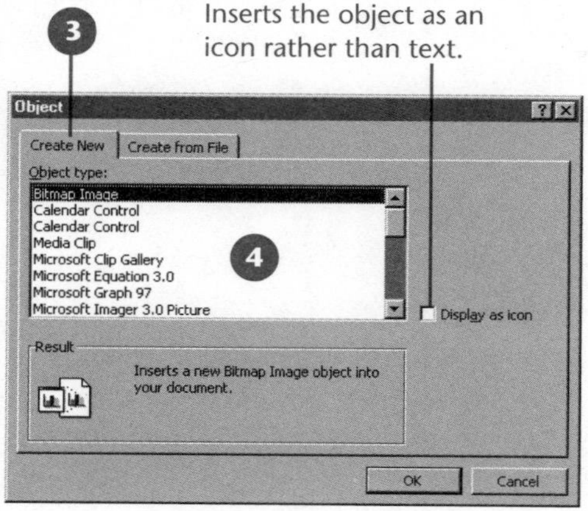

> **TRY THIS**
>
> **Create a travel budget.** *In Excel with columns showing the actual expenses for a trip for one, two, and four people per room write a description of the trip in Word and then link the travel budget below the description. Distribute the Word document to prospective travelers. Update the information as needed from either the Word or Excel file.*

Link an Object Between Programs

1. Click where you want to link the object.
2. Click the Insert menu, and then click Object.
3. Click the Create From File tab or option button.
4. Click Browse, and then double-click the object you want to link.
5. Click the Link check box to select it.
6. Click OK.

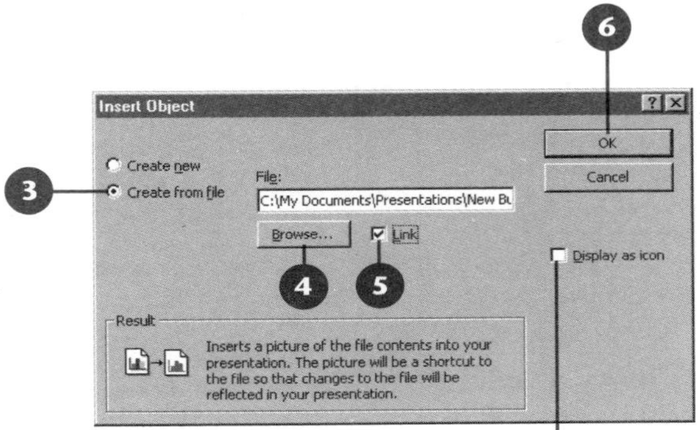

Click this check box to display an icon instead of a picture of the object.

Edit an Embedded or Linked File

1. Double-click the linked or embedded object you want to edit to display the source program's menus and toolbars.
2. Edit the object as usual using the source program's commands.
3. When you're finished, click outside the object to return to the destination program.

The Excel formula bar appears in the Word window so you can edit the worksheet.

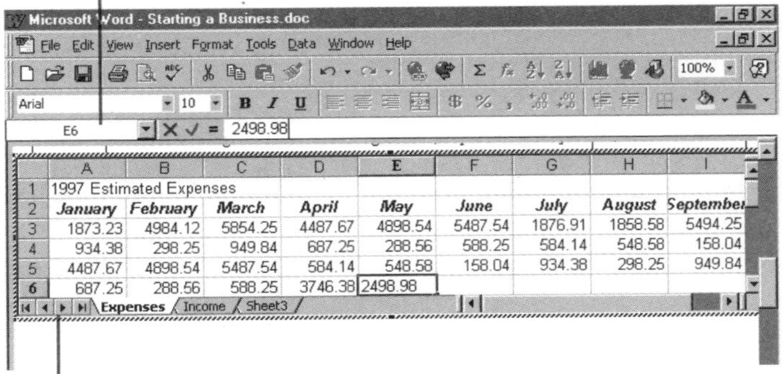

If the object is embedded, the changes are saved only here. If the object is linked, the changes are saved in the source file.

18

Creating Word Documents with Excel Data

A common pairing of Office programs combines Word and Excel. As you write a sales report, explain a budget, or create a memo showing distribution of sales, you'll often want to add spreadsheet data and charts to your text. Instead of recreating the Excel data in Word, you can insert all or part of the data or chart into your Word document.

Copy an Excel Worksheet Range to a Word Document

1. Click in the Word document where you want to copy the Excel range.
2. Click the Insert menu, and then click File.
3. Click the Files Of Type drop-down arrow, and then click All Files.
4. Click the Look In drop-down arrow, and then select the drive and folder that contains the workbook you want to copy.
5. Double-click the filename of the workbook you want to copy.
6. Click the Open Document In Workbook drop-down arrow, and then click the worksheet you want.
7. Click the Name Or Cell Range drop-down arrow, and click the range or range name you want to copy.
8. Click OK.

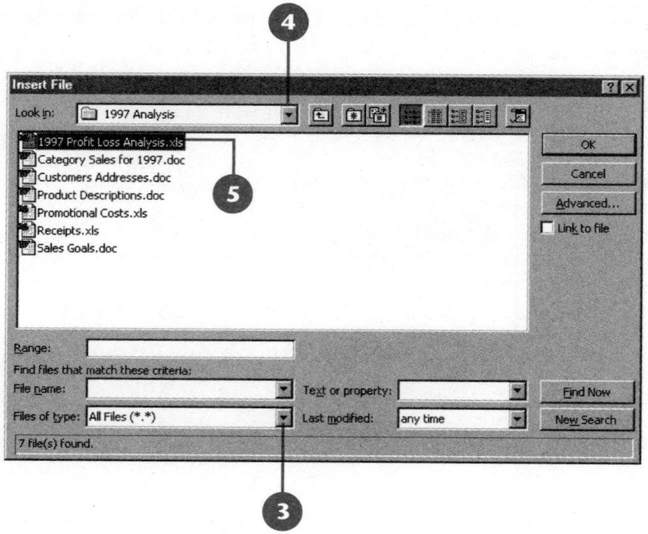

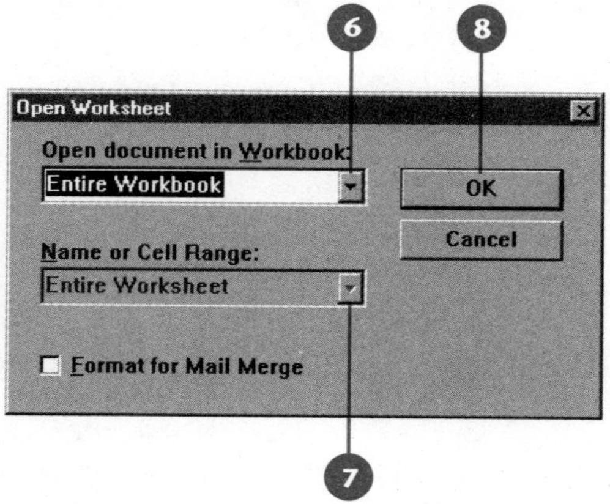

TIP

Import Excel data as a picture. *To save disk space, you can insert Excel data as a picture. Data inserted this way becomes a table that you cannot edit. Select the data you want to import, press the Shift key as you click the Edit menu, and then click Copy Picture. In the Copy Picture dialog box, click OK. Click in the Word document where you want to insert the picture, and then click the Paste button on the Standard toolbar. Drag the picture borders until it's easy to read.*

TRY THIS

Create a new Excel worksheet directly in Word document. *With the insertion point where you want the spreadsheet, click the Insert MS Excel Worksheet button on the Standard toolbar, drag to select the number of rows and columns you want, type the data and format the spreadsheet as needed, and then click outside the spreadsheet to return to the Word window. When you save the file, the spreadsheet becomes embedded in the Word document.*

Embed an Excel Chart in Word

1. Open the Excel workbook where the chart you want to use appears.
2. Click the Excel chart you want to embed to select it.
3. Click the Copy button on the Standard toolbar.
4. Click in the Word document where you want to embed the chart.
5. Click the Paste button on the Standard toolbar.

Handles appear around a selected chart.

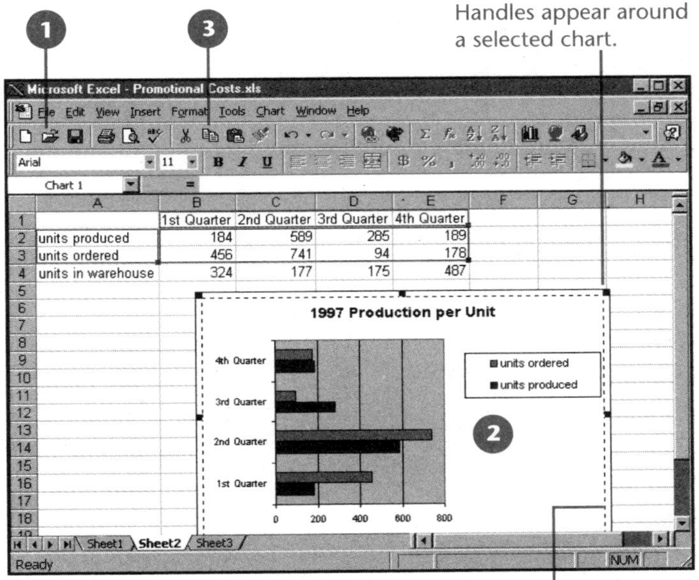

The dotted line shows that the object is being copied or moved.

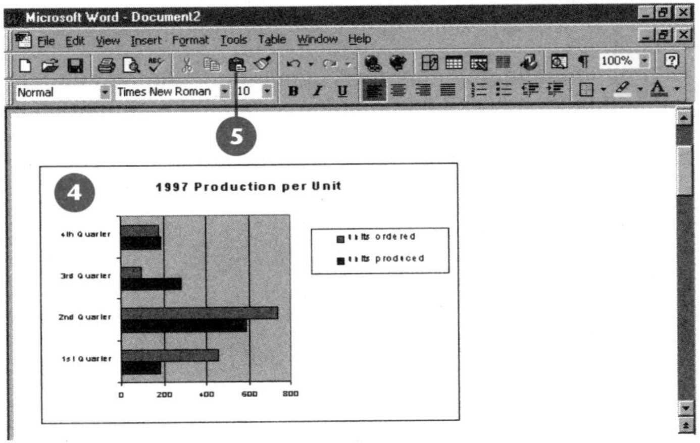

18

Inserting Excel Data in an Access Database

When you import an Excel worksheet into Access, Access creates a new table to store the data. Access will use any labels in the first row of the worksheet for a new table. You can also create a form using Access and then use the form to enter, find, or delete data in Excel.

TIP

Install AccessLinks to choose Access Form. *If Access Form doesn't appear on the Data menu in Excel, then you need to install the AccessLinks add-in program. For more information, see "AccessLinks Add-In" in Excel's online Help.*

Import Excel Data into a New Access Table

1. In Access, click the File menu, point to Get External Data, and then click Import.
2. Click Files Of Type drop-down arrow, and then click Microsoft Excel.
3. If necessary, click the Look In drop-down arrow, and then select the drive and folder that contains the workbook you want to import.
4. Double-click the Excel file you want to import into Access.
5. If necessary, follow the instructions in the Import Spreadsheet Wizard dialog box to set up the data as an Access table.

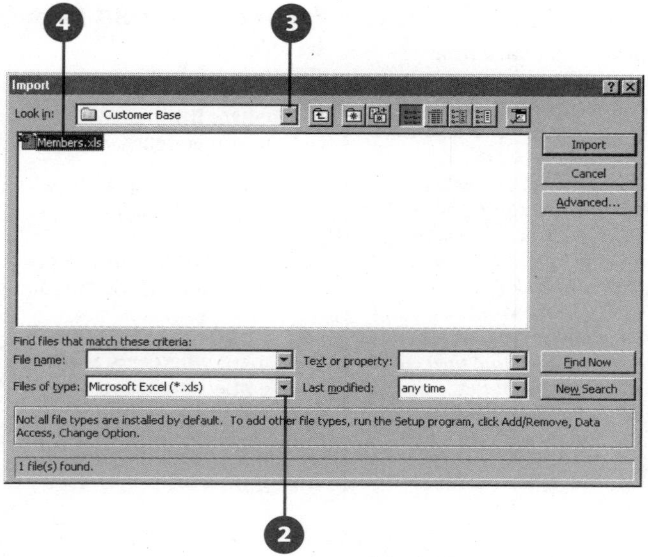

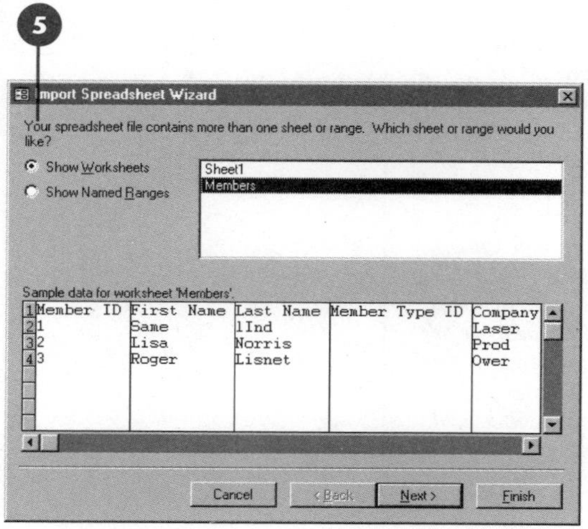

TIP

Create an Access form in an existing database. *In step 4 of "Create an Access Form with Excel Data," click the Existing Database option button instead of the New Database option button, click Browse, and then double-click the database you want to use. Continue with step 5.*

SEE ALSO

See "Charting a PivotTable" on page 153 for information about creating and using Excel PivotTables.

Create an Access Form with Excel Data

1. Click a cell in the Excel worksheet that contains data you want in the Access form.
2. If necessary, click the Save button on the Standard toolbar to save the workbook.
3. Click the Data menu, and then click MS Access Form.
4. Click the New Database option button.
5. Click OK and then click the Forms tab in the Access window.
6. Follow the instructions in the Microsoft Access Form Wizard.
7. Use the form to enter data into Excel.

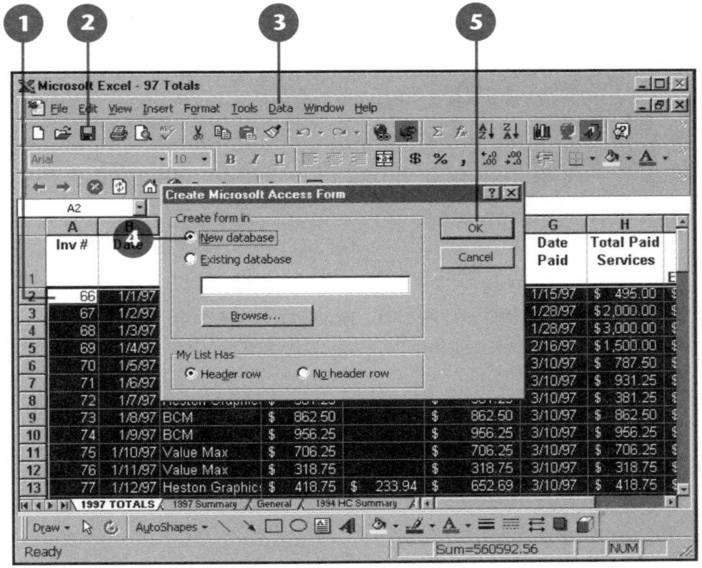

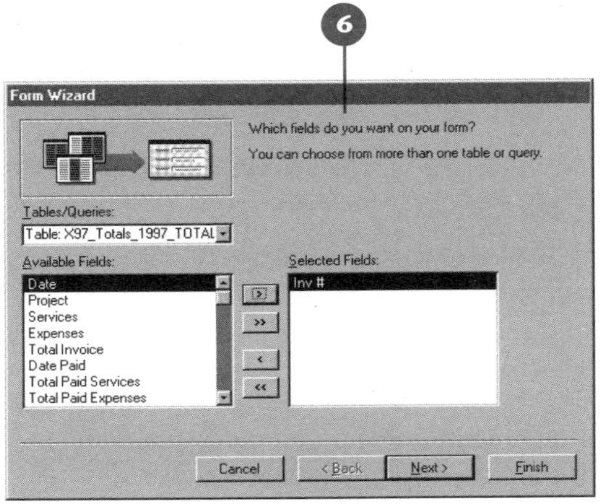

18

Creating a PowerPoint Presentation with Word Text

PowerPoint presentations are based on outlines, which you can create either using PowerPoint or the more extensive outlining tools in Word. You can import any Word document into PowerPoint, although only paragraphs tagged with heading styles become part of the slides. You can also copy any table you created in Word to a slide.

SEE ALSO

See "Applying a Style" on page 93 and "Creating and Modifying a Style" on page 94 for more information about using styles in Word.

Create PowerPoint Slides from a Word Document

1. Create a Word document with heading styles, and then close the Word document.
2. In PowerPoint, click the Open button on the Standard toolbar.
3. Click the Files Of Type drop-down arrow, and then click All Outlines.
4. Click the Look In drop-down arrow, and then locate the Word file you want to use.
5. Double-click the Word document filename.
6. Edit the slides using PowerPoint commands.

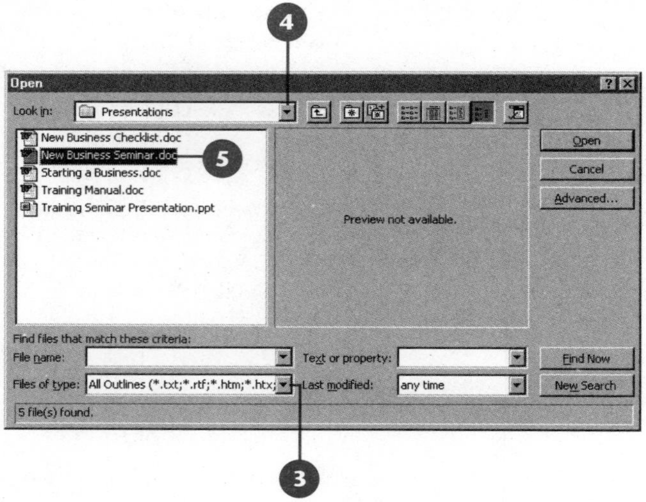

Embed a Word Table in a Slide

1. Click in the Word table you want to use in a slide.
2. Click the Table menu, and then click Select Table.
3. Click the Copy button on the Standard toolbar.

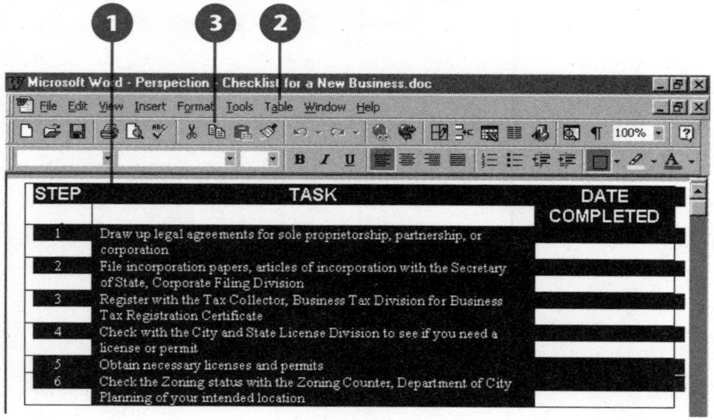

> **TIP**
>
> **Headings in Word become titles in PowerPoint.** *Each Heading 1 style in a Word document becomes the title of a separate slide in PowerPoint. Heading 2 becomes the first level of indented text and so on. If a document contains no styles, PowerPoint uses the paragraph indents to determine a slide structure.*

4. Click the PowerPoint slide where you want to insert the Word table.
5. Click the Paste button on the Standard toolbar.
6. Drag a handle to resize the embedded table.
7. Double-click the table to display Word's menus and toolbars and edit the table using the usual Word commands.

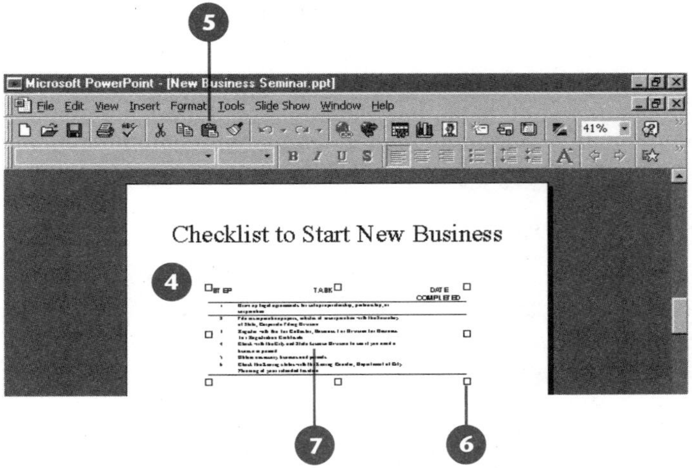

Create a Word Document from a PowerPoint Presentation

1. Open the PowerPoint presentation you want to use as a Word document.
2. Click the File menu, point to Send To, and then click Microsoft Word.
3. Click Outline Only option button.
4. Click OK to save the slide text as a Word file, start Word, and open the file.
5. Edit the text using the usual Word commands.

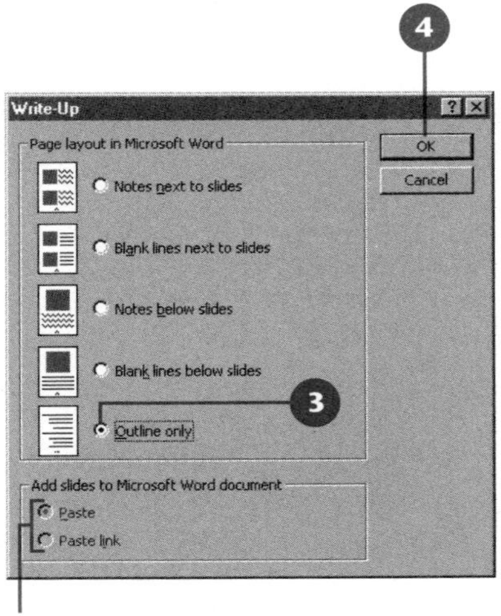

These options are available only when bringing slides and notes into Word. Click the Paste option button if you want to make changes to the Word copy only. Click the Paste Link option button if you want to edit and view the changes you make in both Word and PowerPoint.

18

Personalizing Word Documents Using an Access Database

Access is a great venue for storing and categorizing large amounts of information. You can combine, or *merge*, database records with Word documents to create tables or produce form letters and envelopes based on names, addresses, and other Access records. For example, you might create a form letter in Word and use an existing Access database with names and addresses to personalize them.

SEE ALSO

See "Choosing Templates and Wizards" on page 26 for more information about using wizards.

Insert Access Data into a Word Document

1. In the Access Database window, click the table or query you want to use.
2. Click the OfficeLinks drop-down arrow on the Database toolbar.
3. Click Merge It With MS Word.
4. Click the linking option button you want to use.
5. Click OK, and then follow the steps in the Mail Merge Wizard.
6. In Word, click the Insert Merge Fields button on the Mail Merge toolbar.
7. Click the field(s) you want to insert.

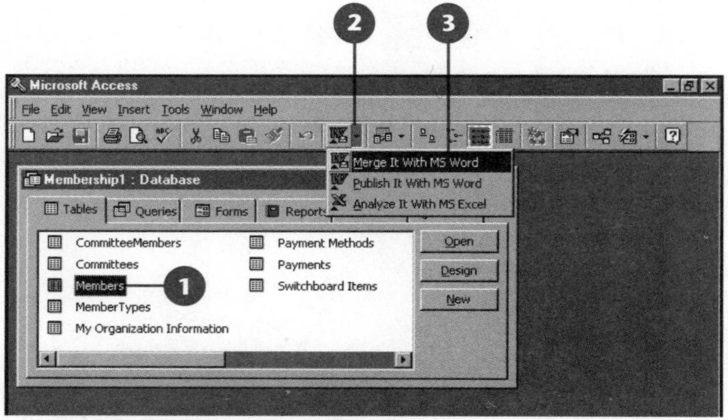

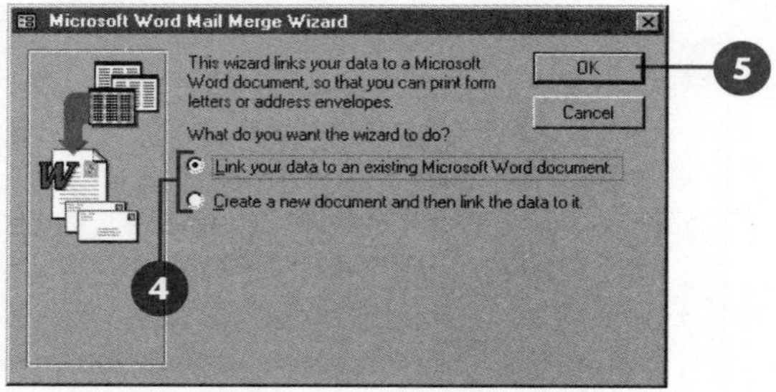

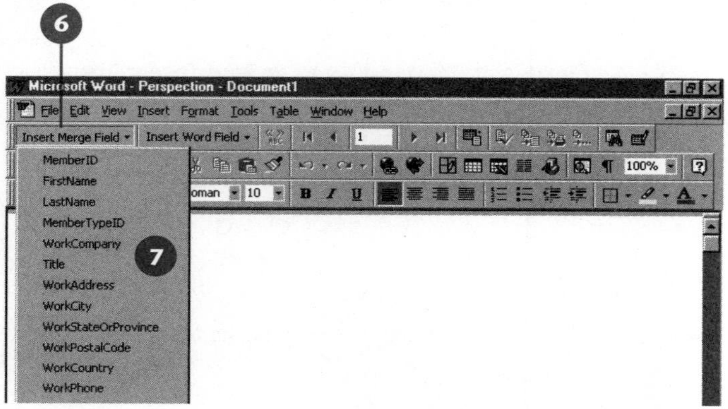

TIP

What is Rich Text Format (RTF)? *Rich Text Format retains formatting, such as fonts and styles, and can be opened from Word or other word processing programs. When you use the Publish It With MS Word command, the output is saved as a Rich Text Format (.rtf) file in the folder in which Access is stored on your computer.*

Create a Word Document from an Access Database

1. In the Access Database window, click the table, query, report, or form you want to save as a Word document.
2. Click the OfficeLinks drop-down arrow on the Database toolbar.
3. Click Publish It With MS Word to save the data as a Word file, start Word, and then open the document.
4. Edit the document using the usual Word commands.

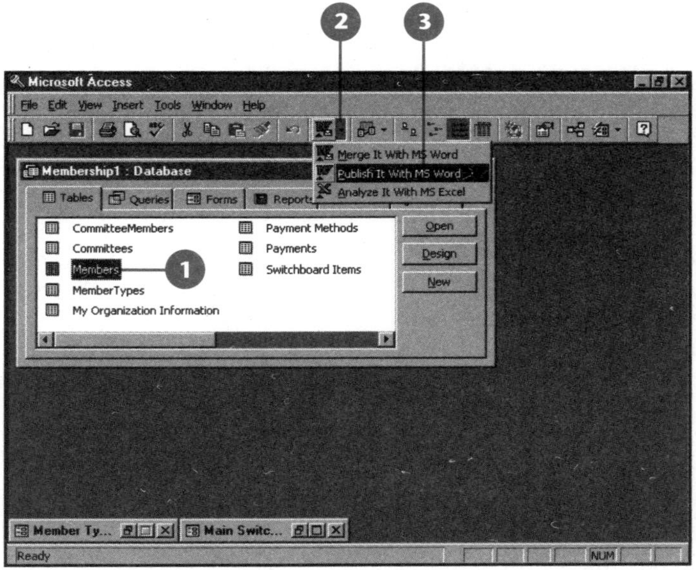

18

Analyzing Access Data in an Excel Workbook

Before you can analyze Access data in a workbook, you must convert it to an Excel file. You can either use the Analyze It With MS Excel command to export Access data as an Excel table file or use a wizard to save the Access data as a *PivotTable*, a table you can use to quickly perform calculations with or rearrange large amounts of data. In the latter, you use *Microsoft Query* to retrieve specific Access data.

SEE ALSO

See "Analyzing Data Using a PivotTable" on page 152 for more information about Excel's Pivot Tables.

Export an Access Database Table into an Excel Workbook

1. In the Access Database window, click the Tables tab.
2. Click the table you want to analyze.
3. Click the OfficeLinks drop-down arrow on the Database toolbar.
4. Click Analyze It With MS Excel to save the table as an Excel file, start Excel, and open the workbook.
5. Use the usual Excel commands to edit and analyze the data.

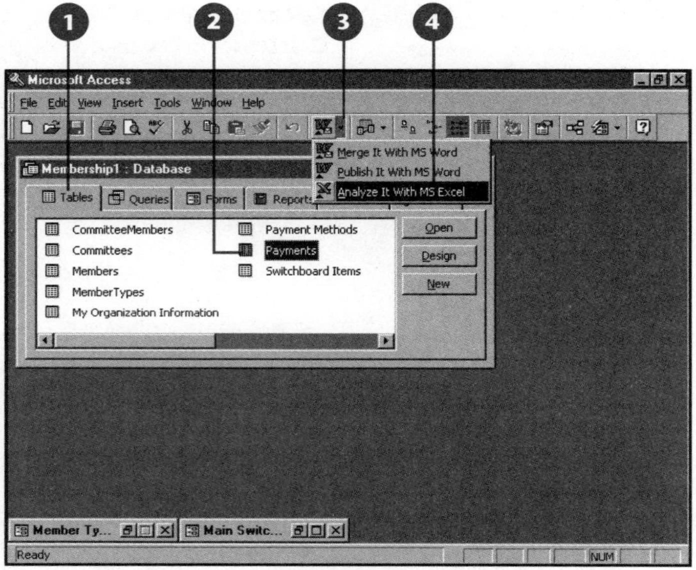

Create an Excel PivotTable from an Access Database

1. In Excel, click the Data menu, and then click PivotTable Report.
2. In the first PivotTable Wizard dialog box, click the External Data Source option button.
3. Click Next.
4. In the second PivotTable Wizard dialog box, click Get Data, and then follow the wizard instructions.

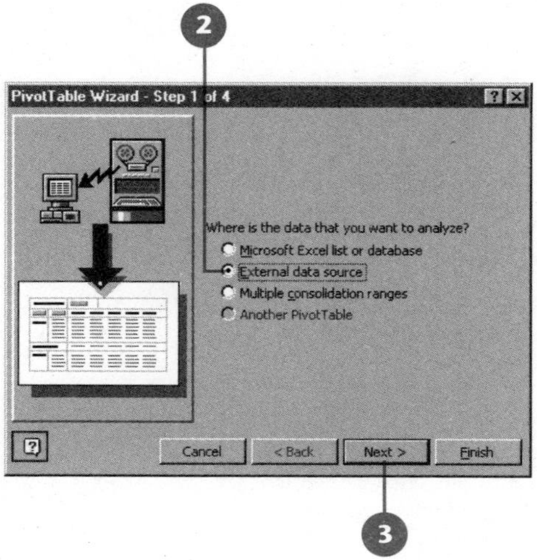

Index

SPECIAL CHARACTERS

A

B

C

D

E

F

G

H

I

J

K

L

M

T

Register Today!

Return this

Microsoft® Office 97 At a Glance, Updated Edition

registration card for

a Microsoft Press® catalog

U.S. and Canada addresses only. Fill in information below and mail postage-free. Please mail only the bottom half of this page.

1-57231-891-0

MICROSOFT® OFFICE 97 AT A GLANCE, UPDATED EDITION

Owner Registration Card

NAME

INSTITUTION OR COMPANY NAME

ADDRESS

CITY STATE ZIP

NO POSTAGE
NECESSARY
IF MAILED
IN THE
UNITED STATES

BUSINESS REPLY MAIL
FIRST-CLASS MAIL   PERMIT NO. 53   BOTHELL, WA

POSTAGE WILL BE PAID BY ADDRESSEE

MICROSOFT PRESS REGISTRATION
MICROSOFT® OFFICE 97 AT A GLANCE,
UPDATED EDITION
PO BOX 3019
BOTHELL   WA   98041-9946